Teaching Adult Literac

Developing Adult Skills

Series Editors: David Mallows and Wendy Moss

The *Developing Adult Skills* series is written to support Adult Literacy and ESOL professionals, particularly those who are studying for the new teaching qualifications. Each book offers strategies and practical tips as well as helping to link theory and practice. The editors and contributors are all experienced practitioners and researchers who share their experiences of meeting the diverse needs of learners.

Titles in the series:

Teaching Adult Literacy: principles and practice

Nora Hughes and Irene Schwab

Teaching Adult ESOL: principles and practice

Anne Paton and Meryl Wilkins

Teaching Adult Literacy

Principles and Practice

Nora Hughes and Irene Schwab
Series Editors: David Mallows and Wendy Moss
NRDC
Open University Press

National Research and Development Centre
for adult literacy and numeracy

The views expressed in this publication are those of the authors and do not necessarily represent the decisions or the stated policy of the Institute of Education.

Open University Press
McGraw-Hill Education
McGraw-Hill House
Shoppenhangers Road
Maidenhead
Berkshire
England
SL6 2QL

email: enquiries@openup.co.uk
world wide web: www.openup.co.uk

and Two Penn Plaza, New York, NY 10121—2289, USA

First published 2010

A catalogue record of this book is available from the British Library

ISBN-13: 978-0-33-5237364 (pb) 978-0-33-5237357 (hb)
ISBN-10: 0-33-523736-3 (pb) 0-33-523735-5 (hb)

Typeset by Kerrypress, Luton, Bedfordshire
Printed and bound in the UK by Bell and Bain Ltd, Glasgow.

Fictitious names of companies, products, people, characters and/or data that may be used herein (in case studies or in examples) are not intended to represent any real individual, company, product or event.

The **McGraw·Hill** Companies

Mixed Sources
Product group from well-managed forests and other controlled sources
www.fsc.org Cert no. TT-COC-002769
© 1996 Forest Stewardship Council

FSC

Contents

Notes on the contributors

Dr Yvon Appleby is Senior Lecturer in the School of Education and Social Science at the University of Central Lancashire. Before this she was Research Fellow at Lancaster Literacy Research Centre working on several NRDC research projects. She is co-author of *Literacy, Lives and Learning* and author of several NRDC/NIACE Practitioner Guides.

Jay Derrick has worked in adult education in the UK since 1975. Since April 2003, when he launched BlueSky Learning Ltd as his specialist consultancy, he has worked on basic skills development in workplaces, teacher training development, and research on assessment for the UK's National Research and Development Centre for adult literacy and numeracy (NRDC) and the OECD.

Sam Duncan has taught adult literacy, English as a foreign language, poetry, and cinema studies in the English further education sector and abroad, and worked in the film and publishing industries. In 2005 Sam joined the Institute of Education, University of London, to teach on the MA in Adult Literacy, Language and Numeracy (LLN) and post-compulsory teacher education courses. She is currently working on a Doctorate in Education, researching the use of fiction in adult reading development.

Judith Gawn is a regional development officer for the National Institute of Adult Continuing Education (NIACE) in London. She was involved in fieldwork for the Improving Formative Assessment project and in the dissemination of effective approaches identified in the research. Before joining NIACE, Judith worked for many years in Hackney and Tower Hamlets as an adult literacy teacher and trainer.

Dr Mary Hamilton is Professor of Adult Learning and Literacy at Lancaster University, member of the Lancaster Literacy Research Centre and the Research and Practice in Adult Literacy group. She is co-author of a number of books including *Local Literacies* with David Barton; *Powerful Literacies* with Jim Crowther and Lyn Tett; and *Changing Faces of Adult Literacy Language and Numeracy: A Critical History* with Yvonne Hillier.

Dr Margaret Herrington, a visiting professor at the University of Wolverhampton, is an experienced adult literacy educator, manager, researcher and author. Since the early 1990s she has worked in higher education, using a 'research in practice' stance on projects in relation to dyslexia and disability and to mainstream 'critical thinking' about dyslexia. Her current research interests are inclusive curricula in HE, developing research in practice and exploring the role of collaborative writing in professional development.

Nora Hughes has worked in the field of LLN since 1979. She taught literacy and numeracy in community, workplace and college settings for many years and now works in teacher education. She is interested in writing development in adult literacy and is currently researching effective practice in teacher education.

Theresa Latham has a background in the further education sector. She worked for the Basic Skills Agency on a range of national projects including the Department for Innovation, Universities and Skills (DIUS) Diagnostic Assessment materials, Core Curriculum Training and DfES Access for All. She works as a freelance consultant. Recent work includes the *Better Teaching Partnership* and *LSIS Migrant Worker Materials*.

Irene Schwab has been teaching literacy since 1974. She has worked in adult, community and further education contexts and is now course leader for the specialist Literacy/ESOL PGCE at the Institute of Education. She was one of the writers and editors of *Language and Power* and is currently working on her doctorate, researching the teaching of critical reading.

Wendy Moss currently manages a teacher training programme for adult educators at City Lit in London. She has published material and articles in adult literacy and learning and contributed to the development of the new teacher training qualifications for adult literacy teachers in England.

Acknowledgements

Our main inspiration for this book has been the adult literacy learners we've worked with for many years, who have shared their ideas and experience with us and whose enthusiasm for learning has made our work so enjoyable.

We would also like to thank the teachers who have participated in our courses at the Institute of Education and have contributed many useful ideas and examples to this book.

The views expressed in this publication are those of the authors and do not necessarily represent the decisions or the stated policy of the Institute of Education.

Introduction
Wendy Moss

Teaching Literacy has been written to support the new specialist qualification in teaching adult literacy that was introduced in England in 2001. Adult literacy has been a key area of lifelong learning since the 1970s. However, much experience and expertise that has been developed by adult literacy teachers has not been recorded. There is also much published research on literacy – both on how it is acquired and its role in society. This research is published in different fields – anthropology, psychology, education and linguistics for example – and in many different countries. It's hard for those working in adult literacy to find their way through, or even access, all this material. The book pulls together research and practice in a coherent and accessible way.

The writers have all worked in adult literacy for many years, as teachers or researchers, and, in many cases, both. The two key writers, Irene Schwab and Nora Hughes, run highly regarded courses for literacy teachers at the Institute of Education, University of London. Much of the book is based on their experience as teacher educators and their, and other writers', long experience of adult literacy teaching. We have drawn on research from many places but particularly that carried out for the National Research and Development Centre for Literacy and Numeracy, and the Literacy Research Centre at the University of Lancaster. The book owes most of all to the sharing of practice by committed adult literacy teachers over many years, many of whose ideas will be here, but not credited.

Who is the book for?

The book is intended to support both teacher trainers and people studying for a teacher training qualification. It is not designed for you if you are an absolute beginner adult literacy teacher – though you may still find it useful – you will find it of more use if you have some experience of working in adult literacy already. In England, you might be completing your first year of training or entering your second year. Or you may be a fully qualified teacher who has become interested in teaching adult literacy and are doing an additional 'specialist' qualification. The book will also be of use to practitioners who want to update themselves and develop their practice.

For international readers, it should be made clear that the book has been written in England, and the government Skills for Life strategy has introduced many common policies, practices and organizations. These are a feature of a particular time and place, so we have tried, where possible, to keep references to these to a minimum.

However, we have to refer to them in places. You will find a glossary at the end of the book which will give you some information about English organizations and terms.

The book has a partner volume – *Teaching English to Speakers of Other Languages (ESOL)*. We do include strategies for teaching literacy to multilingual students. However, we do not discuss in depth how to work with learners who are still in the early stages of learning to speak and understand English. (In the UK, multilingual students in adult literacy classes are generally relatively confident in their spoken English.) You may want to refer to *Teaching ESOL* if you are working with students who are newer to the language.

Those of us who have worked as adult literacy teachers regard it as one of the most privileged roles in education. Our learners are often seen as a social 'problem' and are described in terms of their deficits, but we find learners in our groups who don't at all match this picture: learners who have rich resources, knowledge and skills in many areas of their lives. Often we ourselves are undervalued: many people believe 'basic' literacy must be 'basic' to teach. In fact it is one of the most complex areas of education, needing high levels of empathy, knowledge and skill to do well.

How the book is structured

Any book has to be structured into chapters and sections and these boundaries are always artificial. For example, the chapters on teaching the 'four' skills – reading, writing, speaking and listening – will not offer you an 'off the shelf' plan for a lesson or course. You will need to integrate aspects of each chapter in most sessions with learners. We have also not described in detail common teaching strategies that are easily available elsewhere, for example in the *Adult Literacy Core Curriculum* (DfES 2001). We have assumed you are already familiar with these. What we do hope is that this book will help you to appreciate the significance of certain approaches, to broaden your repertoire and to become a more informed and reflective practitioner as a result.

There is a brief overview of each section below.

Section 1   Literacy in its social context

The social context of literacy looks at broader issues of literacy in society: what do we mean by 'literacy'? What are its purposes? How does national and international policy impact on adult literacy provision? It also places current adult literacy practice in the UK in the context of its longer history.

Who are the learners? discusses literacy learners and their experiences and purposes of learning, drawing on the experience of learners who took part in a large research study in the north of England.

Section 2   Language awareness for literacy teachers

How language works will help you understand the systems of the English Language and consider why understanding something about linguistics and grammar will enable you to support your students.

Language variety explores how we should take account of the multiple language and varieties of English used by our learners and how this relates to issues of identity and power.

Section 3 Teaching and learning literacy

This section discusses in detail how to work with learners on the four key skills of literacy – **Reading**, **Writing**, and **Speaking and listening** – and the underpinning principles behind different approaches. It also gives guidance on **Planning and assessment**. It uses examples of real adult literacy learners and classes throughout.

Section 4 Inclusive learning

Here we focus on literacy learning for two groups that are of particular significance for literacy teachers: **Dyslexia** and **Literacy learning for adults with global learning difficulties**. There are, of course, many other groups we could have considered and we suggest further useful resources in this section. Much literacy learning happens on other courses. The final chapter on **Embedded literacy** offers some guidance for literacy teachers engaged in this work.

Each chapter includes tasks which will help you deepen your understanding of the issues covered. They can be done individually or as a group. We have included a guide to further resources at the end of each chapter should you wish to investigate further.

Section 1

Literacy in its social context

1 The social context of literacy

Mary Hamilton

Understanding literacy in its social context

Introduction

This is an exciting time to be involved in literacy education. Wherever we turn, written texts of some kind are part of our lives. From the MP3 player to the DIY shop, written language, pictures, diagrams mediate our activities and interactions. At the same time, researchers are developing new insights into the importance of literacy for social inclusion – particularly in the light of world economic changes and the growing importance of digital media. In England, the government has put literacy at the centre of its educational policy, both in schools and in the lifelong learning sector. There has never been a time when it is more important to reflect on what we mean by literacy, what assumptions we make about it and what theories should guide practice.

There are long traditions of literacy teaching and research in the English-speaking world that see literacy as a discrete set of skills that can be acquired step by step. Some are foundation skills, such as being able to map words onto sounds using phonics, to spell accurately or form letters through handwriting. Some are more complex linguistic and information-processing skills that enable people to recognize different kinds of texts and to take account of purpose and audience when they read or write. There are continuing debates about what these skills are and about which ones should be included or excluded in definitions of 'basic literacy'.

In this chapter, we maintain that foundation skills are, of course, important, but that literacy is also more than this. To be effective teachers, we need to understand this 'more' – how skills are shaped by the social contexts, purposes and relationships within which reading and writing are used. As an example, something as basic as writing down the bare facts of your life is never done in a vacuum. These facts are written in a CV, a diary or an autobiography. They may be written by another person in medical case notes, given as a speech at a funeral or other ceremonial event, or reported in a police statement. In each situation, the form and process of the writing will be different. Very often the physical act of writing and the materials used to carry it out will be different (a pencil or a computer, a set of notes, a form or a book). Different outcomes will hang on the accuracy of the account, how persuasive it is, or whether the spelling and layout are correct. In other words, literacy is *situated* and embedded in local activities, and can never be pulled out and captured as a separate and unvarying thing.

This perspective, of the contextual and embedded nature of literacy, has become known as **literacy as situated social practice**. It draws on situated theories of learning which see learning as taking place in day-to-day relationships between people in their environment, whether this is a formal college classroom, a workplace or a self-help medical group. It draws a bigger landscape than that of seeing literacy as a set of discrete skills, and is concerned with local differences, diversity and variety as well as with universal principles.

Ways of understanding literacy

Task 1.1

Definitions of literacy
Explore one or two of the following websites for definitions of literacy:[1]

Wikipedia: www.en.wikipedia.org/wiki/Literacy
National Literacy Trust: www.literacytrust.org.uk/Database/quote.html
Canadian Education Association: > Focus on Literacy >Framing the Debate > What is Literacy? www.cea-ace.ca/home.cfm

- How have definitions of 'being literate' changed over the centuries?
- What current definitions can you find?
- Which do you prefer and why?

We have mentioned above two contrasting views of the nature of literacy – the 'discrete set of skills' and the 'situated social practice' accounts – and suggested that we need to draw on both of these in this book. Another important way of understanding approaches to literacy education is to consider the *purposes* of literacy learning and teaching. Literacy is an 'elastic' idea: most people will agree that it is a good thing to have, but it can mean vastly different things from one person to the next. At different points and under different policy conditions, adult literacy has been seen as:

- *a set of functional skills* that help people to meet the demands that society puts on them, especially in terms of employment;
- a civilizing tool, allowing people to *access a literary culture* that is part of their cultural heritage;
- a *means of emancipation*, enabling people to control their lives, challenge injustice and become autonomous, participating citizens in a democracy.

These different perspectives on the purpose of literacy can often exist side by side in different settings, though, at a particular time and place, decisions about policy and practice are usually guided by one dominant view.

If we see literacy as a form of situated social practice, we do not need to search for one true definition of literacy. We can accept that different purposes for literacy exist, and that this will give rise to a variety of literacy education provision, different ways of thinking about teaching and learning and different goals for programmes and policies. Given these inevitable variations, it is probably more useful to use the term **discourses** to describe the different ways of thinking and talking about what literacy is. For example, a programme in a community development setting could be seen as rooted in the **emancipatory discourse** of literacy, enabling people to ask for their rights, manage schooling, access better employment or participate in local democracy. In contrast, an employer-sponsored workplace programme may seem more **functionally oriented**, enabling people to perform literacy tasks needed in their jobs more successfully. This is not to say that different purposes can't be relevant in each setting. The literacy learned in a homelessness project can also be functionally useful, and workplace literacy programmes can be emancipatory.

Literacy as situated social practice

In 1983, Shirley Brice Heath published a study of two communities in the US, documenting the different cultural ways in which very small children were initiated into literacy; these early experiences of literacy enabled them to fit more or less easily into formal schooling. The key idea of a **literacy event** was first coined by her. She identified a literacy event as being any occasion in which a written text is involved in a social interaction (see Heath 1983: 93).

Task 1.2

Everyday literacy events
Think of your own recent experience.

- Do you ever write or give poems to other people? In what context?
- Which languages have you spoken or read during the last two weeks?
- Do you keep family records? What? Where?
- Have you ever written a fan letter?
- Have you ever taken on the job of secretary or treasurer for a local organization?
- When was the last time you asked for help with writing or reading?

For more on literacy events see below.

Another key idea used by researchers – **literacy practices** – is a broader, more abstract one which refers both to people's behaviour and to their understandings of the uses of reading and/or writing. 'Literacy practices' incorporate not only 'literacy events' – observable occasions in which literacy plays a part – but also the ways we understand, feel and talk about those events.

Around the same time as Heath was researching, the psychologists Sylvia Scribner and Michael Cole (1981) were looking the different ways in which literacy was being learned at home and in school in a North African community. They showed that very different literacies resulted from this learning – different scripts, different skills and procedures, different outcomes. Brian Street (1984), an anthropologist working in Iran, also showed how different literacies were acquired in a religious setting, in formal schooling and in the market place. These researchers all showed that literacy skills and practices grow and are shaped within the social system and contexts of which they are part.

David Barton (2007: 29–32) has borrowed the metaphor of an eco-system to describe this – how human activity interacts with the environment. Literacy flourishes in particular 'niches', will take on the characteristics of that niche while other literacies fail to take root, may be diminished or even disappear. For instance, many kinds of specialist workplace literacies flourish – a business or organization will develop ways of keeping records or reporting on its production processes, for example. Reading novels, however, would be inappropriate in most workplaces, except during lunch breaks. Reading and speaking in minority languages very obviously flourishes within communities in the UK, but may be limited within educational or work settings. Train travel favours portable reading that can be engaged with quietly by individuals, whereas a political campaign meeting might involve noisy and collaborative reading, or the drafting of a document.

The social practice approach encourages consideration of how literacy works within the social ecosystem of which it is part. It focuses attention on the cultural, political, economic practices within which the written word is embedded – the ways in which texts are socially regulated and used and the historical contexts from which these practices have developed.

Many literacy researchers lay great store by ethnographic methods – sharing in, and documenting, the everyday context in which literacy is acquired. These methods have become an important resource for literacy studies and for teachers and learners today. Teachers can use this approach to engage with learners in documenting, reflecting on and better understanding the literacy practices in contemporary life in which we all participate.

The perspective of literacy as part of situated social practice, therefore, means not just talking to students about their personal histories but encouraging learners to explore collectively the broader social context in which literacy is used. The topic 'Writing a letter to school', for example, would not only mean practising writing the letter individually, but students finding out together how the school uses the letter and why it is needed, and sharing ideas of what it should contain. It would also mean discussing broader issues such as managing relationships with schools, and ways of feeling powerful around your children's education.

The situated social practice view emphasizes that any teaching and learning activity should take place with the following wider aspects of context in mind:

- what people *do* with texts rather than focusing simply on the texts themselves – literacy events or moments where a text is used in practice; how people help one another to accomplish written tasks (such as writing a letter, filling in a form);
- how reading and writing are embedded in everyday activities (e.g. in weddings, in doing karaoke, in finding your way round a strange town), and how the reading and writing involved in these local 'ecologies' of literacy are formed by cultural convention and reflect and support social relationships;
- how literacy is changing (such as computer-based assessment, sending emails rather than postcards, shopping online, blogging);
- the diversity of different languages, scripts, cultural conventions and modalities (written codes, images, symbols) used in reading and writing. Some of these will be more familiar to particular learners than others. Different literacy activities may also require different physical and cognitive skills (such as using pen and paper or typing with digital keyboard, reading Braille, painting a sign board, reading a graphic novel or a poem, using Arabic, Chinese or English script);
- the existence of 'funds of knowledge' that reside in communities and individuals. These can be valued, drawn on and shared in literacy learning (such as childcare, specialist health knowledge, raising plants for food; travelling in a particular climate).

Documenting literacy as part of situated social practice

As we will discuss later in this book, there are currently two key theoretical perspectives on learning literacy. These match the two approaches to understanding literacy described above.

Theories stemming from a **cognitive** approach focus on how we process language at every level, from recognizing individual phonemes (the smallest unit of sound) to understanding the characteristics of a whole text. Teachers need to work with learners with the full range of these building blocks, which we will describe later as being at 'text', 'sentence' and 'word' level.

The **social practice** theory of literacy takes a different perspective. It looks at literacy *events* and *practices*, i.e. the overall context in which literacy is being used, and considers:

- **participants**: who is involved in an interaction with a written text;
- **activities**: what participants do with texts (and this is not just reading or writing, it can be displaying it, passing it on to others, hiding or even erasing it);
- **settings**: where they do it physically – in the kitchen, on the bus;
- **domains**: the different areas of social life, such as family/household, community/public life/citizenship; workplace; education, commerce, reli-

gion, dealing with public services and bureaucracies; health; children; legal matters. The notion of 'domain' involves values and purposes, not just places;

- **resources**: these might be cognitive skills and knowledge; they might also be paper, a wall or other surface to write on, a computer, a printer, a set of coloured pens or a can of spray paint, a hammer and chisel.

Using these social practice building blocks it is possible to document with learners how literacy fits into their lives, what it means to them and where sources of difficulty or interest might lie. Most important of all, this can reveal why certain kinds of literacy are so important in society, how they are changing and what the significant connections are across time and space.

Task 1.3

Documenting a literacy event
Choose a domain or setting that interests you. Observe one literacy event, e.g. keeping a class register, ordering takeaway food. For something to qualify as a literacy event there must be a written text and at least one person involved. Since you will be recording this event in various ways and talking to those involved, choose an event that you feel confident about approaching. Best of all is to choose something that you are already knowledgeable about and have easy access to, but which might be slightly 'specialist' to other people who are less familiar with it.

Notice the interactions, the visual environment, the texts that are involved and those that are visible in the surroundings. Take written notes of what you have observed and take at least two photographs. Try and get the people and a sense of the activities into your photos; don't just focus on the texts themselves.

Talk to the people involved with the literacy activity and make notes, or a tape recording from your conversations with them.

Write a short account of what you have found out to discuss with others.

For some examples of case studies of a literacy event, see
www.literacy.lancs.ac.uk/resources/studentprojects.htm.

How literacy is changing

One aspect of a situated approach to literacy is to take account of how literacy itself is changing – the skills that are involved, the actual physical form it takes, the value people place on it and the meaning it has within our lives. Literacy practices will probably always change, but we seem to be living through an especially significant period where there is a shift away from traditional print towards carrying out a lot of our reading and writing online, in digital form. Deborah Brandt (2005) has shown how this has happened rapidly in workplaces in recent years, leaving a big 'generation gap'. These changes in knowledge and technologies call into question the nature of literacy and communication.

Task 1.4

How literacy is changing
Carry out the literacy event task above, but do it with two people of different ages, or ask someone to compare how they carry out a literacy event now, and in the past, e.g. communicating with a friend, carrying out a work-related task, obtaining a service such as healthcare.

Literacy: institutions and power

Seeing literacy as part of situated social practice is just one part of a growing recognition that learning and 'knowing' is not simply concerned with individual skills and understanding but the product of social interactions and relationships. Not all forms of literacy are seen as equal. What counts as 'proper' literacy depends on who is using it and why. Not all the participants in a literacy event are immediately obvious. When a care worker fills in a health and safety report, this is likely to have been designed by someone in another agency and passed around the care setting, and will be looked at by others and perhaps checked and evaluated at a future point in a chain of connected events.

Denny Taylor (1996) has coined the term 'toxic literacies' to express the point that literacy can often feel like something oppressive that is used by powerful people and organizations against others, eroding confidence and status and making you feel deficient or out of control. Literacy may feel very different on different sides of the fence – or the desk – for example bureaucrat and job applicant, literacy teacher and learner.

The fact that some literacies are supported, controlled and legitimated by powerful institutions implies that others are devalued. Many of the literacies that are influential and valued in people's day-to-day lives, that are widely circulated and discussed, are not seen as having a place in educational institutions. Neither are the informal social networks that sustain these literacies necessarily drawn upon or acknowledged. Most people have views about who uses 'serious' or 'proper' English.

> **Task 1.5**
>
> **Literacy and power**
> Think about your own reaction to, for example, the following text message:
>
> CU Sun b4 I go xx
>
> Consider:
>
> - Why has this form of literacy developed?
> - What literacy skills are needed by the texter and the reader?
> - Do your learners text, or would they like to text? Would texting be suitable to bring into formal learning activities? If not, why not?

Supporting literacies through lifelong learning policy

These observations about literacy suggest that a learning strategy for adult literacy should pay attention to the social relationships which frame the literacy taught in education, and the power dimensions of these relationships. A lifelong learning strategy for literacy is generally driven by the needs of government and other institutions. This strategy may or may not sustain and develop the literacy practices and funds of knowledge that already exist in civic life. A social practice approach to literacy recognizes these funds of knowledge, and also that people experience changing literacy demands at different stages of their lives (see Chapter 2). It offers convincing evidence of the need for lifelong learning systems which people can access at critical points. Whilst community resources and funds of knowledge exist locally, these are often unevenly distributed. There are uneven and varying levels of formal and informal educational provision available to support them. Formal, structured learning opportunities are one important component of lifelong learning, but they are only one aspect of a solution to sustaining literacies. A wider focus is needed.

Funds could be used to support literacy/lifelong learning in many innovative ways. Some examples are:

- increase the physical spaces available for people and groups to meet/ exchange ideas/display/perform;
- strengthen access points for literacy: libraries/cyber cafes/bookshops/advice centres, etc. so that citizens can access information they are searching for through print, video, electronic forms, etc., engage in virtual or actual meetings with experts;
- strengthen open local government structures that facilitate consultation and access to existing routes for change/citizen action;
- support local media which help circulate and publicize news, events, space for debating issues, ideas;
- provide structured opportunities to learn both content and process skills and link up with others interested in the same issues.

Contexts for adult literacy education: diversity and change

Note: There is a glossary on page 366 to help with some of the names and terms used in this section.

Introduction

The second part of this chapter discusses the diversity and innovation of adult literacy as a field of practice, and the ways in which it has responded to the changing context of adult lives. We focus on the period since the early 1970s when adult literacy became recognized as a field in its own right and a focus for social policy in the UK. We look at the different contexts in which learning has taken place during this time and how these have changed. Each of the sections will be a short overview, with further reading at the end of the chapter. Much of the information and the quotes from practitioners included in this section were collected from the Changing Faces project[2] (see Hamilton and Hillier 2006).

The section aims to set the Skills for Life strategy in a wider perspective. Although this has been an extremely important moment for the development of adult literacy in England,[3] things will inevitably move on and some of the structures we take for granted now will continue to evolve, some will be lost and some sustained as funding changes. A good example of this is assessment of learner progress and achievement. Currently funding in England is linked heavily to targets, achievement and a national test for literacy. However, we may find these emphases being modified in the future as government policy changes.

The longer view: what we have inherited from the earlier history of literacy

Adult literacy has only recently been identified as a field of social policy and education in rich western countries. Up to the 1960s it was seen as a problem for countries without compulsory schooling systems and Western European countries returned statistics to UNESCO recording a zero for illiteracy. Adult literacy first emerged in the UK with the Right to Read campaign in the early 1970s. However, teaching literacy and other basic skills to adults had gone on in various forms throughout the nineteenth and twentieth centuries.

From the mid-twentieth century, the British Army had a programme of education for recruits in their Preliminary Education Centres. Apprentices in the 1960s attended day-release courses including 'general studies' or 'remedial English' at technical colleges. Outside these settings, there were few opportunities for adults to improve their literacy. Some (estimated to be around 5000 in 1972) found their way to the scattered programmes organized by social welfare projects and local authority adult education. Recently arrived immigrants had some opportunities to improve their English Language, for example in the Neighbourhood English Classes, but these were a small part of the patchy provision available for adult learners. Little is recorded about what the learners did or how they felt about what was on offer at the time.

The longer history of how literacy education has developed in the UK is well documented and there are many good sources. We have listed some at the end of this chapter. The roots of literacy education lie mainly with the religious organizations that originally controlled it. The struggle for literacy was central to the emancipatory and self-help political movements of the nineteenth century. All the purposes for literacy – moral and functional and political – that we still debate today – can be seen in these origins.

Adult literacy was greatly affected by the development of free universal primary schooling, which has always been centrally concerned with the teaching of reading, writing and mathematics. It is also important to look at developments in popular culture, and how writing and communication has fitted in to bigger changes in society. As an example, development of a speedy postal service had a big effect on letter and postcard writing in Victorian England and beyond.[4] Similarly, the development of mass media and digital technologies today is affecting how people can access information and entertainment and how print-based literacy is valued.

The wider view: literacy and international movements

International as well as national policies have always affected adult literacy.

From its beginnings in 1948, **UNESCO** has always promoted adult literacy in developing countries without formal schooling systems. Mass campaigns in countries such as Cuba and the Soviet Union were well known, as was the radical literacy work of the Brazilian educator, Paulo Freire, published for the first time in English in 1972. Freire linked literacy learning and political emancipation and his work had a big impact on many literacy practitioners in the UK.

In the 1970s UNESCO funded an ambitious, and largely unsuccessful, programme of employment-related functional literacy, targeting particular groups in developing countries. It designated 1990 as International Literacy Year, and has run world conferences and congresses on lifelong learning, 'education for all' and women's education. Along with the **Organization for Economic Co-operation and Development** (**OECD**) it continues to influence the policy and research agendas of governments around the world.

European Union (**EU**) funding has been another key influence on adult literacy work in the UK. Apart from the volume of financial support given by the EU, the funding is targeted at specific groups, is project-based and has particular auditing mechanisms – all of which are extremely influential in shaping programmes.

The OECD co-ordinated the International Adult Literacy Survey (IALS), which for the first time offered statistical evidence of the 'problem' in Westernized countries. A series of studies carried out in the 1990s resulted in an international league table. This produced the figure of seven million adults in need that has underpinned the current Skills for Life strategy in England (OECD 1997; DfEE 1999).

International agencies continue to be active and influential in the field. They promote assessment frameworks to harmonize standards across the EU countries and beyond (see Lisbon European Council 2000).

Finally, bodies like the **World Trade Organization** and the **World Bank** affect the UK as well as the poorer countries of the South. Through their advice and monitoring, national constraints are placed on public funding, and common strategies are suggested such as the introduction of internal markets and flexible working practices within public services, like education.

Task 1.6

Exploring international developments

List the ways in which international developments affect your own day-to-day work in adult literacy:

How much do you know about the following?

- UNESCOs global monitoring reports on education www.portal. unesco.org/education/en/ev.php-URL_ID=43283&URL_ DO=DO_TOPIC&URL_SECTION=201.html
- The EU's development of key competencies www.eurydice.org/portal/ page/portal/Eurydice/showPresentation?pubid=032EN
- The International Adult Literacy Survey www.statcan.ca/english/ Dli/Data/Ftp/ials.htm

---

Adult literacy since the 1970s – from campaign to Skills for Life

In 1973 a Right to Read campaign was mounted by a voluntary organization, the British Association of Settlements, supported by the BBC. This launched adult literacy as a named field of social policy and educational practice for the first time in the UK, resulting in a new public awareness of the issue. The mobilization of new students and thousands of volunteer tutors created excitement, innovation and a variety of local responses.

Over the next thirty years, literacy classes for adults grew steadily in number. The form of provision changed from one-to-one teaching by volunteers, to small group teaching, drop-in centres and e-learning. Teaching took place in adult and community learning centres, further education colleges, the workplace, in voluntary organizations, and in people's own homes.

During this time, adult literacy was often considered to be a marginal field and had to fight hard for recognition and funding. The Further and Higher Education Act of 1992 brought statutory status to adult literacy for the first time. It became a recognized subject area controlled by further education colleges. However, it was not until the creation of the Skills for Life strategy in 2001 that serious money was committed from central government to develop provision.

Four phases in the development of adult literacy in the UK

Mid-1970s: Literacy campaign led by a coalition of voluntary agencies with a powerful media partner, the BBC.

1980s: Provision developed substantially, supported by Local Education Authority, Adult Education Services and voluntary organizations, with leadership, training and development funding from a national agency (Adult Literacy and Basic Skills Agency, ALBSU, later the Basic Skills Agency, BSA.

1989–98: LEA funding and control of adult education was substantially reduced. Control of much of adult literacy provision was passed to the further education colleges.

1998 to present: Prompted by the OECD international literacy survey, a national Skills for Life strategy was developed, closely directed by central government. £1.5 billion of government money was committed, with unified funding across the learning skills sector through the Learning and Skills Council (LSC).

Despite its high importance for everyday opportunities in employment and education, numeracy has been a much less visible and resourced field than literacy. English for Speakers of Other Languages (ESOL), with its strong links to English as a Foreign Language (EFL), to the politics of immigration and language policy, to debates around language variety, racism and international developments, has an uncertain relationship with 'basic skills'. Policy creates, and sometimes breaks, these links between overlapping areas, which are also specialisms in their own right.

Task 1.7

Different specialisms
In your own employment or teaching practice, note how literacy, numeracy, ESOL and ICT are organized. Are they linked or treated as separate specialisms? How does this affect your work? How does it affect learners?

In the report produced by his committee in 1999, Claus Moser argued that provision was fragmented and inconsistent, and that teachers were poorly equipped and qualified to teach. The result was government action in the form of the Skills for Life strategy, which set ambitious targets for improvement in England. It aimed to set up an infrastructure for the field to support its expansion, including:

- new professional qualifications for teachers;

- new learner qualifications;
- core national curricula in ESOL, numeracy, and literacy;
- materials and training to help implement these changes;
- a media campaign to raise awareness in the public at large and among potential learners.

At the same time, ambitious targets were set to bring in adults to learning for the first time from a range of social groups. 'Hard-to-reach' adults from homeless to young unemployed men were targeted, with the aim of bringing them back into education, training and ultimately employment. Special funds were available to community-based organizations and trade union representatives.

In 2004 the strategy met its aim of 750,000 adults gaining an appropriate qualification at three levels in the new curricula: Entry Level, Level 1 or Level 2.

Separate strategies have been adopted in Scotland, Wales and Northern Ireland. Details of the four strategies can be found at:

- **England**: www.dcsf.gov.uk/readwriteplus
- **Scotland**: Adult Literacy and Numeracy in Scotland (2001) www.scotland. gov.uk
- **Wales**: www.basic-skills-wales.org
- **Northern Ireland**: Essential Skills for Living Strategy (2002) www.delni.gov.uk/essential-skills-for-living-strategy

How the field has grown: learner participation

Adult literacy provision has expanded considerably since its beginnings in the early 1970s. The following table shows how participation has increased:

> **1972**: Survey of local authority provision showed that just 5000 adults were receiving help with reading and writing in England and Wales (Haviland 1973).

> **1976**: 15,000 adults were receiving tuition across England and Wales.
> **1985**: ALBSU estimated 110,000 adults receiving tuition in literacy, numeracy and ESOL.

> **1995–96**: BSA reported that 319,402 people were receiving tuition in England, two-thirds of whom were studying in the FE sector (BSA 1997).

> **2003–04**: DfES (2004a) reported that 639,000 learners had undertaken at least one Skills for Life learning opportunity. By the end of 2004, Skills for Life had reached its target of 750,000 adults passing the national tests for adult literacy, numeracy and ESOL at Level 2.

> DfES (2004) reported that the figures for learners undertaking at last one Skills for Life learning opportunity were as follows:

> July 2000–01   453,000
> July 2001–02   585,000
> July 2002–03   653,000
> July 2004   639,000

2005–06: 2005 target exceeded and a total of 1,130,000 learners had achieved their first Skills for Life qualification.

By 2010: 2.25 million adults should have improved their basic skills as measured by gaining a qualification up to Level 2 in the national qualification framework.

Ideology and ethos: what has changed?

As will be clear from this brief account, people who have been involved with literacy work over the years have seen a major shift in the culture of the field. Changes in accreditation, professional status and the institutions where classes are provided have inevitably led to changes in what is defined as good or bad practice, and what counts as goals for literacy work.

When the literacy campaign began, an ideology of emancipation (or empowerment) dominated. It emphasized support for individual literacy needs and informal, democratic relationships between teachers and learners. There was little specialist training and few teaching materials, so practice was exploratory and improvised. 'In the beginning it was well-meaning, do-gooding people volunteering', one practitioner explained. 'We had ... a lot of emphasis, not on literacy for vocational preparation, but for self-fulfilment, empowerment, being somebody.'

This early work emphasized the diversity of learner needs and the importance of being responsive to these. Central to this approach was support for student-centred learning, enabling students to make active and informed decisions for themselves. The national resource agency, the Adult Literacy and Basic Skills Unit (ALBSU), endorsed this view: 'A participatory approach has been the "bedrock" of adult literacy tuition ... students not as passive receivers but as active participants in their own learning' (ALBSU 1985:5). Entry to what was then termed Adult Basic Education (ABE) was open, groups were mixed ability and there were no screening tests or eligibility criteria. There was a conscious philosophy that ABE should not replicate the experience of traditional schooling, which for many learners would have been before 1950. Many teacher–student relationships strived for equality and mutual exchange of expertise, and the roles of teacher and learner were often blurred, implying the possibility of movement between them.

Through the 1980s public discussions about literacy increasingly became linked to human resource investment. The Skills for Life strategy linked literacy not only to employment prospects but to social inclusion more generally, and particular groups of adults were targeted as learners. Although at the start literacy was said to be part of a broad system of lifelong learning for its own sake, an alignment with vocational training became more explicit over time. In the way it is delivered, adult literacy has moved much closer to the school system and to work-based training.

Where – physical settings and institutions

As we will see in Chapter 2, the range of learners that adult literacy aims to serve is very wide, from those who have recently left school to those who have been away from education for many years; people with different motivations, different past educational and life experiences, different language histories and different employment needs. This means adult literacy provision has to be flexible to accommodate this wide range of learners, wherever possible, offering learning opportunities that are easily accessible and welcoming. Table 11. shows some of the variety of organizations and settings in which adult literacy now takes place.

For people who have had a negative previous experience of education, or can't afford travel, standard college classes are not necessarily the best starting place. A great deal of effort has been made over the years to offer adult literacy in the variety of settings where learners are – from workplaces to tenants' groups, playgroups to prisons as well as in schools, adult community centres, libraries and FE colleges. As you might expect, the facilities available in these different settings vary widely and teachers have often to carry resources with them, including books and laptops.

Table 1.1: Forms of provision for adult literacy in England

Type of provision	Where?
Further education colleges	In main college facilities but also community-based centres and drop-in workshops. A few adult residential colleges exist around the country.
Adult community learning centres	Premises run by local authorities or voluntary organizations that are often multi-functional
Family learning	Primary schools, family learning centres, libraries, football clubs
Learndirect	High street and other venues, drop-in access to literacy programmes on computer or online from home
Workplace learning	Employer premises; private training providers, Jobcentre Plus, trade union centres; online support in national employers
Voluntary community-based literacy	Homeless foyers, centres for young unemployed, drug rehabilitation projects, residents' associations, travellers' programmes
Work-based learning	On-the-job support or as part of vocational training sessions in training bases
Prisons and probation service	In prisons, sometimes with dedicated education facilities; offenders and ex-offenders in community-based venues
Army	On-site, bases in a range of countries. This is one specialized type of workplace. Purpose-built classrooms exist. Soldiers also connect online to UK from overseas bases

For many years, adult literacy could be offered in a wide range of institutions under different names, such as 'Remedial English', 'General Studies' or 'Adult Literacy'. At first there were no purpose-built rooms for the work to be carried out and many learning groups met in makeshift, ill-equipped and inappropriate venues: portacabins, huts at the back of car parks, primary school classrooms with tiny chairs. Teachers pushed for flexibility in the timing and location of courses, and also argued for better practical facilities such as crèches and disabled access. Very few teachers now still work in people's homes, though many travel to community or work-based venues to teach small groups of adults. The nomadic life of the part-time teacher is part of the mythology of the field: 'We were always being moved about from one building to another'; 'I had to cross town to use the photocopier.'

Accessibility and good quality resources are now expected of any provider who receives LSC funding, and Ofsted inspection criteria apply to literacy programmes, wherever they are carried out. Teachers in all settings are likely now to have dedicated teaching space, equipped with appropriate technology and materials and often including some kind of drop-in workshop provision. In further education colleges teachers and learners can usually access the same facilities as others on vocational or other courses.

Who the tutors are and how this has changed

When adult literacy was first established, many of the tutors were volunteers or were taken on as hourly paid part-time tutors. In 1975 when the BBC programmes *On the Move* were broadcast, many people (90 per cent of them women) called to volunteer themselves as tutors. These volunteers were inexperienced in teaching adults, but full of enthusiasm and ideals about social justice. Many were women with young families looking for interesting part-time opportunities to carry on their vocation. Unlike other areas of teaching, no previous training or experience was necessary in the early days.

These volunteer beginnings, and the early marginalized status of Adult Literacy, has meant that developing a professional workforce has always been problematic. There are now more opportunities for training, specialist qualifications and a career structure, but the working conditions are still insecure. This means that it has been difficult to develop stable networks and professional bodies for adult literacy.

When adult literacy moved into the more formal further education sector in the early 1990s, this might have been expected to lead to better working conditions, greater job security and more full-time jobs. However, when the Skills for Life strategy began, statistics still suggested that only one in ten adult literacy or numeracy staff in England and Wales were full-time (BSA 1997). In 2004 a NIACE/TES survey into the Skills for Life workforce found:

> One in seven colleges and adult training centres depends on hourly-paid staff to run their entire basic literacy, numeracy and language courses ... More than half of all the institutions responding to the survey said hourly-paid staff did at least 40% of the work.
>
> (*TES* 2004).

Further education colleges are more likely to have full-time staff, often working as managers who co-ordinate a team of part-time tutors. Agency staff are often employed, especially in job centres and workplace programmes, hired on a temporary basis. Those working in community-based programmes have always depended largely on short-term project funding and have become expert in bidding and proposal writing. In short, the experiences of staff in adult literacy mirror the diversity in the lifelong learning sector as a whole – working conditions and funding depending on the kind of institutional setting they are in.

Professional development has been accelerated by the Skills for Life strategy. Skills for Life also brought requirements for more standardized teaching, record-keeping and performance output measures that some staff have found difficult to deal with, feeling under scrutiny themselves. Some are not paid for the extra time needed to complete the paperwork and worry that these demands detract from their teaching.

Task 1.8

Your entry story

Reflect on your own 'entry story' to adult literacy work. How does it compare with the following?

Interviewer: Can I just go right back to the beginning. What made you go into that prison environment and what made you stay?

Interviewee: Absolutely by default. I lived next door to an assistant governor who could recognize that the education team were always short of teachers ... He asked me to do English Literature at evenings with 21 year old men ... I left [primary school teaching] after my first child – there was no such thing as maternity leave then – and I was going to go back to supply teaching and he offered me this evening work. I hated it. I had never ever had such abuse, such an awakening to the world of prison, and my husband said to me, you do not quit, you've never quit in your life. Give it six weeks. Within six weeks I was hooked. I then enjoyed the environment, enjoyed the challenge, enjoyed the humour, enjoyed the breakthrough. It sounds very altruistic to say changing people's lives, but I knew I did touch lives because I got to the stage where they were asking me to bring a certain piece of work in, to continue with something the next week, to help write letters. The achievement of somebody being able to write, be it four lines to their Mum, was quite touching. And I suddenly thought, I've done it! I enjoyed primary school teaching immensely but this was a new challenge, it was a new dimension, it was a new exciting field and ... in all honesty it just fitted in with my situation. I could do sessional work and I did a lot of supply cover work and really it got under my skin as being a worthwhile challenge.

(Practitioner interviewed for the Changing Faces project)

How and what? Approaches to curriculum

During the first phase of the adult literacy campaign there was little existing wisdom about how to teach this new group of learners. Tutors brought their experience from primary, further or special education, from community development work or from teaching English as a Foreign Language. With minimal resources and institutional support they proceeded to invent a new field. They created methods of teaching, training and managing for adult learning that drew on what they already knew as they responded to the learners who arrived. They developed a range of innovative methods, including approaches to student writing and publishing, functional and linked (now 'embedded') skills.

Because of these origins, teaching in adult literacy has always been eclectic and pragmatic, and teachers have used a range of methods appropriate to individual learners. On the other hand, poor training opportunities have meant that teaching has not been systematically informed by theories that could be useful, especially for teaching those with specific learning needs.

Originally teaching was one-to-one, mainly by volunteers. This was succeeded by group work, partly as funding became available to pay for teachers and to provide appropriate accommodation. Teachers, often with volunteer support, would work with small groups of learners where a low student–staff ratio was promoted. This was important since many learners were taught in mixed-ability groups that were demanding on teachers' time and ingenuity.

By the mid-1990s two-thirds of all adult literacy learners were based in the more formal environment of further education colleges. Computer technologies arrived gradually in adult literacy, offering new pedagogical possibilities. The wider influences of technology and the increasing use of accreditation (see below) changed the nature of the curriculum and methodology. However, learners were still generally taught in smaller groups than in more mainstream provision and were increasingly encouraged to learn through individual programmes agreed with their teachers.

Skills for Life accelerated the trend to more formal and standardized approaches to teaching and learning, with the introduction of a core curriculum, developed from the school English curriculum, which separated skills (not learners) into different levels and a national test that measured achievement across these levels.

Assessment

In the 1970s and 1980s, assessment of learning within voluntary and adult education programmes was conducted informally through discussion and feedback with learners. There was a strong concern not to replicate the negative experiences that some adults brought with them from school. A premium was placed on face-to-face discussion and counselling around student needs and aspirations.

Teachers quickly realized the need to chart progress and plan learning. Systematic, adult-related, though not quantitative, assessment began to develop and teachers had a great deal of freedom to experiment. Records of progress, the forerunners to Individual Learning Plans (ILPs), were introduced and many variations tried out over the years.

At this time, policies that were reshaping other areas of education and training also significantly influenced assessment in adult literacy. The Educational Reform Act in 1988 introduced a national curriculum in schools and testing of children which enabled league tables of achievement to be produced nationally. In 1986 the National Council for Vocational Qualifications (NCVQ) was formed to develop a competency-based framework which would harmonize academic and vocational qualifications and simplify the maze-like world of post-school education and training.

In the 1990s, the earlier informal approaches to assessment were replaced by a new competency-based national qualification (Wordpower) that responded to the need for adult literacy to be incorporated into the national framework for vocational qualifications (NVQs). From 2000 onwards, the competency-based model was further developed in adult literacy during the ensuing Skills for Life era with the introduction of a national curriculum, national testing and a range of competency-based qualifications eligible for funding.

Where are we now? Tensions and enduring struggles

How change has happened

The last seven years have seen big changes in the face of adult literacy as serious amounts of government money have been committed to it for the first time. For staff new to the field, it is hard to imagine adult literacy without Skills for Life. For those with a longer involvement, this recent period has been one of significant and sometimes difficult change, but only the latest in a tumultuous field that has experienced constant reorganization. This seems set to continue with further planned changes to funding and to the government agencies that control the field. This ever-changing landscape has been commented on by researchers (see Edward et al. 2007) who point out both the opportunities and the obstacles this presents to teachers who often find their work being restructured or jobs changing with very little notice. It often feels as though ground is gained and then lost, wheels are reinvented, provision takes two steps forward then one step back. Bev Campbell (Campbell and Bradshaw 2007) has written about the similar experiences of practitioners in Australia and uses the image of the spiral staircase to express this feeling of cyclical change and rediscovery, always in a moving context.

What has been gained and lost under Skills for Life?

We have a field more closely connected to other forms of education and training, offering routes onward for learners. The increased funding, research and policy attention has made adult literacy more visible and given it higher status for tutors and programmes. The diversity of settings is accepted, with Skills for Life courses funded in a range of non-educational settings, like foyers for homeless young people, to ex-offenders and parent groups. The core curriculum, regular inspection and a national test has given a stronger structure to teaching and learning. Teacher qualifications will ensure a more professional workforce.

Alongside these achievements are some danger areas to keep an eye on. The targets may have been achieved at the expense of older learners and those with more complex learning needs. There is more top-down definition of what learners need and it is more difficult to negotiate a programme of learning with students, given the pressures of paperwork and funding categories. We are in danger of losing the more open-ended perspective on literacy as part of lifelong learning to a narrower view of it as functional competencies needed for employment, a trend set to continue with the Leitch (2006) report.[5]

Many tutors are still in precarious positions and working long hours over the odds. We have lost a specialist national agency for adult literacy as the BSA is dismantled. ESOL is being separately treated with the ending of free courses.

In an era emphasizing evidence of achievement, funding is used to steer and reward behaviour which will lead to meeting targets: for learners to achieve qualifications by set dates, and for national standards of professional practice. Practitioners need all the imagination they can muster to make sense of and to shape the frameworks they now work within, while responding to the needs of learners who are as diverse as ever.

One thing that is clear from the discussion above is that the very diversity of the learners, the expectations society holds for literacy and its deep connections with issues of inequality and citizenship will ensure debates will continue about what counts as adult literacy, what the goals of it should be, and the best strategies for supporting learning.

Further reading and resources

Barton, D. (2007) *Literacy: An Introduction to the Ecology of Written Language*, 2nd edn. Oxford: Blackwell.
Barton, D. and Hamilton, M. (1998) *Local Literacies – Reading and Writing in One Community.* London: Routledge.
Barton, D., Hamilton, M. and Ivanič, R. (eds) (2000) *Situated Literacies: Reading and Writing in Context.* London: Routledge.
Hamilton, M. and Hillier, Y. (2006) *Changing Faces of Adult Literacy, Language and Numeracy. A Critical History.* Stoke on Trent: Trentham Books.
Stephens, W.B. (1990) Literacy in England, Scotland and Wales, 1500–1900, *History of Education Quarterly*, 30(4), Special Issue on History of Literacy: 545–71.

Notes

1. You may also want to browse Google Literacy Project website, sponsored by UNESCO: www.google.com/literacy/search.html Use the 'scholar' links to

search for research from UK and use the map to get a feel for the international interest in adult literacy.

2. The Changing Faces project was a research project which charted the development of Adult Literacy, Numeracy and ESOL (ALNE) over thirty years, carried out between 2001 and 2004. A total of 200 interviews were undertaken with practitioners and adult learners, from four case study regions in England. Documentary evidence and an archive of materials were collated, and from this a series of timelines were created.

3. Adult literacy has developed differently in each of the countries of the UK. These differences have become more pronounced since devolution.

4. See Briggs and Burke 2005.

5. In 2006, the British Treasury produced a report, *The Leitch Review of Skills*, which was the result of an enquiry by Lord Leitch into the skill levels of the British workforce. The report warned that Britain would be left behind as a world economy unless it took immediate action to improve work-related skills. The report advised a target of 90 per cent of the workforce to have qualifications at Level 2 (GCSE level) by 2020.

2   Who are the learners?

Yvon Appleby

Introduction

Who are literacy, numeracy and language learners – it's obvious isn't it? They are people who need to learn or improve these skills. You can see photographs and descriptions of learners on posters, in media campaigns (like the Gremlins in the UK) and described in policy documents. Surely we know how many learners there are, how many there should be and what levels they should be achieving? However, as this chapter discusses, what seems a straightforward question to ask becomes less obvious in answering it. This question, at the heart of any teaching and learning, has particular significance for those working in adult literacy, numeracy and language at a time of increased international focus on basic skills and the development of national literacy and numeracy strategies that include teacher training and professional development. The question of who the learners are links policy to what happens in classrooms and to people's everyday lives.

In policy the term 'literacy learner' is used in a general way to define categories, groups and individuals who attend classes or some form of provision to improve their knowledge and literacy skills. The term is constructed through public and policy discourse and is often associated with numbers of people who are identified as needing to learn. Targets of learners to be taught usually accompany this. For example, in the UK the Moser report, *A Fresh Start* (DfEE 1999), identified seven million adults who lacked adequate levels of literacy to be able to function effectively. This definition and estimation of need underpinned the creation of the national strategy Skills for Life (DfEE 2001). In this case people lacking necessary literacy skills were constructed as learners by policy in their absence. This labelling process is mainly external to individuals' lives and meanings around literacy. It relates strongly, although not exclusively, to social factors where lack of literacy becomes defined by policy as an individual responsibility and a social 'problem', one that can be remedied by learning literacy, numeracy or language.

In their book Mary Hamilton and Yvonne Hillier (2006) look at the history of adult basic education, showing how the definition of the literacy 'problem' identified numbers of 'illiterate' and people with low levels of literacy, a number which changed between 1970 and 2000. As we discuss earlier, definitions and numbers are not fixed at this time and are still changing (see for example House of Commons report of Skills for Life 2009). The definition of the 'problem' also shapes the solution; that is, people with low literacy should learn new skills or seek to improve existing ones – in both cases becoming learners. Whilst the term learner is useful in policy and overall planning of provision it does not tell us about these people as individuals, what they are learning, why they want to learn and how this fits in their everyday lives. It tells us who the policy spotlight falls upon, defining them as learners, at various points of its pendulum swing.

If policy uses general definitions and categories, can a more authentic and individual sense of who learners are be gained from classrooms and other learning provisions? This is not straightforward either, as once outside an individual classroom what voices represent the experiences of people who come to learning provision in a range of settings? There are many types of provision ranging from discrete and formal to informal and including various types of embedded learning, both formal and informal. What should be represented: those who succeed, or those who struggle and leave? Should learner voices show the greatest gain or the greatest pain in learning? What is authentic learner experience and who chooses what is represented, and why? Although used for celebrating achievement, or in showing the need for continued funding, this can easily fall into positive confessional accounts. John Preston (2006) calls this 'telling for welfare': narratives that, whilst important in terms of provision, do not adequately represent the experiences of learners. Representing learners within professional circles also runs the risk of exposing power relationships between learners and professionals when deciding what story to include and how it is told.[1] Stories from the classroom and voices of learners may unfortunately, and in spite of a commitment to greater learner representation, tell us more about the provision and providers than they do about the learners.

People use the word 'learner' themselves, particularly when attending some form of learning provision. When people self-identify as learners they have already made the first steps on a learning journey.[2] There is a personal recognition, however fragile, that learning relates in some way to individual history, current circumstances and future aspirations. This could be for concrete everyday things like getting a job, for helping children with homework or being able to manage complicated forms and household bills. It could be for less concretely expressed reasons like overcoming a fear of maths, feeling better about oneself and gaining social confidence by being with others. Or it could be managing to attend a course regularly, something not previously achievable within difficult life circumstances. In other words, there are specific and particular reasons, often linked to everyday experiences, why people come to learn and identify themselves as literacy learners.

There is clearly an overlap between the different ways that 'learner' is used, as some people, identified in policy target groups, also self-identify as learners and take up learning opportunities in literacy or numeracy classes. Whilst there is sometimes a close fit, it is not a simple causal relationship where one thing causes the other to happen. For example, being identified in the media and through policy discourse as having low literacy skills, therefore part of the 'problem', isn't sufficient in itself to make people become learners. Even though they are identified externally as belonging to a target group, therefore as needing to learn literacy skills, they do not necessarily identify themselves as such and do not see the need to learn these skills.[3]

Here there is a mismatch between externally imposed meanings of being a learner and those that individuals hold themselves, as will be discussed later in this chapter.

Does it matter who learners are? Identifying the different ways that the term is used is crucial in terms of practice as it informs understanding of who learners are and why they come to learn – the very basis of pedagogy (the science/art of teaching). If we see learners in the general sense only, used by policy to identify people who in its terms have low or inadequate levels of literacy, then the purpose of teaching is to improve these skills in the most effective way. In this construction of learner, individual progress and success is measured only through external assessment and tests linked to the progress of learning these skills and knowledge. However, where learners are seen as people using different types of literacies in their everyday lives, for a variety of purposes, and who have particular reasons for wanting to learn new skills and develop existing ones, this requires a different approach. Here the motivations and aspirations of the learner need to be understood and connected to the purposes and uses of literacy in their lives in relation to what is being learned.

This is more than a student-centred approach as, whilst it places the learner at the centre of learning, the knowledge and skills being learned relate to existing everyday uses and social practices of literacy. This suggests, as will be shown below, that people as complex, multifaceted individuals learn things of value or importance to them that are connected to and are embedded in their everyday lives. Learning, therefore, is a part of a whole life experience and learning, both informal and formal, needs to relate to that life experience to be useful, meaningful or relevant. Learning is part of everyday life and is not something confined only to classrooms or policy discourses. Rather than talking about learners who are people it might be more useful to think of people who learn a variety of things in different ways throughout their lives.

Task 2.1

Writing a learner case study

Choose an example of a literacy learner represented in the media – this could be from a television advert or a poster. Write a short 'case study' of this person based upon the information given. This could include their appearance, tone of voice, level of confidence, relationship to others and what they are doing. Then choose a learner that you know and write a short 'case study' about them. How do these compare? Swap your case studies with someone else and see if you both have described the people you teach differently to the one constructed in the media. What does this tell us? Can you support people you teach to write about themselves, providing another comparison? What are the similarities and differences in each account?

Adult learners' lives: linking people's lives and learning in a social practice approach

The connection between what literacy, language and numeracy people learn in class and what they use and learn at home was the focus of the three-year Adult Learners'

Lives (ALL) study. Lancaster Literacy Research Centre carried out the ALL study between 2002 and 2005 as part of NRDC[4] research into the national Skills for Life strategy. The overall aim of the project was to develop understanding between learners' lives and the language, literacy and numeracy learning which they engaged in, drawing out implications from these findings for practice and policy. Working in three sites in the north west of England, the project looked at different learning environments, from discrete literacy and numeracy classes to those embedded in other types of provision, including support services within the community. We worked in classrooms with teachers and learners, observing and recording classroom practices, linking this to literacy practices from the everyday lives of people who attended provision. The project produced several reports[5] from this detailed and collaborative research, a book (Barton *et al*. 2007) and several guides for practitioners (Appleby 2008; Appleby and Barton 2008).

The project was rooted in an approach that sees literacy as social practices and that took a social perspective on language, literacy and numeracy. As mentioned earlier, social practices are activities that people carry out in everyday contexts of home, work and community. They are part of, and are shaped by, all other aspects of people's lives including language/dialect, culture, socio-economic factors and other identities. So things like where people live, class background, income, religion, family status and ethnicity are counted as important. The approach acknowledges that people's everyday lives are complex and varied and the roles of languages, literacies and numeracies are equally complex and varied. A social perspective on language, literacy and numeracy teaching and learning meant taking account of this in the classrooms and learning environments we studied. It meant that learners were seen as complex and varied people who had individual histories and current circumstances with hopes and aspirations for the future.

A social practice approach to literacy, in its simplest form, looks at what people do with literacy in their everyday practices.[6] A social perspective to literacy, language and numeracy teaching and learning recognizes that these practices are always embedded in social contexts and purposes – they are not just decontextualized skills learned in a classroom. This approach means recognizing learners as whole people who use literacy, numeracy and language in a range of settings, both inside and outside the classroom. It is therefore different, and in contrast, to a deficit view of learners that sees people as empty vessels to be filled with knowledge.

Using this social perspective enabled us to look at learning from the outside in rather than just from the inside out; that is, from everyday practices of the learners, not just from teaching applied in the classroom. We found that many teachers experience professional tensions in responding to the different ways that learners are constructed. The first, which we identified as 'responsive professionalism', involved tutors listening to learners in order to fine-tune their teaching, making it relevant to people's lives. The second, which we called 'new professionalism', responded to the ability of tutors to fulfil their institutional commitment through adherence to procedures and completing necessary paperwork. Here learners were viewed in more general target-driven terms requiring assessments and monitoring. We concluded that although 'new professionalism' was helping tutors to make their teaching more systematic and fit a core curriculum it was in tension with learners' needs and interests, and made it difficult to always respond to these – the cornerstone of the teaching approach underpinning 'responsive professionalism'. Whilst these are described in terms of teaching, they both rest upon differing perceptions of learners, indicating whether teaching is more responsive to the needs of the curriculum or the learner.

In summary the ALL research found that:

- **Learning is the product of a dialogue between what learners bring and what teachers bring**: To have a dialogue, rather than a monologue, tutors need to understand the complexity of people's life circumstances, which may include health issues, disruption, violence or other hidden difficulties.
- **Tutors need to respond to specific learning contexts and individual learners**: To do this they need to understand the possibilities and constraints of the settings and the circumstances of the individuals they work with.
- **Good personal relationships are important for learning**: This includes recognizing learners as 'whole people' with lives outside the classroom who achieve different forms of learning within it, including what is termed soft outcomes or unrecorded progress.
- **Listening to learners takes time and resources**: Teachers need awareness/training of the need to spend time getting to know how literacy, language or numeracy fits into the lives of the individuals they teach.
- **There are tensions between two types of teacher professionalism for some literacy, numeracy or language teachers**: This tension is generated by differing responses and constructions of the identity of learners inside and outside the classroom.

What was shown by this, and by practitioner research attached to the project,[7] was that seeing a connection between everyday lives and literacy, language and numeracy learning is important in understanding and responding to what people want and need when they come to learn. A social practice approach recognizes that most people use literacy, language and numeracy in their everyday lives in some way and for a purpose. It also recognizes that most people have ways of learning new skills or information and finding strategies for managing their everyday lives. This includes using family, friends and in some circumstances what Jane Mace (2002) identifies as scribes. This approach sees literacy, language and numeracy learning as something that people do in their everyday lives, not only as something that happens in the classroom or in other forms of learning provision. In this way a simple distinction between being and not being a learner becomes less clear as people frequently learn as part of their everyday social literacy practices.

Looking at the connections between everyday practices, how people are identified as learners and how they experience learning is significant in understanding why some people come to learn and why others do not, or drop out. It is also significant in looking at why some learning is successful and some less so. This connection is central in understanding people's participation and engagement in learning. Three questions will structure the next sections that focus on the participation of people in learning – looking at motivation and engagement. The questions ask: what do learners bring? What do learners want from learning? And what do learners feel they are gaining?

What do learners bring?

Learners are whole people situated in everyday lives. As such they have complex lives which are influenced by many different things including socio-economic factors, culture, language, health and sense of belonging. People have differing circumstances; some may work whilst others are unemployed. Some may have one language whilst others are communicating in a second, third or even fourth language. Some may live with poverty, uncertainty, threat or violence whilst others are settled, have adequate resources and feel sustained by their network or communities.

People have existing knowledge and strategies for using and learning literacy; they have hobbies, interests and ruling passions. In *Local Literacies: Reading and Writing in One Community* (2000) David Barton and Mary Hamilton show how people have existing funds of knowledge and also use brokers and local networks of support. Brokers and sponsors are people who become a resource by using their knowledge and skills to help others carry out tasks or learn new skills. By looking at these everyday activities, which included taking minutes for the Allotment Association, writing to a favourite personality or keeping family records, Barton and Hamilton found that people used what they called vernacular, or everyday literacy to negotiate a variety of texts. The texts were varied, things we would recognize from our own lives like junk mail to borrowing books from the library, but importantly they were connected to their everyday lives and activities whatever 'level' of literacy they described themselves having.

People also bring a variety of histories with them, some which relate to their confidence or identity as 'a learner'. In the ALL research we found that many people had previous negative experiences of learning at school and some also experienced this as an adult. Many said they had felt intimidated and bullied at school, which had impacted on what they had been able to learn at the time and affected how they saw themselves now as adults. They had left compulsory education 'not being able to write properly' and many said they had been called, and felt themselves to be 'stupid', 'slow' or 'thick'. More than one person recalled being physically assaulted or being shouted at and one had been thrown across the room for not being able to answer a question. These were powerful negative memories from previous literacy, language and numeracy learning, which some people brought to current experiences of learning. For some, adult literacy learning was also a negative experience involving the humiliation of learning what Elizabeth (pseudonyms were chosen by participants in the project) described as 'the cat sat on the mat type of thing'. For her it was particularly insulting as she was managing life as young widow, doing a day's work, finding babysitters for her children and making a long bus ride to attend class.

People also brought with them many positive things to learning, both from their previous histories and from their current circumstances. Jason, who attended a class as a learner and who also became a co-researcher, shows the different ways in which literacy use and learning is connected to family and community and how people bring a range of both positive and difficult experiences with them. Although the focus of this book is on literacy, Jason illustrates how literacy, language and numeracy are interlinked in everyday life. Whilst they are separated into discrete knowledge and skill areas for teaching, in learning inside and outside the classroom they are mutually reinforcing and interdependent. Whilst Jason was attending a maths class he was using literacy and language skills to be able read material, write answers, record his ILP (Individual Learning Plan), talk to his tutor and apply his maths skills in his everyday and community activities. If we see Jason as a 'whole person' who is learning maths, amongst other things, it is possible to see that the boundaries between literacy and numeracy are not as clearly defined in his life as if we view him simply in educational terms as a 'maths learner'.

Other people that we worked with attended a literacy class to develop or improve particular skills, such as Elizabeth. Elizabeth described herself as dyslexic and because of this found spelling very difficult. She felt confident in her numeracy abilities, particularly 'mental arithmetic' as she was a salesperson, but unlike Jason could not record this in writing. Some adults may therefore view and describe themselves as literacy learners because this is the skill they have come to learn from a class that is identified as such. However, taking a wider angle view shows that there is a relationship between literacy, language and numeracy in people's lives, and as educators it is helpful to understand this to be able to teach effectively (see Appleby and Barton 2009 for a more detailed account of Elizabeth's life careers).

Learner profile 1

Elizabeth was 50 years old when we met her in a spelling class in Liverpool. She explained that the attended this class because she was dyslexic and had had 'a real problem' with spelling all her life. Early on Elizabeth had taken jobs such as working in a toy factory and then a brush factory, which did not need any writing. After her marriage, like many women in her community, she stayed at home to look after her two young children. She said this was expected of women then and she was reasonably happy.

After her husband died unexpectedly in his early forties Elizabeth started work to support her two young daughters. For several years she worked as a barmaid and in low-skilled jobs to make ends meet. At this time she also returned to learning and attended an evening adult literacy class to improve her prospects. She found this patronizing and boring; it did nothing for her confidence so she left. Her father also died at this time leaving her with very little family support.

Elizabeth eventually worked in electrical retail, developing her skills in sales and frequently being recognized and rewarded as the top regional salesperson. She described using many strategies to hide her poor writing skills, although she was always worried about being found out and felt it was weakness in a highly competitive environment. Eventually the stress of maintaining her high level of sales in a hostile environment resulted in a breakdown.

Elizabeth's doctor suggested that as part of treatment she should attend the gym and sign up for a class. Elizabeth said stepping through the local outreach centre to sign up for the spelling class was one of the most terrifying moments of her life and it took her several attempts.

Elizabeth felt that coming to the class enabled her for the first time to learn about spelling and she was able to use her new knowledge in her everyday life, including booking a trip to America online. Importantly, she also described reading for pleasure and was supporting her two daughters to read and continue with their studies. Elizabeth returned to work in another retail store, describing feeling more confident in managing literacy at work and also in recognizing what other skills she brought with her. She planned to buy a car to become more independent – to do this she looked at the paperwork at home, slowly using some of the techniques that she had learned in class.

Like Elizabeth, many people who are learners also support the learning of others within families, communities and at work. This learning is often intergenerational where people share their knowledge and skills across ages and different learning contexts. In a bilingual family literacy class, part of the wider ALL project, we found that mothers were teaching their children how to speak Arabic at home whilst their children were teaching them how to write it. The mothers spoke their own language but had not had access to the alphabet or script when they were young women in their home country. Their children on the other hand were learning to write at Arabic school, attending after going to their English school, but did not have the chance to practise speaking there. The research, looking at connections between home and school, showed that many of the women used and developed methods of teaching that they themselves experienced as literacy and language learners at the bilingual family literacy centre (Gilbert and Appleby 2005). They became insightful teachers, of culture and language, as well as engaged learners participating in their own learning.

People like Elizabeth and the women from the bilingual family literacy centre above bring many things to literacy, numeracy and language learning. As people they use many literacies in their everyday lives, including speaking, visual representation and reading and writing. They have existing, individual and sometimes unique literacy practices to bring to learning. As people they bring understandings that are situated within socio-economic and cultural aspects of everyday lives. They have experience of what it means to be unemployed, a single parent with young children or living in a large multicultural community that they can to contribute to learning. As people they have insights of living and working with others in families, communities and in the workplace. From these they bring practices that travel from one context to another and experience of intergenerational teaching to benefit the learning of others.[8]

What do learners want?

People learn in a variety of ways and settings depending upon what they want and what is available, according to personal choice and individual circumstance. For example, it could be someone attending a *Computers Don't Bite* course because they have just bought a new computer. It could be someone attending a work-based course in the Army to achieve a qualification needed for promotion. Or it could be someone attending a literacy course to give them the confidence and skills to manage their rehab programme. It may be a mixture of several things, for example improving literacy skills to be able to learn to use a computer, which will help the grandchildren with their homework.

What people want from learning is often a mixture of social and economic benefits – some may be immediate and obvious whilst others are longer term and not so clearly articulated. The Wider Benefits of Learning study[9] showed how learning connects to many aspects of people's social and economic lives. Focusing on health, family life and social capital, the authors look at the breadth and interconnectedness of what they term 'learning effects'. They show that there are tangible benefits from learning for both society and the individual (an impossible connection to untangle), resulting in increased economic performance, social integration, improved health and well-being as well as wider benefits for family and communities. These findings were also echoed in an evaluation of the Scottish adult literacy and numeracy strategy[10] that showed a 'virtuous circle' of improvements in confidence, civic participation and learning. The study found that increased confidence and self-esteem impacted on familial, social and work relations, which in turn add to the sum of learners' social capital. They noted that the precise nature of the causal relationship between these factors could not be easily determined.

As with these studies the ALL research found interlinked connections between social, economic and family benefits from learning. From our research people's motivations for learning can be summarized as:

- **Gaining particular subject knowledge**: Many people told us that they came to a particular class because they wanted to know more about English or spelling. For example Susan said: 'I hope to learn a lot of my spellings because when I joined the ICT course I realized that I couldn't spell the shortest word'.
- **Improving wider skills and learning about learning**: In interviews people told us about the other things they were learning about and benefiting from in their class or learning environment. Susan described how learning spelling, what she came for, had added to her wider under-standing of language: 'I think English is fascinating and it's a subject that you can go on and on with. The more you find out about it the more interesting it becomes. I think that's the way learning should be, isn't it?'
- **Making social contacts and developing new social networks and skills**: The social aspects of learning are well documented in both the studies referred to above and others.[11] We found this was an important part of learning, which impacted inside and outside the classroom. Inside the

classroom social contact with the teacher and other learners was significant. For example, Jack, a dairy farmer often working on his own, valued the social aspect of the literacy class where most people were like him. Alfonso said he liked meeting and chatting to new people as it gave him the opportunity to practise his language skills and meet new people where he lived.

- **Developing skills and confidence for finding work or gaining promotion**: Many people want to learn to enable them either to find work or to get promotion in their existing jobs. Abdul wanted to improve his spoken English to get a better job that reflected his previous education and training. When we spoke to him he was working as agency cleaner although he had been a qualified agronomist previously in Iraq. Alfonso was studying to be a chef after finding it hard to get enough work to support his family. Jason, mentioned above, wanted to get qualifications to enable him to get a 'better job' which didn't involve working physically hard and being outside in all weathers.

- **Overcoming school failure and previous negative experiences of learning**: Success at learning as an adult was for some people a primary goal for attending classes or learning provision. This could be subject-specific, for example being able to do literacy after previous failed attempts. Or, more generally, being able to participate and succeed in what is called basic skills learning. Growing up deaf without anyone realizing meant that Susan left school feeling she was a failure. She wanted to learn skills that she had missed at school but also wanted to overturn these negative experiences to see herself, and be seen, as someone that was 'clever enough' to learn, not as someone who 'never put pen to paper'.

What people want from learning varies from person to person and it also changes for individuals themselves as lives and circumstances change. Rick was part of the NRDC Learner Study carried out at Lancaster and Sheffield Universities (reported in Warner and Vorhaus 2008). In the qualitative strand of the study people attending provision were asked how they were benefiting from learning and what they were getting from attending provision. Rick was interviewed as part of the study and at the time attended a literacy class at his local Probation Centre. He shows clearly how what people want changes over time, often as their life circumstances alter.

Learner profile 2

Rick was 38 years old when we spoke to him. He was attending a weekly literacy class working to take the Level 1 test in the learning centre organized by his Probation Service. Rick was given the choice to do a course as part of his Community Sentence, which he agreed to. The course was supported by a facilitator from a private training provider and by a probation support officer.

Rick had worked all his life as a plasterer, managing his own business for 23 years as well as doing contract work in Germany and other parts of Europe. This work was well paid, earning him up to £600 a week. He described the money flowing through his fingers, most of it spent on drinking heavily whilst he was away from his family. He found writing home difficult and was unhappy, depressed and antisocial.

Being in prison gave him the opportunity to think about the future: 'I mean, there's times when I've been in prison people look at you to say, what are you doing that for? But I put all that to the back of my mind; it's peer pressure. At the end of the day it's only about yourself, isn't it?' Rick wanted to change his life and attending class was, as he described it, a stepping stone to be able to achieve this. He explained: 'So this is a stepping stone. For a start, I've already been into college and got the paperwork and that's got to be sent in and hopefully start in September. All my life I've been motivated by money so I've ended up doing things I didn't want to because of money, like working in Germany. I've worked all over the place and I've lived away from my family. It's always been about money at the end of the day, but I don't want that anymore. I'd rather have a less paid job and enjoy the job.'

Rick wanted to do a fitness instructor course at his local college, hoping that learning would help him to find something 'that makes me happy, a happier person'. His goal was 'to wake up in the morning and want to go to work instead of thinking, oh I'm there and I can't do this again ... I want to get up in the morning and think, yes I like that and want to do it.'

Rick shows that people benefit from literacy, language and numeracy at different times in their lives. Although he was unable to write letters or provide quotations as a plasterer, this did not motivate him at that time to become a literacy learner. Now, at this point in his life, he is motivated to become a learner, achieving long-term goals: to change his life to become a happier and more fulfilled person. By accessing learning in prison and the Probation Service, as part of his sentencing, he was able to do this.

Research on provision for disaffected young people in custody and the community[12] shows that many people have strong aspirations, like Rick's, for getting work and being financially independent. Where literacy was linked to work experience and vocational training it was felt by the young people to be relevant, as it contributed directly to what they wanted. They valued this learning more than literacy, numeracy or language taught as a subject within a specific education or education in the community context. Unlike Rick, who at 38 years old was working towards attending college, for many of the younger people this was unobtainable as they did not have the literacy skills or confidence to be able to attend vocational courses at college.

Different types of provision can offer different opportunities for people to achieve what they want from learning. For some adults, being able to learn at work is important as it fits in with their everyday timetables, responsibilities and activities. Being able to study at lunchtime or straight after a shift makes it possible for some people who would otherwise find making the time difficult. Workplace learning can be fitted around work patterns, such as refuse collection or cleaning shifts. It can also be specifically tied into localized need and what people want to learn, for example literacy to support driving tests for staff wanting to be promoted to drivers, or numeracy for learning to operate warehousing systems.[13]

Further education, the largest provider of literacy, numeracy and language, is often able to offer a range of courses. This is shown on the websites of some of the larger colleges (for example www.candi.ac.uk www.citycol.ac.uk; www.ntyneside.ac.uk www.liv-coll.ac.uk/). And increasingly literacy, numeracy and language are being embedded in other curriculum areas, particularly in vocational subjects. This means that people who teach literacy, numeracy and language skills are changing as well as those who might be identified as literacy learners. A series of case studies produced by an NRDC embedding project[14] shows this in more detail, illustrating different ways in which literacy, numeracy and language is being embedded within a range of learning provision. The Literacies for Learning in Further Education project, part of the TLRP (Teaching and Learning Research Programme), is also producing insights into how a range of literacies and literacy practices can be applied to a range of FE teaching and learning environments.[15]

Research in community settings, carried out as part of the ALL project, looked at people who had many complex issues in their lives and the types of literacy, numeracy and language learning they participated in. The project worked with people in a drug and alcohol centre, an organization that supported homeless people, a shelter for young homeless people, a tenants' association and a domestic violence support group. From our research we found that people wanted particular things from learning, often echoing the same things that motivated people with less complex or turbulent lives. For some, it provided a structure to their day, something that was known and stable. For some, it was a place to achieve skills and learning that had been disrupted or hadn't been possible within a negative school experience. For many, what they wanted from learning, like both Jason and Rick above, was a way of constructing a positive future. This was often in terms of work, living independently, being socially confident and belonging to networks and communities (see Appleby 2008).

There are many common aspects to what people want from learning literacy, numeracy and language skills which are individually negotiated in a range of different contexts such as college, prison, the workplace or community provision. The context shapes both what is provided and how learning is individually experienced. The physical learning environment, the structure of the curriculum and expectations around progress and assessment, teaching and learning relationships and levels of support available were all identified as significant factors in the context for learning.

What learners say about learning

By listening to learners it is possible to see what people bring with them and what they want from learning. The process of listening also shows that people have experience of learning in their everyday lives; they are not just learners but are often supporting the learning of others, either directly or indirectly. In the ALL research we found that people were able to talk clearly about what they liked and what was important to them in learning. They were active agents, not passive recipients in the process of learning, both inside and outside of the classroom. People described a mixture of things that were important to them: getting the knowledge, skills or information they had come for from a teacher that was knowledgeable and competent; feeling safe and supported; and meeting and engaging with others. These responses fit within the range of cognitive, emotional and social dimensions of learning.[16] They also resonate with findings from the 2003/04 National Learner Satisfaction Survey (LSC 2005), which surveyed over 43,000 learners receiving tuition or training through further education, work-based learning and adult and community learning providers. The survey found that a large proportion of learners said they enjoyed learning, 'getting a buzz' from it, with almost 50 per cent saying they enjoyed learning for the social aspect. A large proportion in the survey also described increased enthusiasm for the subject, being more confident in the ability to learn, being more creative and prepared to try new things. A significant number mentioned gaining skills for a job whilst others talked of benefits to health and sense of well-being.

Many of these findings, illustrating a learner perspective, were also present in the ALL project. Our smaller scale ethnographically informed research found that several things were important for people to be able to learn successfully. These were:

- **The right time for learning**: The right time for learning is a combination of individual life experiences, purposes and goals with what is available. For some, like Rick above, the right time fitted in with his desire to change his life goals, which coincided with the opportunity and support to learn as part of his sentence. For others the right time was in response to a new job, promotion, retirement or a change of area or country. For many the right time was not always a fixed or secure time, resulting in dipping in and out of learning provision. In some cases, as Sophie below shows, individuals may dip in and out over a period of time.
- **Learning that was useful and relevant to everyday life**: People often said they wanted to learn things that were directly useful and relevant to their everyday lives. This included being able to write a shopping list, write a cheque or address and envelope. It also included being able to use the computer to use chatrooms to meet people, to play games and visit eBay. Many said they wanted to learn themselves to support the learning of others, usually children or grandchildren, and to 'keep up with things'.
- **Learning at the right pace**: Many people said that the pace of learning was important to them. For some it was about not going too fast and having time to repeat things until they felt confident they had understood and absorbed new information. For others, particularly language learners working at higher levels and people with recent experiences of education, a faster pace was preferred that kept up with their developing skills and growing confidence. In both cases people appreciated being able to talk about their pace of learning.
- **Learning that recognized the social dimension of people**: Many people valued the social dimension of learning, of meeting other people and of 'getting out of the house'. People formed friendships and developed support networks which were as important to them as the subject content

they were learning. Many people said being treated as an adult by teachers and other learners was an important factor in participating and achieving. It was frequently compared to negative and demeaning experiences of learning at school, which did not recognize the social dimension of learning or of learners as individuals.

The type of learning people participate in varies, depending on individual lives and circumstances. For some, attending literacy, numeracy or language classes at college or in the workplace may provide literacy, numeracy and language learning at a pace and in an environment that is comfortable. For others this is not the case as they may require more support to manage their lives and learning within a community setting. A practitioner-led study at Broadway Homeless project[17] showed the importance of providing learning that was responsive to the complexity of people's histories and current circumstances and could support plans for the future. The project was based upon practitioner awareness of the difficulties in providing and measuring learning inside and outside the classroom; learning that could be 'officially counted' and that was also useful and relevant to homeless people's lives. The project developed different ways of capturing outcomes of learning, which included social interaction and communication, learning and skills as well as quality of life. They found that improved communication and reduced isolation were key outcomes for people, which reinforced their learning. They describe this as a 'ping-pong effect', between feelings and results, leading to an increase in confidence, which in turn led to an improvement in skills and vice versa.

The 'ping-pong effect' fits Sophie's life and learning below. Sophie, part of the ALL research, said that she wanted to learn and described the things important for her to do this. This included physical and emotional safety, and being treated like an adult – something very different to her experiences at school. She also described things that she didn't want, including being bored by a school approach to basic skills that was uninteresting and didn't stretch the skills that she already had.

Learner profile 3

Sophie at 18 years old was regular attender at Nightcare, a shelter for young homeless people. She had a troubled childhood, as her mother, a teacher, was drug- and alcohol-dependent. Although a bright child, she hated school and often absconded. She was eventually expelled for repeated assault and arson offences. She became homeless at the age of 15 and because of this missed her GCSE exams.

Sophie lived in the Nightcare hostel and went to the day centre attached. This safe space gave her life structure as well as providing a safe environment with food, people and activities. There she learnt often without realizing it as she was involved in arts and craft activities that she enjoyed. She said this was different to learning at school. Sophie had several attempts at going to college but did not manage to complete a course because of the difficulties she was managing in her daily existence where finding shelter, food and safety were her main priorities. The last course she started, on landscape gardening, she left as she became pregnant.

Sophie liked creative and practical activities and found what she called 'basic skills stuff' boring and easy. She enjoyed reading and her favourite author was Virginia Andrews; she said about her books: 'Like it's real life … I can relate to the people, like the stuff that's going on'. Sophie also writes Haiku poetry in French and English and free style writing, often when going through a bad patch.

Sophie was determined to go back to college after the baby was born to take her GCSEs and A levels to enable her eventually to study veterinary medicine or psychology.

Many learners know and are able to say what they want from learning. But achieving this is not always straightforward or easy. The difficulty, particularly for people with complex lives, arises from matching this with what is available. As shown in Chapter 1, what is available is not fixed, as policy indicates who is considered to be 'a learner' and the type of provision and assessment needed to respond to this.

What is more difficult is to find information about why people leave and why they don't come in the first place. People leave learning for a variety of reasons. Some relate to people's life choices or circumstances, others relate to the nature of provision, and some to a mixture of both. This could be moving areas or finding that a course has stopped being funded and is not running any more. Finding out why people don't self-identify as learners, although they are identified publicly as needing to learn, is clearly difficult. One way of approaching this question is to look at existing large data sets of people such as the National Child Development Study. This is a continuing longitudinal study of people born in Great Britain in 1958 that has collected data on medical care, health, cognitive and social growth as well as educational progress. Six survey sweeps at intervals throughout the members' lives (starting at age 7 with the last one at 42 years old) provides information, amongst other things, about people attending adult learning. Mary Hamilton and Yvonne Hillier (2006) used the NCDS data to explore why people do not participate in adult literacy, numeracy or language learning. Their overall analysis suggested three main reasons for non-participation.

The first is that people do learn but it is often part of the informal and often unrecognized learning that goes on in families, communities and the workplace. They suggest that: 'through these informal practices people "just do it", they "get by" and get "settled", supporting and exchanging skills and expertise, fashioning their practical lives and sense of identity within the limits they perceive for themselves' (p. 15). The second reason is that literacy and numeracy can seem irrelevant to people, as it is hidden or embedded in their lives. Any difficulties or limitations are therefore attributed to other factors in their lives. Hamilton and Hillier give the example of where limited literacy or numeracy is associated with a complex range of other factors such as health or long-term disability, which may affect employment opportunities or the ability to participate regularly in educational activities.

The third reason relates to how people's identities are invested in their experiences of learning. For some people learning is experienced as moments of tension and changing identities as well as acquiring new skills. For others, learning may challenge how settled they feel and may be too risky, particularly given past negative experiences of education. Hamilton and Hillier described that 'At 44 years of age, some NCDS members felt they were "too old to learn now" and their attention had shifted to their children's success in education' (p. 15). They conclude that in later life people reach a working compromise between their ambitions and their actual lives. This potential shift in identity is positive for some, like Sophie, above, who saw education as part of a new future, where for others it could threaten support systems and identities built around experiences of exclusion. The work in Broadway homeless project, mentioned above, shows the need to carefully negotiate how learning is integrated into individual lives and circumstances, as a ping-pong effect, rather than destabilizing existing ways of managing.

Conclusion

This chapter started by asking who literacy, numeracy and language learners are. Answering this apparently straightforward question shows the need to be clear about who defines what a learner is, what the definition means and why it is being used. Some definitions are shaped at a particular policy moment, often, as Hamilton and Hillier in their historical analysis point out, responding to wider economic factors and national concerns around employment. These definitions are general, not easily accommodating the experiences of individuals and the variety and complexity of their lives and learning. This general definition makes it easy to categorize and generalize, often completely externally to the individual being labelled. Whilst useful in policy terms, it does not simply or easily translate into real people in the classroom or other learning environments. This explains the mismatch between those who in tests are shown to have low literacy or numeracy levels, and identified as needing to learn, and how they see themselves as not having low levels of skills or needing to learn. The external general definition is at odds with the internal individual meaning.

Where learning is seen as part of everyday life it includes being in families, communities and workplaces as well as in the classroom or other learning environments. This meaning can take into account things that people bring to learning, what people want and what they say about learning. People bring existing knowledge and skills as well as their histories, current circumstances and plans for the future. Some histories and current circumstances include negative experiences of both education and life in general: for example violence, intimidation, poverty or ill health. Other people's histories and current circumstances are more positive – but both need to be taken into account.

Some people are able to progress easily towards their future plans: for example to get a better job or a higher level course. Others take a slower, more interrupted route that may change direction several times or may stop altogether. It is important to acknowledge and support different types of progress, recognizing the variety and complexity of people's lives and their overall goals for learning. In listening to people it is possible to begin to hear what they want from learning, which is frequently a mixture of what could be described as the social, emotional and cognitive dimensions of learning.

Task 2.2

Comparing different aspects of learning
Choose three people you teach. For each make a list of the social, emotional and cognitive aspects of their learning. How are the three aspects of learning different for each person – how do they compare to each other? Can you see any links between these different aspects that might be helpful in supporting learning? Ask learners what they want from learning – how does this compare to your interpretations?

Although someone may come to learn spelling, their overall learning experience is probably a mix of all three dimensions of learning. People know about learning as this is part of everyday social practice; it is not something limited to the classroom. Many people know and are able to articulate what is important to help them learn – although of course this may not always be funded or available.

From a social practice approach and from research in literacy, numeracy and language classrooms we have developed five principles to support social practice pedagogy that recognizes learners as active agents in their lives and learning, both inside and outside the classroom (Appleby and Barton 2008). The principles are:

- **Researching everyday practices:** Teachers and learners can investigate their changing literacy practices and the learning practices around them.
- **Taking account of learners' lives:** People are complex; they have histories, identities, current circumstances and imagined futures. We need to engage with different aspects of people in a teaching and learning relationship.
- **Learning by participation:** Using authentic materials, in tasks for real purposes, helps to make links between learning and literacy, numeracy and language in people's everyday lives.
- **Learning in safe, supported contexts:** Recognizing and valuing the social aspects of learning, including physical and emotional safety.
- **Locating literacy learning in other forms of meaning making:** Recognizing and working with different literacies that include oral, visual, individual and group ways of communicating.

These principles are not simply a blueprint to be followed in classroom or in professional training. Instead they support reflective practice and teacher inquiry, asking teachers to become learners themselves by looking at their own literacy and learning practices inside and outside the classroom. This approach challenges narrow definitions of literacy, of learning and of where and how this takes place. It redefines who we mean when we talk of learners, asks where and how learning takes places and challenges us to change the focus from literacy learners as a generalized 'them' to a more inclusive one that includes all of us.

Further reading and resources

Fowler, E. and Mace, J. (2005) *Outside the Classroom: Researching Literacy with Adult Learners*. Leicester: NIACE.

Lambe, T., Mark, R., Murphy, P. *et al*. (2006) *Literacy, Equality and Creativity: Resource Guide for Adult Learners*. Belfast: Queen's University (www.leis.ac.uk).

Notes

1. Ursula Howard discusses how to represent learners particularly at professional conferences and gatherings without either ignoring or exposing the power imbalance between learners and teachers (see Howard 2004).
2. Jane Ward used a journey metaphor to enable a meaningful dialogue between learners and teachers about progress. This method enabled learners to describe which aspects of learning they were confident with, going fast, and which were more difficult, which felt like being in a cul-de-sac (Ward and Edwards 2002).
3. Although people within the National Child Development Cohort were identified on tests as having low levels of literacy and numeracy, most people didn't see themselves as needing to learn. However, higher rates of ill health and depression have been found in people with below Level 2 literacy skills (Bynner and Parsons 2006).
4. The National Research and Development Centre for adult literacy and numeracy is a consortium of partners led by the Institute of Education. Started in 2003 and funded by the DfES, its remit is to support the Skills for Life strategy by generating knowledge and transforming this into practice.
5. The Adult Learners' Lives project is described in the research reports *Linking Learning and Everyday Life: A Social Perspective on Adult Language, Literacy and Numeracy* (Ivanic, *et al*. 2006) and in *Relating Adults' Lives and Learning: Participation and Engagement in Different Settings* (Barton *et al*. 2006). Both are available at the NRDC website, www.nrdc.org.uk (accessed 24 June 2009).
6. For a detailed account of a social practices perspective, see Barton and Hamilton (2000) and Barton *et al*. (2000). A useful summary and readings can be found in Uta Papen (2005).
7. The ALL project supported several practitioner researchers in its three sites. Findings from their work are available in the report *Listening to Learners* (Ivanic 2004).
8. A literacy as social practice framework illustrates how literacy and learning crosses boundaries between formal learning, informal and everyday uses where people adapt and use 'crossover strategies' for intergenerational and family learning (see Appleby and Hamilton 2006).

9. The Wider Benefits of Learning project looked at benefits to people's family life, health and well-being and civic participation, as a result of learning. The project used a social capital model to assess both informal and formal learning and the interaction between physical and psychological well-being as well as patterns for communication. See *The Benefits of Learning* (Schuller *et al.* 2004).

10. An evaluation of the Scottish Adult Literacy and Numeracy Strategy (Tett *et al.* 2006) also assessed gains in personal and family life, work and public lives through participating in learning. The evaluation found significant increased confidence and improved self-confidence by taking part in learning.

11. The NRDC Research Report on disaffected young people in custody and the community (Hurry *et al.* 2005) found that young people were positive about their experiences of vocational classes, where they felt they achieved something, but frequently disliked literacy and numeracy classes that relied on worksheets, which reminded them of school learning.

12. Hurry *et al.* 2005.

13. The NRDC Research Report on work-based learning explores the effectiveness of workplace basic skills programmes in improving adults' basic skills and on productivity and other lifecourse variables (Wolfe *et al.* 2004, available at www.nrdc.org.uk).

14. The NRDC embedding teaching and learning of adult literacy, numeracy and ESOL described seven case studies including horticulture, Entry to Employment, construction, childcare, nursing and sports showing a variety of approaches and contexts (Roberts *et al.* 2005, available at www.nrdc. org.uk).

15. The Literacies for Learning in Further Education project (LfLFE) is collaboration between two universities and four FE colleges. A major objective of the project is to identify actual and potential overlaps and connections between literacy practices in students' everyday lives, the literacy demands of their courses and the uses of literacy in the workplaces in which they are hoping to gain employment (for more details see www.lancs.ac.uk/lflfe/ accessed 24 June 2009).

16. Knud Illeris (2002) explains that there are three dimensions in the process of adult learning: the social, cognitive and emotional. He sees these as interlinked: 'Learning, development, socialization and qualification are in my conception more or less identical, or at least overlapping functions, to the extent to which it is derailing to try to treat them as separate processes' (p. 17).

17. The Broadway Homeless and Support project took part in the NRDC Practitioner-led Research Initiative, developing an alternative method of recording learning outcomes and progress for vulnerable learners – see NRDC website www.nrdc.org.uk for more details.

Section 2

Language awareness for literacy teachers

3 How language works

Irene Schwab and Nora Hughes

Note: In this section, we have assumed you understand basic grammatical terms. If you are not sure, we have suggested good reference books at the end of the chapter.

We regularly refer to the **learner texts** on pages 129-146 (written by adult literacy learners).

Introduction: Communication in the twenty-first century

Language is a means of communication, one of several used by human beings for self-expression and the fulfilment of personal and social goals. Human communication is multimodal, using linguistic and other means (such as images, sounds and gestures) to convey meaning. Each mode offers particular resources for creating meaning and has limitations on what it can express.

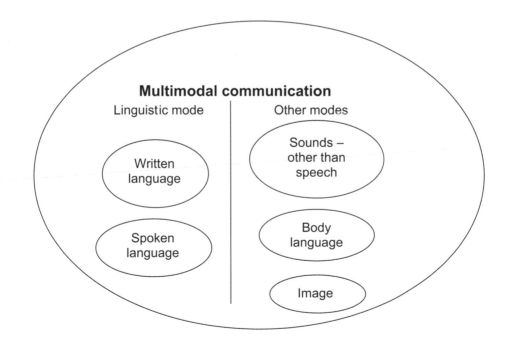

Task 3.1

Multimodal communication
Think about or discuss with a colleague which mode(s) you would use in order to:

- explain to someone how to use a piece of machinery;
- get help in an emergency;
- send a birthday greeting to an old friend.

What does each mode have to offer in these contexts?

Possible responses to this exercise are at the end of the chapter.

We can see each mode of communication as a system, within which we can identify a number of sub-systems. In this chapter we will focus on *language* systems, particularly the sub-systems of written English.

The social context of language use

Language and literacy are purposeful social activities. They are embedded in social practices and reflect prevailing values, beliefs and power relations. Even the most seemingly 'neutral' literacy events have many layers and ramifications, both personal and social. Some of these personal and social issues are illustrated in the examples of literacy learners below.

Example 3.1

Literacy as social practice
In a discussion on form-filling, **Sean** described an experience of filling in a claim form for unemployment benefit, saying it had felt like a 'minefield'. (Personal and social issues: the hidden agendas underlying some questions, not knowing the 'right' answer, his experiences of and feelings about literacy, social class issues.)

Sufia was writing a letter to her mother and grandmother in Somalia. (Personal and social issues: politeness conventions, cultural norms, political background of household separated by war, no access to email, family expectations, differences between generations, personal relationships, her personality and 'voice' as a letter writer.)

In the UK and in the world there are many different language communities. Most adult literacy learners are members of communities whose uses of language and literacy are less prestigious than those of more powerful groups and institutions. For them, one goal of literacy education is to gain access to powerful literacies, whilst at the same time preserving the forms of English on which their personal and social identities depend (**vernacular literacies**). In this chapter, we will consider how an understanding of language and language systems can enable us to support learners in accessing more powerful literacies for their own purposes.

The historical context

There is much talk in the popular media in Britain of 'standards' in language and literacy, implying there is a 'correct' way of using language in terms of grammar, pronunciation, punctuation and spelling. If we take a longer view, we can see that what is considered 'correct' involves many shifts and reversals over time. For example, the 'rules' and conventions of English grammar, punctuation and spelling were different in Shakespeare's time to those of today. Spelling was much more flexible and writers would vary their spelling of a word according to how it looked on the page. From an historical view of language and literacy, 'standards' are in fact temporary and provisional.

Human language is continually evolving. One significant result of recent technological development is the globalization of communication. The advances in technology have created new 'literacies'. The shift from page to screen has led to the establishment of new genres (types of text such as email, text messages, web page design) and new written conventions (e.g. new forms of address, new vocabulary, new layout conventions and an increasing informality of style associated with electronic genres). Co-existing with this process are differences and inequalities between societies, in terms of access to new technologies, and the different uses of oral and written language within them.

Some of the impact of these new literacies can be seen in the example below.

Example 3.2

Using new literacies
Sufia comes from a village community in which oral language still has primacy over written language and where people's relationship to literacy is different from in the UK. As a girl she attended primary school in a neighbouring village but had no secondary school education. In her adult education class she downloaded images of Somalia from the internet with the help of another learner and wrote a short piece about her country. She put the final text together electronically and shared it, orally and through the class magazine, with her community of learners.

Similarities and differences between languages

Human languages are diverse and change over time. However, they share universal characteristics. They are composed of signs (oral, written, visual or gestural) that can be combined to generate an infinite number of meanings, using sets of rules or principles. All human languages have a range of functions. M.A.K. Halliday, a functional grammarian, summarized these as:

- **ideational**: our ability to name, classify and organize our world, through language;
- **interpersonal**: our ability to use language to develop and maintain relationships with people – for example, answering and responding to questions, persuading and being persuaded, expressing distance or closeness;
- **textual**: the ways we use principles, rules and conventions to construct meaning e.g. grammatical and syntactic rules, structures for expressing formality or informality.

All languages can be used to perform these functions and they share a surprising level of similarity. For instance, speakers in all languages have conventions for how to indicate the time of an action or event but do so in a wide variety of ways. In English, the time an action is happening is indicated through changes in the verb: *I am going* (present), *I went* (past), *I will go* (future). However, in British Sign Language, a visual language, the past is indicated by the signer sweeping their hand behind them.

The similarities and differences between languages are particularly significant for bilingual learners in literacy classes and for those whose spoken variety of English differs from the standard variety. We discuss these issues in more detail in Chapter 4.

Similarities and differences between spoken and written language

'I can say it but I can't write it down' is a common frustration expressed by adult literacy students. Conquering the differences between oral and written language is difficult for newer readers and writers, particularly as they tackle more formal written texts. There are probably no *absolute* differences between speech and writing, but there are features that are more typical of speech, particularly informal speech, that are less common in writing. So for many literacy learners, learning to write means learning a range of new linguistic structures and conventions.

The key differences between speech and writing stem from the fact that speech is 'live':

- The structure of speech is heavily influenced by the speed at which it is produced – there is only so much information a listener can process at one time. So speech is in short 'chunks' rather than well-formed sentences.
- In speech, much meaning is expressed non-verbally through body language, intonation or stress.
- Speakers can usually be much less *explicit* than writers, because they are communicating with someone in the same time and space. For example, if a friend and I are in my kitchen, and the friend asks if I have seen her

mobile phone, I might say *It's over there*. This would be a perfectly meaningful utterance. However, if she asked me by email, replying *It's over there* would be meaningless. I would have to expand my reply and be more explicit. I might write: *You left it on my kitchen table when you were over last night.*

- Interpersonal functions are more significant in speech. Informal speech is full of appeals to the listener for empathy (*Don't you think?; Isn't it?*), or phrases to check understanding (*Do you see what I mean?*) In writing, these again have to be made explicit.

Consider the oral text below. Which features would not be typical of a written text?

Example 3.3

Features of spoken language
('...' Signifies a pause.)
I'm so sorry ... really sorry ... the trains were a nightmare ... I got to Euston right and it was packed ... you know packed ... you couldn't move ... so there's a woman at the turnstile and I said to her 'What's going on?' ... she says there's been an accident somewhere ... 'You'll be hours', she says ... and I think oh god! ... have you ... have you started? ... erm ok ... no problem good to see you all ... I feel bad being late ... being so late you know.

You may have noticed some or all of the following:

1   The speaker does not use sentences. In fact a sentence is a written construction, not an oral one. Speakers generally speak in **idea units** of seven or eight words or less.
2   In the first line of the text (*I'm so sorry ... really sorry ... the trains were a nightmare*) the speaker does not *explicitly* say why she is sorry (she is late) or that his or her lateness is due to problems on the trains. But that meaning is still conveyed.
3   Other features typical of oral language appear in the text:
     - repetition: e.g. *it was packed ... you know, packed ... you couldn't move*;
     - pauses, stops and starts and fillers: e.g. *erm ok*;
     - use of *and ... and ... and* to connect idea units;
     - appeals to the listeners: e.g. *you know*;
     - use of direct speech: I said '*What's going on?*'; '*You'll be hours*' she says;
     - ability to shift tense in speech (in stories, speakers will often shift from past to present tense for dramatic effect): '*You'll be hours*' *she says ...and I think oh god!*

When a writer is developing her skills, then, she is doing far more than putting oral words on paper. She is learning the language of writing rather than speaking. The more formal the writing, the further, generally, it is from everyday speech, so the more explicit it needs to be, and the more complex the sentence construction. We will compare the grammar and organization of oral and written texts further on in this chapter.

Language systems

Human language is multidimensional. In contemporary linguistics, these dimensions are sometimes referred to as **discourse**, **grammar** and **lexis.** In the current adult literacy core curriculum in England the framework used is **text**, **sentence** and **word**, which is roughly equivalent.

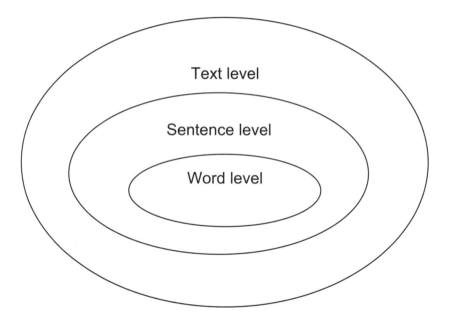

The levels are interrelated and all of them operate together whenever language is used. For example, when we read, it is not enough to recognize individual words. To be sure of their meaning, we need to consider them in the context of the sentence, the text as a whole and the wider social context. When we write, we choose words that make sense in the sentence *and* fit with our overall purpose.

Example 3.4

Interrelation of text, sentence and word level
Dear Mr Barnes
Thank you for your letter, which I <u>received</u> on 19 February.

In certain very crucial ways, text-level organization underpins all language use. In the example above, it determines the layout, structure and word choice. There are conventions in the UK about the opening lines in formal letters, and this writer is following the rules. The writer has also used the word *received*, instead of the more common word *got*, in order to achieve the formal **register** associated with business letters. By following the rules, the writer probably has more chance of achieving results from her letter.

Pragmatics is the study of how written and oral language conveys meaning above and beyond the literal meaning of words and sentences. We can use language to be formal or informal, polite and distant, or warm and close. Following the appropriate convention in letter writing is similar to choosing appropriate clothes for work, a night out or a wedding.

At the same time, language is a code made up of sub-systems (such as **grammar**, **phonology** and **morphology**) each with its own identifiable patterns and mechanisms. For example, the spelling of the word 'received' follows current patterns of English spelling and the **morpheme** 'ed' is used to signal that the action happened in the past, in accordance with the grammar of standard written English.

The point here is that all linguistic operations are both 'technical' and strategic. To use language effectively, we have to know the code *and* be able use it strategically to achieve a particular communicative purpose.

In the next section we will discuss a number of linguistic concepts, at text, sentence and word level, together with suggested applications to adult literacy teaching.

Text focus

When we consider oral or written language at **text or discourse level**, we are studying the rules and coventions that govern the overall structure of a text. As we will see, these are very much determined by its social purpose.

The term **discourse** is used in many different ways. For the purposes of this section we will draw on two main meanings of the word **discourse**:

1   A connected piece of speech or writing.
2   The topics and types of language associated with particular contexts. (e.g. the discourse of international football, the discourse of party politics in the UK).[1]

The words discourse and text are sometimes interchanged, but text more often refers to written language, particularly a recognizable unit with a beginning and end and a clearly discernible function (e.g. an email, a webpage, a letter).

Discourse analysis is concerned with:

● how the various elements of a text work together, such as headings, images and vocabulary
● the relationship between the text and its social context, and the use of language to achieve a purpose.

Critical discourse analysis adds an extra dimension to this way of looking at texts. It suggests that texts are not neutral, but embody the social structures, beliefs and values of the societies that use and produce them. When reading or listening, we therefore need to look below the 'surface' features of a text at the ways in which particular sets of beliefs and values are being exemplified and how we are being influenced. In terms of writing and speaking, the implication is that we need to be aware of the values implicit in what we write or say, and the means we use to influence the reader or listener.

Genre, register and 'voice'

One important way of looking at discourse is by examining **genre**. Genre theory is concerned with identifying the typical features of a particular kind of text. In order to understand or produce a text, we need to know the conventions of the genre to which the text belongs. 'Reading' a text includes bringing knowledge of these conventions and understanding how they are being used by the writer. 'Writing' includes reproducing the language and organizational features associated with the genre. Examples of genres[2] are stories, instructions, reports, persuasive texts such as adverts, letters, emails or academic essay writing.

Genre conventions are changing. Users of electronic media, in particular, have created, and continue to create, new genres and new conventions, some of which are controversial. For example, a question often debated in the media is whether the language of text messaging is creative, or a symptom of linguistic 'decay' and loss of 'standards' in language use.

Generally people of higher status and more power in a society will control the higher status and more complex written genres. Enabling learners to reproduce more powerful genres is an important part of literacy education, enabling people to have their views heard and access their rights as citizens and consumers.

Register

Register refers to the features of a text that make it distinctive to a particular context, for example the degree of formality or the choice of style and vocabulary, as in college reports, coursework for counselling training or legal documents. One aspect of genre change is the way in which the register of different genres shifts over time. For example, the relatively formal register that used to be associated with many workplace texts, such as memoranda, has given way to the more informal register of email; even very formal business letters are a little less formal now than they were half a century ago.

One of the skills involved in reading is recognizing the register of a text and responding accordingly. One dimension of writing is writing in a register that is in keeping with your intentions as author, within the possibilities of the genre. In the following example, two adult literacy learners try out writing in different registers.

Example 3.5

Using different registers
(See **Texts 1a and 2a** in the learner texts.)

Two young learners enjoy reading fiction, particularly romantic novels and horror stories.

Geraldine wrote a synopsis of a Mills and Boon novel that she wanted to recommend to others. She gave a sense of what it would be like to read the book, by using the register of romantic fiction in her synopsis.

Sharon tried her hand at writing a 'scary story'. This was her first attempt at writing fiction and she found it difficult to write in a recognizable register, which made the story less effective. Working on this aspect of her writing would increase her pleasure and satisfaction in the writing process.

Voice

When learners, teachers and researchers discuss what helps people become more confident writers, they often refer to the importance of a writer finding his or her **voice**. In fact, voice is both a social and an individual dimension of writing. All users of language have many different voices, reflecting the identities they assume in different contexts.

Example 3.6

Finding a voice

(See **Texts 1b and 1a** in the learner texts.)
Look at the two texts written by **Geraldine**:
- a letter to her local councillor;
- a preview of a romantic novel.

The texts were written for different purposes, in different domains of her life. In each text she has produced the register of a particular genre, and within this register she has expressed an individual voice.

Roz Ivanic (1997) coined the phrase **the discoursal self** to convey the idea of multiple identities and multiple voices. To be effective writers, we need a repertoire of voices for the different types of text we might want to use in different domains of life. Developing a repertoire of written and oral voices is part of becoming more literate.

Coherence

Coherence in a text refers to its underlying structure, organization and connectedness. In a coherent text, all the different elements combine to create the overall meaning of the text and achieve its communicative purpose.

In multimodal texts, coherence works across the different modes: captions, headings, sentences, punctuation marks, links, still and moving images, sounds – all of these must be relevant, interconnected and organized on the screen or the page in such a way as to achieve the desired effect(s).

Coherence is one of the qualities that make a text effective. In the example given below, we describe an adult literacy activity where the teacher is encouraging learners to develop coherent texts.

Example 3.7

Creating coherent texts

'I visited a car mechanics course in which literacy learning was "embedded". On the afternoon of my visit, learners were using their mobile phones to take photographs of operations in the workshop. The next step would be for them to download the photographs and put them into a set of instructions, combining and organizing words and images to produce a coherent whole.'

(Adult Literacy Teacher Trainer)

In more traditional written texts, coherence is achieved by such devices as headings, subheadings and paragraphs. These devices are often referred to as **signposting**, because they guide the reader through the text, making the underlying structure clear.

Sequencing is an important element in creating coherent texts in both reading and writing. Sequencing can be *logical* (for example constructing or following an argument in an essay) or *chronological* (constructing or following a sequence of events in a narrative).

Example 3.8

Sequencing in texts
(See **Texts 3 and 2a** in the learner texts.)
Eddie wrote this short *explanatory* text when he went to a further education college to seek help and advice. In the text, he explains why he wants to work on his reading and writing. This is an example of a coherent text, in which a logical progression of ideas is marked by two short paragraphs.

(The difficulty for the reader caused by **Eddie's** unconventional spelling is a separate issue).

Sharon's 'scary story' is a *narrative* text. In the first few sentences the sequence of events is fairly clear, but by halfway through the reader has lost the plot. **Sharon** needs support to develop this aspect of her writing, in order to make it more effective.

Coherence and meaning making

In discourse theory, another important dimension of coherence is **meaning making** – the idea that the meanings in a text are not only created by the writer but by the reader bringing her own knowledge and understanding to the text (e.g. knowledge of the context, the genre, the language used in the text).

Communication is made possible by the shared knowledge of reader and writer. Where there is no shared knowledge, there is no meaning. If a text contains numerous references to things unknown to the reader, she will be unable to make sense of it.

Task 3.2

Identifying assumed knowledge in a text

The following article was taken from the Arsenal Football Club website.

What shared knowledge is *assumed* by the writer?

Chelsea 2–1 Arsenal
Carling Cup Round 4

Arsene Wenger has complete confidence in his Carling Cup kids now and feels many will put up a serious battle with many first-choice players for a starting berth.

Before all the red cards and recriminations began, Arsenal youngsters actually put in a sterling effort against a full strength Chelsea Side in Sunday's final at the Millennium Stadium. Having beaten Premiership level XIs from Everton and a handy Liverpool team at Anfield, Wenger now feels many of his starlets can step up.

(From www.arsenal.com accessed 28 February 2007)

Possible answers are at the end of this chapter.

Coherence and learning style

Coherence in reading, writing, speaking and listening can be relatively easy or difficult for people to achieve, depending on their individual cognitive abilities and on the type of text they are dealing with. For example, **Sharon** finds it difficult to maintain a sequence when writing, but she can do it more easily if she draws a visual mind-map and refers back to this as she writes. Other people find sequential texts (instructions, narratives, arguments etc.) difficult to follow, but may have less difficulty navigating a webpage, whose overall structure is not linear or sequential, but spatial, and where visual modes are used alongside the linguistic mode.

Cohesion

Cohesion is one of the means by which coherence in spoken and written discourse is achieved. Cohesion is achieved through making linguistic links between different parts of a text, giving it a clear structure. These links operate at text, sentence and word level.

Grammatical cohesion

Grammatical cohesion includes devices such as **connectives**, **ellipsis** and **referencing**.

Connectives are words or phrases used for the purpose of making logical or temporal (chronological) connections between different parts of a text. They are also called *discourse markers*.

For example, in **Text 3**, which is an explanatory text, **Eddie** uses **logical connectives** (*because* and *so*). In **Text 4**, **Sean** uses **temporal connectives** to develop a narrative sequence (*on my first day back, as a young boy, now, still,* etc.), and **logical connectives** to clarify ideas, make links and develop an argument (*in the first place, although, that is not to say, as a consequence,* etc.)

Ellipsis means omitting from a sentence material which is logically necessary but which can be understood from the context. The reader supplies the missing words by making links in her mind as she reads. In **Text 1b**, **Geraldine** uses ellipsis effectively when describing her grandmother's situation and her wishes with regard to where she lives:

> She likes where she is now <u>and does</u> not want to be moved … she has a health problem <u>and has</u> also just lost my granddad Paddy.

Ellipsis improves the 'flow' of a text by removing unnecessary repetition. Without ellipsis, these sentences from **Geraldine's** text would be clumsy and repetitive and would slow the reader down:

> <u>She</u> likes where she is now and <u>she</u> does not want to be moved … <u>she</u> has a health problem and <u>she</u> has also just lost my granddad, Paddy.

Referencing is the use of words, such as pronouns (*he, she, it*), demonstrative pronouns (*this, these*) and the definite article (*the*), to refer backwards or forwards within a text, or outwards to the world These are called **anaphoric**, **cataphoric** and **exophoric** references respectively. Referencing makes the reader make connections with other parts of the text and with the broader social context in which the text is situated.

Effective referencing adds to the overall coherence of a text, while unclear referencing causes the reader to lose the sequence of ideas or events. For example, in the extract above, it is clear who **Geraldine** is referring to when she uses the pronoun *she*, because it refers back to *my Nan Brigid* mentioned in the previous sentence (**Text 1b**), whereas in **Text 2a,** by **Sharon**, the use of the pronoun *they* is confusing, as is the use of the definite article *the*, in this sentence by the same writer:

> Then <u>they</u> stop running because <u>they</u> saw <u>the</u> other person on the way back to their car.

Which *other person* is the narrator referring to? Although the use of *the* suggests writer and reader already share this knowledge, no *other person* has previously appeared in the story. The reader is therefore unable to form a clear picture of events at this point and literally loses the plot.

Lexical cohesion

Lexical cohesion is achieved by using words and phrases which are semantically linked (linked in their meaning). These **lexical sets** relate to key themes or **messages** in the text. For example, in the text below, words to do with languages (*languages, spoken, speakers*) are repeated several times. Another lexical set, words to do with <u>danger/dying</u>, is highlighted.

Example 3.9

Lexical cohesion
Ninety percent of the world's languages may be <u>in danger</u>. Around 6,000 languages are currently spoken in the world. Of these, half are <u>moribund</u>, in that they are no longer learned by the new generation of speakers. A further 2,500 are in <u>a danger zone</u>, in that they have fewer than a hundred thousand speakers. This leaves around 600, a mere ten per cent of the current total, as likely <u>survivors</u> a century from now. Of course, languages inevitably split, just as Latin eventually split into the various *Romance* languages. So some new languages may emerge, but the diversity will be much reduce
(Gardiner 2000: 23)

Rhetorically, lexical cohesion in this text contributes to the building up of two interrelated themes: the world's rapidly changing linguistic landscape and the loss of (or dying) abundance and diversity which the writer associates with this.

In **Text 2a**, **Sharon**, notwithstanding her difficulties with grammatical cohesion, has achieved a degree of lexical cohesion by using the words *run* and *running* several times, thereby creating an impression of continuous movement and an atmosphere of fear in the story.

Task 3.3

Referencing and lexical cohesion

1 Analyse **Sean's** text (**Text 4**) in terms of:
   a) **Referencing**. Look at the underlined words in the first two paragraphs. Identify the kind of **references** (anaphoric, cataphoric or exophoric) used by **Sean**.
   b) **Lexical cohesion**.

   - Make a list of words and phrases **Sean** uses relating to *education* in the first two paragraphs.

   - Find a semantic set relating to **Sean's** *feelings about learning as an adult.*

2 Comment on **Sean's** control of these two forms of cohesion.

Possible answers are at the end of this chapter.

The importance of focusing on discourse

Adult learners are active users of language. They may want to enhance their ability to participate in particular literacy practices, or to extend the range of contexts in which they can do so with confidence.

Developing skills and strategies at text/ discourse level can strengthen learners' identities as readers and writers and can facilitate the development of their natural communicative ability, enabling them to use language and other modes of expression effectively for their own purposes.

Sentence focus

Grammarians have traditionally looked at the rules of texts at sentence level, particularly the **syntax** and **morphology** of sentences. (However, linguists are now increasingly studying the 'grammar' of whole texts as we can see from the section above).

What is grammar?

This is apparently a straightforward question, but the answer is very complex. There are many different views about what grammar is.

- A **prescriptive** grammarian thinks that there are fixed underlying rules to language and we need to learn, and adhere to, the rules.
- A **descriptive** grammarian believes that language cannot be separated from its use, and the role of grammarians is to study and *describe* the rules about the way it is used in different oral and written contexts.
- **Functional grammar** is one kind of descriptive grammar. A functional grammarian considers how language in use is organized to fulfil specific communicative purposes or *functions* i.e. what is the speaker/writer **doing** with language?

Task 3.4

Different approaches to grammar
Read this sentence written by **Flora** (Text 5a):

Rosa Parks famous because she refuse to give up she seat to a white man.

What would proponents of each of the above viewpoints have to say about this sentence?

Possible answers are at the end of this chapter.

As discussed in the last section, we don't believe grammar can be discussed in terms of 'right' or 'wrong', or in terms of absolute rules. Grammar is more appropriately seen as sets of conventions about language use, and conventions change. They change across time according to region and according to whether the grammar is relating to speech or writing. These changes, for us, make nonsense of the idea of a single unchanging grammar.

Grammar is about making meaning and is influenced by who is talking and who is listening (or who is writing and who is reading); it's about purposes and functions. Above all it's about communication. Without grammar the language would be so chaotic and random that communication would be impossible.

Understanding the grammar of written text involves analysing both the sentence (**syntax** and **punctuation**) and words (**morphology**). We will discuss morphology in more detail under **Word Focus** below.

Syntax

Syntax concerns the rules of organization of a sentence – how words are ordered and sentences constructed. The following task illustrates this.

Task 3.5

The importance of syntax

Consider some of the ways in which the sentence *I am now using grammar* can

be rearranged. Which of these are acceptable in English?

1 I am using grammar now.
2 I am now using grammar.
3 Am I now using grammar?
4 Grammar now I am using.
5 Now using grammar I am.
6 Grammar I am now using.
7 Using now am grammar I.
8 I grammar using now am.
9 Using am grammar now I.

Comment 3.5

In English, some of these (1–3) are perfectly acceptable (although with slightly different meanings); some are just about possible (4–6); yet with others we would struggle to understand the sentence (7–9). The individual words are the same, but the rules of English syntax make some combinations meaningful and some almost meaningless.

Everyone who can speak English has first-hand experience of grammar. When we speak, we automatically choose syntax that makes sense and accords with the rules of whichever variety of English we speak. We have learned this through long experience with the language. If we listen to children learning to speak, we can see this learning process in action: for example, the child who generalizes from hearing the regular past tense of *walk* (walked) and *talk* (talked) produces *goed* and *drinked*.

The syntax of speech and writing

We looked at some of the differences between speech and writing in the last section. There is a significant difference between the syntax used in conversational speech and that used in formal writing. As we discussed, speakers can usually draw on intonation, rhythm, gesture and facial expression to make their meaning clear, but for writers all the meaning has to be carried in the text itself.

Example 3.10

Comparing the syntax of spoken and written texts
Consider the texts below. One is spoken and one is written. Both have the same topic.

Sample 1

>   *A*: I came back and I can't get it to come on.
>   *B*: Was it OK before you went?
>   *A*: Yeah fine.
>   *B*: OK well just move this.. no? Well push any of these ... no didn't work ... you probably have to hit this one ... this one here.
>   *A*: Oh great. It's back on ... what happened?
>   *B*: It was asleep ... if you're away from it for a while it goes to sleep and you need to press that one to get it started again.

Sample 2
Sleep mode: Computers go into a power-saving sleep mode when left idle. The screen goes blank and the hard disk stops, but everything comes back on within a few seconds after the keyboard is touched. Computers can also be put into the sleep mode manually.

(Adapted from Di Nuccio *et al.* (1994: 85))

These texts illustrate some typical differences between the grammatical conventions of the two modes, particularly between informal speech and more formal writing. Below are some of the key ones.

The sentence is a feature of writing, rather than speech

>   OK we'll just move this ... no? ... Well push any of these ... no, didn't work ... you probably have to hit this one ... this one here
>
>   (**Sample 1**).

We have already mentioned that the sentence is a feature of written rather than oral language. The equivalent in informal speech is the 'idea unit' or 'chunk' of meaning.

Speech typically links idea units by using simple co-ordinating conjunctions such as *and* and *but* or no explicit co-ordination at all. However, this does not mean that speakers do not express complex relationships between ideas. They use intonation, gesture, rhythm, body language and context to indicate these.

The sentence is characteristic of writing. Writers have to link ideas in a sentence explicitly, and can use a wide range of connectives to show relationships – cause, purpose, contrast, time, order, etc. – to form complex sentences, as in the one below:

>   The screen goes blank **and** the hard disk stops, **but** everything comes back on within a few seconds **after** the keyboard is touched
>
>   (**Sample 2**).

Speech has a higher incidence of function words

Certain types of words such as conjunctions, prepositions, articles and pronouns have little or no **lexical** meaning. They are called **function words** and their role is to indicate grammatical relationships with other words in the sentence.

According to Halliday (1985), everyday speech uses a higher proportion of function words. Writing tends to use a higher ratio of **content words** (those with lexical meaning) which include nouns, verbs adjectives and some adverbs. Some of the content words used in **Sample 2** are: *computers, keyboard, goes, touched, stops, blank.* Writing also tends to use more complex modification in noun phrases (see below), as in *a power-saving sleep mode.*

Questions and commands are much more typical in everyday speech

There are several questions and commands in **Sample 1**, but none in **Sample 2**.

Speech doesn't use punctuation

Punctuation is, obviously, a feature of writing, not speech. If we were to *hear* the text in Sample 1, we would be able to tell where the sense boundaries were through the use of stress, intonation and phrasing. The use of punctuation is essential in written texts because these non-verbal signals have to be replaced.

It can be seen from the above that new readers or writers may be fluent in the syntax of speech but need to acquire some different rules and conventions when they start to write.

What sort of grammatical knowledge is useful?

There is much debate amongst policy makers, researchers, teachers and the public about the value of teaching grammar to support accuracy and quality in writing.[3] The task below considers its value in adult literacy teaching.

Task 3.6

Is grammar useful for literacy teachers?

Can you think of any specific ways in which grammar can be useful to learners you work with?

Does it make a difference which level these learners are working at?

Comment 3.6

This is a subject for debate. We might argue, however, that for some learners:

- understanding the **metalanguage** of grammar (the language used to talk about language) enables teachers and learners, at any level, to engage in dialogue about language – how it is used, and how it can be used effectively;
- knowing the terminology can enable teachers and learners to compare English with other languages, or to compare different varieties of English;
- an understanding of language itself is part of a wider understanding of the world.

We could see grammar as a structure, or framework, on which we hang elements of language. We would argue that literacy teachers need to know how to describe and talk about how the different parts of that structure work.

Elements of a sentence

M.A.K. Halliday (1985), who founded functional grammar, describes language at sentence level in terms of a rank scale with a hierarchy of components building upon each other from the smallest part, the morpheme, to the largest, the clause complex. In writing, a sentence can be interpreted as a clause complex.

Below we show how a sentence can be broken down into its various grammatical elements:

- morpheme (elements of a word that carry meaning in their own right);
- word;
- phrase;
- clause;
- clause complex.

Example 3.11

Elements of a sentence

Sample sentence:

Although often overlooked, morphemes are important as they are the building blocks of words.

Elements

Morpheme:	Examples of morphemes are <u>over</u> + <u>looked</u>; <u>block</u> + <u>s</u>.
Word:	We will all recognize the term *word*. Here, however, the term means more than the separate words in a sentence. It relates to the word class to which each word belongs, e.g. <u>morphemes</u> (noun) <u>are</u> (verb) <u>of</u> (preposition) <u>although</u> (connective) <u>the</u> (article)
Phrase:	<u>the building blocks of words</u> is an example of a phrase (a chunk of meaning).
Clause:	Examples of clauses used here are: <u>morphemes are important</u> (main clause) <u>as they are the building blocks of words</u> (subordinate clause).
Clause complex:	This is a combination of clauses. For example, <u>Although often overlooked, morphemes are important as they are the building blocks of words</u>.

Each of these elements is described in more detail below:

Morphemes

Morphemes are the structural elements of words. To understand how a word is built out of morphemes can help us to understand how it is constructed, where it comes from, what word class it is and what work it is doing in the sentence. It can also help both with reading the word and spelling it (see **Word focus** below).

Word classes

Some people might remember with horror school English lessons, struggling to come to terms with **parts of speech** and identifying them in sentences (called **parsing**). The term **parts of speech** has generally been replaced with the term **word classes**. An understanding of word classes can be useful in giving the teacher and learner a shared language, in particular to talk about aspects of reading and writing.

In English, words can often be more than one word class depending on how they are used in context.

Task 3.7

Word classes and context
What word class is the word round in each of these sentences – noun, verb, adjective or preposition?

- They went **round** the corner.
- As they **round** the corner, they see their friends.
- She bought a **round** of drinks.
- There were **round** beads and square ones.

Possible answers are at the end of this chapter.

It can be seen from this exercise that word classes relate to the context in which the word is used. An understanding of this is especially useful to bring to reading when, perhaps, the content is obscure, and the vocabulary unfamiliar.

Open and closed word classes

There are **closed** and **open** classes of words. Closed classes contain a finite set of words, formed many years ago and relatively unchanging. Open classes contain an infinite set of words. New words are constantly added to this set while, at the same time, new meanings regularly emerge for existing words.

Task 3.8

Open and closed word classes
Look at the list of new words for 2008 on the website: www.askoxford.com/worldofwords/newwords/?view=uk
    What word classes are represented by these words? Why do you think these word classes are open classes and others are more fixed and closed?

Possible responses are at the end of this chapter.

Using knowledge of word classes to make sense of texts

A fluent and experienced user of the English language will follow the rules of syntax unconsciously, without necessarily being able to name the different word classes or sentence constituents.

    The advantage of knowing the metalanguage, however, is to enable readers to follow this explanation and then to discuss it with others. It not only deepens their understanding of this text, but also equips them to tackle other texts in the future. In addition, it gives them the tools to exploit a wider range of effects in writing.

Phrase

Every sentence, every clause is made up of phrases. One of the advantages of analysing language in terms of phrases rather than individual words is that words that go together in terms of meaning can be seen as one unit. This 'chunking' of words in meaningful units can be used to break up a sentence when reading, or build up a sentence when writing.

Phrases, or 'chunks', are named according to the most significant element or **head word**. If the head word is a noun, it becomes a **noun phrase**; if it is an adjective, it becomes an **adjective phrase**, etc. Sometimes one sort of phrase can be embedded in another as in:

> The flowers in the garden are dying because of the drought.

The flowers in the garden is a noun phrase (the subject of the verb) but it also contains a preposition phrase telling us where the flowers are situated (in the garden). This preposition phrase, in turn, contains another noun phrase (the garden).

At a simple level, we know that every sentence has a verb. However, learners are often surprised when the verb turns out to be not one word but several, e.g. I would have gone skating if it hadn't been so cold. Identifying the **verb phrase** may help learners to recognize that they need to check for all its different elements.

There are similar advantages to recognizing a noun phrase. Seeing it as one unit emphasizes the connections between the head noun itself and the *modifying* elements, e.g. in the sentence above, *flowers* would be the head word, but by making a connection between the flowers and the place where they are to be found (in the garden), we know:

- not to put a comma after *the flowers*;
- to use a plural verb because it relates to the (plural) *flowers* not to the (singular) *garden*, even though the *garden* is nearest to the verb.

Single adverbs, adverb phrases and preposition phases can all act as adverbials.[4] One of the functions of an adverbial is to give additional information about the action which is described in the rest of the sentence. For example, they might describe where, when, why or how something happened. We can see how this works in the following extract from **Wayne's** writing (**Text 9**).

> I have made a lot of changes in myself over the last two years. I can't believe how irresponsibly I used to act before I came here.

If **Wayne** had not used adverbials it would look like this:[5]

> I have made a lot of changes. I can't believe how I used to act.

Wayne's use of adverbials not only extends the information given but makes it more coherent. The adverbials used here (in bold) indicate the place, time and manner of each action.

> I have made a lot of changes **in myself** (Where have you made changes?) **over the last 2 years** (When did you make changes?).

> I can't believe how **irresponsibly** I used to act (How did you act?) **before I came here** (When did you act like this?).

Task 3.9

Working with phrases
Text 5b was written by **Flora**, a learner from West Africa who uses a Nigerian variety of English. Her narrative, originally in the form of an informal letter, describes a recent party she has attended.

1   Identify the different types of phrases in **Flora's** text. We have underlined them below. You will need to look for:
- noun phrases;
- adjectival phrases;

- adverbials.

2   In what ways has **Flora** made good use of phrase structure and what help might she need to develop this piece of writing?

Flora's text

I like to tell you about <u>my cousin wedding</u>. I went to <u>her wedding</u> <u>last</u> <u>Saturday the ceremony</u> was in the church, <u>bride and bridesmaids</u> are <u>looking</u> <u>so wonderful</u>. I enjoy <u>very much</u>.
   Then <u>after church</u> we all went to Highgate Hotel, in the Hall <u>the decoration</u> was <u>very beautiful</u> and food was <u>very delicious</u> we all enjoy <u>very much</u>.
   After the food we all have drink and disco and dance <u>until the midnight</u>. The Party was <u>so enjoyable</u>.

An understanding of noun phrases is particularly useful for writing development. Two pieces of writing by **Geoffrey** (**Text 6**) and **Sharon** (**Text 2b**) illustrate this:

Example 3.12

Geoffrey

Jim Reeves
   My hero is Jim Reeves. I don't know him personal but I heard his records and he was <u>a great singer</u> he died at the age of 30 in a plane crash he has <u>a great</u> <u>talent</u>.

In the text above, **Geoffrey** has written a short piece about someone he admires. He uses **pre-modification** in his noun phrases, but he uses a single pre-modifying adjective repetitively (*great*). By offering a range of possible modifying adjectives, the teacher can assist **Geoffrey** to extend his vocabulary. A quick glance through a thesaurus or a brainstorm would offer words like *remarkable, immense, enormous, famous, impressive, fantastic*, etc., which **Geoffrey** could discuss and choose from.

Example 3.13

Sharon

It was <u>a fine sunny day</u>. <u>The beautiful young woman</u> was walking down <u>the long dirty street</u>. She was wearing <u>a new blue coat</u> and she was carrying <u>a shiny big handbag</u>.

Sharon has taken on board her teacher's advice about pre-modification, but has applied it mechanically, creating a pattern of two adjectives for each noun which can become boring and repetitive.

Sharon's teacher might want to have a dialogue with her about what good writers do i.e.:

- vary her modification of nouns: using pre-modification and post-modification;
- have a larger range of adjectives at her disposal (use of thesaurus);
- use a variety of ways to modify nouns: adjectives, preposition phrases, nouns, prepositions and relative clauses.

Sharon's teacher could suggest she looks at some models of narrative texts focusing on how noun phrases are constructed and used.

Clause

A sentence is always made up of one or more clauses. There is always at least one **main clause** which can stand on its own (e.g. **Rose invited me to her birthday party**). This can be extended by adding more clauses – **main** or **subordinate**. The various ways of doing this are illustrated below:

> <u>Rose invited me to her birthday party</u> **and** <u>I was looking forward to it</u>.

In this sentence each of the two clauses which are connected by *and* is equally independent and has equal value in the sentence, so they are **co-ordinate clauses**.

> <u>Rose invited me to her birthday party</u> **because** <u>she is my closest friend</u>.

In this sentence, the first clause makes perfect sense on its own, but the second clause, introduced by *because*, does not. As a result, the second clause is termed a **subordinate clause** as it is dependent on the main clause. A subordinate clause can never exist on its own.

> Rose, **who** <u>is my closest friend</u>, invited me to her birthday party.

This sentence includes an example of an **embedded** subordinate clause. The embedded clause <u>who is my closest friend</u> is both dependent on and nested inside the main clause.

It is helpful to be able to recognize a main clause as it will help identify the main point of a sentence (especially useful in long, complex sentences). Recognizing a main verb can often be crucial for correctly assigning number, tense and aspect to the verb or for determining who or what is the main agent in a sentence.

The clauses in a sentence are connected by conjunctions. In the case of two or more main clauses these are **co-ordinating conjunctions** (for example, *and, but, or*). Subordinate clauses are usually joined to the rest of the sentence by **subordinating connectives** (like *and* in the first sentence above) or **relative pronouns** (like *who* in the third sentence). These can be placed between the clauses they connect, or at the beginning of the subordinate clause. So, if the subordinate clause is at the beginning of the sentence, the connective will be at the start of the sentence, which can seem counter-intuitive. Compare the placing of connectives in the following two sentences:

> Rose invited me to her birthday party **even though** it was on a Sunday.

> **Even though** it was on a Sunday, Rose invited me to her birthday party.

Connectives are important clues in a sentence, especially one that is long and complex. They indicate the relationship between events and states. They can indicate time (*as soon as, while*); place (*where, wherever*); manner (*as if*); condition (*if, unless*); similarity (*as, like*); reasons (*because, since*); purposes (*so, so that*) and results (*so, so that*). They can also signal a contrast with what has gone before (*although, despite the fact that*).

A common problem with beginner writers is to over-use short, simple sentences consisting of a single main clause (see **Flora's** text above) or to over-use compound sentences with clauses joined together by *and*. Exploring different *types of sentences* can help new writers extend their repertoire.

Sentence

Types of sentence

Sentences can be simple, compound or complex. These do not relate to the relative sophistication of the writing; they are grammatical terms:

- a **simple sentence** has a single main clause and one main verb;
- a **compound sentence** has two main clauses joined by one of a small group of co-ordinating connectives (for example *and, but, or*);
- a **complex sentence** has one main clause and one or more subordinate clauses, usually joined by subordinating connectives or by relative pronouns.

Choosing sentence types

Different sentence types have different uses and effects. **Compound sentences** might allow a writer to balance out two points in a sentence, or set one against another. For example:

> I am against the war in Iraq and I think we should pull out now.

> I am against the war in Iraq but I understand the reasons we are there.

Complex sentences allow greater nuances to be made inside one sentence, for example:

> Even though I understand the reasons we are there, I am against the war in Iraq, because the end can never justify the means.

It is true that beginner writers tend to use simple sentences, but it is not true that good writers use only complex sentences. Good writing contains a variety of sentences. Learners need to be aware of the range of sentences and the range of ways in which they can be connected – by word order, use of connectives and punctuation.

In the next task we look at an example of an excerpt from a speech by Martin Luther King (one very famous for its effectiveness). It illustrates how different types of sentences are used to create an effect. (**Note**: a speech is an unusual form in that it is both a written and a spoken text and contains features of both.)

Task 3.10

The effectiveness of varying sentence type
This extract from a famous speech by Martin Luther King is made up of both simple and complex sentences.
How does he use these to create an effect?

I have a dream
Go back to Mississippi. Go back to Alabama. Go back to South Carolina. Go back to Georgia. Go back to Louisiana. Go back to the slums and ghettos of our northern cities, knowing that somehow this situation can and will be changed. Let us not wallow in the valley of despair.

I say to you today, my friends, even though we face the difficulties of today and tomorrow, I still have a dream. It is a dream deeply rooted in the American dream.

I have a dream that one day this nation will rise up and live out the true meaning of its creed: 'We hold these truths to be self-evident: that all men are created equal.'

I have a dream that one day on the red hills of Georgia the sons of former slaves and the sons of former slave owners will be able to sit down together at the table of brotherhood.

I have a dream that one day even the state of Mississippi, a state sweltering with the heat of injustice, sweltering with the heat of oppression, will be transformed into an oasis of freedom and justice.

I have a dream that my four little children will one day live in a nation where they will not be judged by the color of their skin but by the content of their character.

I have a dream today.

I have a dream that one day, down in Alabama, with its vicious racists, with its governor having his lips dripping with the words of interposition and nullification; one day right there in Alabama, little black boys and black girls will be able to join hands with little white boys and white girls as sisters and brothers.

I have a dream today.

Comment 3.10

Martin Luther King is renowned for his power of expression. Part of his skill in this speech is his control over the syntax.

He alternates very long complex sentences with short simple ones, for example:

> I have a dream that one day, down in Alabama, with its vicious racists, with its governor having his lips dripping with the words of interposition and nullification; one day right there in Alabama, little black boys and black girls will be able to join hands with little white boys and white girls as sisters and brothers. (57 words)

and:

> I have a dream today. (5 words)

We might note also his use of effective phrases to create atmosphere. He uses post-modification very powerfully, e.g. noun phrases such as <u>Alabama, with its vicious racists, with its governor having his lips dripping with the words of interposition and nullification</u> and adjectival phrases such as <u>sweltering with the heat of injustice, sweltering with the heat of oppression.</u> (**Note**: in this case the head word of the phrase is a participle being used adjectivally.)

Functions of sentences

Sentences, as well as being of different types, also have different functions.

There are four basic sentence functions:

- statement;
- question;
- instruction/command;
- exclamation.

How might this knowledge help learners?

The commonest sentences are statements, and learners' first writing will probably consist mainly of positive and negative statements. Learners are most likely to use questions and exclamations in narrative writing, and will come across instructions in a range of texts such as recipes. For these two functions, the main issues for learners relate to changes in word order and punctuation.

Instructions are ubiquitous: cooking from a recipe; operating home entertainment equipment; health and safety at work. They can be clearly distinguished from other types of text by their use of imperative forms of the verb (take a large cabbage; chop it up) often placed at the beginning of the sentence. Recognizing an imperative can help early readers to identify a set of instructions more quickly and to use them consistently in their writing.

Questions are noted by the inversion of the subject and verb (Are you coming?) or the inclusion of an interrogative word at the beginning of the sentence and a question mark at the end. (What are you doing? Why are you ringing?) Bilingual learners may need to practise forming a question in English. All learners can explore the different responses elicited by open and closed questions.

Exclamations are most common in informal letters and stories. They are useful to help learners see how punctuation can replace intonation in speech.

Punctuation

The grammar of a sentence includes punctuation as well as syntax. Traditionally written sentences start with a capital letter and end with a full stop, question mark or exclamation mark depending on the type of sentence. Other punctuation marks (commas, colons, semicolons, apostrophes, speech marks, etc.) operate within sentences indicating phrases, clauses, shortened forms, ownership, direct speech, etc. Punctuation has a close relationship with the syntax of the sentence. It is particularly difficult for new readers and writers to develop accurate punctuation skills, as the function of punctuation depends on an explicit or unconscious use of the grammar of the written sentence. The sentence – particularly in its complex forms – does not feature in conversational speech, as we have seen. We will discuss the development of punctuation skills further in Chapter 6.

Word focus

Lexis, or vocabulary, is seen in recent research as one of the four key components of learning to read (Kruidenier 2002). When reading, if we can recognize a whole word and access it from our lexical memory, it saves us from having to decode it letter by letter or sound by sound. But we can't keep it in our lexical memory unless we know what it means. Similarly, in writing, being stuck for a word because we can't spell it is frustrating. We either need to know how to spell the word or have strategies for recording what we want to say and checking spellings later.

We all know more words than we are likely to use. You might recognize a word like *antidisestablishmentarianism*; you might even know what it means, but you would be highly unlikely to use it in your everyday speech or writing. We call this our **passive vocabulary**. The words we actually use are our **active vocabulary.**

I (the writer) and you (if you are a fluent English user) will share a very similar active vocabulary. Most of our active vocabulary will be common words including all the *function* words. There are some words in my active vocabulary which might not be in yours because they relate to my work, my hobbies, my family life, my friends and social life and my community involvement. The active vocabulary that I draw on for speaking purposes will not necessarily be the same as that I use for writing (think of words like *furthermore*, *faithfully* or *yeah*, *sort of*, etc). As my life changes, my literacy practices will also change, and words might move from one vocabulary to the other.

When I read, I will come across words that I know, but am unlikely to use myself. For example, I might read an article in a scientific journal or a nineteenth-century novel and whilst I have no trouble understanding what I read, I would be unlikely to reproduce it. Glancing at an article on drugs in a popular science magazine, I see words like *arrhythmia*, *off-label*, *prostaglandin*, *jollies*. They are not words I would use myself, but I can interpret them enough to understand the article.

For reading it is enough to have passive vocabulary; for writing we need an active vocabulary. What does this mean to someone who is learning to read and write? How many words might this be? Well, as always, there is disagreement among linguists.[6]

Many literacy teachers in the UK use the Dolch list – 220 words said to cover 50–75 per cent of all reading.[7] One researcher (Nation 2002) estimates that someone knowing the most common 2000 word families has a coverage of 80–95 per cent of most written English texts depending on topic and style. These are called high-frequency words and would include most of the 176 function words as well as some content words. However, to read fluently and independently, a reader needs to be familiar with 98–99 per cent of the words in a text (McShane 2005). Research shows that vocabulary knowledge is crucial for getting meaning from text and for giving choice and control over the writing process (National Reading Panel 2000). While studies agree that knowledge of vocabulary is important for developing reading skills, they also show it is normally extensive reading that helps develop a wide vocabulary.

Task 3.11

What do we need to know about a word?
Consider what we mean when we can say we know the word *gregariously*.

What sorts of knowledge about the word do you need to have in order to recognize and use it in speech and writing?

Your answers will fall into the areas of:

- **phonology**: how the word is pronounced (speech) and the sound–symbol correspondence (for spelling);

- **morphology**: how the word is built (the significance of the *inflection -ly*);
- **semantics**: the meaning of the word.

And maybe also:

- **collocation**: what other words it is most frequently used with.
- **graphology**: the formation of letters and how these are combined in writing;
- **etymology**: the word's derivation;

We deal with each of these categories below.

Phonology

> Beware of heard, a dreadful word,
> That looks like beard and sounds like bird,
> And dead: it's said like bed, not bead,
> For Goodness' sake don't call it deed!
> Watch out for meat and great and threat,
> They rhyme with suite and straight and debt.[8]

As we all know, the sounds of English sometimes seem to have a rather random connection with the letters used to write it. It is often stated that English spelling is impossible to learn because of the number of irregular words. How true is this? It is not a simple task to check. Trying to assess what percentage is actually irregular is hard as it is hard to define irregularity and even harder to define a word.[9]

There seem to be only about four hundred everyday words in English which are totally irregular i.e. follow no known patterns. Unfortunately, however, the ones that are irregular are among the most commonly used. Nevertheless phonemic knowledge can still be helpful in the learning of spelling. Crystal (2003: 72) quotes a major 1970s US study of a computer analysis of 17,000 words that found 84 per cent were regular to some extent and only 3 per cent were so unpredictable that they had to be learned by heart.

There are two aspects of phonemic knowledge that are useful for decoding or spelling: **phoneme–grapheme** (or sound–symbol) correspondence and **onset-–rime**.

Learning **phoneme–grapheme** correspondence is called **phonics** in the UK and **alphabetics** in the US. It means understanding how the sounds of a word match with the letters representing those sounds. The issue (which will be explored further in Chapter 6) is how to help learners manipulate the complex rules for how sounds in English can be represented, so that the sound system becomes a help rather than a hindrance to learning. A further difficulty, illustrated in Example 3.14, is that the correspondence between sounds and symbols differs according to the variety of English, especially in the case of vowel sounds.

Example 3.14

Variation in sound systems
A teacher from Manchester who told her London group that the word *stuck* rhymed with *book* was met with incredulous stares.

Teachers also need to be aware of the unstressed English vowel sound called a *schwa*. This is the sound in words like about, baker, possible, second, suppose. It is the most common vowel sound in spoken English but can be spelled by using any of the vowels. It is therefore almost impossible to judge how to spell it just from the sound. It can cause a major spelling problem.

Phonemes

Phonemes are the smallest sound units possible. In the word *rat* there are three phonemes corresponding to the sounds r-a-t; in *rant*, there are four: r-a-n-t.

In English sometimes we use two or more letters together to make a single sound (**digraph** e.g. *th* or *ea*; **trigraph** *tch* or *sch* or *our*), so *read* has three phonemes: r-ea-d and *this* also has three: th-i-s.

There are 44 phonemes in the English language, 24 consonant phonemes and 20 vowel phonemes.[10]

Many languages show consistency between written symbols and speech sounds, which makes their orthography **transparent** or **shallow.** English has a more irregular grapheme–phoneme correspondence (known as **opaque** or **deep** orthography). We see one phoneme can be represented by a variety of graphemes, for example:

- the phoneme /ʃ/ in *pressure, sugar, **sh**ape, addition, **ch**ef*;
- the long vowel sound /eɪ/ in *ma**d**e, pain, reign, neighbour, café, station, break, maelstrom, ballet, day, ley lines, chez*

Or alternatively, the same graphemes can have several different sounds in the words: *soul, foul, should, route* or *chemistry, chef, cheap*.

Another way for learners to fit sound and symbols together is to use **onset and rime,** which has had good results with children (Goswami and Bryant 1990). This uses syllables as the basis for sounds. If a word is broken into syllables, each one has an onset (beginning) and a rime (end) e.g. *cheap* has *ch* (onset) and *eap* (rime). Some teachers and learners find these are easier to remember.

One other aspect of phonology teachers might want to consider is the placing of stress on words and how it can change the meaning, thus affecting both reading and spelling. Words like *refuse, contract, record, present* are pronounced differently depending on whether they are being used as a noun or a verb. Despite the difference in stress (in British English), it helps to know that *advertisement* is from the same root word as *advertise* in order to spell it accurately.

Morphology

As mentioned above, morphology is primarily concerned with the structure of words and morphemes, units of meaning, are the building blocks of words. To understand how a word is built out of morphemes can help us understand how it is constructed, where it comes from, what word class it is and what work it is doing in the sentence. It can thus help with decoding a word, understanding its meaning and spelling it.

There are two types of morpheme, **bound** morphemes and **free** morphemes.

Free morphemes are units of meaning that can stand on their own. Examples of free morphemes are the word *cat* and the two parts *copy* and *right* of the word *copyright*. They can be lexical or content words (an open group such as *pan* and *cake*) or function words (a closed group) as *in* and *to* in *into*.

Bound morphemes are parts of words which cannot stand on their own, such as prefixes and suffixes, e.g. *ing* in *packing*. They too can be divided into two groups:

Derivational morphemes make new words by changing the grammatical category e.g. thought-*less* (noun to adjective) ; kind-*ly* (adjective to adverb); care-*ful-ly* (noun to adjective to adverb).

Inflectional morphemes never change the grammatical category. What they do is show the grammatical function of a word (Standard English has only eight inflectional morphemes: two are attached to adjectives (comparative *-er* and superlative *-est*); two to nouns (plural *-s*; possessive- *'s*); and the rest to verbs (*-ed, -s -ing, -en*). It seems to be inflectional morphemes that cause the most difficulty for adult literacy learners; derivational morphemes are more likely to trouble bilingual learners.

Task 3.12 asks you to look at **Grace**'s use of morphemes (**Text 7**). She uses quite a few inflectional morphemes and has some problems in this area.

Task 3.12

Using inflectional morphemes
The words underlined are those which use inflectional morphemes in Standard English.

- Which of the eight kinds of inflectional morphemes are represented?
- Which does **Grace** use correctly and which does she have problems with?
- Can you make a guess as to why these are difficult for her?

I went to Rose birthday party and it was so nice.

   She nineteen year old and there was a lot of visitor that she invite to the party and did rent a big hall for the all night party.

   My friends Rose spend a lot of money of the birthday Party eat special food like Rice and yam all kind of drink and she bake cake of the party we all was dancing in the hall.

   And she invite all her family and her brother and sister to the party and all her visitor and friends from school all of them was in party.

Possible answers are at the end of the chapter.

The following excerpt from from **Malika's** writing (Example 3.15) also contains some examples of inflectional morphemes:

Example 3.15

Malika (Text 8a)

Racism

In this <u>day's</u> racism is growing a lot. We should respect all groups of <u>peoples</u> no matter they are white, black or which religion they are. Or any country they came from.

Malika has made two morphological errors, the second of which is characteristic of someone who does not have English as her mother tongue.

- *day's* – she has added the apostrophe*'s* where it is not needed, so she has used an inflectional morpheme incorrectly. She may have meant *These days …* which should have been represented by a plural *s* ending;
- *peoples* – she has added the plural *s* where none was needed, which shows she has made an error about the plural of *person;* she has correctly remembered it is irregular but she has forgotten that it has no *s* to denote plural.

Wayne's piece (Text 9) shows a third use of inflectional morphemes:

Example 3.16

Wayne (Text 9)

How have you been I hope you have been OK, I doing good I have made a lot of changes in myself over the last 2 <u>year's</u>. I can't belive how <u>irresponsible</u> I used to act before I came here. Life <u>seem's</u> so different now I have responsibility, I can't wait to come home and face up to my <u>responsibilitys</u>.

Wayne's home language is English. He makes four errors in morphology:

- Two of these, *year's* and *seem's*, are adding an apostrophe where none is needed. He obviously has some knowledge of apostrophes as he has used one correctly in *can't*, but maybe he understands their use in shortened forms but still is unsure about their use for possession.
- *Irresponsible*: he has omitted the adverbial ending (not changing *-le* to *-ly*). This is likely to relate to his language variety (London) where the adverbial ending is often omitted.
- *Responsibilitys:* a spelling error where **Wayne** does not know or has forgotten that the *y* following a consonant changes to *ies* in the plural.

Fluent speakers of English (whatever their language variety) who are inexperienced in writing often have difficulty with inflection. This may be due to the lack of stress on the inflection in fluent running speech, or elision (merging of one word into another), which is also a characteristic of fluent speech. (Try saying *he walked to the car and opened the boot* rapidly, as you might do in conversation. The sounds of the *-ed* endings of the verbs almost disappear.)

They may also have been exposed to many non-standard uses of the apostrophe, and this is bound to contribute to their own usage. The use of the apostrophe is an area of language use that is currently undergoing change. Teachers might want to discuss with their learners the value of learning to apply the formal written conventions for apostrophes.

Semantics

Semantics is concerned with meaning, as expressed in language or other systems of signs. In reading, coming across an unfamiliar word can make us reluctant to read on; in writing it can make us nervous that we have used the word wrongly.

Example 3.17 is an extract from the Tesco website.[10] Even if all the words are known to you, some are used in a legal sense here and meanings might not be exactly the same as those you are used to. 'Terms and Conditions' may never actually be read by a customer of Tesco, but they could be important.

Example 3.17

Examining lexical meaning in a text

Terms and Conditions

Intellectual property

The content of the Tesco.com Site is protected by copyright, trade marks, database and other intellectual property rights. You may retrieve and display the content of the Tesco.com Site on a computer screen, store such content in electronic form on disk (but not any server or other storage device connected to a network) or print one copy of such content for your own personal, non-commercial use, provided you keep intact all and any copyright and proprietary notices. You may not otherwise reproduce, modify, copy or distribute or use for commercial purposes any of the materials or content on the Tesco.com Site without written permission from Tesco.com.

No licence is granted to you in these Terms and Conditions to use any trade mark of Tesco.com or its affiliated companies

(Extract from www.tesco.com accessed 30 March 2009)

Understanding the exact meanings of words is always important in legal language. So how could we work out the meaning of *non-commercial* in the text above?

The prefix *non* means *not*, so we know that *non-commercial* must be the opposite of *commercial*. So if we know the word *commercial*, we can work out *non-commercial* because it is the opposite (**antonym**). If we didn't know the meaning of *commercial* and asked someone, they might say it is about 'selling', 'making money', 'trading'. These would be **synonyms** of the word (words/phrases that have the same or similar meanings). Dictionaries rely on synonyms to give us meanings of words. So both synonyms and antonyms are useful for defining meanings of words.

If we didn't know the term *copyright* in *The content of Tesco.com site is protected by copyright, trade marks, database and other intellectual property rights*, we might be able to link it with the other words it is listed with (*trade marks*, *database*) under the overall heading of *intellectual property rights*. *Copyright* is a **hyponym** of *intellectual property rights* (its **superordinate**) i.e. It is subsumed under that heading. This again helps us with the meaning – we know roughly what *copyright* must mean, even if it doesn't give us such an exact meaning as a synonym or antonym.

Too many hyponyms in texts make them more difficult to access. The text is more accurate – as each word specifies a particular aspect of the meaning of the superordinate term – but the content is correspondingly more dense.

Homonyms, homographs and homophones

Other terms which describe relations between words are **homonyms, homographs** and **homophones**. The terminology can confuse the teacher, just as these types of words are often confusing for the learners.

	Written form (spelling)	**Spoken form (pronuncia-tion)**	**Origin**	**Meaning**
Homonym	same	same	different	different
Homophone	different	same	different	different
Homograph	same	often different	different	different

Examples

Homonym	*mean* (intend); *mean* (average); *mean* (unkind) *light* (shine); *light* (not heavy)
Homophones	*knew* and *new*; *rain, reign* and *rein*
Homograph	*wind* (noun – type of weather); *wind* (verb – to roll up) *lead* (verb – conduct); *lead* (noun – a metal); *moped* (verb – behave miserably); *moped* (noun – small motorbike)

We should remember that words can be homophones in some varieties and not in other varieties: *merry, marry, Mary* could be homophones for a speaker of American

English but not for a British English one; as might be *do* and *due*; a southern English speaker might hear *court* and *caught* as homonyms but a Scottish speaker would not.

While it is true that homonyms and homographs can cause problems for learner readers, and homophones for learner writers, it is best to deal with such words in context, as and when they cause problems, rather than try to cover large numbers of similar words at once.

Connotation and denotation

Every word has a dictionary definition called its **denotation** – its *explicit* meaning. But words can also have less definable or *implicit* meanings: for example, a feather is something that covers a bird, part of its plumage, but it can also mean anything that is light or even trivial by association. (He was an intellectual featherweight.)

A **connotation** is what is implied by a word about a feeling, an emotion, or a value judgement. The implication may be what an individual feels, but is more likely to be formed by the values of society or a cultural group within society. So, for instance, taboo words are those that society looks down upon. Words to do with bodily functions (e.g. *shit, f*ck*) come from the Anglo-Saxon; they have been in the language for a long time and are not intrinsically or linguistically any worse than the euphemisms acceptable by society, but they have connotations of rudeness and dirtiness that are generally known and understood by members of that society.

Other connotations are more subtle – as explored in the task below:

Task 3.13

Connotation
A recent newspaper billboard stated:

Travellers set to occupy marshes.

The local council have given the land to the travellers. What connotations, however, might be suggested by the verbs: *set* and *occupy*?

Possible responses are at the end of this chapter.

A *critical approach* to language use is intended to make explicit these intentional or subconscious expressions of values and beliefs.

Advertisers and other writers of persuasive texts make full use of connotations and it is one way in which a control of language is useful for recognizing where these are being utilized and being able to make personal use of them to write effectively.

Collocation

Another feature of understanding meanings of words is related to how and when words go together with other words to create different meanings. This is called **collocation**. For example, in the Tesco terms and conditions above, the word *trade* appears in the first line. We may know several words that are often used with *trade* (trade *description*, trade *union*, trade *name*, trade *route*, trade *wind*, *Board of* trade, *passing* trade as well as phrasal verbs such as trade *off*, trade *in*, trade *down*). If we are aware of these possible collocations, fluent readers will predict the next word, *mark* from this set and will glance at *'mark'* to confirm they are right. (We will also use other clues such as the context and our knowledge of syntax).

Thornbury (1998: 8) says words 'hunt in packs', which is a good way of conveying the notion of collocation. Encouraging learners to draw on this knowledge may help them predict a word they have difficulty reading. Of course, as with any context-bound use of language, it often relies on culturally specific knowledge; collocations can often be colloquial or idiomatic and it cannot be assumed that they will always be known or understood. Learners may know about *half-term* or *half-time*; they might have come across *half a pint, or half a dozen*, but would they know *at half cock; how the other half lives; not half; one's other (or better) half*?

Task 3.14

Collocation
List some collocations for these words: **right, youth, computer**.
   Which collocations might make it easier to read for a learner? Which might make it more difficult?

Possible answers are at the end of this chapter.

Graphology

'Good', that is neat, legible handwriting, used to be an important element of mastering writing. With the accessibility of computers, it has become less and less important, although many learners might still feel that their handwriting lets them down sometimes. As well as lessening the strain of having to write neatly, computers have changed the nature of writing in a variety of ways (see Chapter 6).

Etymology

Etymology is the study of the origins of words. Understanding where a word has come from is helpful for a number of reasons: it can help with some of the vagaries of English spelling (e.g knowing that the origin of *debt* is the Latin *debitum* can be useful for remembering the silent *b*); it can help interpret unfamiliar words (knowing that *psycho* comes from the Greek word for mind or soul can help with interpreting psychological, psychoanalysis, psychosomatic); it can also help some learners use their own first language to access words in English which might be unfamiliar.

Applying knowledge of language to literacy learning and teaching

In this chapter we have examined different aspects of written and spoken English – at text, sentence and word level. In this final section, we will consider how this knowledge can be helpful in adult literacy teaching.

In order to plan effectively, teachers need to identify the linguistic elements of a group or individual learning goal, using their knowledge of language to break it down into component skills, knowledge and understanding. There are two reasons for doing this: to make the hidden sub-skills of language and literacy more visible, and to approach the learning in manageable stages.

Course and lesson planning also draw on 'diagnostic' or in-depth assessment, through which a tutor identifies individual learners' strengths and areas for development. In a one-to-one tutorial she gives feedback, draws on the learner's own insights into her use of language, and negotiates priorities for learning.

In Example 3.18 we show how knowledge of language can enable us to analyse a learner's writing to show her strengths and areas she could work on further, using the text/sentence/word framework.

Example 3.18

Using knowledge of language to carry out a diagnostic analysis of a learner's writing
Text 1b: Geraldine

Strengths and areas for development
Text level
Geraldine's text-level writing skills are strong and they are very much in evidence in this text. These skills include:

- Genre knowledge: ability to produce the language and format of a particular genre (formal letter of request)
    - Uses formal register, standard layout, standard greetings.

- Ability to create coherent text
    - Makes use of shared knowledge of context
    - Organization of ideas
        - Introduces herself
        - States the purpose of her letter
        - Elaborates, lists arguments
        - Issues a challenge to the reader and reiterates her request
        - Thanks the reader and signs off.

- o Grammatical cohesion

    - Uses discourse markers to signpost the main ideas: logical connectives *because, and, also, if*

    - Uses pronoun references effectively with no confusion or loss of clarity: *I, you, she*

    - Uses ellipsis to produce fluent sentences: and [she] does not want to be moved, and [she] has also just lost.

- o Lexical cohesion

    - Uses theme words: gypsies site, travellers on the road, my Nan on the road, etc.

    - Makes positive affirmations: has lived there 20 years, likes where she is

    - Makes frequent negative statements and commands: don't close down, does not want to be moved, wouldn't be good, you don't want.

- • Pragmatic competence and rhetorical skill
    - o meets the information needs of the reader
    - o uses rhetorical strategies to heighten the impact of the text

Sentence level

- • Grammar
    - o Uses compound sentences

        - Sentences are well constructed, but punctuation is not used consistently to mark sentence and clause boundaries – see below.

    - o Varies the length of sentences. This is effective because:

        - Variety makes the text more readable

        - Contrast works well rhetorically (e.g. between the long explanatory sentences of the middle paragraph and the short sentences in which she makes a direct challenge to the reader).

    - o Uses a range of tenses accurately

        - Present simple tense, with Standard English subject–verb agreement: *she likes, she does*

        - Present perfect tense: has lived there for ..., has just lost ...

    - o Sometimes gets confused when expressing negation: I am writing to ask you don't to close down ... a move right now would don't be good.

- Punctuation
  - Uses full-stops accurately at times
    - To mark short sentences which are clear units of meaning: You say you Don't want Travellers on the Rd. If you don't wanna see my Nan on the Rd Don't close down were she lives.
  - Gets confused when the meaning spans sentence boundaries:
    - The whole middle paragraph is punctuated as if it were a single long sentence.
  - Doesn't understand that punctuation is based on sentence and clause boundaries, not on units of meaning – this is logical but doesn't correspond with current conventions.

- Capitalization
  - Uses capital letters accurately at times:
    - At the beginnings of clauses and sentences
    - To mark the name of a person or place.
  - Sometimes uses capital letters rhetorically to highlight significant words: *Site, Now, Problem, Right Now, Don't close, Don't want …*
  - Her inconsistent use of capital letters suggests lack of proofreading skill e.g. she uses a capital for her own name in the opening sentence but not at the end of the letter.

Word level

- Vocabulary
  - Uses words accurately and effectively in terms of their meaning.
  - Range of vocabulary in this text is fairly limited.

- Spelling
  - Spells most common words and personal key words correctly, including difficult words: *Hackney, gypsies, Travellers,* **Geraldine**, *Brigid, Paddy.*
  - Spells some words according to how she pronounces them: *jas, wanna.*
  - Has difficulty with consonant clusters
    - poblem for p<u>r</u>oblem
    - ack for as<u>k</u>
    - G dad for <u>gr</u>anddad.
  - Has difficulty with visual memory of some common or familiar words: *writing, site, heart.*

- When she can't attempt a word, she sometimes writes only a small part of it, often only the initial letter. This is a good strategy for maintaining fluency and achieving her communicative purpose
  - *R* for writing
  - *S* for site
  - *h* for heart.

Chosen areas to work on

- Text level
  - Spacing of paragraphs: this is an easy thing to learn and will immediately improve the visual effectiveness of her text.

- Sentence level
  - Basic sentence and clause structure and how punctuation relates to this: this will improve the clarity of her writing.
  - Capitalization: she wants to understand what the basic conventions are; in the longer term she can go back to using capital letters for rhetorical effect.

- Word level
  - Individual spelling programme with a specialist tutor: this should help her understand her strengths and difficulties with spelling and develop strategies for improving it.

Conclusion

We have considered various aspects of language in this chapter and argued that it is essential for a literacy teacher to have an understanding of how language works in order to support learners in developing their written and spoken language. A fundamental principle is that there needs to be a clear connection between this application of linguistic knowledge and the social context of the learners. This can be achieved through ongoing dialogue between learners and teachers focusing on a wide variety of texts and contexts and on their own uses of language.

Tasks possible answers and comments

Task 3.1
Multimodal communication

How to use a piece of machinery – assuming this is an oral task, you will probably use spoken language and gesture/body language. You might also use images (e.g. a drawing).

Get help in an emergency – spoken language (you may shout for help), gesture, sound (you may sound an alarm).

    Send a birthday greeting to an old friend – written language, image (a card with pictures).

    You may have considered the following reasons why these modes are useful:

- Gesture and body language, and visuals are particularly useful for supporting spoken language when demonstrating or instructing.
- Intonation and other sounds are useful for quickly indicating danger or the need for help.
- Written language gives you the ability to connect with somebody who is not in the same physical space as you, and pictures can convey a feeling, attitude or meaning – often more powerfully than words.

Task 3.2

Identifying assumed knowledge in a text

This text relies on a considerable amount of assumed knowledge by the reader – of football in general, and about Arsenal football club and its recent history.

    You need to know that Arsene Wenger is the current manager of the Arsenal team, that the Carling Cup kids are junior players, that the 'starting berth' is the chance to be booked to play for an adult team, what a 'red card' means and what happened at a recent match – to identify just a few. For the audience for which this is intended, however, this text would make perfect sense.

Task 3.3

Referencing and lexical cohesion
    1 **Analysing Sean's text (Text 4)**

a) Referencing

On my first day back in education as an adult at Shoreditch college in Hackney, was very daunting. In the first place it was hard to relate to **the** (*cataphoric*) boy who from the age of four to sixteen didn't enjoy his time at school also in Hackney and Tower Hamlets. As a young boy at school I was very unfortunate to have gone to school in **the** (*exophoric*) early 60s and 70s where their was some very strange ways of teaching. Although the schools were clean and well kept the standard of education was not.

Most of the teachers in the main were exstremly nice people Some of **their** (*anaphoric*) teaching texneces left a lot to be diseared, not to be disrespectable to the indivigle involved, I personally think that the laid back and right-on atictute was not the right way for me; that is not to say that I would have liked to have been tort in the fashion of my perants generation where **the** (*anaphoric*) children were ruled by fear. Respect in my opinion is earned. If unlike me you got off to a good start at school, the schools I attended where very good, nice clean buidings, friendly environment, clean and well maintand, Teacher perants, and school children all very positive.

For these children it must have been a very empowering, and a good grounding For a postive adult life. But for me and a lot of my classmates **this** (*anaphoric*) was not the case,

If like now as an adult I have children of my own, and know that if a child is left behind it is very difficult for **them** (*anaphoric*) too catch up later on in todays climate most teachers and perants are aware of **this** (*anaphoric*) and as a consequence in the modern method of teaching **this** (*anaphoric*) doesn't happen (or not too often)?

So getting back to my first day at collage, I was very surprised that I was looking forward to going so much. As a youngster I lived around Hoxton and the Hackney area, and I can tell you that **the** (*anaphoric*) building has changed so much For the better in 30 years since I was young. The building I was now going into was clean, new, modern, and above all welcoming, The posotive feelling I got just for going into **the** (*anaphoric*) place was great. I Still get and have some pange of aprehenchon about education I know I will come out of **this** (*anaphoric*) with something quite posotive. I hope to come out of this exspirence with some academic qualification and a beter understanding of schooling.

b) Lexical cohesion:

- **Education:** *education, school, teaching, education, teachers, taught, schools, school children;*
- **Feelings about learning as an adult**: *daunting, positive; welcoming; looking forward; positive feeling; pangs of apprehension; quite positive.*

2 Comment on Sean's control of cohesion

Sean seems to be skilled at both referencing and using a range of lexical sets. His references cover a range of types and he doesn't assume knowledge internally or externally to the text that is inappropriate.

In terms of cohesion, he is not repetitive and shows an ability to keep to themes well. He shows a good range of semantic choices when commenting on the quality of teaching in his school.

Task 3.4

Different approaches to grammar

We can speculate here that a prescriptive grammarian would be concerned that **Flora** broke many of the rules of Standard English in this sentence and would consider it as simply inaccurate. Both the descriptive grammarian and the functional grammarian would treat this text non-judgementally as the writer's actual use of language and that of her speech community (though they may want to point out the differences with Standard Written English and encourage her to use the latter in more formal written forms). Both the descriptive and functional grammarian would consider context and purpose. A functional grammarian's analysis would focus particularly on what the speaker or writer was trying to do with this text. They would consider its construction, and, in speech, the prosody, and examine its interpersonal effectiveness. For example, in writing, using non-standard grammar could establish identity and a sense of honesty with a reader.

Task 3.7

Word classes and context

Round is used in these sentences as a

- preposition;
- verb (round<u>ed</u>);
- noun;
- adjective.

Task 3.8

Open and closed word classes

The new words you will find on the website will vary according to the time you look.

You should notice that they are all 'content' words – nouns, verbs and adjectives. These are the words we use to name, label and categorize our world, so they expand as we have new experiences and new ways of looking at these. Other word classes are function words (e.g. prepositions, determiners). These underpin language, allow us to link content words together in endless variations of meaning. As they are the *scaffolding* of meaning in a sentence, they are less subject to change.

Task 3.9

Working with phrases

Flora has produced an effective narrative that communicates clearly an outline of the main events and gives some descriptive detail about the occasion. How could she be supported to make it more effective?

a) **Noun phrases**

In terms of noun phrases, she has achieved some variety: as well as single nouns (church, Saturday), there are some noun phrases consisting of two nouns (bride and bridesmaids) a noun preceded by the determiner (the ceremony; the decoration); or a possessive pronoun (her wedding). There is one instance of a noun pre-modified with a possessive noun (my cousin wedding) and this is the only example of a noun phrase that consists of more than two words

Although at times **Flora** has attached a determiner appropriately, at other times she has shown she has some problems e.g In Standard English, we might expect *the* food or *the* bride and bridesmaids and we would not say *the* midnight.

A literacy teacher might be able to help her make her writing more expressive by expanding the noun phrases, by increasing her ability to pre-modify and also to consider post-modification e.g the ceremony was in the *old stone* church *on the corner.*

b) **Adjectival phrases**

Flora uses a limited range of adjectival phrases: two modified by *so* (so wonderful; so enjoyable) and two by *very* (very beautiful; very delicious). Her teacher could help her consider other ways of modifying adjectives (really enjoyable; truly delicious). She could also look at other ways of modifying nouns e.g. *the moving ceremony, her fabulous wedding.*

c) **Adverbials**

Flora uses preposition phrases to add detail about the time and place of events.

> Time – *last Saturday; after church, until (the) midnight*
> Place – *in the hall*

Flora also employs an adverbial phrase to indicate the degree to which something occurred (*we all enjoy <u>very much</u>; I enjoy <u>very much</u>*). Again she could consider a range of ways of explaining this: '*we greatly enjoyed it*'; '*I really loved it*'.

Adverbials can greatly increase the information supplied by the verb or noun alone and extended use beyond time and place to indicate manner, frequency, purpose can all be helpful.

For further ideas for building up phrasing, see Chapter 6.

Task 3.12

Using inflectional morphemes

Inflectional morphemes	Correctly used for Standard English	Incorrectly used for Standard English
Noun plural	<u>brother and sister</u> – we do not know whether she has one of each (in which case this is correct) or more than one (in which case she has omitted the plural s) <u>friends</u> – correct plural	<u>year</u> – plural s omitted <u>visitor</u> – plural s omitted (twice) <u>friends</u> – plural s put in incorrectly
Noun possessive		<u>Rose</u> – possessive 's omitted
Verb past -ed		<u>invite</u> – present tense should be past simple (twice) <u>bake</u> – present should be past simple
Verb present /past continuous -ing	danc<u>ing</u> – past continuous	

Comment 3.12

Grace uses a West African variety of English and in her variety, inflections are not used in the same way as in Standard English (SE). In particular, we can see that the plural -s and the past -ed are areas where **Grace's** variety diverges from SE. This would be a major area of discussion for **Grace** and her tutor (see Chapter 4).

Task 3.13

Connotation
Commentary
This is a possible response to this task:

The verb *set* means here 'intend' but has the connotation of (a) agency by the travellers and (b) determination in the face of opposition.

Occupy is a term with strong connotations. Armies *occupy* territories, demonstrators *occupy* buildings. It suggests an aggressive or illegal act in the face of opposition

The effect of using *set* and *occupy* by the newspaper is to suggest that the travellers are about to perform an action that is opposed, and perhaps illegal but they are determined to carry it through. In fact they are moving, perfectly legally, into land they have been offered by the authorities.

TASK 3.14

Collocation
Possible answers
These are some examples of collocations. You may have thought of others.

Right	right time; turn right; right on; right away; right hand; right and left; right and wrong; right turn; turn right; right time; right hour; in the right way; yes, right!
Youth	youth work; youth training scheme; youth project; youth today
Computer	computer disc; computer terminal; computer mouse; computer screen; computer programme; computer disc; home computer

---

Comment 3.14

The usefulness of these collocations to learner readers depends on how familiar they are linguistically and culturally with the expressions.

Right on, for example, is particular to a particular culture and age group.

Although the collocations linked with *computer* are relatively neutral, they depend on the learner having some knowledge of computers and computer jargon.

Further reading and resources

Crystal, D. (2004) *Rediscover Grammar*. Harlow: Longman.
Thornbury, S. (1997) *About Language: Tasks for Teachers of English*. Cambridge: Cambridge University Press.

Notes

1. Adapted from Carter, R. (1995) *Keywords in Language and Literacy* pp. 38–9 London: Routledge.
2. The term 'text type' is commonly used in literacy teaching. We prefer the terms 'genre' and 'genre knowledge'. Some linguists distinguish between 'text type' and 'genre'. However, here we will treat them as meaning the same.

3. See for example Andrews *et al.* (2004).
4. Adverbials can also be clauses and can have other functions in the sentence.
5. We have corrected the errors in this extract in order to make it easier to see the grammar.
6. A rough estimate made by David Crystal is that there are between half a million and two million words in the English language (excluding very technical/colloquial/regional ones). A university graduate might know 15,000–30,000; an average person maybe 12,000–15,000? Crystal's calculations lead to a middle-aged female secretary having an active vocabulary of 31,500 and a passive one of 38,500 (higher than Shakespeare, who was estimated to have used 20,000–30,000 different words in his writing!).
7. The Dolch word list should be used with care; it was published in 1948 and thus represents language common in the early twentieth century; it was compiled from young children's reading programmes; it excludes common nouns. These days we have a number of electronically compiled examples of texts which draw on authentic examples of written and/or spoken language and represent a more accurate picture of how language is actually used.
8. This poem has variously been attributed to Richard Krogh in Bolinger, C. and Sears D. (1981) Aspects of Language, New York: Harcourt Brace Jovanovich, p. 283; to T.S.W in Yule G. (2006) *The Study of Language*, Cambridge: Cambridge University Press, p. 39, and to Anon elsewhere. For other poems about the difficulties of English spelling see: www.spellingsociety.org/news/media/poems.php (accessed 30 March 2009).
9. For example: are compound or hyphenated words one word or two? Are inflected words like dance, dancing, dances, danced one word or four? Do we include proper names, loan words, dialect words?
10. For the full list with the phonemic symbols see: www.teachingenglish. org.uk/download/phonemes.shtml (accessed 30 March 2009).
11. Tesco is a British supermarket.

4   Language variety

Nora Hughes and Irene Schwab

Linguistic diversity

Many literacy groups, particularly in urban areas, are made up of people from a wide range of backgrounds, including learners whose home language is a regional variety of English and bilingual learners who speak another language or languages at home. This has implications for learning and teaching. To work effectively with linguistically diverse groups, tutors must know something of the cultural backgrounds and language communities to which learners belong, their language and literacy practices and the resources they bring to learning. They also need some understanding of how people become more confident and proficient users of a language or language variety that is not their 'mother tongue'.

Language communities

The learners who feature in this chapter are members of different language communities. Each person has a unique language history, reflecting his or her linguistic heritage and current language use, and a number of social roles and **discoursal** identities – ways of using spoken and written language in different domains of their lives. The choices they make are affected by the relative power and prestige of the languages and language varieties available to them.

Language histories: heritage and change

Geraldine (Texts 1a, 1b) is a 17-year-old woman who lives with her family on an official Travellers' site in an inner London borough. At home she speaks mainly Irish English, the variety spoken by her parents and extended family. Her linguistic heritage also includes knowledge of Gammon,[1] the traditional language of the Irish Traveller community. In social contexts outside the Traveller community, the greatest influence on her speech is London English, a rich vernacular which itself reflects the diverse influence of generations of native and settled communities. As a writer of formal texts, **Geraldine** uses Standard English, which she aspires to use more confidently in the hope of getting a qualification and a job.

Geraldine's history illustrates not only language change from generation to generation but also individual variation and choice. People adapt their language according to context and purpose and develop new ways of using language in the pursuit of their life goals.

Dulcie (Texts 10a, 10b, 10c), having been brought up in rural Jamaica, is a speaker of Jamaican Creole, a language used by the whole community for everyday communication but not for official or formal purposes, when Standard Jamaican English would be employed. This was the variety which was used in the media and taught in school. **Dulcie** switches between these two varieties depending on who she is speaking to, and her written English draws on both varieties, together with the London English she has heard all around her for the last forty years.

Malika (Texts 8a, 8b, 8c), as an Arabic speaker, is a member of a large international language community. Her linguistic repertoire includes: classical Arabic, the language of the Quran; Standard Arabic, the official language of the Arabic-speaking world; and Moroccan Arabic, the spoken variety used by the Moroccan community at home and abroad. She also has a little knowledge of French and Spanish, both of which she studied at school.

More recently, **Malika's** main language, apart from Arabic, has been English, which is increasingly important to her as a citizen, parent, neighbour and friend and which, as a powerful global language, brings many potential benefits and opportunities.

Language and power

All the learners represented in this chapter are aware that language hierarchies exist. They know implicitly, if not explicitly, that using Standard English, the most prestigious variety of the world's most powerful language, can open many doors. For example, they use it in their role as citizens, knowing that only this form of English is regarded as 'correct' or acceptable. They also aim to use it in educational contexts in which gaining a formal qualification is a central goal.

Like many others who were educated in the Caribbean under Colonial rule, **Dulcie** was taught that her own Creole language was 'not a proper language', and was punished for using it in school. Now, however, young people of Caribbean origin are reclaiming Creole (sometimes called Patois or Patwa) as their heritage and often use it as their preferred language for communication among their peers; it has achieved high status among young people of various backgrounds as the language which can express and maintain their social group identity. However, ironically, this revival as a youth language may have reduced its respect among older members of the UK population, even though it is taken much more seriously now in the Caribbean itself.

For **Malika** and **Geraldine** another aspect of language inequality is the high status of English compared with the languages of their ancestors and communities. Gammon is a minority language with no prestige in mainstream European societies except as an object of research for scholars. Arabic has a distinguished history as the language of an ancient religion and culture revered by millions of people worldwide, but Asian and African languages are not always accorded the same respect as European languages. For example German, unlike Arabic, is commonly offered as a GCSE subject in UK schools, despite the fact that it is not in widespread use in the community in the same way as Arabic.

For another learner, **Aftab**, a Sylheti speaker, there are also issues of inequality. Sylheti is not a high-status international language, nor is it even an official language of Bangladesh. It is not seen as 'useful' in mainstream British society or associated with 'success' in national civic life.

Language and identity

This privileging of some languages and language varieties over others, and the consequences for language and literacy learning, are important issues for teachers to take account of in their work. Despite the relatively low status of their home languages and language varieties, literacy learners are often proud of their linguistic heritage. As the terms 'mother tongue', 'home language' and 'community language' suggest, language is at the core of everyone's personal, family and community identity.

In adult literacy education there is a strong tradition of celebrating linguistic diversity, whilst also helping learners develop the knowledge and skills they need to make effective choices in their language use, including the use of Standard English whenever they judge this to be necessary or desirable.

History of the English language

"Language is a dialect that has an army and a navy.[2]"

The history of the English language is one of constant change and development. The oldest varieties of English are only about 1500 years old and, as a language we would recognize today, it is perhaps barely 500 years old. The factors that cause languages to change are related to those which cause society to transform; in the case of English we can clearly follow these through a series of invasions and occupations. The process by which English has developed over the years, grafting new vocabulary from a number of languages onto a basic grammar from the original language, could be seen as a process of **creolization**.[3] The historical processes that saw those in power imposing a new language as a way of controlling the indigenous population can be seen in the history of Africa, the Caribbean and other parts of the world.

The birth of English

What we know as English began around the fifth century with the invasion of groups of peoples who spoke West Germanic dialects – Angles, Saxons and Jutes. They imposed these on a country that still spoke mainly **Celtic languages** (now preserved in Welsh, Irish and Scottish Gaelic). We call the language they introduced Old English.

Like modern German, **Old English** was an inflected language with endings showing the function of the word; word order was variable. We would find it hard to recognize Old English as the language we use today, although there were certainly some words that would be familiar (e.g. *hūs* – house; *wīfman* – woman; *lufu* – love; *ic*-I; *wealcan* – walk) This first form of English was developed and changed over the years by a series of invaders and also by trade and by contact with other countries.

In the seventh century, the conversion of most of the population to Christianity meant that the Church had a powerful influence. **Latin**, the language of the church, became important in England, as elsewhere in Europe. Whereas it never gained a hold under the four centuries of Roman occupation, it now became the language of prestige and scholarship. It was at this time, not during the Roman occupation, that many Latin words entered the language (e.g. *candle, devil, wine, angel*).

The invasion of the Vikings from Scandinavia brought **Old Norse**, another Germanic language, into the country. Many Vikings settled in the north and east of England and their language mixed in with the prevailing dialects being used there. Although the use of Old Norse itself died out, many Scandinavian words entered the language (e.g. *egg, sky, give, take*).

In 1066, the Normans invaded. The name Norman, meaning *North man*, shows they too were descended from Vikings who had invaded northern France. Their language was a variety of French which had been influenced by Old Norse as well. **Norman French** became the language of government, law and the court. Latin was still in use by the church and for scholarship; ordinary people still used their local variety of English. Many words coming into the language at that time (like *prison, castle*) were representative of the rule of law imposed on the populace. The language of the conquerors was seen as the language of power and culture; English was seen as a rough and inferior language.

In the early thirteenth century, Normandy was taken over by the French whose court, using the Parisian dialect of French, was the most powerful in Europe; their influence also permeated England and **Parisian French** also became an influence on the English language, especially in relation to administration (*e.g. parliament, government, manor*), and culture (*e.g. art, beauty, romance*).

During the thirteenth century the rise of the English middle classes meant that the language they spoke also gained a higher status. In 1362, for the first time, the king's speech at the opening of Parliament was in English. In the same year an Act of parliament was passed making English, not French, the language of the law (although records were still kept in Latin). Moves were made to teach schoolchildren in English rather than French. The English of this period is now known as **Middle English** and there were a number of regional varieties of this language with different pronunciation, grammar and vocabulary.

The development of Standard English

The idea of a standard version of written English first began to take root during the 1300s. One of the six varieties in use at the time, the **East Midlands dialect,** began to be seen as more important than the others. There were three main reasons for this: it was used by the middle classes in and around London, which was the centre of government, law, the court and culture. The two universities, Oxford and Cambridge, were also within this area, so this was seen as the dialect of educated people. In 1476 Caxton introduced printing and he printed material in the East Midlands dialect, which helped that dialect to spread and gave it greater status. As its influence grew, it became known as **Standard English**. This influence became even greater when education became compulsory in 1870 and all children were taught in this variety. Children were led to believe that this was the correct version and their own spoken variety was less correct.

English as a global language

Just as historical socio-political reasons led to Standard English becoming the most powerful dialect in the United Kingdom, they also led to English becoming the powerful force it is in the world today. British colonial expansion in the seventeenth to nineteenth centuries brought English to the countries they colonized as a way of maintaining control and assimilating the local population. This is why Australia, New Zealand, Canada, the United States, South Africa and many countries in Africa, Asia and the Caribbean now use English as their first or as an official language. In the twentieth century the military might of Britain gave way to American economic and military power. The pre-eminence that English has in today's world is more due to American dominance of the world economy than anything connected with Britain. The US now has 70 per cent of the world's mother tongue English speakers.

The rise of multinational companies, the dominance by the US of the press, broadcasting, technology, entertainment (particularly cinema and popular music) and the use of English as the international language of science, scholarship and business have led to it becoming a world language. English is the language of international communications; the content of the internet is said to be 80 per cent English;[4] it is used for international maritime communications (Seaspeak) and for international air traffic control (Airspeak).

Its use all over the world has led to developments of many different sorts of 'Englishes'. English is spoken not just with a different accent but with different elements of grammar, vocabulary, collocations and idioms drawn from local languages. This has led to the formation of hybrid languages such as Singlish used in Singapore, drawing on English but also on local languages, such as Chinese and Malay.

How does this affect literacy learners?

The education system is designed to promote Standard English as the variety of English necessary to get on in life. Whilst accepting that access to this is important, it can be helpful for learners to realize that Standard English is only one variety of English amongst many and its current status as the norm is related to historical and political reasons rather than ones of intrinsic superiority. Everyone uses a slightly different variety of English related to when, where and how they were brought up. This is called an **idiolect** and it is closely related to one's identity. These varieties show difference but, in linguistic terms, Standard English is no better than Creole, Indian English, Scots, Geordie or any other variety that might be used. Speakers of these varieties may have been told that their language is 'bad English' or 'broken English' and it can be helpful to explain and discuss how this came to be.

Whatever their language background (and groups are always made up of individuals with different language backgrounds), it can be empowering to see that all varieties of English have rules and logic behind them. Whether each variety is right or wrong depends on the context in which it is being used and the purpose to which it is being put. What is important is that people are able to communicate clearly and effectively in language that is appropriate for its purpose.

It is hard to say when a variety stops being a dialect and starts being a separate language. Dialects of a language are sometimes seen as a continuum with total mutual intelligibility at one end and complete unintelligibility at the other. But mutual intelligibility can depend on so many things – like speed of delivery, knowledge of local issues and accent. What is termed a language might have more to do with the political status of its speakers and its acceptability as a means of communication than intelligibility. For example, Hindi and Urdu are closely related but are seen as separate languages because they are the national languages of the separate political nations, India and Pakistan, whereas Mandarin and Cantonese are seen as dialects of Chinese because they are spoken in a single country, although their oral forms are mutually unintelligible.

Caribbean Creole languages

Dulcie's spoken language is the one she grew up with, Jamaican Creole. In Creole languages, although the words are familiar to us as English words, the underlying grammar is based on that of West African languages. Creole languages are spoken by millions of people in the Caribbean and all over the world. They came into existence through the processes of exploration, trade, conquest, slavery, migration and colonialism that brought together the people of Europe and the people of the rest of the world. The relationship between these peoples has been on a very unequal basis and Creole languages often came into being under the harshest conditions.

Between the seventeenth and nineteenth centuries, large numbers of people were taken by force from West Africa to work as slaves on sugar plantations run by Europeans in the Caribbean. The African people who were taken as slaves spoke a number of different languages, mainly from the same language family – now known as the Niger–Congo family of languages from West Africa and Southern Africa. On the long and horrific boat journey across the Atlantic (the Middle Passage), speakers of the same language were deliberately separated in order to lessen the risk of rebellion; in order to communicate both with each other and with the slave traders who had power over them, the captured West Africans were forced to learn some words of the European languages such as English, French, Spanish, Dutch and Portuguese. These words were put together into a limited type of language which was used for communication between the slave traders, the plantation owners and the different groups of West Africans, none of whom could understand each other's languages. Linguists call this type of language a **pidgin** language. A pidgin is nobody's first language but is purely a transactional means of communication. In time, this developed into a full language, called a **Creole** language, which could express everything its speakers wanted to say. It became the mother tongue of the slaves and their descendents and also the descendents of the slave owners in the Caribbean.

In Jamaica, the language drew on the words of English but maintained the grammatical structure of the African languages originally spoken by the slaves. A Creole language is one that has grammar and some pronunciation patterns which come from a non-European language but uses words which come from a European language. **Jamaican Creole** uses English words but has the underlying structure of West African languages. Other Creole languages draw on vocabulary from other European colonial powers (e.g. French, Dutch, Spanish) but have grammar patterns similarly from West African languages.

The Europeans who ruled the Caribbean tried to dismiss the Creole languages as 'baby talk' or 'broken English'. They did not allow it to be used in schools and made no effort to devise a writing system to write it down. Thus, for a long time, it remained primarily an oral language.

Today Jamaican Creole (often known by its speakers as **patois** or **patwa**) is not only written down but has a thriving literary tradition, both in the Caribbean and in Britain. There is a dictionary of Jamaican Creole[5] – a sign of how seriously it is taken – and new projects to develop its use in government and education in Jamaica.[6]

Commentary

Text level

In the samples of **Dulcie's** writing below we can see that **Dulcie** writes exactly as she speaks; she has understood the connection between speech and writing. However, she is not writing in Standard English because she does not speak Standard English. In each of these three samples **Dulcie** has also written in the appropriate genre. The first two samples are an autobiographical narrative; in the third she has reproduced the style and register of a typical Agony Aunt column. Although the texts are short, in each case she has created a narrative flow with a clear orientation at the beginning, a more developed middle section and ending with a personal comment. It may be that **Dulcie's** experience of the story-telling tradition of the Caribbean (with its roots in African traditional practices) has been a model for her to draw on. Similarly, her position as a senior and respected member of her community might have given her experience in offering advice in a way that would be accepted and valued by those who sought it.

Sentence level

A reader unused to **Dulcie's** variety of language might argue that her writing is 'ungrammatical'. If we look at it in more detail we find that, on the whole, she has followed known grammar patterns quite accurately; it is just that they are not English grammar patterns.

Jamaican Creole grammar has a number of differences from Standard English grammar. Among these we might note:

1 Creole does not use an *s* to denote 3rd person singular. This is known sometimes by teachers as subject–verb agreement
   Dulcie uses this construction several times. See **Text 10(a)**:

   He <u>see</u> my sister ...
   ... and he <u>tell</u> she that he <u>ask</u> me ...

   Text 10c:

   ... and see how he <u>take</u> it.

2 Creole has fewer pronoun forms than Standard English, so a single form might be used for the subject or object pronoun in a sentence.
   Dulcie uses the subject form of the 3rd person singular pronouns in object position. See **Text 10a**:

   ... and he asked me to let <u>he</u> take me home.
   ... and he tell <u>she</u> ...

3 Plurals of nouns are sometimes marked by adding -*dem,* rather than by adding an *s*, especially when referring to people (e.g. *di man dem =* the men); at other times the Creole plural is the same as the singular.
   Dulcie talks generally about her initial views of urban London, employing the singular form of the nouns. See **Text 10b**:

   I thought the house was a factory

4 Creole doesn't use the copula (the verb *to be* acting as a link between subject and predicate).
   Dulcie doesn't always use the copula and, on occasion, also doesn't use the auxiliary verb *to be*. See **Text 10c**:

   My advise to go away ...

5 In Standard English the past tense is usually marked (*walk–walked,* *eat–eat<u>en</u>*); in Creole the past tense is often not marked so that it can look the same as the present tense.
   Dulcie uses this construction several times and, because of the context, it is always clear that she means something that happened in the past. See **Text 10a**:

   When I first <u>meet</u> my husband ...
   He <u>see</u> my sister the next day ...
   ... and he <u>tell</u> she that he <u>ask</u> me to take me home ...

There are many other differences between Standard English and Creole grammar which are not represented in these samples of **Dulcie's** writing.[7] However, Creole, like English, is a dynamic language and is constantly changing according to where and how it is used. When speakers of Creole have left the Caribbean and moved to other countries like Britain, the language they use has been affected by other varieties of English they have come into contact with. In London, a new form of Creole, sometimes called London Jamaican (because Jamaican is the dominant Creole language used in London) has developed and is used both by settlers from the Caribbean and by young people of other backgrounds anxious to be linked with the prestige form of youth culture associated with the language.

Dulcie is not involved with youth culture but she has lived and worked in London for nearly forty years and, consciously or unconsciously, she has modified and changed the form of language she uses. Some people argue for a type of continuum with Standard English at one end and Jamaican Creole at the other, with versions more or less affected by one variety or the other at different points on the continuum. This is the **bidialectism** view, where **Dulcie** would be seen as having access to more than one point on the continuum of dialects of English. However, as we have shown, Creole is not just a version of English but a separate language in its own right so it cannot be a continuum of varieties of English. **Dulcie's** position is perhaps more akin to bilingualism.

Although we can see elements of Creole grammar in **Dulcie's** writing, she does not use Creole all the time. If we look again at the five Creole features we examined before, we can see that in each case she also uses the Standard English version:

1   subject–verb agreement. See **Text 10c**:

   ... and do has he <u>likes</u>
   ... and see how she <u>takes</u> it.

2   Pronouns. See **Text 10a**:

   ... and I was afraid of <u>him</u>.

3   Plurals. See **Text 10b**:

   Maybe after <u>times</u> goes
   ... (although this could be seen as an error in both languages).

4   Copula. See **Text 10a**:
   ... for I <u>was</u> so shy

Text 10c:

   I think the best idea <u>is</u> to inveited the family for tea

5   Past tense. See **Text 10a**:

   ... and he <u>asked</u> me to let he take me home
   ... and he <u>asked</u> me if I <u>would</u> take a drink

Text 10b uses past tense throughout.

It is not that **Dulcie** has tried to use either Standard English or Creole and got it wrong. It is a complex situation where the language form she uses has been influenced by the two languages she has access to, which have elements that overlap but also elements that are quite different. This variety of language is sometimes called **British Black English**.[8]

Word level

At word level, the differences between the two languages are not as obvious, as Creole makes use of recognizable English words. Although, in general, **Dulcie** uses vocabulary well known to an English speaker, she sometimes uses words and expressions that might be unfamiliar. See **Text 10c**:

... to fool her up ...

Or constructions that are grammatical but seldom used in Standard English. See **Text 10a**:

... take a drink
... for I was shy

Text 10c:

... for a little time ...

Phonology

There are also aspects of her spelling that relate to the pronunciation of Creole[9] (for example omitting the final consonant in certain consonant clusters and adding an *h* in front of words beginning with a vowel). See **Text 10a**:

... all you are going through With your husban ...

Text 10c:

he only trying to fool her up and do has he likes

So although **Dulcie** often uses Creole, she does not do so consistently. This is because she has lived in England for many years and is used to hearing Standard English spoken around her and used on the radio and TV. Although she does not read much, she occasionally sees a newspaper or magazine; she sees the Bible, the hymn books and, of course, has been attending literacy classes, which have taught her aspects of Standard English grammar. Her writing contains elements of the languages and varieties of language she has been exposed to.

> **Task 4.1**
>
> **Identifying features of a language variety**
>
> Look at the writing of **Leon**, another writer of Caribbean origin (**Text 11**). **Leon** was born in England, attended school there and has never been to the Caribbean, but his language – both spoken and written – has many similarities with **Dulcie's**.
>
> Which of the features of Caribbean Creole, noted in **Dulcie's** writing can you recognize here?

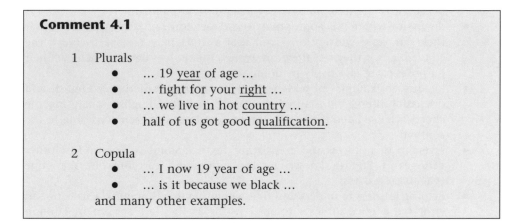

> **Comment 4.1**
>
> 1 Plurals
>   - ... 19 <u>year</u> of age ...
>   - ... fight for your <u>right</u> ...
>   - ... we live in hot <u>country</u> ...
>   - half of us got good <u>qualification</u>.
>
> 2 Copula
>   - ... I now 19 year of age ...
>   - ... is it because we black ...
>   and many other examples.

However, we can also see signs of another variety of English that **Leon** uses – London English. **Leon** was born and brought up in London; he went to school there and most of his friends – whatever their parents' origins – were also born there. His speech and therefore his writing have been influenced by this variety as well.

What will help Dulcie and Leon improve their writing?

If the teacher marks **Dulcie** or **Leon's** work with Standard English in mind, the work will come back covered in red pen. This is discouraging and never helpful to learners. Both writers have written according to the variety of language or languages that they use in speech, so just telling them that it is wrong is disrespectful and will not help them to improve their writing. What will be helpful to them?

Most people who have more than one variety at their disposal (Standard English and their regional variety) are used to code-switching in everyday speech. Because we write less often than we speak, we are not so accustomed to doing this in writing. Just as it is helpful for the teacher to understand how different varieties of English impact on a person's literacy use, so too is it for the learners. The teacher needs to find ways to discuss the issues with learners so that they can make informed choices about which variety to use.

They can do this by:

- sharing with learners some of the political and historical factors in the formation of Standard English and Creole and the reasons why some languages and varieties of language have greater power and status than others;
- discussing how accent, pronunciation, spelling, vocabulary and grammar relate to spoken language;
- pointing out which elements of the writing emanate from, for example, Creole, which from regional English varieties and where Standard English is being used. The terminology may need to be explained;
- discussing where it is appropriate to use each variety, bearing in mind that these are only conventions, and that writers may choose to break the conventions if they feel they can express themselves better or achieve their purposes more effectively by doing so;
- looking at examples of texts written in different varieties of English and discussing them, 'translating' them into Standard English, analysing the effects achieved and evaluating the pros and cons of each according to the context;
- reversing this process and 'translating' texts in Standard English into other varieties of English known by the group and carrying out the same evaluation process;
- helping learners to understand that when they say 'somefink' this is not an error but a good attempt to spell words as they are spoken in London English, using the sounds accurately. However, in this case the *f* sound has to be represented by the digraph *th*, just as in the word *washed* the *t* sound is represented by – *ed*;
- using phonics with care as in Creole, and in many varieties of English, sounds are pronounced very differently; in Creole *pot* and *pat* sound alike; in London English the rime sound in *with* and *live* is the same.

Language variety and reading

This is an extract from a miscue analysis of **Dulcie** reading *The Book Boy* (Trollope 2006).

Example 4.1

She is
'She's in the bike shop.'

                              say amazing   get
Ed took a step forward. He said, amazed, 'But she hasn't got a bike, she couldn't
...'

        say
'No,' Becky said, 'she couldn't. She hasn't. But Scott has.'

             was
Craig said, 'Scott?' His eyes were twice their usual size. '*Scott?*'

       say   look   smile
'Yes', Becky said. She looked up and smiled right at them. 'Yes, Mum is in
                            give
a room at the back of the bike shop. With Scott. She gave Scott the money to

put down on a bike.'

        shout
'I'll kill her!' Ed shouted. 'I'll kill them both!'

         say
'And in return,' Becky said, taking her time, 'Scott is teaching her to read.'

In reading this passage, **Dulcie** makes nine miscues (one of which is repeated four times). Seven of these (arguably even eight) are due to her reading the passage in her own language variety i.e. substituting her Creole version of the past tense which looks like the present and not using a contracted version of *she is*. She is not entirely consistent in this. As with her writing, she sometimes uses Standard English, showing her easy familiarity with both varieties. As she reads, she does not recognize these as errors, so does not self-correct, and she is able to make perfect meaning from what she reads. Her use of her own language variety is not causing her a problem with comprehension and there would be little point correcting her, unless she needed to be able to read aloud with accuracy.

Languages and language varieties

Geraldine and **Dulcie** make use of their **vernacular** (or non-Standard) varieties of language for everyday use. Some learners might be happy to write in their own variety of language; others may want to use Standard English only. As tutors we are able to support learners in the way they choose to write and discuss with them the reasons why they might decide to use different varieties in different contexts and for different purposes. In some cases this will mean they use their own variety or their own language, rather than Standard English.

One way of assisting learners to make real choices is to look at what languages (and varieties of languages) have in common and what is different about them. Bilingual learners may not be aware that the way they write something reflects the syntax, morphology or pragmatics of their first language rather than English usage. Likewise, when we hear a turn of phrase all around us all the time, it is not always easy to know if that is because it has particularly common usage in our language community or whether it is because it is a Standard version. It can need explicit teaching to differentiate.

Ideas are often expressed in very different ways and this can cause problems for learners trying to write something in an unfamiliar language. If a learner says, 'I go home now, yes?' it can be understood perfectly by her teacher and anyone else in the room, but if the same sentence appeared in a written text the reader would have more difficulty, so for writing the learner needs to use English constructions more accurately.

Working with bilingual learners in literacy groups

In this section we explore ways in which literacy tutors can work effectively with bilingual learners alongside learners whose home language is English. We do not offer guidance on ESOL teaching, which is a separate specialism with its own theory and methodologies. However, in the bibliography you will find textbooks and other sources in which ESOL approaches and techniques are explained.

Reading, writing, speaking and listening: issues arising for bilingual learners

In order to work effectively with this group of learners, tutors need to consider what is involved in reading, writing, speaking and listening in a second or additional language. Bilingual learners who have been appropriately placed in literacy groups are fluent speakers of English and can participate fully. However, they are dealing with a language they did not grow up with and each of the four language skills presents particular challenges for them; issues can arise at text, sentence and word level that would not come up if they were operating in their home languages.

Cultural knowledge

As discussed in Chapter 3, **pragmatics** is the study of how language conveys meaning above and beyond the literal meaning of words and sentences. It is concerned with the cultural norms and conventions that govern the use of language, which, like other aspects of language, may not be obvious to the user; we all internalize the norms of our home language and society and tend to assume that the way we use language is 'natural'. For literacy learners and tutors, one of the benefits of working in linguistically diverse groups is that it can raise everyone's awareness of the cultural dimension of language.

Reading and listening involve, among other things, understanding **exophoric references**[10] – references to things outside the text that the writer and reader, or speaker and listener, both know about. This depends on shared knowledge which is often cultural in the broadest sense of the word, encompassing familiarity with national media, music, sport, famous people, food and drink, festivals, customs, ways of doing things that are culturally specific and yet taken for granted by people from that culture.

When planning a reading or listening activity, it is a good idea to check for culturally specific content and explore this in advance with learners.

In one well-known example (Glover *et al.* 1990: 85–8), a written text features a child who is very attached to her *piggy bank* but eventually destroys it. This is easy to understand if you know about piggy banks, but utterly baffling if you don't. Not only is the collocation of *piggy* and *bank* surprising, but the fact that the child smashes her beloved *bank* or *piggy* to pieces is confusing for a reader from a culture in which piggy banks do not exist.

Cultural knowledge is equally important for writing and speaking. 'Appropriacy', knowing the 'rules of the game', understanding the relationships between participants, using language or gesture to achieve particular effects – these are all much easier in a language and culture we have known from childhood.

Example 4.2

Applying for a job
Cultural norms in job seeking are very varied. They depend on broader social relations within a culture and on the 'expected' behaviours of the people involved. For example, in a letter of application or a supporting statement, the applicant must get the balance between assertiveness and deference, and in an interview the 'right' body language is equally crucial.

When working with literacy learners on these skills it is important to avoid implying that 'the way we do it here' is the best or only way, and to ensure that bilingual learners, who may be used to very different cultural norms, have access to the broader cultural knowledge they need for the context.

Discussing these issues explicitly can help all learners in the group become more aware of them, and enable them to make informed choices.

Genre conventions

Reading and listening include bringing genre expectations to a text (the reader or listener thinks 'Ah, it's that kind of story/ joke/ article'). Familiarity with the genres of a language enables us to predict their content and style and interpret the way language is being used by the writer or speaker.

Speaking and listening depend on knowledge of politeness conventions, which vary from one language to another, for example knowing how to interpret the 'moves' made by a speaker or using appropriate 'body language' or verbal 'softeners' in different kinds of interaction.[11]

Writing involves reproducing the format and register of established written genres, as discussed in Chapters 3 and 6. Sometimes there are specific conventions or expectations associated with more formal texts like academic essays or business letters.

Example 4.3

A letter of request
In a Chinese letter of request, stating the request at the outset, before explaining the reasons for making it, could seem abrupt, whereas in English it is generally expected.[12]

Such differences are lessening as a result of the 'globalization' of literacy, with the spread of American and Western European norms and standards worldwide. But cultural variation is still an issue for bilingual learners when writing formally in English, and one which literacy tutors need to be aware of.

Grammar

When reading and listening we use our knowledge of grammar to understand and interpret what is being said: if someone writes *I walked to work*, we know she is referring to a past action because she has used the past tense form of the verb *to walk*. Reading and listening in a new language involve recognizing the grammatical forms of the language and getting meaning from them.

For the 'productive' skills of writing and speaking, grammar presents an additional challenge, as the writer or speaker not only has to understand these forms but produce them accurately enough to make her intended meaning clear. In this extract from **Aftab's** text (**Text 12**) the use of the present tense form of the verb in the fourth sentence is ambiguous:

> My name is **Aftab**. I born in Bangladesh. I came England in 96. I stard to work smool job in Hotel But it <u>is</u> very hard for me Becoze I <u>have</u> family problem.

At this point in the text the reader is unsure whether **Aftab** means it is still hard for him and he still has a 'family problem', or whether he is referring to a situation in the past. In the next sentence it becomes clearer:

> So I live this job. Now I have new job and I can look my family.

Working with **Aftab** on this text could include asking him what his intended meaning was when he wrote *It is very hard for me becoze I have family problem*, and teaching or revising the past tense forms of the verbs *to be* and *to have*, as there is evidence in the text that he is familiar with this tense even if he does always use it accurately (*I born, I came, I stard*).

As discussed earlier in the chapter, a writer or speaker uses different kinds of grammar according to the social context she is in. For example, she would aim to use Standard English in a formal letter or job interview, but is more likely to use the grammar of her local variety of English when socializing with friends or neighbours. As Roxy Harris points out (1995), a bilingual learner's use of English is influenced by the spoken variety of the region she has settled in.

So bilingual learners, like others in literacy groups, need knowledge of the grammatical differences between Standard English and their local variety of English, in order to make informed choices when writing and speaking.

But a more fundamental issue for a bilingual learner, in terms of grammar, is the fact that there are likely to be significant differences between the grammar of her home language(s) and the grammar of English. Languages convey grammatical meaning in a wide variety of ways involving many different aspects of grammar. The examples we give below are not comprehensive but are intended to give a sense of the kinds of sentence-level issues that can arise for bilingual learners, particularly when writing or speaking in English.

Word order differences

An English sentence typically employs a word order of subject, verb, object (SVO):

> The woman   eats   an apple.
>
> **Subject   verb   object**

However, not all languages order sentences in the same way. For example, Japanese, Amharic, Bengali and Turkish use SOV; Welsh and classical Arabic use VSO:

> *canodd Gaenor cân hyfryd* (Gaenor sang a beautiful song)[13]
>
> Literally: sang Gaenor a song beautiful (VSO).

In Sylheti the word order of a question is exactly the same as for a statement. As in English, the rising intonation indicates that it is a question, although the interrogative particle *ni* is generally added at the end of the question, e.g:

> *tumi musulman* (You are a Muslim.)
>
> *tumi musulman ni?* (Are you a Muslim?)

Word order and morphology/inflections

In some languages such as German, the order of the words is less important than in English because the meaning can be worked out from the **inflections**, i.e. the ending of each word indicates what that word is doing in the sentence.

For example:

> 1 Ich möchte, daß der junge Mann dem Lehrer den Stuhl gibt.
>
> 2 Ich möchte, daß dem jungen Mann den Lehrer der Stuhl gibt.

In these two German sentences the word order is the same. However, they have very different meanings:

> 1 I'd like the young man to give the chair to the teacher.
>
> 2 I'd like the chair to give the teacher to the young man.

The difference is in the use of inflections. In German the word for *the* changes according to whether it belongs to the subject (der Mann), the object (den Lehrer) or whether it includes a preposition (dem Mann – to the man). Likewise the adjective (jung – young) is inflected according to whether it modifies the subject (junge) or object (jungen). The role of each word is thus indicated clearly wherever it is placed in the sentence.

English has very few inflections and therefore word order is much more important in determining meaning. A learner who is used to using an inflected language may well try to make changes to the article, the adjective or the noun itself as all of these can be inflected; she may also not pay so much attention to word order as this may not be so important in her home language.

Word class differences

In English we are used to seeing sentences in terms of word classes like nouns, verbs, adjectives and prepositions etc. Although all languages have these concepts, they do not all express them in the way that English does. We have seen how Creole does not use a copula; neither does Bengali or Russian. So learners who have languages like these as their mother tongue might easily omit the verb *to be* in their writing. A Sylheti speaker(**Aftab**) stated:

> I born in Bangladesh (*was* omitted)

Prepositions can also cause difficulties to speakers of other languages. Turkish is an **agglutinative** language which means that suffixes are attached to root words to make more complex words, phrases or even complete sentences. So for example, prepositions are not separate words but appear as suffixes of nouns, e.g.

> Bankaya (to the bank); Bankadan (from the bank)

Otele (to the hotel); Otelden (from the hotel)

In Bengali **post positions** are used instead of <u>pre</u>positions.

These different ways of using prepositions can cause general confusion with English prepositions, especially as, being small and often unstressed words, they can be difficult to hear. Typical problems might be omitting the preposition; using the wrong preposition; using a preposition in the wrong place or where it is not needed.[14]

- I go Bangladesh.
- He hit me in my arm.
- I told to her.

The grammar of British Sign Language

British Sign Language or BSL is not English. It is a language in its own right, with its own word order and grammar. It uses hand signs and facial expressions as a visual form of communication and the grammar is completely different from English grammar. For example:

- it does not use the verb *to be*;
- it does not use articles such as *a, an, the*;
- verb phrases, which might in English be represented by several words, are inflected by changes of speed or placement, so are indicated by only one sign.[15]

The word order of a BSL sentence is also different from English, presenting the topic first and then a comment on it. So for example, *What is your name?* in English becomes *Your name what?* in BSL, or *Turn right at the traffic lights* in English becomes in BSL *traffic lights* (one sign) signed first, followed by *turn right* (one sign).

This means that in terms of literacy, a BSL user can be in the same position as a bilingual learner; her language is organized differently and this will impact on her interpretation and production of written text. It is important to discuss with the learner how these differences impact on her learning and how best to draw on her knowledge of language structure and vocabulary.

Similarly, when working with any bilingual learner on a point of grammar (for example one that has arisen in her writing), it can be helpful to explore grammatical differences between English and her home language, using the learner's implicit or explicit knowledge of language as a resource for learning.

Punctuation

Punctuation conventions vary from one language to another. When a literate learner's home language has the same script as English, punctuation is unlikely to present difficulties for her when reading, as she only has to recognize punctuation marks which are already familiar to her. It is more of an issue in writing, as a writer makes punctuation decisions based on the conventions of the language she is writing in.

Example 4.4

Marking sentence boundaries

In Arabic the use of full stops and commas is more flexible than in English. By contrast, the 'rules' for marking sentence boundaries in English are rather rigid, based on syntactic units which don't always correspond to natural pauses or units of meaning.

When a learner's home language has a different script from English, or if she has had limited access to literacy as a child, learning punctuation involves getting to know a whole new set of symbols and understanding their use in written texts.

Vocabulary

It is highly likely that a bilingual learner's vocabulary in English will be less extensive than that of a learner whose home language it is, as she has not been accumulating a 'mental lexicon' of English words since childhood and needs opportunities to do so as an adult, acquiring words and phrases for different contexts.

Pre-teaching vocabulary before a reading, writing, speaking or listening task is a way of ensuring that bilingual learners have the resources they need for the task, and gives them an opportunity to develop vocabulary for an authentic communicative purpose.

Sometimes the words a bilingual learner does not know, which native speakers of a language take for granted, are not long, 'difficult' or formal ones. They can be short and 'easy', but may be relatively uncommon and express slightly different meanings from more common alternatives.

Example 4.5

Less common words

Malika was reading a story in which one of the characters 'grinned'. She was baffled by the word and was unable to work out its meaning from the context.

When planning a reading activity, it is useful to think about words that bilingual learners may not have come across before, and consider whether their meanings can be deduced from the context.

Word meanings

Understanding, interpreting and using words depends on knowing their explicit meanings and also their connotations and likely collocations, as discussed in Chapter 3. These processes are more difficult in an unfamiliar language and culture.

Identifying the register of a word and using it appropriately can also be tricky, especially as there may be differences not only between English and the learner's home language but also, in the case of learners from former British colonies, between British Standard English and the Standard English of their country of origin. This is often reflected in the degree of formality that is considered acceptable in certain contexts. For example, the use of the word *esteemed* in the salutation *Esteemed colleagues* at the beginning of an email or letter, might be considered appropriate in some cultures, whereas in a contemporary British workplace text a more usual greeting would be *Dear colleagues*.

One implication for teaching is the need to make these aspects of language explicit, discussing them as they arise in written and oral activities.

Another issue that can arise with vocabulary is the fact that some words of the same origin in English and the learner's home language have evolved to the point where their meanings are completely different. For example, in Spanish *embarazada* means *pregnant*, not *embarrassed*, and *exito* means *success*, not *exit*. These words are called 'false friends' because their apparent 'closeness' is misleading.

Spelling

The English spelling system is alphabetic, and is therefore likely to be easier for learners whose first language is alphabetic than for those who have grown up using a different kind of script. However, the fact that English has an 'opaque' orthography, compared with the more 'transparent' orthographies of other alphabetic languages, such as Turkish or Spanish, can cause confusion or difficulty for any learner.

Another issue for bilingual learners is that some of the sounds of English may not exist in their home languages, while others may be represented by different letters or symbols.

Handwriting and keyboarding

Handwriting and using a keyboard can be challenging for learners who are used to a script with different characters and directionality (top to bottom or right to left). Even for those whose home languages use the same script, keyboarding can be an issue when the keyboard has a different layout.

Both handwriting and keyboarding are likely to be difficult for learners who have had little or no previous experience of literacy in any language. In the case of handwriting, it is helpful to provide clear handwritten models of learners' own words, and invite them to copy and practise these for use in their own texts, giving guidance on the mechanics of the process if they need it (for example how to hold the pen or which direction to take when forming letters).[16]

Phonology and pronunciation

Teaching pronunciation is not a primary aim of literacy education and in many cases is inappropriate or unnecessary, but there are occasions when a bilingual learner asks for help with pronunciation. A 'rule of thumb' is for the learner to aim for *comfortable intelligibility*; which the tutor can help with by modelling pronunciation and giving guidance.[17]

Phonology and spelling

At word level, speaking involves articulating the smallest units of sound in a language, such as **phonemes** (single sounds) and **consonant blends or clusters** (two or three separate sounds together). Some of these sounds or combinations may not exist in a learner's home language, which can have an impact on how she spells.

Example 4.6

Consonant blends
In **Text 8b**, **Malika** inserted a vowel between the *d* and the *r* in the word *drinking* (she wrote *dirinking*). Her spelling of the word seems to have been affected by her pronunciation – when she speaks she tends to add a brief vowel sound between the two consonant sounds, reflecting pronunciation patterns in Arabic.

It can be helpful to discuss and compare pronunciation patterns in the learner's home language and English. In **Malika's** case, discussion might focus on English consonant clusters that do not exist in Arabic, which she would then look out for when proofreading her writing.

The concept of **interlanguage** from second language acquisition theory[18] applies to spoken as well as written language but can be particularly helpful to literacy teachers when assessing bilingual learners' writing.

Interlanguage refers to the **language system** used by a learner at any particular stage of learning a new language. It contains elements of her home language and the new language, and is both systematic (showing recognizable patterns) and variable (showing inconsistencies).

In this extract from **Malika's** text (**Text 8c**), the use of the **past participle** as an adjective is sometimes correct (*scared*, *pleased*), but on two occasions she has confused it with the **present participle** (*exciting* for *excited* and *embarrassing* for *embarrassed*):

My daughter Khadija was five years old and she start school. She was very happy and <u>exciting</u>. Khadija wasn't <u>scred</u> ...

I still remember that day Jane invited us for tea ...I was <u>pleased</u> ... But when Jane handed me my tea I dropt it by accident and it goes all in the sofa. I was <u>embarrassing</u> and I wanted help her clean the sofa ...

A person's interlanguage is constantly changing as new elements are added. The order in which these are acquired is not dependent on her language background, but sometimes there are recognizable instances of language transfer.

I have family problem ... I have new job

In this extract from **Text 12**, **Aftab,** a Sylheti speaker, has got close to the two constructions he was aiming for (*I have a family problem* and *I have a new job*) and his intended meaning is clear; he has used English word order, which is different from Sylheti, but has left out the indefinite article, reflecting the fact that in Sylheti this word class does not exist.

A learner's interlanguage shows how she is actively looking for ways of expressing meaning, sometimes applying mechanisms from her home language and at other times applying **hypotheses** based on knowledge of the new language. Not all errors are due to language transfer; they can be because a learner's knowledge of an aspect of language is incomplete, or because she is not aware of irregularities or variations in the new language.

Example 4.7

Text 8c
Malika's spelling of *dropped* as *dropt* reflects the standard pronunciation of the word (after an unvoiced final /p/ the -*ed* ending is pronounced /t/).

She may also be generalizing from words such as *crept* and *slept*, in which there is a more obvious match between the spelling and the sound.

Either way, her spelling of *dropped* as *dropt* suggests that she is not aware of the different ways of representing the sound of the consonant blend *pt*, and is assuming that English spelling is more consistent than it really is.

Implications for practice arising from the concept of interlanguage include:

- look for evidence of the learner's communicative strategies and explore these with her;
- notice patterns and inconsistencies and consider the possible reasons for these;
- teach language that the learner is already trying to use, which will serve her communicative purpose in the text;

- be aware of possible **language transfer** and discuss this with the learner if appropriate.

Analysing learners' writing

In this section we will focus on two samples of **Malika's** writing, **Texts 8c** and **8b**: a personal narrative and an email to her local councillor (see learner texts).

Commentary

Text level

Malika's text-level writing skills are strong in many ways. *Friendship* is an engaging story from her own life, in which she describes her feelings and narrates an anecdote to illustrate the theme of friendship; she develops this theme, taking a new paragraph for each stage in the growth of the friendship and using temporal connectives to mark the passage of time (*four years ago, but that day, I still remember*). These features of a personal narrative are similar in most languages. She wrote this draft without the support of a tutor.

In the email to her local councillor she has also produced an effective text, but in this case the tutor provided essential *scaffolding*[19] related to the norms and conventions of formal letters in English. Before **Malika** composed her email, the tutor discussed with her the context and purpose of the writing, then elicited, modelled and explained the typical features of a letter of request and the sequence in which they occur:

- Opening paragraph: state the purpose of the letter.
- Middle paragraph(s): give background information and provide evidence.
- Final paragraph: make a request for action.
- Closure: politely put pressure on the recipient of the letter to respond (*I look forward to hearing from you*).

For **Malika**, this explicit modelling of a formal genre is very important. It gives her access to communicative strategies in written English which she needs in order to achieve her vocational and other goals. Learners from English-speaking backgrounds may also need explicit teaching of formal genres; the difference for a bilingual learner is that the conventions of these genres in her home language may be different.

Sentence level

Punctuation and capitalization

Malika's use of capitalization is mainly accurate, despite the fact that there is no distinction between upper and lower case letters in Arabic script. Likewise her use of punctuation: she has only made one error involving the use of a comma instead of a full stop, despite the fact that in Arabic the use of full stops and commas is much freer than in English:

> ... I was little bit nervous and shy because I met other parent and teacher, <u>all</u> this people they new for me ...

This accurate use of punctuation marks and capital letters in English is probably evidence of **Malika's** transferable literacy skills. She understands the role of these symbols in written texts, and has been able to draw on her experience of literacy to learn a new set of conventions in another language. A learner with more limited experience of literacy would be likely to find this much harder.

Grammar

This is a more difficult area for **Malika**, as for many language learners. Getting to grips with the grammatical system of a new language is not easy, especially when it differs significantly from the grammar of the learner's home language.

English verb tenses present a challenge for most learners, whatever their language background. Additionally, there are differences between Arabic and English **past and present tenses** which make it easy for Arabic speakers to get confused when using these tenses in English. In **Malika's** two texts the use of tenses is fairly accurate on the whole, but sometimes there is a mixture of past and present tenses even in the same sentence:

> We <u>drink</u> tea ... and we <u>became</u> friends.

> I <u>am writing</u> to complain about things that <u>happen</u> last week ...

However, she uses these correctly in other parts of the two texts, which suggests that she knows the verb forms but applies her knowledge of them inconsistently. The tutor could check **Malika's** knowledge of the tenses and ask her to proofread her text to find and correct inconsistencies.

Malika's use of articles is also inconsistent. She uses the **indefinite article** (*a*) correctly twice:

> Jane is like <u>a sister</u> for me ...

> One man had <u>a dog</u> ...

but she omits it on four occasions when it is needed:

> little bit nervous (a little bit nervous)

> long chat (a long chat)

> lot of children (a lot of children)

> broken bottle (a broken bottle)

This is almost certainly an example of language transfer: there is no indefinite article in Arabic and Arabic speakers often omit it in English.

The **definite article** (*the*) is used in both Arabic and English, but there are differences in the way it is used, which are reflected in **Malika's** texts. She has used it correctly several times, including:

> the sofa
>
> the play area
>
> all the time

but she has omitted it three times when it is needed:

> same age (the same age)
>
> same thing (the same thing)
>
> same area (the same area)

and she has used it on one occasion where it would not normally be used in English:

> the Finsbury Park (Finsbury Park)

Malika has learned about articles in English and uses them correctly at times, but overall she is still unsure of them and needs explicit teaching on this issue.[20]

Word level

Vocabulary

Malika's English vocabulary is more than adequate for writing a personal narrative at this level of literacy; for example, she uses a range of adjectives to describe feelings:

> happy, excited, scared, nervous, shy, pleased, comfortable, embarrassed

As mentioned earlier, she does not always know less common words (such as 'grin') and would benefit from developing her vocabulary further, incorporating a wider range of words and phrases for different contexts.

Spelling

Spelling is a particular strength of **Malika's**, demonstrating her ability to absorb a new spelling system, even one which is notoriously 'opaque'. She has made only two spelling mistakes in the course of two texts, a remarkable feat considering the difficulty of English spelling. This suggests that spelling is not a priority area for development.

Approaches to formative feedback

Earlier we applied the concept of **interlanguage** to analysing bilingual learners' writing, and in Chapters 6 and 8 we explore other approaches to formative feedback. Additional points to bear in mind when working with bilingual learners could include:

- Check what the learner already knows: ask questions, give prompts, offer alternatives. For example in response to:

  I met other parent and teacher, all this people ...

  the tutor could ask:

  'Did you meet <u>one</u> parent or <u>more than one</u> parent?'

  'What letter can you add to the word *parent* to show that you mean more than one?'

  'Do you mean all <u>this</u> people or all <u>these</u> people?'

- *Reformulate* if necessary: provide the language needed if the learner does not know it. For example:

It goes all in the sofa	It went <u>all over the sofa</u>
He was dirinking beer,	He was drinking beer,
even his son was with him	<u>even though</u> his son was with him

- Practise as needed, inviting the learner to come up with more examples:

  It went all over the sofa

  It went all over ...

- Model the correct structure and invite the learner to identify the pattern:

  Khadija was excit<u>ed</u>

  Khadija wasn't scar<u>ed</u>

  I was pleas<u>ed</u>

  I was embarrass<u>ed</u>

- Select points of language to work on, on the basis of:
  - suitability for level
  - usefulness / motivation / communicative purpose

  My daughter <u>was frightened of</u> the dog

  He was drinking beer, <u>even though</u> his son was with him

Conclusion

In this chapter we have seen how linguistic diversity in literacy groups creates both opportunities and challenges for tutors. Every learner has a unique language history and uses language in particular ways. Being an effective literacy teacher depends on noticing how people use language, being aware of issues that can arise for different groups and exploring these with learners.

Further reading and resources

Crystal, D. (2003) *English as a Global Language*, 2nd edn. Cambridge: CUP.

Harris, R. (1995) Disappearing language: fragments and fractures between speech and writing, in J. Mace (ed.) *Literacy, Language and Community Publishing: Essays in Adult Education*. Cleveland: Multilingual Matters.

Saxena, M. (1994) Literacies among the Panjabis In Southall, in M. Hamilton *et al.* (eds) *Worlds of Literacy*. Clevedon: Multilingual Matters.

Notes

1. Derived from Gaelic vocabulary and English grammar.
2. Weinreich (1973).
3. See the section on Caribbean Creole Languages in this chapter.
4. Crystal (2003): 118–19.
5. Cassidy, F.G. and Le Page, R.B. (2002) *A Dictionary of Jamaican English*. Barbados: University of the West Indies Press.
6. www.mona.uwi.edu/dllp/jlu accessed 12 June 2009.
7. For a detailed linguistic analysis, see Patrick, P. (2003) Jamaican Creole morphology and syntax privatewww.essex.ac.uk/~patrickp/papers/JamCreoleGrammar.pdf accessed 12 June 2009. For a more accessible version see Mark Sebba's 'A' level unit, *Creole English and Black English* (2002) on his website, www.ling.lancs.ac.uk/staff/mark/resource/creole.htm accessed 1 June 2009.
8. Sutcliffe, D. (1982) *British Black English*. Oxford: Blackwell; also Sebba, M. (2002) *Creole English and Black English*. www.ling.lancs.ac.uk/staff/mark/resource/creole.htm
9. Sebba, M. (1993) *London Jamaican*. Harlow: Longman, p.153–9.
10. See Chapter 3.
11. See McCarthy, M. (1991) *Discourse Analysis for Language Teachers*. Cambridge: Cambridge University Press; or Carter, R. and McCarthy, M. (1997) *Exploring Spoken English*. Cambridge: Cambridge University Press.
12. See Kirkpatrick, A. (1993) Information sequencing in Modern Standard Chinese, *Australian Review of Applied Linguistics*, 16(2); and Kirkpatrick, A. (1993) Information sequencing in Modern Standard Chinese in a genre of

extended discourse, *Text*, 13(3) – discussed in Liddicoat, A.J. and Crozet, C. (2000) *Teaching Languages, Teaching Cultures*. Sydney: Applied Linguistics Association of Australia.

13. Thanks to Gaenor Kyffin for the Welsh sentence and its translation.
14. See Hall, D. (1998) *Assessing the Needs of Bilingual Pupils: Living in Two Languages*. London: David Fulton.
15. See DfES (2001) *The Adult ESOL Core Curriculum*. London: DfES; and DfES (2002) *Access for All*. London: DfES.
16. For more guidance on developing literacy with bilingual learners, see Williams (2003); and Spiegel, M. and Sunderland, H. (1996) *Teaching Basic Literacy to ESOL Learners*. London: London Language and Literacy Unit/ London South Bank University.
17. For approaches to teaching pronunciation, see our partner book: Paton, A. and Wilkins, M. (2009) *Teaching ESOL*. Maidenhead: Open University Press.
    .
18. For discussion of the concept of 'interlanguage', see Gass, S.M. (2001) *Second Language Acquisition: An Introductory Course*, Mahwab, NJ: Lawrence Erlbaum Associates; also Mitchell, R. and Myles, F. (2001) Second language learning: concepts and issues, in C.N. Candlin and N. Mercer (eds) *English Language Teaching in its Social Context – A Reader*. London: Macmillan.
19. See Chapter 6.
20. See our partner book, Paton and Wilkins (2009) *op. cit.*

LEARNER PROFILES and TEXTS

Geraldine

Social and educational background

- Aged 17
- Lives with her family on an official Travellers' site
- Attends a pre-vocational literacy course for young people provided by a training organization

Language use

- Knows Gammon, Irish English, London English, Standard English
- Speaks Irish English at home and London English with friends outside the Traveller community
- Reads and writes mainly in Standard English

Examples of literacy practices

- Exchanges numerous text messages with friends
- Enjoys reading romantic fiction
- Writes to the authorities on behalf of her community, with support from tutors
- Reads about issues she cares about on the internet

Goals and aspirations

- To gain qualifications and get a job, if possible as a journalist

Text 1a: Geraldine

Mills and Boon

Her New Life

Hayley was on her way two her new Flat and Life in london. Having just moved to london after the Death of Her mother She Has No friends No family and No job She moved two London Hoping to make a New life for Her Self and find her father. Lil dose she No she will also Meet Her future Husband.

Callum loved He's life the way it was He definitely wasn't Looking for Mrs Right. until She walk into He's life and Took over He's mind and Body But What is she Hiding from him?

Tender Romance ... love affairs that last a lifetime

Text 1b Geraldine

Dear Sir/Mardan

   My name is Geraldine McGarry I am 17 years old.
   I am R ing to ack you dont to close down the gypsies S in Hackney because My Nan Brigid has lived there for over 20 years She likes were she is Now and Dose not want to be moved also She has a h Poblem and has also jas lost My
   g Dad Paddy and a move Right Now would Don't Be good.
   You say you Don't want Travellers on the Rd. If you don't wanna see my Nan on the Rd Don't close down were she lives.

Thank you
Yours Faithfully
geraldine McGarry

Sharon

Social and educational background

- Aged 17
- Attended a comprehensive school to age 16
- Was identified as have mild global learning difficulties and received additional support at school
- Attends a pre-vocational programme for young people at an FE college

Language use

- Speaks London English at home and with friends
- Uses Standard written English at college

Examples of literacy practices

- Reads popular fiction, particularly horror stories
- Exchanges text messages with friends
- Keeps a diary intermittently

Goals and aspirations

- To develop her writing skills and general confidence
- To be able to read and understand more difficult texts
- To get a job eventually, perhaps in catering as she enjoys cooking

Text 2a Sharon

Scary story

   I walk into the woods at nighttime and try to get my dogs and then I saw werewolves running towards us. We run to get to my car. I got one of my dogs into the car. I went to get the other one. Then I running for it. The dog survice and I tripe over and then I saw the dog get into the car myself and I drive off and the werewolf was running behind us. Then they stop running because they saw the other person on the way back to their car. The dog ran to my car. I opened the door to let him in and the family didn't make it. So I had to look after the dog for them.

The end

Text 2b Sharon

It was a fine sunny day. The beautiful young woman was walking down the long dirty street. She was wearing a new blue coat and she was carrying a shiny big handbag.

Eddie

Social and educational background

- Age and educational background unknown
- Worked as a building site labourer for twenty-four years
- Had time off for an injury and recently has only had temporary jobs
- Has just joined a literacy class

Language use

- Writes in Standard English
- Other language use not known

Examples of literacy practices

- Reads the sports page in the daily paper
- Reads formal letters (e.g. from local council) and would like to read them more confidently

Goals and aspirations

- To gain a qualification as a bricklayer and find secure employment
- To read science fiction novels

Text 3 Eddie

I word lick to be a backlald Be cors I lick dowing ti and I am fade up being out for work.

So I hope to line to reder and writ ti word holp me a lont.

I would like to be a bricklayer because I like doing it and I
am fed up being out for work.
So I hope to learn to read and write it would help me a lot.

Sean

Social and educational background

- Aged 41
- Attended primary and secondary school but truanted frequently
- Has a manual job in the Cleansing Department of the local council
- Has just started a pre-Access programme at an FE college

Language use

- Speaks London English at home and with friends
- Uses standard written English at college

Examples of language and literacy practices

- Reads widely, particularly history books and articles from websites
- Helps his 11-year old son with homework

Goals and aspirations

- To improve his writing skills
- Eventually to study history at university

Text 4 Sean

Personal Narrative

On my first day back in education as an adult at Shoreditch college in Hackney, was very daunting. In the first place it was hard to relate to the boy who from the age of four to sixteen didn't enjoy his time at school also in Hackney and Tower Hamlets. As a young boy at school I was very unfortunate to have gone to school in the early 60s and 70s where their was some very strange ways of teaching. Although the schools were clean and well kept the standard of education was not

Most of the teachers in the main were exstremly nice people Some of their teaching texneces left a lot to be diseared, not to be disrespectable to the indivigle involved, I personally think that the laid back and right-on aticttute was not the right way for me; that is not to say that I would have liked to have been tort in the fashion of my perants generation where the children were ruled by fear. Respect in my opinion is earned. If unlike me you got off to a good start at school, the schools I attended where very good, nice clean buidings, friendly environment, clean and well maintand, Teacher perants, and school children all very positive.

For these children it must have been a very empowering, and a good grounding For a postive adult life. But for me and a lot of my classmates this was not the case,

If like now as an adult I have children of my own, and know that if a child is left behind itis very difficult for them too catch up later on in todays climate most teachers and perants are aware of this and as a consequence in the modern method of teaching this doesn't happen (or not too often)?

So getting back to my first day at collage, I was very surprised that I was looking forward to going so much. As a youngster I lived around Hoxton and the Hackney area, and I can tell you that the building has changed so much For the better in 30 years since I was young. The building I was now going into was clean, new, modern, and above all welcoming, The posotive feelling I got just for going into the place was great. I Still get and have some pange of aprehenchon about education I know I will come out of this with something quite posotive. I hope to come out of this exspirence with some academic qualification and a beter understanding of schooling.

Flora

Social and educational background

- Aged 55
- Came to UK from Nigeria 25 years ago

- Works as a dinner lady in a secondary school
- Attended primary school in Nigeria
- Has been attending literacy classes in her local FE college for several years

Language use

- Speaks Yoruba at home with her family and friends
- Speaks a Nigerian variety of English to friends, colleagues and classmates

Examples of literacy practices

- Reads menus and food packaging at work
- Reads the Bible at home
- Writes informal letters to her family in Nigeria
- Deals with forms and informal letters with support from her son

Goals and aspirations

- To be able to write longer letters back home
- To read aloud in church
- To deal with bureaucracy more independently

Text 5a Flora

Rosa Parks famous because she refuse to give up she seat to a white man.

Text 5b Flora

I like to tell you about my cousin wedding. I went to her wedding last Saturday, the ceremony was in the church, bride and bridesmaids are looking so wonderful. I enjoy very much.

   Then after church we all went to Highgate Hotel, in the Hall the decoration was very beautiful and food was very delicious we all enjoy very much.

   After the food we all have drink and disco and dance until the midnight. The Party was so enjoyable.

Geoffrey

Social and educational background

- Aged 48
- Attended a special school for children with mild learning difficulties (but now diagnosed as dyslexic)
- Had a job as a school keeper for many years but illness now prevents him from working and he lives on Incapacity Benefit

Language use

- Speaks London English
- Uses Standard written English at college

Examples of literacy practices

- Uses the internet to find out about his condition and possible new treatments
- Reads medical pamphlets, drug packaging

Goals and aspirations

- To use email to keep in contact with other sufferers of his condition
- To read novels and newspapers
- To record his life story

Text 6 Geoffrey

Jim Reeves
My hero is Jim Reeves. I don't know him personal but I heard his records and he was a great singer he died at the age of 30 in a plane crash he has a great talent.

Grace

Social and educational background

- Aged 24
- Came to UK from Nigeria 5 years ago
- Attended primary school in Nigeria
- Has three small children and is a full-time parent
- Has recently started attending a literacy class at an FE college

Language use

- Speaks Igbo and English at home
- Speaks English with friends and classmates

Examples of literacy practices

- Reads magazines and letters from home
- Corresponds with family in Nigeria

Goals and aspirations

- To help her children succeed educationally
- To get a qualification and a job when her children are older

Text 7 Grace

I went to Rose birthday party and it was so nice,
  She nineteen year old and there was a lot of visitor that she invite to the party and did rent a big hall for the all night party.
  My friends Rose spend a lot of money of the birthday Party eat special food like Rice and yam all kind of drink and she bake cake of the party we all was dancing in the hall.
  And she invite all her family and her brother and sister to the party and all her visitor and friends from school all of them was in party.

Malika

Social and educational background

- Aged 29
- Came to the UK from Morocco 10 years ago
- Attended primary and secondary school (to age 16) in Morocco
- Attends a pre-GCSE course at an adult education centre

Language use

- Reads the Quran in Classical Arabic
- Speaks Moroccan Arabic at home and with friends
- Reads and writes in Standard Arabic
- Uses English in a range of formal and informal contexts

Examples of literacy practices

- Sends emails to relatives living abroad
- Spends time reading from Arabic and English language websites
- Reads correspondence from her daughter's school and helps with her homework
- Reads a story to her daughter every night

Goals and aspirations

- To gain a qualification and get paid work as a community interpreter/translator

Text 8a Malika

Racism
    In this day's racism is growing a lot. We should respect all groups of peoples no matter they are white, black or which religion they are. Or any country they came from.

Text 8b Malika

Dear Councillor O'Sullivan

    I am writing to complain about things that happen last week in the play area in the Finsbury park.
    I went to the park on Saturday with my daughter and when we arrived to the play area there was lot of children and parents, it was very busy. One man had a dog and also he was dirinking beer, even his son was with him. My daughter frighted from the dog and I am very annoyed about this.
    We went back to the park on Sunday and there was broken bottle on the ground. This very dangerous and I am worried about same thing happen again.
    Please could you do something about this?

    I look forward to hearing from you.

Text 8c Malika

Friendship

Four years ago I met Jane. My daughter Khadija was five years old and she start school. She was very happy and exciting. Khadija wasn't scred because it was her friends with her in the same school and now she is older they go to school together and go back home together.

But that day I was little bit nervous and shy because I met other parent and teacher, all this people they new for me, but day by day I used to this people, some of them became my friends.

I still remember that day Jane invited us for tea. Her daughter Sonia is same age as Khadija and they live near, in same area. I was pleased and when we arrive to their flat she said sit down, make yourself comfortable. But when Jane handed me my tea I dropt it by accident and it goes all in the sofa. I was embarrassing and I wanted help her clean the sofa, but Jane laughed and said don't worry this happens all the time.

Morning time the next day I went back to her house with some nice cakes I made. We drink tea and long chat and we became friends. We always help each other and Jane is like a sister for me.

Wayne

Social and educational background

- Aged 32
- Attended primary and secondary school in London, but truanted regularly
- Currently attending a literacy class in prison

Language use

- Speaks London English
- Uses Standard written English for writing

Examples of literacy practices

- Writes letters to his family
- Reads a national newspaper

Goals and aspirations

- To get a job when he comes out of prison

Text 9 Wayne

> How have you been I hope you have been OK, I doing good I have made a lot of changes in myself over the last 2 year's. I can't belive how irresponsible I used to act before I came here. Life seem's so different now I have responsibility, I can't wait to come home and face up to my responsibilitys.

Dulcie

Social and educational background

- Aged 57
- Came to UK from Jamaica 40 years ago
- Had very little schooling in Jamaica
- Works as a school meals assistant
- Has been attending an evening community literacy class for some years

Language use

- Speaks Jamaican Creole at home and with friends and family
- Uses Standard Jamaican English for more formal interactions

Examples of literacy practices

- Reads the Bible, hymn book and the church newsletter
- Pays the family bills and deals with official correspondence

Goals and aspirations

- To improve her general reading and writing skills

Text 10a Dulcie

> When I first meet my husband I was come from Uncle's and he asked me to let he take me home. I did not answer and he asked me if I would take a drink. I did not take it for I was so shy. He see my sister the next day, and he tell she that he ask me to take me home and I was afraid of him.

Text 10b Dulcie

When I first came to England I was frightened to see England. I thought the house was a factory. I did not have any coat so I was cold.

Text 10c Dulcie

Problem Page

Dear Doris

I am verry sorry to see all you are going through With your husban. My advise to go away for a little time and see how he take it. Maybe he don't love the girl.

he only trying to fool her up and do has he likes. I think the best idea is to inveited the family for tea and disguss the promblem With your Mother and see how she takes it. Maybe after times goes she will calm down and give you that house.

Leon

Social and educational background

- Aged 19
- Born in London of Jamaican parents
- Attended primary and secondary school in London
- Lives in a flat with his partner and baby son
- Currently unemployed

Language use

- Speaks London Jamaican English

Examples of literacy practices

- Uses the Internet and plays computer games
- Reads job adverts
- Reads a national Black newspaper and the local paper

Goals and aspirations

- To get a job so that he can support his family

Text 11 Leon

> As we know this country is going down the slidehill. I now 19 year of age and I was born in this country and I am black and I proud of it. But if a person prejudice against me. I prejudice against them. It not because I not prejudice I can't not stand stupid people who beat us up for fun. All this time some of white people got somefink against us. Why is it because we live in hot country or is it because we black, I don't know, but half of us got good qualification but can't get no jobs because we black. And half the population of people is black and we getting a good telling off because of We the one can't get no job. Half of us black kids was born in this country and we got right to stay on it. We are fed up of this harassment on us. It is time for us black white and Indians people to fight against this evil sin because it will break the race marriage so you fink about it. Will you let them threat you no well fight for your right.

Aftab

Social and educational background

- Aged 35
- Came to UK from Bangladesh 12 years ago
- Works as a waiter in a local restaurant
- Attended primary school in Bangladesh for four years
- Used to attend ESOL classes intermittently
- Now attends a literacy class at an FE college

Language use

- Speaks Sylheti and Standard Bengali
- Reads and writes a little in Standard Bengali.
- Recites passages from the Quran in Classical Arabic
- Speaks Sylheti at work and with family and friends
- Speaks English with neighbours, classmates and teachers at his children's school

Examples of literacy practices

- Reads letters from his children's school
- Looks through Bengali and English language newspapers
- Writes down orders from restaurant customers

Goals and aspirations

- To get a better job

Text 12 Aftab

> My name is Aftab. I born in Bangladesh. I came England in 96. I stard to work smool job in Hotel But it is very hard for me Becoze I have family problem So I live this job. Now I have new job and I can look my family. So I think must I addmeshon in College so when I look for batter job no problem for me. If I can write good English is batter for me.

Zahra

Social and educational background

- Age and background unknown
- Originally from Somalia

Language use

- Speaks Somali and English
- Other languages unknown
- Reads and writes in Standard English

Examples of literacy practices

- Not known

Goals and aspirations

- Not known

Text 13 Zahra

I Have a Dream …

I have a dream that one day the people of Somalia will stop the war. I have a dream that one day this nation will rise up and join hands and rebuild their destroyed country and bury their differences.

I have a dream that one day the nation of Somalia will be transformed into an oasis of freedom and justice. I have a dream that one day the nation of Somalia will live by the true meaning of their beliefs.

I have a dream that one day the people of Somalia will create equal rights for men and women.

By Zahra

Joyce

Social and educational background

- Aged 66
- Came to UK from Jamaica in the 1960s
- Attended school in Jamaica to age 14
- Attends literacy and cookery classes in a community centre

Language use

- Speaks Jamaican Creole at home
- Uses Standard English in more formal contexts

Examples of literacy practices

- Corresponds regularly with relatives
- Reads newspapers, magazines and church literature
- Reads cookery books and sends recipes to magazines and websites

Goals and aspirations

- To read more widely
- To write her autobiography

Text 14 Joyce

My journey (extracts)

It was a hot summers day in June 1974, when I boarded the Pan Am aircraft in Kingston Jamaica destination London England. The land that pave with that proverbial gold.

The plane journey was something I can never forget, I was sick all the way the experience was unforgettable.

....

It turned out to be a bit of a struggle, but many jobs, colleges and three kids, six grandchildren later, I am still waiting to find my share of the gold England possess. Still living the dreams of one day.

George

Social and educational background

- In his 50s
- Born and raised in London, with foster parents after his father died
- Went to a special school for children with learning difficulties

Language use

- Speaks English and a bit of French

Examples of literacy practices

- Reads social sight signs
- Looks at pictures in newspapers
- Identifies texts by type (so is good at telling what's a potentially important formal letter) and has a network of friends to help him read them

Goals and aspirations

- Works as a volunteer at an old people's home, loves it and wants to continue with this

Text 15 George

Lost Family[3]

I am George Cochran. I am a kind person, a bit quiet.

I was seventeen and my dad had a heart attack.
He got old. He really got old. And then he died and is buried in Archway.
I really missed him. I miss him and I miss my mum. It's not the same when you're in with foster parents. It's not the same. People want to move on.
I haven't got his furniture. All his stuff has been cleared. I don't know if he ever had any money.
I bought a grave stone for him and I put some flowers on it. I like to visit his grave because it's a memory of him.

Yvonne

Social and educational background

- Aged 38
- Came to UK from Ghana 8 years ago
- Sings in a Ghanaian group
- School education in Ghana was disrupted because of illness
- Attends a literacy class in a community centre

Language use

- Speaks Twi with family
- Speaks Ghanaian English in a range of formal and informal contexts

Examples of literacy practices

- Deals with forms and formal letters/emails, with support from her family
- Exchanges greeting cards with friends and relatives

Goals and aspirations

- To read song lyrics
- To write personal letters

Text 16 Yvonne

I when to the market to do some shopping When I got to the market I bout som potato and sping some fiurut which onions and rice some maket And yam and fish and shacken and some first milk Some cod and chips I bout some orange jues and Banana.

And come back home.

NOTES

1. From reading material accompanying the national training course to launch the English Department for Education and Skills (2001) *Adult Literacy Core Curriculum in England*.

2. From NRDC practitioner guide: Grief, S. and Chatterton, J. (2007) *Writing*. London: NRDC/ Leicester: NIACE, p. 17.

3. This piece won a prize in the NRDC *Voices on the Page* competition in 2007. See www.nrdc.org.uk/voicesonthepage. Accessed 24 June 2009.

Section 3

Teaching and learning literacy

5 Reading
Irene Schwab

Introduction

Most adults, even those with limited experience of reading, will have been exposed to innumerable texts during their lifetime. In this chapter we will show how literacy learners can build on this experience and extend their existing literacy practices.

Learners often feel that improving their reading is a priority for them. They know that having more choices and more control over their lives depends on having access to the print and electronic texts which surround us all today. A recent study by the National Research and Development Centre (NRDC) noted that 'learners may not be making enough progress in reading because not enough of the class session is spent on reading activities' and 'a larger proportion of adult literacy sessions needs to be devoted to reading activities and specifically focused, quality reading instruction' (Besser *et al.* 2004). We will explore below some ideas for focusing on reading with groups of learners.

You will find that, in many cases, we have not distinguished between beginner readers and others at a more advanced level because we feel that most approaches and activities are suitable for any learner reader at any level. When working with beginner readers, the teacher may choose shorter, simpler texts; she may make more use of language experience and spend more time on decoding techniques, but in principle the methods and techniques are similar to those used with more skilled learner readers. In addition, because they have all experienced the print and technology-rich twenty-first-century world, adult beginner readers are also able to be critical and analytical about the texts they read.

Leon (Text 11) is a young man of 19 whose parents originated from the Caribbean. He felt that school had little to offer him when he was younger, but now that he has family responsibilities and is looking for a job, he is interested in developing his reading skills to improve his employment prospects. He is also a conscientious parent who would like to be able to read to his young son and, when he is older, help him with his homework.

Geoffrey (**Text 6**) is a middle-aged single man who has a disabling condition, so is unable to work. He has to spend a great deal of time at home alone and is sometimes bored by the TV. He has a computer and has begun to surf the net and communicate with others who suffer from the same condition. In particular, he is not convinced the hospital is providing the best care possible so he is interested in finding out more about his condition with the aim of challenging the medical staff.

Flora (**Text 5a** and **5b**) a 55-year-old woman from Nigeria, is a devout Christian and attends Church regularly. She reads her Bible at home and would love to be able to read aloud to the rest of the congregation in church. **Flora's** children are grown up and she now lives alone. She would like to be able to deal with forms, leaflets and the bureaucracy of life without always having to call on her son.

Note: Text numbers in bold refer to Learner profiles and texts.

Leon, **Geoffrey** and **Flora** have individual motivations for reading which are related to their own interests and social practices. They are also involved in many communal literacy practices, for example **Leon** with his son, **Geoffrey** with other sufferers of his condition, **Flora** with her fellow worshippers.

In addition, they take part in shared reading practices in a weekly literacy class that they attend. Amongst other work, they have been reading *The Book Boy* (Trollope 2006)[1] together over the past ten weeks. They have finally finished the book and are having an animated discussion about the characters they have been reading about: 'Did Alice do the right thing?' 'What will happen to her?' 'What would I have done in the same circumstances?' Suddenly **Geoffrey** says, 'Why are we getting so excited? It's only a book!' and there is a stunned silence. The whole group has been lost in another world. These readers come to literacy classes to improve their skills, but they are also learning that reading can be entertaining, and they can lose themselves in a gripping novel just like any other readers.

We read in many different ways, in different domains of our lives and for many different purposes. Generally speaking we read because we want something from the text; we want to find something out – the end of a story, what we have to do to operate the DVD player, what is going on in the world, how to cook a particular dish, whether to vote for one party or another. If we don't get what we are after, the reading has not been successful. We have to make meaning from what we read; how we access that meaning is a complex issue.

Let us first examine how a fluent reader approaches the reading process.

Practices of fluent readers

and getting a sense of what is happening in the world. Or we might scan the newspaper deliberately looking for the particular article we have in mind and ignoring all the others.

On the other hand, we can pick up a piece of junk mail from the doormat and bin it, hardly giving it a second glance.

We can do this because we have a clear purpose for reading. If the text does not fit our purpose, we can choose not to read it at all. If there are no immediate obvious benefits in the leaflet, we will set it to one side. We can make a quick decision based on our ability to skim (read through quickly for an overview) or scan (read through quickly looking for a particular piece of information).

The ability to use these rapid reading skills depends first of all on our understanding that these are techniques we can use for approaching texts. We can give ourselves permission to look quickly at a text rather than scrutinize it thoroughly because we can predict its content, to a large extent, by knowing its genre.

In the case of *Curry in a Hurry* we know it is a leaflet and, furthermore, the manner of its arrival (pushed through the letterbox) alerts us to the fact that this is advertising something and that its purpose is to persuade us to spend money on the product. We can recognize the genre immediately because of the shape, format and language of the leaflet. It is similar to the countless other fast food leaflets that arrive on the doormat.

We recognize this genre through a variety of features:

Text level

- **Layout**: The design of the leaflet (using diverse print sizes and fonts, capitals and lower case, different colours, brightly coloured bubbles containing important and enticing information, print turned at 90 degrees) is intended to lead our eyes to significant information items.
- **Use of images**: In this case, photographs of a meal on a table which tell us immediately it is about food.

Sentence level

- **Lack of complete sentences**: There is almost no punctuation and only one full sentence. Information is all at the phrase level and therefore easy to access.

Word level

- **Key words**: The words in the biggest print size (**Curry in a Hurry**) indicate both the name of the restaurant and the type of food it serves; other important words like *free* and *halal* (in Arabic) stand out because of their size and location on the page.
- **Lexical sets which emphasize the message**: There is a lexical set of food words and phrases e.g. *cuisine, restaurant, takeaway*, and another set concerned with speed and convenience e.g. *hurry, home delivery, collection, open 7 days a week including bank holidays, everyday.*

If you decide the leaflet is worth reading, you **make a decision on how to read it.** For a fluent reader, this is likely to be instant and unconscious. The strategy we pick for any reading task depends on our context and purpose for reading. For example:

- **Scanning**: If you were alone and very hungry and wanted to eat as soon as possible, you might **scan** the leaflet to find out delivery times.
- **Skimming**: If you had friends over unexpectedly (some of whom are vegetarian) and needed to feed them, you might **skim** through to get a sense of what dishes are available.
- **Reading for detail**: If you had a limited amount of cash, you might read the **detail** to work out whether you could put together an affordable order.
- **Critical reading**: If you had several such leaflets, you might read it **critically**, assessing the range of food, prices etc. and comparing this one with the others.

Your purpose for reading thus determines your approach to a text. You will draw on your *schema* (see below) of 'takeaway curries' and there may be particular questions you ask of the text (How soon can I get my meal? Will it be quicker if I pick it up or should I let them deliver? What must I order to get my free lager?). Your reading will be geared towards answering those questions.

Having determined how you are going to read the leaflet, you **start reading**. If a text contains elements which we struggle to understand, we draw on a variety of strategies. A fluent reader starts from the premise that it is intended to make sense, so we won't be happy until we have found the sense in it. This might involve strategies:

- for predicting from what we already know about the background and subject of the text, making sense through linking it to our prior knowledge;
- for understanding the text as a whole, drawing on our understanding of how writers make texts coherent and cohesive;
- for making sense of the way the text is structured by drawing on our knowledge of the conventions of grammar and punctuation;
- for working out words we don't know (using strategies like decoding by sounding out; using analogy with other words; using our knowledge of morphology; using a dictionary or asking others).

You may use one of these strategies more than others or you may use several of them simultaneously.

Once you have read as much as you need or want to, you will have a **response to the text** which will be based on your needs and purposes for reading and your interpretation of its contents.

You may, after all, decide to throw the leaflet away, or you may store it somewhere to use later; you may discuss the leaflet with others, perhaps reading it out loud, or passing it around; you may use the leaflet to make an order, which might involve finding the telephone number, perhaps preparing a list, reading it aloud and responding to enquiries about your address. Reading the leaflet is not an isolated activity; it is a *literacy event*.

The reading curriculum

What are the implications for teachers of an understanding of what fluent readers do?

The act of reading we have just examined consisted of activity by one or more people around a text with clear stages: before reading, during reading and after reading. Each of these stages is necessary whether you are a fluent reader or one who is just beginning. The reading curriculum will obviously vary according to the contexts and purposes of the learners, but teachers of reading at all levels will want to address the following key elements of the reading process:

Before reading
- enabling learners to recognize and utilize genre features to understand and interpret texts;
- assisting learners to use what they already know about the content and context of the text to predict what they are likely to meet when reading it;
- helping learners become conversant with the different styles of reading above, so that they can choose the one most appropriate for their purpose. New readers often feel they have to read every word of a text to make sense of it.

During reading
- helping learners to recognize that this stage is only one part of effective reading;
- enabling learners to acquire a variety of skills and strategies to decode and comprehend the text.

After reading
- encouraging learners to reflect on and be critical of what they read;
- supporting learners to respond to the text.

How people learn to read

Most of the research around developing reading skills has, quite naturally, been carried out with young children learning to read. Although we may well find much that is also relevant for adults, there are aspects of their situation that are quite different.

Task 5.2

Learning to read as a child or an adult

How might learning to read as an adult be different from learning as a child?
Note down some ideas.

Comment 5.2

You may have considered that adults:

- bring their greater life experience to the texts they read;
- already possess some familiarity with a wide range of texts;
- have generally had some previous reading instruction – with varying
  degrees of success – and their earlier experiences of education will
  affect both their current attitude and the reading techniques at their
  disposal;
- hold a variety of different motivations and purposes for reading that
  relate both to their everyday lives and to their future aspirations. This
  will affect the contexts in which they learn, both formal and
  informal.

The adult learner's experience can be both a resource to draw on and a
challenge. They may originally have been taught in ways which you, as a teacher, do
not feel are the most helpful to their current learning: perhaps they rely overmuch on
an alphabetic approach (naming each letter) or they feel they have to look up every
unfamiliar word in a dictionary. The challenge as a literacy teacher is to work with
learners to help them understand their personal approaches to reading. We can
discuss with them their current skills and strategies and, by making these explicit, we
can explore together how they might best approach reading effectively.

Theoretical perspectives on reading

There is a long history of debate about the best way to approach the teaching of
reading with children. Research with adults has been very limited. Apart from the age
of the learners and their much greater experience of life, the context of adult learning
is very different.

In the past, reading has been approached from two widely differing viewpoints.

From a **cognitive perspective** reading is seen essentially as a *bottom-up*
process. That means the process of reading begins with the text and the reader starts
with the symbols on the page. She moves from the smallest units of print up to the
sentence and from there to the text as a whole, aiming for automaticity in word

recognition. Decoding words by sounding out is a slower process, used by readers when they meet words they don't recognize. A reader would work towards fluency and automaticity in recognizing words independently of their context. Materials for use with this approach tend to use strictly controlled vocabulary relating to the words and patterns that have already been learned.

The **social view** is that reading starts with what is already in the reader's head. She uses her background knowledge to make a prediction of what is likely to be found in the text and reads to confirm that prediction. She will only need to read enough of the text to confirm or reject the prediction, not necessarily every word, and certainly not every letter. This is called a *top–down* process as it starts with an overview of the whole text and moves towards the parts. Often called the **whole language** model, it proposes that learners need to work with authentic examples of different genres and whole books, which connect with their purposes for reading and their wider reading practices.

Some theorists have proposed a solution that combines elements of both traditions, which they call an **interactive model**. This views reading as a complex interaction between the writer of the text and the reader, implying a balanced approach to the teaching of reading, drawing on both theoretical models.

Keith Stanovich (1980) has proposed an amended version of the interactive model, the **interactive compensatory model**. He suggests that better readers make less use of context because their recognition of words is efficient and automatic, but less skilled readers find such cues useful while they are learning to compensate for less automaticity.

The Rose Review (2006) into the teaching of early reading, aimed mainly at teachers of young children, recommended that teachers use the **simple view** of reading. The simple view (Hoover and Gough 1990) proposes that there are two sets of abilities that contribute to reading: *word recognition ability* (the ability to read and understand the words on the page) and *language comprehension ability* (the ability to understand language we hear and language we read). These can be represented on a diagram with two axes:

The simple view of reading

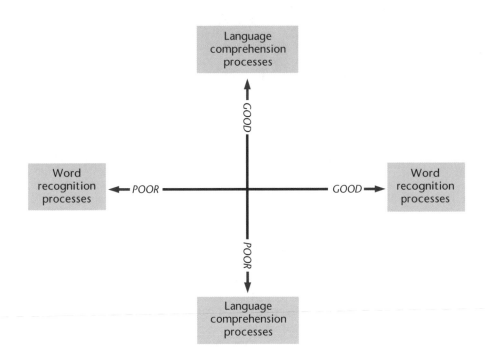

Both dimensions are seen as essential to reading, but it is recognized that learners may not perform or progress equally well in each. The challenge for the teacher is to devise appropriate teaching techniques and activities to develop skills in both dimensions.

The diagram below[2] takes into account that the ultimate aim of reading is to have a complete understanding of a text. It shows in greater detail the skills and knowledge needed for the processes shown on the two axes of the diagram above. It demonstrates that the 'simple' view is actually far from simple.

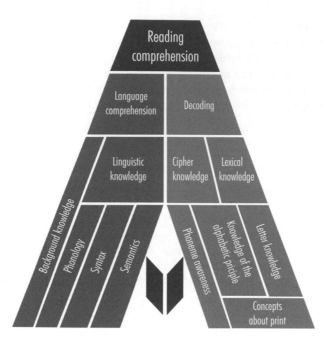

Diagnostic assessment of reading and formative feedback

As most learners will come to the literacy class with some previous experience of learning to read, it is useful for the teacher to establish what strategies they already use and how successfully they are using them. There are a number of different ways she can do this, but one of the most effective is for her to listen to learners reading aloud and to record any hesitations, omissions, insertions, repetitions and, most importantly, substitutions for the words on the page. The term 'miscue' is used where what is read does not accord with what is written in the text. The analysis of miscues helps the teacher to determine how effectively each cue (syntactic, semantic, graphic and phonic) is being used to interpret the text.

This is not a precise scientific tool; it relies on the teacher's categorization and analysis of miscues, which can be subjective. However, even though it takes time and practice, many teachers find it a useful way of investigating how learners read.[3]

The teacher can record the learner's reading on a photocopy of the text (a running record) or by taping the reading and analysing it later (a miscue analysis). Keeping a running record[4] is not as time-consuming as a full miscue analysis and sometimes can be completed in a classroom situation, where learners read aloud within the group.

At the end of the reading, the teacher asks some questions to ascertain how well the reader has comprehended what she has read. From these 'windows on the reading process'(Goodman 1973: 107), the teacher can gain insight into which cues are being used effectively and which might need further practice.

Below is a small extract from a running record of **Geoffrey's** reading. He has chosen a passage about traffic control.[5] **Geoffrey's** substitutions are written above the text. Where he corrected himself the code *SC* has been used.

Task 5.3

Running record of reading

- What might the record below tell us about **Geoffrey's** reading?
- How could the teacher feed back to him?

Speed bumps

doubts
No one <u>denies</u> that speed bumps help to control traffic. Not only do they

count
reduce traffic speed but they also <u>cut</u> the number of vehicles in the area of the bumps.

dangerous
However, speed bumps are unpopular. They are <u>a danger</u> to cyclists and

ambulances SC   *at a speed*
cause problems for <u>emergency</u> vehicles, which need to travel <u>at speed</u>.

a driver brakes
Local residents complain about the extra squealing noise as <u>drivers brake.</u>

Exhaust fumes fill the air as cars slow down and then speed up again.

are talking
Bus services suffer and people <u>taking </u>children to school find it difficult

---

Comment 5.3

Oral questioning after the reading made it clear that **Geoffrey** had understood the gist of the passage. Although we would need a longer extract to make an accurate assessment of his reading, **Geoffrey's** running record indicates that he is making some use of all four cues, although not always consistently. He is already beginning to monitor his reading for meaning and he could build on this to draw more effectively on the reading skills he already has.

The best way to give detailed feedback is for the teacher to have some time with **Geoffrey** alone or while the rest of the group are working independently. If she has taken his writing away to do a miscue analysis, her feedback may come later when she has analysed his miscues and then she can play the tape to

Geoffrey and they can listen together to his reading and discuss it. The nature of her feedback would depend very much on whether his responses to her questions after reading indicated he had understood what he had read.

If **Geoffrey** had not understood the text, she might ask him to read the text (or part of it), through again. It may be that silent reading, or reading aloud, stopping at the end of each sentence or paragraph to check understanding, would be helpful for his comprehension.

As **Geoffrey** has understood the gist of what he was reading, the teacher can engage in a dialogue, which could include an opportunity for **Geoffrey** to respond to the text by giving his own opinions about the use of speed bumps in his area. She might make other formative comments such as some of the following:

- You read that very clearly **Geoffrey**, well done. You can see that I was able to hear every word you read as I've recorded it here on the page. You paused at the full stops and you put real expression into your reading. Have you been practising reading aloud?

- There were 93 words (in this extract) and there were only seven places where you read something different from what was on the page. And the miscues you made show that you were making good sense of what you were reading. Look at this one – you read 'as a driver brakes' for 'as drivers brake'. What's the difference in meaning between what you read and what's on the page? How does it look different?

- See where you read 'ambulances' whereas in the text it says 'emergency'. You certainly got the right sort of vehicle, which needs to travel at speed. Emergency vehicles can be ambulances. Then you corrected yourself. Can you remember why you went back and changed the way you read it? Maybe you made a guess without looking closely enough at the word itself and then when you read on, you realized that ambulances vehicles doesn't go together. So you did just the right thing by predicting what the word might be and then going back and looking again when your prediction didn't work. That's exactly what good readers do – monitor their own reading.

- Now, here you read 'count' where it says 'cut'. You made good grammatical sense of it – you used the right sort of verb, but let's look back at the sentence and see who or what might be doing the counting or cutting?

Using texts for teaching and learning reading

Choosing and simplifying texts

A text used for classroom purposes may be any text that is interesting and relevant for the learner(s). Learners might bring in texts that they want or need to read or theteacher might provide a text to focus on. Any genre of text might be studied and authentic texts are usually the best examples of different types of genres. Realia such as newspapers, leaflets, manuals, recipes, letters, adverts, food packaging, forms, websites, mobile texts as well as items for entertainment such as books, stories, poems and song lyrics can all be useful. Understanding the features of the genre – format, structure and language – will make these more accessible.

One reason for a reader struggling is that she may be faced with **inconsiderate texts**. These are texts that have a difficult structure or vocabulary, or both. For a learner to be able to access the content independently without strain, the vocabulary needs to be about 98–99% familiar (McShane 2005). If a text seems too difficult for an individual or group, however, it does not necessarily need to be abandoned if there is interest in its content. There are a number of ways the teacher can facilitate access to a text if learners are motivated to read it:

- the teacher, or one of the stronger readers in the group, could read it out to the other learners;
- the learners might read just a small part of the text and the teacher reads out or summarizes the rest;
- the group could use collaborative reading techniques e.g. paired reading or reciprocal reading (see below);
- the teacher could simplify the text for classroom use;
- the teacher could use a combination of these for different members of the group or at different times.

Simplifying texts is commonly carried out by literacy teachers to make texts more accessible to learners. There are formulae like SMOG[6] which give a readability level for written material, or you could just apply common sense, which is often just as effective, if less scientific!

To make a text easier to read:

- leave out irrelevant information peripheral to the main idea;
- replace long and difficult words with easier synonyms;
- shorten longer sentences;
- make complex sentences into simple or compound ones;
- use active verbs rather than passive ones;
- make the print larger and use a font which is clear such as Arial or Comic Sans;
- ensure there is plenty of white space around the text;
- use bold type or a box for emphasis rather than capitalization (lower case letters have more distinguishing features than capitals as they extend above and below the line);
- add in extra headings and spaces;
- make use of illustrations and captions.

You might, however, choose to leave in certain difficult words because they are easily decoded or because they are crucial to the meaning or interpretation of the text. They could be discussed or defined before reading. The important thing is to retain the main ideas and format of the original text as these are important for indicating features of the genre.

Remember that what makes a text difficult to read does not just involve its physical appearance, but also pragmatics – the invisible meanings which depend on shared knowledge and assumptions between the writer and the reader. The effective teacher of reading will be able to use what the learners already know as a basis for developing their reading skills.

Using learner-produced texts – the language experience approach

As we see above, the reader will look for what he or she expects to be there. The **language experience** approach builds on this expectation by making the text as familiar as possible through the use of the learner's words. It is particularly useful for working with beginner readers.

Language experience makes use of learners' own speech to provide a text for them to read back. The teacher may talk to the learner and jot down an extract from what he or she says. This may be just one sentence or it may be two or three. He or she then writes it out clearly for the learner to read back. The reading matter is thus made up of the learner's own language patterns and content, so he or she is likely to find it easier to read.[7]

The effectiveness of this approach depends on the words being recorded as exactly as possible, using the learner's own syntax. An illustration of this is provided by Julia Clarke (Schwab and Stone 1986).

> When a student dictated the sentence 'I took my motor-bike to pieces', I suggested that we write 'I took my motor-bike to bits' (thinking bits would be more useful for later phonic teaching). This confused the student who continued to read 'pieces' where I had written 'bits'. So, I eventually changed the written sentence to 'I took my motor-bike to pieces', whereupon he read 'I took my motor-bike to bits'. We finished by tearing the paper it was written on to bits (or pieces)!

Whether the words are changed by accident or design, the results are the same; the learner is not able to use memory and familiarity in deciphering the message and is not able to make the vital link between spoken and written language. So whatever the learner's variety of English, her exact words are important. The use of memory here is not 'cheating'; it is serving a similar function to that of a child 'reading' stories she has heard countless times. Familiarity with the style, syntax and rhythms of reading matter is an essential part of understanding what is being read.[8]

The tutor can build on the initial process of word recognition by making some copies of the text. The learner then:

- cuts up the sentences and matches them with the original;

- removes the original and sequences the sentences;
- cuts the sentences into parts (phrases or words) to match and sequence these;
- reorders the cut up words to make new sentences;
- replaces words within a sentence with new words and reads the transformed sentence.

Using multimodal texts

An interest in technology is what motivates some people to develop their reading skills. New genres such as web pages, social networking sites, email and texting have arisen through the growth of new technology and are likely to continue to develop rapidly. The new electronic texts have implications for the teaching and learning of reading.

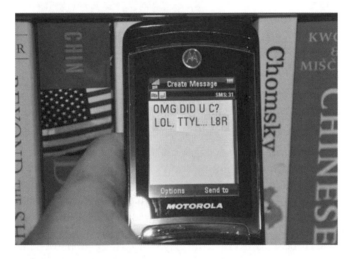

(blog.westervillelibrary.org/teens/wp-content/uploads/2008/02/cell-phone-texting.jpg)

Many young people (and older ones too) read texts prolifically. It may be the main thing they read on a daily basis. Teachers can draw on this literacy practice, making use of texting to teach aspects of reading both because it can be highly motivating and because it may help build learners' skills at code-breaking, which could be transferable to other types of codes or conventions.

Other issues arise from reading web pages:

- Different modes of communication can be used simultaneously; for example, a web page may use images, sound, video and animation as well as written text. Reading on a screen thus involves understanding how to interpret these different modes in order to access information.

- A typical web page will not be organized in a linear way like a printed page but will appear as a visual display. Important elements might be placed anywhere on the screen and could be indicated by images rather than words. Learners who have been taught to read a page of print from top left to bottom right will need to adjust to this new approach.

- To find more information about a subject of interest, a reader does not turn to the index as one might in a book, but follows a hyperlink, which might take her to an entirely different site. Each choice forms new connections and creates new hybrid texts. This involves an element of risk not found with books. Teachers can help learners build their skills and confidence in following links by modelling the process.

- Unlike conventional libraries, access to texts on the internet is available 24 hours per day with no closures for weekends and holidays and no need for intermediaries. This promotes independence in choosing reading material and is a tremendous resource for self-study.

Reading on the internet thus requires a different approach from reading the traditional printed page. If a teacher has use of a data projector, she can model how to read a web page and follow hyperlinks, showing learners how to use the structure and format of these types of text to access information.

The rapid growth of new technology is motivating and empowering for learners. Young people, in particular, often bring to the learning situation great skills in using technology, providing an ideal opportunity for teachers and students to learn from each other.

Ways of teaching and learning reading

As we have seen, reading is a holistic activity which involves a number of different skills and sub-skills. In examining them in more detail below, we have chosen to use a model developed originally in Australia by Allan Luke and Peter Freebody (Freebody and Luke 1999), and named by them the four resources model. They suggest there are four resources needed for effective reading:

- code breaking;
- meaning making;
- text use;
- text analysis.

We feel this model is useful for examining the different elements involved in the development of reading skills because all of these elements are considered equally important for all learners. They can be applied to any text, with learners working at any level. Each is necessary but not sufficient for learning to read and all four need to be tackled simultaneously for reading to be learned effectively.

The value of this model is the recognition that the acquisition of literacy skills is a complex and many-faceted issue, which involves developing a variety of skills. A beginner reader can be critical about the texts she reads and a developing reader still needs to find a way through the codes and conventions that characterize different genres of text. An effective literacy teacher is one who is able to apply all four of these resources appropriately to meet the needs and goals of every learner in every context.

We will examine the four resources one by one give examples at the end of the chapter of how they can be combined around a particular text.

Code breaking

Decoding

     5   £   ♀   ♫   +   ☺   ♥   z

The symbols above all stand for abstract ideas or concepts. None of them can be interpreted without knowing what the symbol stands for.

The written language is a type of code. If it weren't, we would be able to read it as soon as we could speak. To be able to 'break the code', we need to understand the meaning of each symbol and how it fits with the whole. In the case of written English, the symbols are letters (or they can also sometimes be numbers, punctuation marks or other symbols like smileys).

Decoding in reading involves a sequence of two steps:

- understanding that spoken language is made up of sounds and that each word is made up of a sequence of these sounds (phonemic awareness);
- understanding that **phonemes**, the sounds of spoken language, have a relationship with **graphemes**, the symbols of written language (phonics).

If a reader is able to match sounds with letters, she is on the way to breaking the code and reading the word.

Phonemic awareness

Unlike many children beginning to learn to read, most adults already have some phonemic awareness, but this might not be secure and it might not extend to all sounds. Work can usefully be done with learners to help them notice sounds and manipulate them in spoken language as a preparation to working with written language. Kruidenier (2002) suggests blending and segmenting may be the most effective skills to concentrate on.

> **Phoneme blending:** listening to a sequence of phonemes and combining them to form a word, e.g. what word is /b i t/?

> **Phoneme segmentation:** breaking a word into separate sounds, e.g. how many sounds are there in *shop*?

Activities could consist of short oral games using cards, pictures and actual objects as resources. Many materials have been produced to help children develop these skills and some of these might be adapted for use with adults.

Phonics

Alongside developing an awareness of spoken sounds, researchers agree that progress in reading depends on having knowledge of the sound–symbol relationships of the language. An understanding of phonics enables the reader to work out how to say any new word she comes across as long as it has a regular sound–symbol correspondence. This is an immense advantage to a learner as, once the pattern is learned, it can be applied to other unfamiliar words and they can be decoded in the same way. If you know *quick*, you can work out *quilt, quibble, quiz* and even words you may never have come across before, like *quidditch*; if you can read *able*, you can also read *cable, table* and *stable*.

However, many English words do not have this regularity and then the reader who is relying primarily on phonics can have difficulties (e.g if you know *rough*, it doesn't help you with *through, cough, though*; likewise, how far does *able* help with *vegetable, reliable*). Most words have some phonic cues. A systematic phonics approach would encourage the learner to try all the possible alternatives. However, this requires a fairly comprehensive understanding of phonic strategies, including an understanding of word stress, which some learners find difficult to acquire.

Another issue with this method is that although the reader may be able to pronounce the word, it does not mean that she has been able to understand it. Teachers may be familiar with the phenomenon of 'barking at print' where a learner reader seems to be reading the words of a text, and is able to say them aloud, but is not getting any meaning from the text. This can be because she is slowly decoding every word and the effort of doing this fills the working memory so there is no spare capacity to hold on to the meaning.

In any literacy group there will also be a range of different language varieties in use with words pronounced in different ways (different from the teacher and from other group members). Teachers would need to recognize that a sound–symbol relationship that works for one learner might not work for another, particularly in the case of vowels.

Teaching and learning phonics

There are many available resources for working on phonic instruction, most of which, however, are devised for children, so teachers of adults will have to choose with care, or make their own resources. Research indicates the important factor in teaching phonics is that it needs to be systematic and explicit.

This raises a dilemma for teachers who are working with groups of adult learners from diverse backgrounds. Although children today are introduced to sound–symbol relationships at an early age in school, adult learners might have received their education at a time when this was not taught, or they may have been educated in a country where a different system was used, for example in the Caribbean, where a system of using the names rather than the sounds of letters was employed. Adult learners come with varying amounts of phonic knowledge and skill and with different potential to use decoding strategies.

For these reasons, some teachers find a systematic use of phonics very difficult to achieve. They do the best they can to use phonics effectively by having an overall view of the phonic patterns that will be most useful to the learners in their group and introducing and practising them in ways that match the learners' needs and interests. They might decide on a useful set of sound–symbol relationships (not necessarily every single one) and introduce them in as logical a sequence as possible. Teachers who make use of the 'teachable moment' (spontaneously making a teaching point out of a question or dealing with an issue as it arises) may wish to maintain a flexible approach, to meet the needs of their learners.

An order for teaching phonics is suggested in the National Adult Literacy Core Curriculum (DfES 2001). For beginner readers, initial consonant and short vowel sounds are seen as the first step. It is not helpful to persist in practising phonic distinctions if the learner finds it difficult to discriminate between them. For example, in a variety of English spoken in South East London, *i* and *e* sound very similar, as in *will* and *well*. Some learner readers are likely to find using other cues to identify a word, such as visual ones, and context, to be more effective.

There are currently a number of different approaches to phonics instruction, and the effectiveness of each approach is hotly debated. The following are definitions of the three most well-known systems – **synthetic**, **analytic** and **onset-rime** phonics.[9]

Analytic phonics – an approach to the teaching of reading in which the phonemes associated with particular graphemes are not pronounced in isolation. Children identify (analyse) the common phoneme in a set of words in which each word contains the phoneme under study. For example, teacher and pupils discuss how the following words are alike: *sat, sit, sale and sun.*

Synthetic phonics – refers to an approach to the teaching of reading in which phonemes (sounds) associated with particular graphemes (letters) are pronounced in isolation and blended together (synthesized). For example, children are taught to take a single-syllable word such as *sit* apart into its three letters, pronounce a phoneme for each letter in turn /s, æ, t/, and blend the phonemes together to form a word.

Onset-rime phonics – uses syllables rather than individual phonemes. The onset is the part of the syllable before the vowel; the rime is the vowel and whatever follows in the rest of the syllable. Some teachers and learners find that rime patterns are easier to learn because they are more predictable than individual phoneme–grapheme patterns.

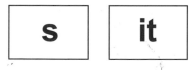

Research by Medwell *et al.* (1998) with schoolchildren suggested that it doesn't matter much which system of phonics instruction is used. The important factor is 'embedding word and sentence-level aspects of reading and writing within whole text activities which are both meaningful and clearly explained ...'

A research report on effective practice in reading by the NRDC (Brooks 2007) found that many teachers who used phonics gave misleading information to learners or did not have any clear system for structuring their phonics teaching. The key to success with phonic instruction, according to Usha Goswami (2002), is informed teachers.

Using phonics effectively involves the following:

- Being explicit as to what is being learned and why.
- Seeing phonics not as an end in itself but as a means to an end. No amount of practice in decoding is useful without applying it to a variety of texts in a range of contexts. It should therefore be applied in small doses, and not for whole lessons.
- Being 'systematic' in phonics instruction with children has traditionally involved using books written for learners with strictly controlled vocabulary which introduce sounds in a set sequence. Learners only have to deal with phonic patterns they are familiar with, so these texts are seen as easier to read. Some learners find them awkward and inauthentic as the language used is, by its very nature, unnatural. As we argue with reference to the language experience approach, learners find it easier to work with language patterns they are familiar with. One option is to use authentic genres of text and draw the learner's attention to phonic aspects of these in a systematic way. Texts that can be particularly useful for practising phonics are poems, song lyrics and advertising jingles with memorable rhyme sequences that help with phonic analogies.

Teaching and learning whole word recognition

The ability to recognize whole words makes reading speedier and more efficient than decoding every word. For a beginner reader, the words to concentrate on might be:

- key words for the individual learner – those relating to their names and addresses and personal details for the rest of their family and friends;
- high-interest words relating to work, hobbies and interests; these might include technical and specialist words;
- common words: those on the Dolch list are frequently used by literacy teachers. However, any list should be used with discretion; it is not designed for learners to work through word by word.[10]

Ways to help learners recognize and remember useful words include:

- flash cards (making use of different colours, fonts and pictures to assist);
- using these cards for games: like pelmanism, snap, bingo and matching;
- physically moving around plastic, magnetic or foam letters to build words;
- cloze exercises where words have to be chosen to fit a particular context;
- visual methods where significant parts of the written word are stressed, for example by underlining or with a highlighter;
- morphological methods where word structures are examined and roots, prefixes and suffixes are explored;
- other ways of analysing words like examining syllables, compound words, word origins;
- implicit methods whereby the learner is repeatedly exposed to situations where these words are used in a variety of texts and a variety of writing situations;

- ICT methods drawing on interactive programmes devised to practise using particular word sets.

Decoding for more advanced readers

Decoding is often seen as a tool for beginning readers. However, it can usefully be sustained with more fluent readers who might come across unfamiliar words when reading technical or other specialist texts.

Using the same techniques, better readers can:

- decode longer words using knowledge of sound–symbol patterns – these words are often of Latin or Greek origin and therefore have more logical spellings and, ironically, can sometimes be easier to decode than shorter words;
- make use of a knowledge of morphology to analyse the structure of words and their function in the sentence;
- make use of a knowledge of etymology to make analogies with other known words of similar origin;
- make use of the clues in the context in which the word is to be found.

Task 5.4

Decoding for more advanced readers[11]
In the article below, what strategies might help to decode the underlined words?

> **From backbenches to the bedroom, the BlackBerry is taking over**
> According to the emerging etiquette of the online era, it's the height of rudeness to take out your handheld device and check your emails while friends or colleagues are talking. But what if they've been talking for seven hours? ...
>
> Perhaps it was only a matter of time before BlackBerrys and other wireless communication gadgets were permitted inside the chamber of the House of Commons. But given the usual pace of change at Westminster, you might have been thinking in terms of geological time. Instead this week – just four years after BlackBerrys arrived in the UK – parliament's modernisation committee demanded that tradition give way, meaning that the ubiquitous email device will probably soon conquer the heart of British democracy.

Comment 5.4

Phonics would help to some extent with all of these words. Whilst many are irregular, none of them are completely so, although one might have to work through various sets of grapheme–phoneme correspondences to decode some of them. Some longer words such as *ubiquitous, communication, committee* are in fact very regular.

Morphology might also help with some words e.g. *emerging, rudeness, wireless*.

Etymology might help with some words such as *democracy, geological'*.

Compound words such as *handheld'* or *online* could be worked out.

An understanding of the **context** and **background knowledge** might be necessary to access the meanings of some words e.g. *Westminster, backbenches, parliament*.

Words which might cause particular difficulties:

- *etiquette, conquer*: <u>qu</u> pronounced in k as in French rather than the more usual kw as in English;
- *BlackBerrys*: one might expect a plural of *–ies* (as with the fruit – blackberries) but the capital letter alerts the reader to the fact that this is a product name and therefore doesn't follow the usual rules (as does the capital *B* in the middle);
- *parliament's*: although this word can be read phonically, most people do not pronounce the *i* in the middle, so would find it hard to break down the sounds.

Other conventions of written language

Decoding when reading involves an understanding of the phonic code, but there are also other codes or conventions to explore with learners, for example:

- **genre / text type**: recognizing what language and structural devices are used in different genres (see below);
- **diagrams and charts**: e.g. knowing that the same information can be presented in, for example, a pie chart, a bar chart or a line graph;
- **map reading**: involving a complex set of skills which include using an index, understanding grid referencing, knowing the conventional colours, symbols and abbreviations used to denote features, understanding scale and reading the key or legend;
- **word order**: as discussed in Chapter 3, the syntax of English demands a particular word sequence, so *The man bit the dog* and *The dog bit the man* have different meanings;
- **punctuation**: e.g. knowing whether a sentence is a question or a statement and therefore knowing both the intonation to use when reading and the type of response that might be required;
- **numeracy**: knowing, e.g. that fractions can be the same as decimals and percentages; that 'two and two makes four' or 'two added to two equals four' is the same as '2+2=4';

- **text language**: the meaning of certain combinations of letters, numbers and emoticons to make words and phrases for texting.

Meaning making

TASK 5.5

Constructing meaning from texts

Consider the two texts below. The first is an extract from the Convention for the Protection of Human Rights and Fundamental Freedoms 1950.[12] The second is from an email that was circulating in 2003.

What makes it difficult to read these texts?

What strategies can you draw on to read and understand them?

Sample 1

Article 58 Denunciation

A High Contracting Party may denounce the present Convention only after the expiry of five years from the date on which it became a party to it and after six months' notice contained in a notification addressed to the Secretary General of the Council of Europe, who shall inform the other High Contracting Parties.

Such a denunciation shall not have the effect of releasing the High Contracting Party concerned from its obligations under this Convention in respect of any act which, being capable of constituting a violation of such obligations, may have been performed by it before the date at which the denunciation became effective.

Sample 2

Aoccdrnig to rseearch at Cmabrigde Uinervtisy, it deosn't mttaer in waht oredr the ltteers in a wrod are, the olny iprmoatnt tihng is taht the frist and lsat ltteer be at the rghit pclae. The rset can be a ttaol mses and you can sitll raed it wouthit porbelm. Tihs is bcuseae the huamn mnid deos not raed ervey lteter by istlef, but the wrod as a wlohe.

Comment 5.5

Both these texts are difficult to read, but for different reasons. Even though we are able to use our usual decoding strategies in Sample 1, we might find it hard to understand because of its long and complex sentences and unfamiliar vocabulary. Sample 2 might cause us some decoding problems, but we can probably make sense of what it says. In both cases, the difficulties we encountered may have impeded our ability to predict what we were about to read.

If we are confident readers, we will have strategies for finding out the meaning of words we don't know, or don't know in this context; we can break down sentences into smaller units, and use clues in the text (such as linking words and referencing) to make sense of its organization. We will also draw on our knowledge of genre, register and our understanding of the context, the subject and the world outside the text to make informed predictions.

Constructing meaning can be seen as the ultimate goal of reading. *Constructing* meaning is not the same as *getting* meaning. Constructing meaning is an interactive process which involves the reader bringing a number of different resources to the text and actively using them to create a meaningful interpretation.

What did you bring to the texts above in order to understand them?

- **An expectation that the text will make sense**, which leads you to persevere and search for meaning in spite of the difficulties.
- **Your knowledge of the world outside the text**, which you will bring to the reading process.
  - For example, in Sample 2, the word *research* might point towards a place where research is carried out, so you might expect a word like *university* to follow. And Cambridge can be guessed as a well-known university.

- **Your knowledge of texts** will lead you to recognize the genre of the text.
  - Sample 1 is a section of a legal document so you might expect specialist (and sometimes archaic) vocabulary and complex syntax carefully constructed to ensure that it cannot be misconstrued.

- **Your critical faculties** will be engaged as you start reading. You might start asking questions of the text to investigate claims like *According to research ...* or 'How might the issue of *denunciation* affect me?'.
- **Your knowledge of syntax** will tell you that texts are divided into discrete sentences, each one of which will make sense on its own. Within each sentence you will know what word classes to expect in particular places in the sentence.
- **Your knowledge of semantics** will tell you that only certain words will make sense in this context, for example collocations like *the human mind*.
- **Your knowledge of word structure and morphology** will lead you, in Sample 2, to rearrange words into known patterns. For example, *Taht* is an unlikely letter combination in English but *that* is well known; *iprmoatnt* is most likely to end in *ant* as this is a common English ending.

Therefore, as we can see summarized in the diagram below, the reader brings a variety of skills, knowledge and resources to the reading process:

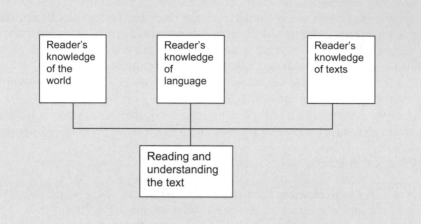

As long as we expect something to hold some meaning, we will try our best to use all the resources and strategies at our disposal to make sense of it. As reading is an interactive process it will be a combination of what the text provides and what the reader brings to it.

Interpreting a text is a combination of processes that take place before, during and after looking at the text itself.

Pre-reading processes – the importance of context

Understanding the context of a text helps us interpret the meaning where more than one meaning might be possible.

To understand the word *BlackBerry* in Task 5.5, we can make use of two types of context:

- **Linguistic context**: *BlackBerry* in combination with words like *handheld device, email, wireless communication gadgets* tells us that it is a phone we are talking about rather than a fruit.
- **Physical context**: if we know it is to be found on the business pages of the newspaper, rather than the features or the cookery section, we can use its physical context to guess the particular meaning intended here.

The advertisement example below demonstrates further how reliant we are on context to make sense of texts.

The advertisement is one of a series for the *Economist* magazine which depends upon us recognizing their consistent style and colour to identify the product. Some of the posters don't even mention its name.

They work because the viewer uses prior knowledge to decode the adverts:

- **about the world**: the magazine *Reader's Digest;*
- **about other texts:** the *Reader's Digest* publishes short or condensed articles which have popular appeal and which aim to inform their readers;
- **about the creator:** aspiring to appeal to an informed and intelligent reader and aiming to make the reader feel informed and intelligent for having interpreted the adverts.

When texts refer to other texts this is termed **intertextuality**. The *Economist* campaign, in turn, has inspired other adverts which draw upon its renown; adding another layer of intertextuality and, for the inexperienced reader, maybe further difficulties.

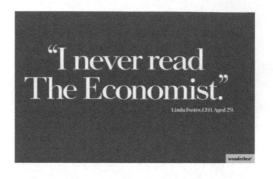

Using schemata

As can be seen from the above, one thing readers bring to the meaning-making process is their knowledge and understanding of the world.

A **schema** is a mental representation of the world which allows us to recognize and remember information by making links with what we already know. Our schema of a form will enable us to recognize it when we see it and thus differentiate it from a leaflet or other printed matter and to know what to do with it – i.e. fill it in.

Look at the text below. It is the first paragraph of an article in *OK* magazine.[13]

> Just as viewers were beginning to nod off with the constant bickering and bitchy backbiting inside the house, Big Brother jumped in to sort things out and sent in four brand-new shiny housemates for the girls (and boys) to play with. But they weren't just any old housemates, mind! They were four fit, walking and talking straight men, which certainly gave the man-hungry girls in the house something to chew on – well for five minutes at least, before they started having another bust-up over toast or bananas.

In order to make sense of this paragraph you would need to know who Big Brother is; what house is being talked about; who the housemates are; and why they needed 'sorting out'. In fact, far from setting the scene for an article on this TV programme by giving useful background information, this opening paragraph assumes the reader will already bring a great deal of background knowledge to the text. Readers will have a Big Brother schema that will enable this new information to be stored alongside previously understood information about this programme so that readers will immediately be able to make sense of what they read.

Activating our Big Brother schema will enable us to comprehend this text. By making use of intertextuality we can uncover a further layer of meaning by drawing on our knowledge of the original Big Brother in George Orwell's *1984*, in order to understand who Big Brother is and why he might have such power over the housemates.

Text schemata, like genres, enable us to recognize a text type and therefore make predictions about its content. A well-known experiment carried out by Bransford and Johnson (1972) gave the following passage to three groups of people, telling them before or after they read it, or not at all, what it was about.

The procedure is actually quite simple. First you arrange things into different groups. Of course, one pile may be sufficient depending on how much there is to do. If you have to go somewhere else due to a lack of facilities that is the next step, otherwise you are pretty well set. It is important not to overdo things. That is, it is better to do too few things at once than too many. In the short run this may not seem important but complications can easily arise. A mistake can be expensive as well. At first the whole procedure will seem complicated. Soon, however, it will become just another facet of life. It is difficult to foresee any end to the necessity for this task in the immediate future, but then one never can tell. After the procedure is completed one arranges the materials into different groups again. Then they can be put into their appropriate places. Eventually they will be used once more and the whole cycle will then have to be repeated. However, that is part of life.

Those who were told before they read that it is about washing clothes were able to remember significantly more than those who were unable to activate a schema. This example illustrates not only the importance of knowing the context of a text in order to understand it, but also how helpful it is if a schema is activated before approaching a text.

Task 5.6

Activating schema
How might you activate a group of learners' schema before reading the Big Brother text above?

Comment 5.6

Some ideas you might have suggested are:

- Ask questions such as: Have you heard of Big Brother? What do you know about it?
- Write *Big Brother* up on the board and elicit what they know about it already.
- Ask learners in the group to share between them the knowledge they already have on this subject.
- Explain to the group they are going to read about Big Brother and ask them to think of some questions they would like answered when they read the text.
- Ask the learners to predict what might come up in a text about Big Brother.
- Ask them if they have heard of *OK* magazine and what they might expect to be in it.

> - Use any images, headings etc. in the article for prediction and to set the context.
> - Start with a game or task to set the scene. For example, images of different types of houses including the Big Brother house; pictures of the housemates; a quiz on what people might argue about.
>
> These strategies build on what the learner already knows and assist them with making predictions about what they will encounter in the text. Reading it will confirm or deny what they have already suggested. The teacher can then assist the learners in monitoring their reading to see how well it fits with what they already know.

Example 5.1

The importance of schema
Cheryl, a learner on a childcare vocational course with embedded literacy, was given an article to read which described how a therapist had used hypnotism to enable a client to go back to her childhood and thus gain a better understanding of events in her early life. Cheryl had never come across the concept of hypnotism before and was unable to make any sense of the entire article, even though in other ways the level of the text was appropriate for her.

This example shows the importance of choosing texts to use in the classroom that relate to people's lives. If a reader has no schema for 'hypnotism', then it will not be possible to activate it. If such a text is important or necessary for the learner to read, then the concepts need to be taught before the text is approached. On the other hand, many adult learners come with considerable experience and knowledge about the world and it is likely that they will know more about certain subjects than the teacher does. By choosing appropriate texts, the teacher will be able to build on their current funds of knowledge and also develop and extend them.

Reading and understanding

Effective comprehension of a text depends both on understanding its **explicit** meaning and being able to read between the lines, interpreting the **implicit** meanings.

Texts are not neutral and they do not exist in a vacuum. Every text is produced within one social, political and cultural context and is read in another. The writer of the text will have composed it for a specific purpose and it will communicate a particular perspective. By understanding this viewpoint and exploring what tools the writer has used to create it, the reader will be better able to make a critical judgement about what it is saying and whether they agree. It may seem obvious that we need to read political pamphlets and advertisements critically, but in some other texts the manipulation of the reader can be much more subtle. A reader who is able to interpret texts critically is a powerful reader.

In the last few years research on comprehension has led to a variety of conclusions. The National Reading Panel report (2000) concluded that effective strategies for developing comprehension have two themes:

- the application of **comprehension strategies** (and teaching to develop those strategies);
- the importance of **vocabulary development** (and teaching to extend vocabulary development).

We will look at these two aspects of making meaning in turn.

Comprehension strategies

Most teachers associate making meaning with the development of comprehension skills. The National Reading Panel (2000: 4–5) defines comprehension as 'understanding a text that is read or the process of constructing meaning from a text'.

In order to 'construct meaning' the reader must actively engage with the text. 'Meaning making' is the ultimate goal of all readers, from those taking their first steps in reading to those who are comfortable with a wide variety of genres.

Reading any sort of text will be part of a literacy event in which there will always be at least two participants – the writer and the reader. The writer will have constructed the text in a particular way to fulfil a particular purpose, knowing that, unlike oral discourse, she may never meet the other participant – the reader.

In the absence of the author, readers must reconstruct what the writer had in mind from clues both within the text and from their own prior knowledge – of the world, of texts, of how language works – all stored in their working memory. If they are not able to do this, a problem with comprehension occurs.

Recognizing that a problem exists is the first step towards finding a solution. A good reader will recognize the problem and decide on a strategy to resolve it. One way a teacher can help a learner with comprehension is to teach her strategies she can use when comprehension breaks down.

The strategies we use depend on our context; if we are at work, or with others we trust, we might turn to them and ask for help. This is what a learner might choose to do in a classroom situation. However, if there are no others around to ask, or if we feel it might be humiliating to ask, we need to have other strategies to draw on. Developing such strategies is an important part of becoming an effective reader.

There has been some research on effective strategies for improving comprehension. The National Reading Panel (2000) noted seven key strategies: comprehension monitoring, co-operative learning, using graphic organizers, answering and generating questions, story structure and summarizing. It also found that teaching a combination of these techniques is likely to be most effective.

What the teacher can do

Before reading

- Devise and model activities that will help learners to: Activate their prior knowledge. (Discussing vocabulary, content and exploring background knowledge is especially useful where cultural or language differences might prevent understanding.)
- Help learners to predict what the text might contain or ideas it might express, for example by using headings or images. Record the group's ideas and explore links between them (perhaps by using a mind map or another type of graphic organizer).
- Suggest some questions they might like to have answered by reading the text.

During reading

- Model prediction strategies (point out the basis for your predictions, then draw attention to evidence which confirms or refutes them). Putting text onto a PowerPoint can be helpful for a collaborative group prediction activity (see below).
- Ask questions, either allowing learners to look back at the text, or encouraging them to work together to reconstruct meaning. You should ask both factual questions and those that need higher level thinking skills. A range of such questions is discussed below.
- Draw learners' attention to aspects of the structure of the text and model how you use them to access meaning – headings, subheadings, introduction, conclusion, topic sentences and paragraphs.
- Model using clues in the text to make sense of new words: using context, grammar, skipping a word and returning to it, rereading a sentence or paragraph; reading on to grasp the meaning; using a dictionary; talking to others.
- Encourage *learners* to ask questions such as: What's going on here? Why did it say that? Why did the author include this information? What's the connection with the last section? How does this information fit with what I read before? Are the two authors saying different things? How could the ideas be reconciled?
- Summarize what has been read after each section.
- Use reciprocal reading (see Example 5.2).

Example 5.2

Reciprocal reading[14]
Reciprocal reading is a way of combining several methods for supporting comprehension which helps learners to develop self-monitoring skills while reading in a supportive and collaborative environment.

It is easiest if learners work in groups of four, but other groupings are also possible. The teacher could model the comprehension process first, showing how she interacts with the text by asking questions, summarizing after each section, clarifying difficult words or sections of the text and predicting what will come next. Learners join in with this process and as they become more skilled at it, the teacher releases control and readers use these strategies independently. In their groups, readers either take turns at the teacher role or they can split it up between them so each group member has some responsibility for interpreting the text.

The four roles are:

> **Questioner**: poses questions about the section read, to be answered by reading on.
> **Clarifier**: clarifies any unfamiliar or confusing words or concepts.
> **Summarizer**: highlights the key ideas in the section read.
> **Predictor**: offers and/or invites guesses about the next section of the text.

Obviously, roles can be alternated so everyone gets a turn at each. Although it might take a while for learners to get used to this way of organizing their reading, it has long-term benefits in the development of active reading skills, reasoning and problem solving.

After reading

There are a variety of ways of helping learners review what they have read and deepen their understanding:

- Summarizing in their own words.
- Using diagrammatic ways of summarizing such as:
    - semantic (mind) maps, spidergrams or other diagrams to show links between ideas or words
    - tables or grids to organize information under headings
    - timelines to show the sequence of events.

- Questioning.

Using questioning

It is common for teachers to address questions to the learners after they have read something. There are a number of ways of classifying questions which can be helpful to the teacher who is trying to use questioning as a tool for developing reading skills rather than just assessing them. Two key ones are:

- Bloom's taxonomy;
- question–answer relationship (QAR).

Bloom's revised taxonomy

Benjamin Bloom[15] suggested that questions could operate at different levels, requiring different levels of thinking. His classification of question types has recently been revised by a group of cognitive psychologists led by Lorin Anderson (Anderson and Krathwohl 2001). The taxonomy has been represented as a triangle with questions requiring 'lower order' thinking skills at the bottom and 'higher order' skills at the top.

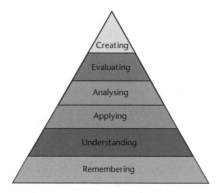

The kind of question a teacher asks can encourage basic or higher level interpretation. If a teacher asks factual questions, learner readers will focus on facts when they read. If she asks questions that need higher level thinking and use of background knowledge, they will tend to think that way when they read.

Teachers often focus on factual questions with beginner readers but if they use the full range at all levels, learners are encouraged to become active critical readers from the start.

Question-answer relationship approach

QAR is another useful way of organizing questioning to support comprehension development.

QAR was developed by Taffy Raphael in the late 1970s (Raphael *et al.* 2001). It helps the learner to understand that the text on its own cannot yield answers to all questions. Sometimes the answers can only come through the reader's own ideas and experience of the world; this encourages critical thinking and active engagement with the text.

QAR divides questions into different types:

- **Right there questions**: the answer is directly stated in the text.
- **Think and search questions**: the reader must search and combine information from different parts of the text to find the answer.
- **On my own questions**: this requires the use of prior knowledge combined with text information. These can be further subdivided into:
    - on my own: readers use their own ideas and experiences to answer the question;

o   <u>author and me</u>: readers think about how the text and what they already know fit together.

Task 5.7

Using questioning

Using Bloom's Taxonomy and QAR

Read the article below and categorize the following questions using the **QAR categories**:

1   Where is the teashop?
2   Do you agree that the Tea Cosy Rooms sounds like 'the scariest place ever'?
3   Make a list of the rules Mr Daly has set in his shop.
4   What rules (if any) do you think a tea shop should have?

And these, using the categories of **Bloom's revised taxonomy**:

5   What would you say to Mr Daly if he asked you to leave for dunking your biscuit? Why?
6   What does the term 'eccentric' mean? Give an example of how Mr Daly is eccentric.
7   Mr Daly says the menu and setting at his teashop is based on 'high tea at the Ritz'? What do you think this means? Why should it mean people ought to behave in a certain way?
8   What do some people describe Mr Daly as? Are they serious? Does he agree?
9   Write a short dialogue between Mr Daly and one of his customers.

Storm in a teacup[16]

An eccentric tea shop owner is causing a stir by barring people who flout a strict set of rules. David Daly warns customers they will be asked to leave his Brighton shop if they dunk their biscuits. Other rules include not putting your elbows on the table, not insulting the Queen, never handling sugar cubes and not sipping from teaspoons, reports the *Brighton Argus*.

Customers have jokingly described Mr Daly as a Fascist and even set up a website and discussion forum. One described Tea Cosy Rooms as 'the scariest place ever' while another said she had witnessed ejections for 'biscuit wetting'.

Another customer said: 'If you dare talk when the piano lady is performing you are out.' Banging a teaspoon against a cup and using a mobile phone is banned outright, as is talking 'louder than two shakes of a tea cup'.

Mr Daly says the menu and setting is based on high tea at the Ritz. The 30-year-old says he is far from being a Fascist and is actually 'very nice' in real life. He said: 'People have to obey the rules and if not they are asked to leave. It is the art of tea drinking – this is not going to Starbucks with a mug of coffee.'

> ## Comment 5.7
>
> **Note**: The example questions below have been jumbled up for the purpose of providing an activity for teachers. When devising a set of questions for learners, you would normally start with lower order questioning and move towards those requiring higher order thinking skills.
>
> **QAR categories**
> 1   Where is the teashop in the article? (Right there)
> 2   Do you agree that the Tea Cosy Rooms sounds like 'the scariest place ever'? (On my own – author and me)
> 3   Make a list of the rules Mr Daly has set in his shop. (Think and search)
> 4   What rules (if any) do you think a tea shop should have? (On my own)
>
> **Bloom's revised taxonomy**
> 5   What would you say to Mr Daly if he asked you to leave for dunking your biscuit? Why? (Evaluating)
> 6   What does the term 'eccentric' mean? Give an example of how Mr Daly is eccentric. (Understanding + applying)
> 7   Mr Daly says the menu and setting at his teashop is based on 'high tea at the Ritz'? What do you think this means? Why should it mean people ought to behave in a certain way? (Analysing)
> 8   What do some people describe Mr Daly as? Are they serious? Does he agree? (Remembering)
> 9   Write a short dialogue between Mr Daly and one of his customers. (Creating)

DARTs (**directed activities related to text**). DARTs are techniques to be used by the teacher to assist learners to create meaning from difficult or 'inconsiderate' texts. The acronym was developed by a team from Nottingham University (Lunzer and Gardner 1984). They consist of a variety of activities and are best done in pairs or small groups as the discussion element is crucial.

Reconstruction activities (the teacher needs to modify the original text)

These activities can help learners develop an understanding of the structure of different text genres

- **Text completion** (cloze): Learners predict deleted words, sentences or phrases. Beginner readers can be offered a list to choose from, but ideally learners should be allowed a free choice of words to ensure engagement with meaning.

- **Diagram completion**: Learners predict deleted labels on diagrams using other texts for reference.
- **Completion activities with disordered text**: Learners sequence cut up segments of text or classify sections under headings.
- **Prediction**: Learners predict the next part of the text.

Analysis activities (learners use unmodified text)

- **Underlining or highlighting**: Learners search for relevant keywords or phrases according to a given subject (a point of view; a topic).
- **Labelling**: Learners label segments of text (using a set of headings provided).
- **Segmenting**: Learners break up text into paragraphs or logical sections.
- **Making diagrams**: Learners construct diagrams to show relationships e.g. flow diagrams, mind maps.

Developing vocabulary

Learners may well have a large oral vocabulary (words they use and understand in speaking and listening) but a smaller reading vocabulary (the store of words they read and understand in print). Further, there are different levels of understanding a word. Although they may have a deep understanding of words that they use frequently (knowing all their different meanings), they may only have a shallow knowledge of a word that is heard rarely, so they may only be aware of a single meaning.

Two key issues relate to vocabulary in reading. First, decoding a word is only helpful if it is already in the reader's oral vocabulary. Secondly, it is hard for readers to make sense of a written text unless they understand almost all the words (McShane 2005).

Learners can be stuck in a vicious circle. They might find texts from unfamiliar contexts hard to read because they involve knowledge and experience outside their own areas of expertise, together with new vocabulary. As these texts are such a challenge to read, learners may not choose them very often, so they will not develop their vocabulary through reading. It is therefore not practical to expect learners spontaneously to pick up knowledge of words as they read. Vocabulary instruction is necessary and studies do seem to show that implicit or explicit vocabulary teaching leads to better comprehension of texts as a whole.

Implicit instruction. This consists of exposure to words through wide reading and might rely on a range of texts which introduce a wide variety of vocabulary, or it might focus on deeper development of key vocabulary in a particular subject area. The texts chosen need to introduce some new words but should not be too challenging. If there are too many unknown words, the reader will not have enough contextual clues to make sense of the new vocabulary.

Explicit instruction

This can take a variety of forms:

- **Pre-teaching** words before reading a text.
- **Multiple exposure**: teaching words that learners are likely to come across in real-life situations (and by implication not worrying too much about those that are obscure). Useful words might be those that help in making sense of the structure of texts (*therefore, in contrast, however, although*), those useful for understanding a particular text to be read or those key to the learners' situations and interests (e.g. related to their work or hobby).
- **Active engagement**: ensuring that new words are used frequently in oral and written tasks.
- **Strategies for learning words**: e.g. teaching prefixes and suffixes and demonstrating how they alter the meaning and function of base words; looking at word origins; teaching strategies for using context cues to work out the meaning of unknown words, for example, noticing an explanation following the word; teaching how to use a dictionary; encouraging learners to record vocabulary in their personal dictionaries.

TASK 5.8

Developing vocabulary

Geoffrey found the text below on the BBC News website.[17] He has been investigating alternative medicine and would be interested in reading it.

If you were helping him with the vocabulary, which words might you choose to focus on and why?

Homoeopathy's benefit questioned

A leading medical journal has made a damning attack on homoeopathy, saying it is no better than dummy drugs.

The Lancet says the time for more studies is over and doctors should be bold and honest with patients about homoeopathy's 'lack of benefit'.

Heavily diluted solutions are used in homeopathic remedies

A Swiss–UK review of 110 trials found no convincing evidence the treatment worked any better than a placebo.

Advocates of homoeopathy maintained the therapy, which works on the principle of treating like with like, does work.

Continuing dispute

Someone with an allergy, for example, who was using homoeopathic medicines would attempt to beat it with an ultra-diluted dose of an agent that would cause the same symptoms.

The row over homeopathy has been raging for years.

In 2002, American illusionist James Randi offered $1m to anyone able to prove, under observed conditions in a laboratory, that homeopathic remedies can really cure people.

To date, no-one has passed the preliminary tests.

In the UK, homoeopathy is available on the NHS. Some argue that it should be more widely available, while others believe it should not be offered at all.

> **66 Many previous studies have demonstrated that homoeopathy has an effect over and above placebo 99**
>
> A spokeswoman from the Society of Homoeopaths

In 2000, the UK Parliamentary Select Committee on Science and Technology issued a report on complementary and alternative medicine.

It reported that 'any therapy that makes specific claims for being able to treat specific conditions should have evidence of being able to do this above and beyond the placebo effect'.

Comment 5.8

Geoffrey is interested in alternative medicine so a lexical set of words on this subject might help him interpret other texts he reads on the subject as well as this one. It might include words like: *homoeopathy, therapy, homoeopathic remedies, complementary* and *alternative medicine*. The teacher might help **Geoffrey** understand and develop this set by drawing a semantic network (sometimes known as a mind map) on the board so that he can see the relationships between these words.

In this particular article, he would need to be clear about the meaning of words that would help him to follow the argument, i.e. that some doctors are questioning the value of homoeopathic treatment. These might include: *dummy drugs, placebo, ultra-diluted, agent*.

In terms of the background or world knowledge needed to understand the article, it might help to explain that *The Lancet* is a leading medical journal, what a *review* consists of and the role of a *Parliamentary Select committee*.

Further work on the key word *homoeopathy* might include investigating its etymology and the alternative spelling (it is often spelled *homeopathy*) so that he can Google it for more information; **Geoffrey** might also find it useful to work on other words with the same root e.g. *homoeo*pathy, *homoeo*path(s), *homoeo*-pathic or allo*pathic,* tele*pathic,* psycho*pathic.*

It would be helpful for the teacher to pre-teach some words before **Geoffrey** tackled the article, so that he could read it more independently. She could also help him to learn key vocabulary by recycling it in post-reading activities.

There are other difficult words in this article e.g. *advocates, illusionist* and *preliminary* which may not be so crucial for its comprehension. If **Geoffrey** is concerned about them, he could look them up in the dictionary or the teacher could just tell him their meaning when he gets to them. It is best not to overload either the pre-reading or the reading stage with new words, so if there are too many of these, the text is too difficult. However, 'passionate interest' in a text might overrule any other considerations as the learner will be so highly motivated to read it.

Text use

Making meaning for different purposes

Task 5.9

Making meaning for different purposes
What reading might take place in the following situations?

1   Taking a bus.
2   Shopping in the supermarket.
3   At work in an office.

Comment 5.9
This is by no means comprehensive but your list might have included:
1   Reading a timetable, fare guide, map, instructions for buying a ticket, safety notices on the bus, advertisements, various street signs, shop and street names.
2   Reading shopping list, labels, signs, notices about discounts, special offers and competitions, recipes, packets, sell-by dates, instructions for cooking items or for parking in the car park.
3   If you work in an office – notes, memos, faxes, emails and attachments, formal letters, signs, instructions, websites, reports, manuals, regulations.

Education is just one domain in life and texts produced specially for the classroom may not resemble those used in everyday life. The teacher has to be careful that learners are not only developing skills for the community of practice of the classroom but for those in other areas of their lives. She can, however, ensure that the tasks set to practise newly acquired reading skills are as authentic as possible and match what learners might do with those texts outside the classroom. One facet of the teacher's role is to find meaningful texts and assist the learners to do meaningful things with them.

For example, if you were practising finding information, instead of just giving learners a handout you might need to model the whole process: deciding where to look, choosing several information sources (including some that you will later need to reject), selecting the most useful ones, using their organizational and structural features to locate the information needed, assessing the quality and usefulness of the information uncovered and maybe making a comparison between more than one source. For beginning readers, the teacher will be doing most of this and explaining how she is doing it, but gradually learners will become more independent in the process.

Activities around texts can be set at varying levels of difficulty. For example, looking at a TV guide, a beginner reader might be asked to find the column that deals with BBC1; a more confident reader could check what is on two different channels at 9.00; a more experienced reader might compare programmes in two newspapers or magazines and see which offers the most useful information about the evening's viewing. On the other hand, there are some tasks which can be offered to learners at any level and they will complete the task according to their skill level, for example comparing programmes in two newspapers or magazines to see which has the most accessible layout and why; discussing why a programme might have been put on at a particular time. If the task is appropriate, even quite complex texts can be used in the classroom.

Text analysis

Critical reading

Texts are social constructs that reflect ideas and beliefs held by their writers at the time of their creation. Every text is constructed within a historical, social, cultural and political context and it will have been formed by these factors.

In some, this will be overt (see the election leaflet below); in other cases it will be less obvious. The institutions of society serve to promote the interests of some groups and individuals while marginalizing others. Texts are neither natural nor neutral but are often constructed by particular institutions and bound up with producing and maintaining unequal arrangements of power.

Interpreting a text is always the result of interaction between the writer and the reader. The writer has produced the text for a purpose and the way it has been constructed will relate to that purpose.

Task 5.10

Critical reading
Read the text below to answer the following questions:

- What type of text is this?
- Who wrote it and for what purpose?
- What devices does the author use to achieve his or her purpose?
- How successful is he or she in achieving his or her purpose?

Matthew Penhaligon—
Your choice for a cleaner, safer Hackney

Dear Friend,

My name is Matthew Penhaligon, and I am proud to be the Liberal Democrat candidate for Mayor of Hackney.

Below you'll find a little bit more about me and the Lib-Dems and overleaf my six pledges to make Hackney a better place for all of us.

For too long, the people of Hackney have been poorly served by their council. We need a change and the Liberal Democrats are that change.

Matt Penhaligon

Comment 5.10

You may have noticed the following features of this text, which was, in fact, from a mayoral election leaflet in May 2006:

- Use of the genre of a personal letter to create a friendly feeling (*Dear friend*) and signing off with an informal font as if it were handwritten.
- Use of a photo of the candidate to accompany the written text, showing him to be smiling and informally dressed, creating the image of an affable and approachable person.
- Use of compound sentences to create an informal tone – almost like speech.
- Use of present and future tenses to show optimism for the future, except when talking of the past problems of a council that is not Liberal Democrat.
- Use of first person singular pronouns (*I, me, my*) to personalize the appeal and use of the first person plural (*we*) to show affinity with the readers. Use of the second person (*you*) to appeal directly to the reader as a person.
- Use of words like *pledges, change* (repeated) to demonstrate commitment to the promise of a new regime.
- Use of words like *proud, better* also to show optimism for the future.

In many texts the writer's purpose is not as evident as this. Just by reading a newspaper article we might not be aware that newspapers are owned by individuals or conglomerates who have a particular view of society.

A critical reading of a text involves considering the writer's intentions and making a judgement about what we are reading. We might ask questions about the text. Who wrote this text? What was their purpose? How are they implicating me in this? Is this the way I want to be implicated? What words have they used? What phrases and grammar? How have the layout and images been used? Is there another way it could have been written and why wasn't it written that way?

Using genre knowledge to become a critical reader

At the start of this chapter, we discussed how readers draw on their knowledge of different genres to make sense of texts. We can develop and extend learners' genre knowledge by analysing the devices used by a writer to achieve her aims, for example the general 'design' of the page – the layout of the text, the images chosen to illustrate it (and how they are used), the grammar of the sentences, the words chosen. As discussed earlier, this detailed questioning of the text has been called 'critical discourse analysis'. It can be done at any level with any text.[18]

Below is an example of questioning which one literacy teacher used to interrogate a text, in this case the front cover of a novel.[19]

Example 5.3

Interrogating a text

Much information can be gleaned about this book before it is even opened. Here are some questions you could use to discuss this text with learners:[20]

- What is the title of the book? How do you know?
- What is the name of the writer of the book? How do you know?
- Looking at the title, can you guess what the book might be about? What information helps you?
- Looking at the name of the writer, can you tell if it's a man or a woman? Can you tell anything else about the writer?
- Look at the picture on the front cover.
- What can you see? What does it tell you about what might be in the book? Are there any people represented in the picture?
- Where are they (foreground or background)?
- Why is the picture in black and white and not in colour?
- Read the subtitle ('*A James and Sinclair mystery*') What is a mystery? Who might James and Sinclair be? Do you think they solve the mystery or make it? What do we need to know about them?
- What is the point of the question at the bottom of the page? Why does it refer to 'your life'? Does it make you want to read the book?
- What genre is this book? (You could show some other titles or online images of book covers).
- How else could the cover have been designed? What effect would this have had on the message the reader gets?

Why is this exercise useful?

- Book covers contain a great deal of information and can help learners decide whether they want to read that book.
- The cover of a book can start the process of prediction. We already know some things about the book and have started asking questions. This leads to active reading to find answers to those questions.
- Book covers are a genre with predictable features. There is certain information you will always find on a cover which will generally be laid out in a particular way. This is not random; it is designed not just to give impartial information, but to make it inviting to the reader. As with any text, it can be analysed critically. We could ask:
    - Why has it been designed in this way?
    - Who designed it? What was their purpose?
    - Does it achieve its purpose?
    - What is the effect of the language, layout, images?
    - What other way could it have been designed? What effect would this have had?

This type of reading involves looking at both what is there in the text and what is not there. Even an apparently neutral, scientific label on the food we buy at the supermarket may not be telling the whole truth. If we go to a shop and buy a product with one of the labels below, we might feel that the label is helpfully guiding us towards healthier choices. However, as we hover over the fridge, making our decision, we might also wonder just how obliging the supermarket is being.

Developing critical reading skills

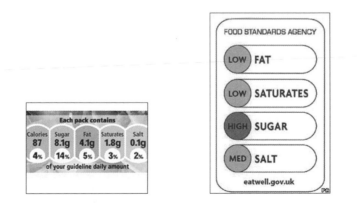

Critical reading is about interrogating (asking questions of) the text. Gunther Kress (1985) developed a framework of three questions which could be applied to any text in the pre-reading, while-reading or post-reading stages:

1 Why is this topic being written about?
2 How is the topic being written about?
3 What other ways of writing about the topic are there?

These questions might lead us to consider the whole issue of food labelling, the role of the government and the supermarkets and the effect on the consumer. Although food labels are comparatively small texts, they might play a large role in many learners' lives. By careful questioning, learners will be able to see them in their social and political context and explore the implications of their content.

Example 5.4

Using questions to develop critical reading
Some questions we could apply to the food labelling texts:

Pre-reading

Do you read food labels? If so, what information do you expect to get from them? Are all foods labelled? Why or why not? How are they labelled? Why do supermarkets do it? Are they doing it voluntarily? Do you agree it should be done?

During reading

Information is being presented in two different ways. What is the difference between these two ways? Do they both give the same information? If you wanted to know how much fat is in this product, which label would help you most? If you were shopping in a hurry, which would give you information quickest? Is one easier to understand than the other? What makes it easier? Can you see anything which might suggest one label has government approval? Why might the government approve one and not the other?

Post-reading

Which way of labelling do you prefer? Why do you think supermarkets might prefer one way rather than another? How do you think supermarkets should label food?

This approach encourages readers to reflect on what they read and take a critical stance. It is sometimes called 'reading between the lines' because it is about looking below the surface meaning to understand the ideas that inform that meaning.

Although an understanding of how a text positions us does not necessarily mean that we can do anything about it, becoming more critically aware can lead to greater control over our lives. It enables reading to become a stimulus for critical discussion and possible action.

It is true that critical reading, like critical thinking, is a higher order skill. However, most learners have experience of critiquing spoken texts (TV programmes, sermons, speeches) or visual ones (advertisements, shop displays), so this is not a new concept. As we saw with the food label example, any learner at any level can read a text critically, given an appropriate text with support through discussion and collaborative activities.

Putting it all together

Below are two activities around integrating some of the above ideas within a single text. Whilst you would not want to apply too many different techniques to a text at any one time, this shows a range of possibilities from which a teacher could select.

Working with a text on PowerPoint

ICT can be an effective resource to teach reading skills, particularly when texts are projected onto a screen or whiteboard. This focuses the whole group on the same text, encouraging collaborative work and allowing you to choose how much text you focus on at any one time. For beginner readers one sentence might be enough. Another advantage of using a projector is that you can adjust the text to suit the learners – you can change the font and the size of print; you can also alter the background colour (helpful for dyslexic learners) and you can embolden or underline elements of the text you wish to focus on.

Task 5.11

Working with a text on PowerPoint

The following text (shown on slides) is taken from a short book about the inventor, Elijah McCoy.[21]

Look at the activities suggested and consider whether they could be seen as:

- code breaking;
- meaning making;
- text use;
- text analysis.

You can use the slides to support prediction and schema activation as with this text (Slide 1).

Have you ever heard the expression 'The real McCoy?'

Can you give an example of when it might be used?

Slide 1

Then you could show the text, bit by bit (Slide 2). This can be helpful if learners are apt to lose their place in a text or if large amounts of texts are rather overwhelming.

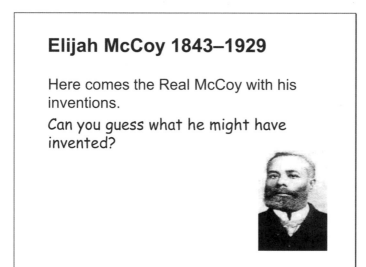

Elijah McCoy 1843–1929

Here comes the Real McCoy with his inventions.
Can you guess what he might have invented?

Slide 2

You could leave out words, as in a cloze exercise, for the learner to fill in with whatever makes sense (Slide 3). This encourages reading for meaning. Learners can discuss what might fit in the gap. On an interactive whiteboard, you can even write in the suggested choices and see how they look. By considering what makes sense syntactically and semantically, the learners are discovering how use of context can help them to make more logical and accurate guesses when they come across an unfamiliar word.

Elijah McCoy

He was born in Canada where his parents went to escape from ...

As a young man he was interested in machines and tools. He enjoyed watching them move.

Slide 3

The actual word can be shown on the next slide (Slide 4). Sometimes the group might argue that the word they chose was more effective than the original – which is all part of seeing themselves as active readers engaging with the text.

Elijah McCoy

He was born in Canada where his parents went to escape from slavery.

As a young man he was interested in machines and tools. He enjoyed watching them move.

Slide 4

You could focus on specific aspects of the text, for example (Slide 7),
- noticing the simple past endings;

- searching for words with the same root such as *invent-* (*invented; invention; inventions*).
- breaking new words into syllables as in *lub/ric/ants* or *pat/ent/ed;*
- sound patterns like oy (McCoy) and oi (oil).

Elijah McCoy

Before McCoy, every machine had to be stopped for oil to be put in to cut down wear and tear. This cost time and money. McCoy invented the 'Drip-cup' and 23 new lubricants. The first was patented in 1872.

Slide 5

Another advantage of using an interactive whiteboard is that you are able to jump out of the PowerPoint presentation to the internet to check details like the position of Michigan on a map (referred to on Slide 6) and return easily to the text.

Elijah McCoy

His fame spread all over the world. People used to ask about the oil in a machine 'Is it the real McCoy?' because his oils were so good. Eager to get on, he produced two or three new inventions every year – for example, an ironing board and a lawn sprinkler, as well as new brands of oil.

He started his own company in Michigan to sell his inventions.

Slide 6

A small amount of text on a slide could also be helpful for fluency practice with the teacher or the learners demonstrating different ways of reading the text aloud. The group could discuss which they think is the most effective rendition (Slide 7).

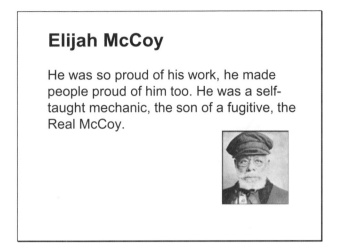

Slide 7

After reading, the teacher might focus questions on aspects of meaning, for example the genre features or critical thinking (Slide 8) or on further research (Slide 9). Again, a click of the mouse could lead on to useful linked readings or images.

Questions

- What sort of text was this?
- How do you know?
- Do you think the writer admired McCoy?
- How do you know?

Slide 8

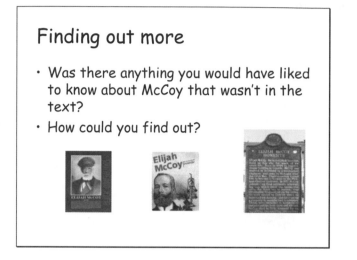

Slide 9

Comment 5.11

The suggested activities are categorized below.

- **Code breaking**: Activities for Slide 5, 7.
- **Meaning making**: Activities for slide 1, 2, 3, 4, 6, 7.
- **Text use**: Activities for slide 7, 9.
- **Text analysis**: Activities for slide 8.

In any one session, however, you might only choose to do one activity with a text, for example a cloze exercise that runs through the whole text, but it would always be good practice to have a discussion of some sort about the content of the text.

Health and safety poster[22]

On an embedded literacy course, learners often have to read and understand texts about health and safety. Instructions, like any other text, can be explored in a number of different ways.

Task 5.12

Applying the four resources model

How might you apply **the four resources** model to the Dermatitis text on the next page with a group of learners on a vocational catering course?

1   What questions could you ask to help them create meaning from this text?
2   What further activities might you suggest?

Make some suggestions under the headings:

- Code breaking
- Meaning making
- Text use
- Text analysis

Comment 5.12

Below are some questions you could ask learners to support their response to this poster. Some of these might be quick oral questions; others might become part of larger activities – oral or written. Of course, you would never do all these things with any one learner or group; they just show a sample of the range of possibilities at different levels.

Code breaker

- What is **dermatitis**?
- Can you break it into syllables to make it easier to read? Are there any smaller words inside it that might help with reading it?
- How did you work out how to read it? Letter by letter? Sound by sound? Break it into syllables?
- Are there any other difficult words in this poster? Can you use the same techniques to work out how to pronounce them?
- What other words end in *itis* like dermatitis? What do these words have in common?
- Can you think of any other words that have the same root word as dermatitis? What do these words have in common?
- **Dryness** and **redness** both have the same ending. Can you think of other words with this ending? What do these words have in common?
- In the thesaurus, some other words for redness are: blush, rosiness, ruby, glow. Why did the writer not pick one of these words?
- How would **flaking, scaling, swelling** be written without the *ing* ending?

Health and Safety Executive

Skin checks for dermatitis

Regularly check your skin for early signs of dermatitis

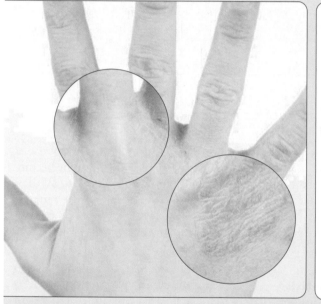

Look for...

Dryness
Itching
Redness

...which can develop into **flaking, scaling cracks, swelling** and **blisters**

If you think you may have dermatitis, report it to your employer

Contact name

Your employer may need to refer you to an Occupational Health Doctor or Nurse

www.hse.gov.uk

Meaning maker

- Does the text remind you of something that has happened to you or to someone else you know?
- If you saw the logo HSE what might you guess this text was about?
- What might you predict was in the poster?
    - if you saw the heading Skin checks for dermatitis?
    - if you saw the image of the hand?
- What did you feel as you read the text? What made you feel that?
- What message is the author presenting? What are the main ideas presented?
- What do the pictures tell us? Why are there six different images of hands?
- Did the poster raise any questions for you? What more would you like to know?

Text user

- What is the purpose of this text? How do you know?
- How can you find information in this text?
- Why has the writer presented the text like this? Do you think it works?
- Where would you find a text like this? Who would read it?
- How are the language/layout/images the same or different from other similar posters you have seen?
- If you wrote a text like this, how would you present it?
- What will you do with this text? What might others do with this text?
- If you were going to put this text on the web, what changes would you make?

Text analyst

- What is the text trying to make you think or believe?
- Is this text fact or opinion? How do you know?
- How would the text be different if it was aimed at a different group of people (Doctors? Employers? Cchildren?)
- Why do you think the author chose these words/pictures?
- Who does the text represent? (Who is shown in the text?)
- Is there anyone not represented by the text? (Who is not shown in the text?)
- There are some instructions in the text. Should you follow them? Why or why not? What might happen if you do (or don't) follow them?
- Who is responsible for your health and safety at work according to this poster? Is this how it should be?

Some examples of follow-up activities are shown below.

Code breaker	Meaning maker	Text user	Text analyst
Compare this text with another poster or another set of instructions. What features do they have in common? (e.g. imperative verbs, some sort of listing; images).	Do some more investigations into work-related dermatitis. Look at leaflets and websites; talk to people who have suffered from it. Having done your research, would you want to add any information to this poster?	Reproduce this information in a different format for a different purpose e.g. in a leaflet; as a web page; as a narrative of your own (or a colleague's) experience of work-related dermatitis.	Design a poster on work-related dermatitis from a different point of view e.g. for a trade union; for the employer; for occupational health professionals. How is each poster different?

Developing fluency

In the National Reading Panel report (2000), fluency is seen as one of the four basic constituents of reading skill. Fluency is a combination of speed and accuracy in decoding and word recognition, and **prosody** (using appropriate rhythm, intonation and expression while reading).

Without fluency, comprehension is compromised. The reader has to put in too much effort and will struggle to get sense out of the text. Yet, some comprehension is needed for fluent reading as it involves interpreting what is being read; grouping words into coherent phrases; using knowledge of words and punctuation for intonation and expression. A learner needs to develop an awareness of how to use all the available clues in the text like punctuation, different types of print (e.g. bold/italic) and signpost words/phrases, etc.

For readers to be able to read for enjoyment, fluency is a vital skill to master. It is particularly important for learners like **Flora**, who want to be able to read aloud in front of others.

Below we discuss some methods for developing fluency in reading.

Guided repeated oral reading

This method involves repeated reading of the same text with teacher feedback. Learners might need to read a passage several times until they feel they have mastered a fluent rendition. They might be assisted by the teacher (who could model the reading), other learners or an audiotape.

Burton (2007) describes various methods used by teachers with adult learners to develop fluency, among them:

- **paired reading** in which the learner reads alongside another more skilled reader; when she feels ready, she continues reading alone;
- **choral reading**: a group version of the above. Some learners enjoy doing this, but others might feel uncomfortable, so make sure you check with the group first;
- **repeated reading** of one passage so that faultless fluency is achieved;
- **modelled (echo) reading** where the teacher reads aloud and the learner repeats.

Reading aloud to the teacher is the traditional way to enable a teacher to hear how the learner is reading and offer support. However, this can be rather redolent of school and some members of the group might become disengaged when they have no role other than listening. One way of involving all the learners present is for them to work in pairs or small groups, reading to each other and supporting each other (see the section on reciprocal reading). Preparing for a performance or presentation to the rest of the group can provide an authentic purpose for group activity.

Interest in this type of reading can depend on learners' own purposes for reading aloud – they might want to be able to read aloud to their children or for religious purposes, in which case practice might meet their own goals. Recordings can be a useful resource, to listen to a model reading or to practise for a performance. (It is important to remember that this type of reading aloud is meant to be a learning experience, not an assessment.)

For fluency practice the text should not be too difficult. It has been suggested that you need to use materials at the learner's *independent reading level* (readable with 98–99 per cent accuracy or no more than two errors in 100 words).[23] It is also important that the text used is short enough for repeated reading to take up only a short time. Learners will feel more confident reading aloud if they have had a chance to read through the text silently first.

If a reader is stuck on a word or misreads it, the teacher should allow some time for the learner to self-correct. Research is divided on the sort of prompts that might be offered. One project with children shows that rime hints by the teacher are more helpful than whole-word prompts (Moseley and Poole 2001). However, Keith Topping (1995), in his work on paired reading with children, suggests that after allowing four to five seconds the whole word should be given to avoid comprehension breakdown.

With research divided, this might be a useful discussion to have with the learners. What would they like to happen when they get stuck on a word? Do they want someone to give them the word? Would they like to be given a clue, such as the first letter sound? Or do they want to be left to work it out for themselves? A small group reading together might want to decide on their ground rules before they start.

Sustained silent reading

Many studies show a correlation between extensive reading and improved reading achievement: better fluency; better vocabulary; better comprehension; broader knowledge of the world. However, we can't be sure that this is a cause and effect process. Does more reading make better readers or do better readers read more?

What the research does show clearly is that self-study outside the classroom will help to develop learners' skills and independence (Brooks *et al.* 2007).

How can a teacher help with this?

- Take a group to the local (or college) library. Hold a session there. Enlist the help of librarians – show that they are human too. Devise activities that help learners discover the layout of the library, the range of resources on offer and the procedures for using the equipment and borrowing resources.
- Bring in some books and other print resources and lay them out in the classroom. Allow learners to browse. Devise activities that encourage them to explore these resources and explain how they can be followed up outside the classroom.
- Set projects on subjects that interest the learners, which can be researched outside the classroom.
- Model using the internet to find information. Set tasks like webquests[24] that help learners navigate the internet to find information.
- Help learners find and use search engines to discover websites that relate to their current literacy practices around their interests. Show them how hyperlinks can be followed to explore subjects further.
- Make a list of websites that offer interactive activities to help develop their reading skills.
- Make use of free newspapers and magazines which learners can take home with them.
- Inspire learners by encouraging them to read writing by other literacy learners.[25]

Developing reading skills further/reading for study

Some learners find that when they start new academic or vocational courses, they are required to read longer and more complex texts. However, there isn't necessarily a point at which a learner stops being a literacy student and becomes another sort of student or a reader of different kinds of texts. Literacy learners such as **Geoffrey**, described at the beginning of this chapter, may have difficulties with many types of text, but he is able to read and understand quite complex texts relating to his medical condition. He is fully conversant with the relevant vocabulary and probably understands the detail better than many people with apparently higher literacy skills.

Longer texts which have a more complex structure and which may contain a number of ideas can be a challenge to those who are not used to them. Learners may need some support navigating through them and finding the information they seek.

There are a number of models for developing reading comprehension skills beyond beginning levels. One that many learners find useful is **SQ3R** (Survey, Question, Read, Recite, Review) (Robinson 1970). SQ3R is a technique that learners can use by themselves to develop the effectiveness of their study skills. It helps readers clarify their purpose for reading and then read and take notes to fulfil that purpose as efficiently as possible.

- **Survey**: Skim read the chapter/text/article; look at headings and sub-headings, pictures and captions, introductory and concluding paragraphs, italicized or bold text.
- **Question**: Ask yourself what you already know about the subject and what you need/want to know about it; at each section turn headings into questions.
- **Read**: At your own pace; read text actively to answer your questions; stop and reread parts that are not clear.
- **Recite**: Say aloud to yourself, or jot down, key points that sum up the section and answer your questions. It is important to use your own words, as this helps the memorizing process.
- **Review**: You will end up with a list of key points that provide a rough outline of the chapter. Cover up your list and see if you can recall them.

Conclusion

We are all aware of being faced with an ever-increasing quantity of print, both on screen and on the page; in this technological age, it is supplemented with information in other modes which make it both more accessible and more difficult to interpret. In some educational texts, reading is called a receptive skill. We have demonstrated in this section that it is a much more active process than this, involving a complex set of actions and responses on the part of readers in their search for meaning. The effective literacy teacher will build on learners' current knowledge and practices to develop their skills and strategies, so that they are able to understand and deal with texts in all their forms and in all contexts.

Further reading and resources

Burton, M (2007) *Reading, devloping adult teaching and learning: practitioner guides.* Leicester. NIACE

McShane (2005) *Applying Research in Reading Instructions for Adults: first steps for teachers*, Washington DC. National Institute for literacy.

Notes

1   *The Book Boy* by Joanna Trollope is one of the *Quick Reads* novels for adults who are new to reading.
2   See www.sedl.org/pubs/sedletter/v11n01/images/frameworkgraphic.gif accessed 3 June 2009.
3   Further information about this technique is available on: www.dfes.gov.uk/readwriteplus/bank/Miscue%20Analysis.pdf accessed 3 June 2009.
4   The running record is a system developed by New Zealand educator Marie Clay and detailed in the 1993 edition of her book, *An Observation Survey of Early Literacy Achievement.* Auckland: Heinemann Education.

5 Extract taken from *Skills for Life Learning Materials*, E3, Unit 3, page 11. www.dcsf.gov.uk/readwriteplus/Learning_Materials_Main accessed 12 June 2009.

6 For a simple interactive way to calculate the readability level of a passage see www.literacytrust.org.uk/campaign/SMOG.html accessed 3 June 2009.

7 Further ideas for using language experience can be found in Mace, J. (2004) Language experience: what's going on? *Literacy Today*, 39 (June) www.literacytrust.org.uk/Pubs/mace.html

8 The language experience methodology used by ESOL teachers differs in this respect. They usually record learners' utterances using Standard English grammar. Teachers of bilingual literacy learners will need to use their own judgement here.

9 www.literacytrust.org.uk/Database/Primary/phonicsdef.html accessed 3 June 2009. The definitions used there have been taken from Greg Brooks's report (2003) *Sound Sense: The Phonics Element of the National Literacy Strategy – A Report to the Department for Education and Skills.* Sheffield: University of Sheffield.

10 A more recent list is that devised by Fry: www.usu.edu/teachall/text/ reading/Frylist.pdf accessed 12 June 2009.

11 *Guardian*, 23 June 2007: 11.

12 Hirst, T. (1998) *Butterworths Personal Injury Litigation Service: A Guide to the Human Rights Act 1998: A Special Bulletin for Personal Injury Lawyers.* Carlisle: Butterworths.

13 *OK!* 26 June 2007: 102.

14 Sometimes called reciprocal teaching; developed in the mid-1980s by A. Brown and A. Palincsar.

15 Benjamin Bloom (1956) published a taxonomy of intellectual behaviour important to learning. Bloom, B. (1956) *Taxonomy of Educational Objectives, Handbook I: The Cognitive Domain.* New York: David McKay Co. Inc.

16 'Storm in a teacup', 13.38, 8 August 2007. www.ananova.com/news/ lp.html?startingAt=11&keywords=Quirkies&menu accessed 25 June 2009.

17 news.bbc.co.uk/1/hi/health/4183916.stm accessed 12 June 2009.

18 For some examples in an ESOL context, see Wallace, C. (1990) Developing a pedagogy for critical iteracy with ESOL learners, *Language Issues*, 4(2).

19 Newland, C. (2006) *The Dying Wish* (Quick Reads). London: Abacus.

20 Thanks to Hilary Buck for this activity.

21 Text from Forde, F., Hall, L. and McLean, V. (1988) *Black Makers of History: The Real McCoy.* London: The Bookplace.

22 www.hse.gov.uk/skin/posters/dermatitis.pdf, accessed 6 June 2009.

23 This is in contrast to the *instructional reading level*, which is 95–97 per cent accuracy.

24 For an explanation see: www.teachingenglish.org.uk/think/resources/ webquest.shtml and for some examples see www.webquest.org/ index-resources.php Both accessed 6 June 2009.

25 For example: *Your stories* on BBC Skillswise www.bbc.co.uk/skillswise/ yourstories/ or the NRDC *Voices on the Page* Storybank www.nrdc.org.uk/ voicesonthepage.asp accessed 17 June 2009.

6 Writing
Nora Hughes

Introduction

- What writing do literacy learners do and aspire to do?
- What skills and knowledge do they bring?
- How can tutors support them in developing their writing further?

The learners whose writing we discuss in this chapter, and who are profiled in the learner texts, have varied experiences of and motivations for writing. They want to become more skilled and confident writers and see writing as a means to fulfilling their goals and aspirations.

For some people, these relate to their role in the family and the community. For example, **Malika** uses writing as a parent, friend and neighbour and would like to be a community translator. Others need writing for study or employment. **Eddie** wants to get a place on a bricklaying course, while **Sean** aims to study history at university and needs academic writing skills. Some people have more personal motivations for developing their writing. **Joyce** loves corresponding with friends and would like to write her autobiography.

These learners bring many skills and abilities as writers and communicators. One of the principles underpinning this chapter is that effective teaching of writing depends on recognizing learners' strengths and building on them.

How the chapter is structured

We begin with an overview of theory and in the remainder of the chapter we suggest ways of putting theory into practice.

Part 1: Themes from contemporary theory

As with reading, there have always been 'wars' over writing; some of these have been resolved over time and competing theories have been incorporated into established practice.[1] A recent example is a debate about syntax. Andrews *et al.* (2004) suggests that children improve their sentence structure primarily through reading and develop it further through free writing. The counter argument is that they need to study and practise it explicitly.[2] More recently there have been debates about text messaging and its impact, positive or negative, on young people's ability to write more formally.[3]

Overall, there has been less research into how people learn to write than how they learn to read and much of it has been carried out with children. In this chapter we do not analyse any one theory in detail or judge competing theories, but explore ideas and approaches which, in our view, can be usefully applied to adults.

Two bodies of educational theory that are currently influential are **cognitive** and **social practice** theory, which both offer important insights.[4] In terms of writing development, cognitive theory focuses on writing as an individual, internal activity and the sub-skills that make up the writing process, while social practice theory is concerned with what people *do* with writing and the kinds of learning that will enable them to participate in real-life events and practices in which writing has a central role.

Purposes for writing: the concept of genre

The concept of **genre** is central to a social practice view of writing. Genres are conventional ways of using language, in different contexts and for different purposes. Genres evolve over time and vary across cultures, but at any one time there are genres that can be easily recognized and whose purpose is clear (see Chapter 3). In a social practice view of writing, developing **genre knowledge** is part of becoming an effective writer.

The original aim of a **genre** approach was to empower people from marginalized communities by teaching them to reproduce **powerful genres** such as academic essays, formal letters and reports. Another, more contemporary aim is to recognize and enhance people's everyday writing practices, including less prestigious and more personal genres, like shopping lists, notes or greeting cards.

Funds of knowledge

The concept of 'funds of knowledge' comes from a social practice view of learning. When applied to writing, it refers to learners' knowledge of familiar genres and ways of using language, acquired through their experience of literacy in everyday life. It also encompasses the personal and social resources they bring, such as cultural knowledge, values and motivations for writing.

When approaching a writing task, often a learner will understand the social context better than the tutor and can make judgements about how to address the reader. An example of this is **Geraldine's** letter to her local councillor (**Text 1b**), in which her knowledge of the Traveller community and her political astuteness make the letter particularly effective. Similarly, in more informal types of writing such as text messages or emails to friends or family, people know the conventions of their own cultures and subcultures and use this knowledge to make decisions as they write.

What teachers have to offer is explicit knowledge of how language works, how texts are constructed and the conventions of different kinds of writing, particularly more formal genres. So writing development can be seen as a shared construction of knowledge between learner and teacher.

Critical literacy

The concept of 'critical literacy' is central to a social view of writing. Essentially it means that writing is not neutral: a writer makes choices that reflect her view of the world and 'position' the reader.

Task 6.1

Consider these extracts from texts. First, what genres do you think they are taken from? Secondly, what 'critical' choices have the writers made?

    1a Happy birthday! Lots of love xxx
    1b Best wishes for your birthday.

    2a I would be grateful if you would give this matter your urgent attention.
    2b If I do not receive the full amount within one week I shall be obliged to take legal action.

    3a Government troops killed twenty people when they opened fire on a group of civilians.
    3b Twenty people were killed in an incident involving soldiers and civilians.

Comment 6.1

1a and 1b are birthday greetings expressing different degrees of intimacy. 1a is intended to be more intimate than the more formal, distant comment in 1b (though it is worth remembering that within different cultures intimacy and distance are expressed differently).

2a and 2b are from letters of complaint. In these the writer chooses whether to make a polite request or issue a threat.

3a and 3b are from news reports. When a journalist reports an incident, she can make clear *who* did *what* (3a), or she can disguise this by leaving out the subject of the action (*Government troops*) and using the passive voice (*were killed*) (3b). The passive voice gives an impression of objectivity and lack of personal involvement, which can disguise the writer's real position.

Motivation and confidence

In both a cognitive and social practice view of writing, motivation and confidence impact on people's development as writers. A cognitive psychologist, Keith Stanovitch, coined the phrase 'the Matthew effect'[5] to describe the downward spiral of lack of opportunity, loss of confidence and loss of motivation that mars many people's experience of formal learning (Stanovitch 1986). Cognitive theorists see this primarily as an individual experience; they analyse the impact of negative feelings on a learner's progress. Social practice theorists argue that confidence and motivation are linked to social factors, including inequality in the education system and institutional barriers based on class, race, gender and other factors; they give higher priority to the development of critical literacy skills as a tool for empowerment.[6]

In the field of adult literacy these issues are particularly significant; some learners, however confident they are in other aspects of their lives, see writing as something to fear rather than something which they can use for their own purposes. They need constructive feedback on their writing, recognition of their strengths and a chance to explore wider issues, including issues of power.

Creativity can be a key to alleviating anxiety and unlocking potential. **Sean** Taylor, in his article 'Improving on the blank page' (in Mace 1995), describes how participants in a poetry workshop, using the metaphor of a key, discovered that writing could be an 'ally' rather than an 'enemy'. Grief and Chatterton (2007) agree and offer examples of the use of creative tools to stimulate and encourage writing.

'Higher order' and 'lower order' skills

For most people, writing is more difficult than reading. While reading involves interpreting a code, writing involves using it with enough precision and skill to achieve a purpose.

Writing involves both 'higher order' and 'lower order' skills.[7] All human activity is made up of this combination. For example, higher order skills in gardening include planning the layout of the garden and choosing plants according to an overall design. Lower order skills include watering the plants and digging.

Task 6.2

Identify the higher and lower order skills involved in:

- listening to a party political broadcast;
- cooking a meal.

Comment 6.2

A person listening to a party political broadcast uses higher order skills to identify the speaker's intentions, noticing how she uses language to influence her audience. Lower order skills include hearing individual words and following the order of words in a sentence.

A person cooking a meal envisages the end product and uses all the different elements – ingredients, utensils and procedures – to achieve that end. Envisaging, designing and synthesizing are higher order processes, while turning on the gas and chopping vegetables are lower order.

In writing, higher order skills include organizing ideas and choosing language according to audience and purpose. Lower order skills include spelling and keyboarding, which rely mainly on memory and hand-eye co-ordination rather than higher order thinking.

A writer will find it difficult to create an effective text – one that is coherent, articulate and fulfils the writer's purpose – if she has difficulties with lower order skills such as spelling. This kind of difficulty can slow down the writing process and prevent the writer from fully expressing her ideas. Higher order thinking uses a lot of brain capacity and therefore writers need 'automaticity' in the lower order skills. But for many adult learners automaticity is difficult to achieve and producing a written text can mean struggling with every word.

Automaticity: 'getting the words down'

'A beginner reader is not a beginner thinker'.[8] Learner writers who have difficulties with lower order skills must draw on other strategies when writing, so that they can produce a text that conveys their ideas and achieves their communicative purpose. In **Text 1b**, **Geraldine's** strategy was to 'leapfrog' over unknown spellings, often writing only the first letter of a word and leaving the rest blank, in order to concentrate on building a persuasive argument.

This kind of strategy is good for producing a first draft, as it frees up the brain for the challenge of composition. In a finished text, however, unconventional spelling can make things difficult for the reader, slowing down the reading and undermining the clarity of the text.

'Correctness' and effectiveness in writing

Some choices made by writers, even if they are not 'correct' in terms of standard written English, reflect a spoken variety and do not impede communication. For example, in **Grace's** text (**Text 7**), the absence of plural and past tense markers does not seriously affect the clarity of the writing:

> I went to Rose birthday party and it was so nice,

> She nineteen <u>year</u> old and there was a lot of <u>visitor</u> that she <u>invite</u> to the party and did rent a big hall for the all night party.

But sometimes grammatical errors cause confusion, throwing the reader off course and making the writing less effective. In the first sentence of **Sean's** text (**Text 4**), his use of an adverbial phrase as the *subject* does not make sense, and the reader is forced to reread the sentence in order to understand the meaning:

> On my first day back in education as an adult at Shoreditch college in Hackney, was very daunting.

Nonetheless, it is important not to confuse the skilful use of written language with 'correctness'. A correctly spelt and punctuated text is not the same as an effective text, as we can see from **Texts 1a** and **2a**. **Sharon's** *Scary Story* (**Text 2a**) is more 'correct' at sentence and word level than **Geraldine's** *Her New Life* (**Text 1a**); there are far fewer errors of punctuation, capitalization and spelling, but as a text it is less effective. While *Her New Life* has a clear structure and is written in the style of popular romantic fiction, *Scary Story* is less coherent and the 'voice' is not so easy to recognize.

An experienced writer can make choices about whether or not to follow standard conventions of grammar and punctuation. However, there is often a penalty to be paid for not obeying the 'rules'. A good literacy teacher will see beneath the 'surface' errors in learners' writing to the 'deeper' text-level qualities, but an employer or examiner may have a more superficial view and assume that a writer is incompetent.

Skills and strategies

For all these reasons, learners need support from teachers to develop writing skills at every 'level' of the process. Writing is difficult because it demands control over 'technical' aspects, such as punctuation and spelling, as well as 'strategic' ones like design, organization and register. The communicative toolkit of the writer is a mixed bag of higher and lower order skills.

The aim of literacy education is for people to develop enough confidence and control to be able to write for their own purposes. The extent to which they can do this, and the means to achieving it, will depend on the individual. For example, it is unlikely that an older person who is learning to read and write for the first time will acquire full automaticity in the lower order skills of writing, as she has not had an opportunity to learn the alphabetic code at a time in her life when this would have been achievable. But she can develop skills, strategies and confidence as a writer, provided she has access to learning that meets her needs, and can draw on support for writing, inside and outside the classroom.[9]

Learners working at higher levels of literacy, who may, for example, want to pass examinations, need to develop more independence and accuracy in their writing and be able to 'code-switch' between standard and non-standard usage according to their audience.

Cognitive overload

The concept of **cognitive overload** is an important one for writing, because writing involves a combination of complex processes, any one of which can present a challenge. It is often best to work on one new skill at a time, focusing primarily on one aspect of writing and providing **scaffolding** for the rest, so that the demands on the learner are realistic.

For example, when working on a text-level skill like organizing ideas in a text, learners could use a bank of words or sentences, as discussed later in the chapter; when working on sound-symbol correspondence they might read a text in which the syntax and vocabulary have been simplified to avoid distracting from the spelling pattern(s).

The impact of new technology

As the cartoon character says, digital technology is changing what it means to write:[10]

Writing on a computer or mobile phone involves using 'non-traditional' skills. For example, a writer using digital technology can easily create **a multimodal** text, incorporating images and sounds which contribute to the overall meaning[11] Contemporary writing also involves new styles and ways of interacting with the reader which are increasingly global, rather than specific to any one language or culture (see Chapter 3).

Another issue is the impact of computers on the writing process. For example, a computer makes drafting easier by speeding up the production of letters and enabling the writer to cut and paste chunks of text. It can also help with technical problems such as spelling, though it cannot remove them completely. If **Eddie** (**Text 3b**) had written his text on a computer, a squiggly red line would have told him that 'backlald' (for 'bricklayer') was incorrect, but the spellchecker would only have given him 'backland' and 'backlands' as alternatives, leaving him unable to come up with the spelling he needed.

The writing cycle

In a cognitive approach to writing there are distinct 'stages' that writers go through to produce texts. Among these are:

- generating;
- focusing;
- structuring;
- drafting;
- revising;
- editing.

Writing can also be seen as a cyclical process. For example, when revising a piece of writing, a writer often has new ideas which lead her to refocus, restructure and redraft her text.

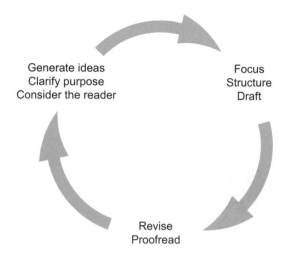

Generate ideas
Clarify purpose
Consider the reader

Focus
Structure
Draft

Revise
Proofread

The social practice view additionally stresses how the writer makes 'critical' choices throughout the writing process. For example, she might reconsider the stance she has adopted, as in Example 6.1, later in this chapter.

Learning to write by writing

People learn to write, not just by doing grammar or spelling exercises but by composing whole texts, with support from teachers focusing on both the technicalities of writing and on the wider social context that 'gives writing its meaning and power'.[12] There is a degree of consensus on this: in a social practice view, writing skills must be contextualized if learners are to develop the *genre knowledge* needed for the real world; in a cognitive view learners need to practise composing texts in order to understand the writing process as a whole, rather than just parts of it.

Top-down and bottom-up approaches

There is disagreement, however, when it comes to beginning writers. Government policy for primary schools has veered between a **top–down** and a **bottom–up** approach. In a top–down approach the starting point is whole texts and developing a sense of self as a writer; in a bottom–up approach people learn to put individual speech sounds (phonemes) into writing, before moving on to words, sentences and, eventually, texts.

In **Synthetic Phonics**, a controversial bottom-up approach outlined in Chapter 5, learners are discouraged from writing their own texts until they have mastered a certain number of sound–symbol correspondences and can consistently produce accurate spellings within this range. In the field of adult literacy most people see this approach, if followed strictly, as unrealistic, particularly in view of the limited time adults have for learning; it could result in them never writing a single real text, much less developing a sense of self as a writer.

On the other hand it is important to be aware that producing a written word, let alone a whole text, is a challenge for beginner writers. In a top-down approach, teachers deal with this by providing **scaffolding**, such as word and sentence banks, to support people in constructing texts; they work on sub-skills like spelling outside the composing process, using material from learners' texts to generate patterns and explore strategies.

A writing curriculum

In a social practice view of writing, the curriculum comes from the contexts in which people write and their purposes for writing; in a cognitive view it is based primarily on a progression of skills. In most literacy courses these perspectives are combined.

When literacy is embedded in a vocational subject, the writing curriculum covers genres such as reports, job records, job applications and CVs. In discrete literacy classes it is designed around a wider range of genres, reflecting the interests of the group. 'Bringing the outside in' is characteristic of a social practice view of writing.[13] It means using class time to explore the range and scope of the writing people do in everyday life, and the skills and knowledge about writing that they bring.

As discussed in Chapters 3 and 8, in-depth diagnostic assessment enables tutors to investigate with learners the skills they already have and the areas they need to work on. An example of diagnostic assessment of a piece of writing (**Geraldine's Text 1b**) is given at the end of Chapter 3.

Where to begin

On vocational courses the order of the curriculum is usually fixed but in less formal provision there is more flexibility and learners' own priorities are the starting point. In this case there are strong arguments for beginning with personal writing, especially personal narrative, rather than with formal, impersonal texts:

- Personal writing has a role in developing a writer's 'voice', building confidence and allowing people to experience writing as an 'ally' rather than an 'enemy'.
- The language of a personal text is closer to the language of speech, making it easier to move into the medium of writing.
- A personal narrative is based on a sequence of events; it is easier to sequence events chronologically than to sequence ideas logically, as required in many types of formal writing.
- There is evidence that adult learners are highly motivated by this kind of writing.[14] Student publications, in which personal narrative is the predomi-

nant genre, have a long history in adult literacy, comprising not only commercial publications but booklets and class magazines produced by learners and teachers.[15] The aim is to celebrate people's writing, create a wider audience and develop a *sense of authorship*, which in a social practice view of writing is part of becoming a confident writer.

Part 2: Developing writing at text level

'Authoring'

Text-level writing skills are sometimes referred to as 'authoring' skills. Authoring means creating a text that conveys the meaning, and has the impact, the writer intended. It means using words and images **rhetorically** to achieve a purpose, whether this is to tell a good story, express how we feel or persuade someone to do something.

Using learners' writing as models of 'authoring'

There is a tradition in adult literacy, of using learners' writing to demonstrate particuar qualities, as in the examples below.

In this short descriptive text[16] the author, who is a beginner writer, uses adjectives simply but effectively to give the reader an impression of her home and how she feels about it:

> My house is big.
> My kitchen is nice.
> My bedroom is warm.

In **George's** piece (**Text 15**)[17] the directness of the language and the repetition of key words and phrases create a powerful effect:

> It's not the same when you're in with foster parents. It's not the same. People want to move on.

In **Zahra's** piece (**Text 13**) a single visual image, the national flag of Somalia blowing in the wind, symbolizes the author's 'dream' of national unity and an end to conflict. She has used an image to enhance the meaning and impact of her words.

Reading as inspiration for writing

Zahara wrote her piece in response to Martin Luther King's famous speech, showing how reading can be a source of inspiration.

Literacy tutors also use 'hot' topics to stimulate writing, as in this example:

> *What credit crunch? City bankers receive £13bn bonuses this year*[18]

In the process of articulating their own views, learners gain valuable practice in text-level skills, including sequencing ideas, building an argument and using specialist language such as *credit crunch*, *banker*, *financial system*, *bonus*, *risks*, *rewards*, all of which can equip them to engage more confidently in debates on issues of concern to them. Difficult texts can be simplified to enable learners at all levels to participate (see Chapter 5).

Writing tasks arising from this topic could include a letter to the editor or an article or opinion piece for the class magazine or group blog.

Using new technology to develop 'authoring' skills

Using a computer makes it easy to produce a multimodal text, which can be shared online or incorporated into a group document. Inexperienced writers, by using photos, video clips, sound clips and other features, can create whole texts with relatively few written words, for example a poster to publicize an event, a PowerPoint slideshow or a blog. Blogsites such as this one are relatively easy to use:

Sharon's first blog on this site consisted of a photograph downloaded from her mobile phone and a caption:

Tuesday, 27 January 2009

Rebel

This is my cat Rebel.
Posted by Pet owner at 10:44 2 comments

In all these activities, a range of text-level skills are developed, including visual design, writing headings and captions and using the language and style of an online network or discourse community.

Genre and purpose

Authoring also means producing a text that 'works' and which the reader will recognize as belonging to a particular genre. For example, a recipe needs ingredients and instructions; a story needs a sequence of events and sufficient background information for the reader to make sense of them.

Key features of genres

Genres have recognizable features in terms of their organizational structure, visual format and language, for example:

Structure

Typically, a writer follows a set pattern according to the *purpose* of the text:
Argument essay:

1   Set out the main arguments.
2   Elaborate, illustrate, give evidence.
3   Summarize, restate the arguments.

Formal letter (or email) of request:

1   State the purpose of the letter/email.
2   Make a case, give evidence and background information.
3   Ask the recipient of the letter to take action.

Personal narrative:

1   Set the scene (themes, people, events).
2   Develop the narrative (and themes).
3   Close the story (and resolve the themes).

Format

Texts are often recognizable by how they look on the page or screen:

EDUCATION AND QUALIFICATIONS

1989–1994 St Ann's Secondary School, Hackney

GCSE English, RE, History

2005–2006 East London Community College

City & Guilds Level 2 Certificate in Adult Literacy

EMPLOYMENT

1999–   Finisher, John Brown & Co Ltd

Clothing manufacturers

Hackney, London E9 5JK

The woods are lovely, dark and deep,
But I have promises to keep,
And miles to go before I sleep,
And miles to go before I sleep.[19]

We can tell from a quick glance that the first of these is a CV and the second is a poem or song. A closer look confirms this: the first text has the standard headings and content of a CV; the second one has a line that is repeated word for word, a powerful device used in poems and song lyrics but less likely to be found in more 'functional' kinds of writing.

Language

The language of a text reflects its purpose. In the extract from the Robert Frost poem above, the sound of the words and the rhythm of the lines reflect the poet's feelings. In other kinds of writing, other aspects of language have a particular role to play, as in the examples overleaf.

Tense and narrative: in a story, verbs in the **past continuous** (pc) tense tell the reader what was going at the time the events took place, while verbs in the **past simple** (ps) tense narrate the events themselves:

> Daylight <u>was fading</u> (pc) and the wind <u>was howling</u> (pc) in the trees. She <u>felt</u> (ps) a light tap on her left shoulder and <u>screamed</u> ... (ps)

Imperative for instructions: in a recipe, the **imperative** form of the verb is used for giving instructions:

> <u>Peel</u> the bananas ... <u>boil</u> them together with the cinnamon ... <u>Bake</u> ... in the oven ...

Discourse markers: in a narrative, **temporal connectives** mark the passage of time and in an explanatory or persuasive text **logical connectives** mark a sequence of ideas, as discussed in Chapter 3. Learners' texts featured in this book include a wide range of connectives, including **temporal connectives**:

> on my first day back, as a young boy, now, the next morning

and **logical connectives**:

in the first place, so, because, although, as a consequence

Genre techniques

In a genre-based approach to writing, learners identify, analyse and practise all these features. Activities progress from teacher-led analysis and modelling, through shared authorship to independent writing, as described in textbooks dedicated to this approach.[20]

Text analysis

In a genre-based approach tutors use model texts to illustrate the typical features of genres. They ask questions, give prompts and invite discussion of key features, many of which learners know implicitly from their experience as readers.

In the following text, the layout and structure, the use of subheadings and the imperative form of the verb are all features of the genre:

Baked Bananas

Rating: ***** Reviews: 1

Serves: 4
Country: Aruba

Ingredients:

4 ripe bananas
2 tbs cinnamon powder
3 tbs vanilla extract
1 cup sugar
4 cups water

Method/directions:

Peel the bananas and boil them together with the cinnamon, vanilla extract, sugar and water for about 20 minutes.

Bake the bananas in the oven at 275° for 10 minutes.

Serve with favorite ice cream.

(*Caribbean Choice* website, www.caribbeanchoice.com/accessed 4 January 2008)

A text like this makes a good model: it is authentic and accessible, and for people who want to send in their own recipes to the website, as two of the learners in this chapter (**Joyce** and **Sharon**) have done, the simple structure is easy to imitate.

As we discussed earlier, texts written by learners themselves, with errors corrected, can also be used as models. **Malika's** personal narrative (**Text 8c**) and **Geraldine's** letter of request (**Text 1b**) show how language can be used effectively within the conventions of a genre. In *Friendship,* **Malika** tells a story, describes her feelings and develops a theme. In her letter of request to a local councillor, **Geraldine** gives convincing evidence to support her case and ends the letter with a direct challenge to the reader:

> You say you don't want Travellers on the road. If you don't want to see my Nan on the road don't close down where she lives.
> (Note that **Geraldine's** spelling has been amended in this extract.)

Exploring critical choices in writing

A model text like **Geraldine's** letter can also be used to discuss the critical choices made by a writer, for example the way she positions the reader or the point of view she puts across in the text.

In some kinds of writing, the main issue affecting the choices made by the writer is the balance of power between writer and reader.

Task 6.3

The balance of power between writer and reader:

- Can you think of a type of text in which the writer has more, or less, power than the reader?
- What difference does the balance of power make to how the writer approaches the task?

Comment 6.3

Most people, when dealing with an official form, such as a benefit claim form, have less power than the people who produced it. As a writer, the claimant is in a powerless position: she must word her answers in a way that will satisfy the reader, who has the power to refuse her benefit.

Form-filling is often taught as if it were a purely 'neutral' way of using literacy, when in reality there is often a power relationship involved.[21]

When working on this kind of form-filling it's helpful to discuss the wider social context, including issues of power, and focus on how to use writing to gain the desired outcome.

In the example below, the reader is in a position of power. A literacy group decided to write to the centre manager asking for better facilities. They were aware of the imbalance of power between them and their reader and discussed at length how to approach the task. They asked the tutor to provide support and she did so by facilitating group discussion about 'tactics' and choice of language.

The learners decided to use 'posh' language in order to be taken seriously. They asked the tutor for difficult spellings and vocabulary, for example *facilities, conditions, communities, progress, opportunity, ventilation*.

After reading the first draft, they decided to change their stance on a particular issue: one member of the group expressed concern that the letter contained a complaint about ESOL groups enjoying preferential treatment and in the end everyone agreed that it would be better to ask for good facilities for all users of the centre. This was the final result:

Example 6.1

Taking power as writers

Dear Ms Smith

Facilities in the learning centre

We are a group of learners who attend an English class at the centre two mornings a week. Our classroom is very small and there is only one window. We have one computer between ten of us. We feel that these poor conditions do not help us to learn.

We all study hard and value our lessons. Learning to read and write is very important to us. Some of us want to get jobs. All of us want to become more independent and play an active part in our communities.

We know that people who come to ESOL classes have bigger class-rooms and better facilities. They make very good progress and we would like the same opportunity to do well. We think that everyone who uses the centre should have good conditions. We would like you to give us a bigger room with proper ventilation and more computers.

We look forward to hearing from you on this important issue.

Yours sincerely

Modelling the construction of text

Modelling is a standard technique used in a genre-based approach to writing. In the example above, the tutor modelled the construction of the text using a digital display board. She discussed the process with learners, emphasizing the choices they could make as authors and pointing out typical features of the genre, such as the conventional closure, *Yours sincerely*, and the final sentence, which politely urges the recipient of the letter to respond:

We look forward to hearing from you on this important issue.

Scaffolding

Another classic genre technique is **scaffolding**. As with a literal, physical scaffold, the aim is to provide support for as long as it is needed. Scaffolding takes many forms, gives varying degrees of support and is reduced or withdrawn as the learner's skills and confidence grow.

At text level, scaffolding can take the form of a **writing frame**. This often consists of a skeleton text with key features provided, such as beginnings of sentences, as in this example of a health and social care report:

Report of visit to ... (name/address of client)

On ... I visited Mr/Ms ...

I arrived at ...
Mr/Ms ... was ...
She/he told me that ...
I offered to help by ...

I would recommend ...

The point of this approach is to enable learners to reproduce the features of a genre by giving them language and structures to practise with until they are able to produce their own texts independently.

However, some learners find this kind of frame difficult to use. For example they get confused trying to finish another person's sentences, particularly if the constructions used are unfamiliar. The challenge for literacy teachers is to find a form of 'framing' that is flexible enough to provide structure whilst leaving scope for independent thinking and expression.

Grief and Chatterton (2007) explain how **Zahra (Text 13)** used a simple frame based on Martin Luther King's famous line, 'I have a dream', to develop her own piece of writing. The frame gave her a basic structure and a stimulus to express her own ideas and feelings.

An approach used in ESOL contexts which can be adapted for use with literacy learners is *Reflect*[22]. Participatory tools and techniques, including visualization (graphics created by learners themselves), are used to explore issues of importance to them.

Learners choose a familiar object as a metaphor. A river, for example, represents the passage of time and is used for developing narratives or comparing a past time with the present. Learners begin by generating and sharing ideas, as in the example below:[23]

Example 6.2

Using visualization

Learners in East London used the metaphor of a river to explore changes in the lives of their community. They divided into two groups – one group discussed changes for the better, while the other group focused on changes for the worse. They created pictures to represent their ideas visually:

Changes for the better

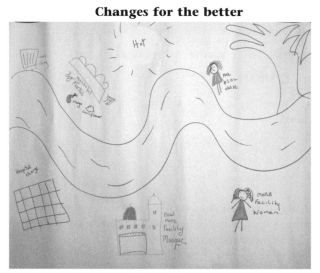

Changes for the worse

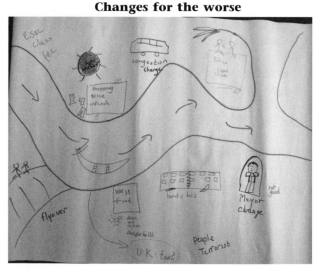

After discussion in separate groups, they came together to share ideas, develop themes and review and practise the language needed for communicating these.

In a literacy context this kind of collaborative process can be used as a starting point for writing.

Exploring register

Using and maintaining a recognizable **register** in a text is one of the things that makes it effective.

One way of exploring register is for learners to compose contrasting texts. These texts can be part of a **genre set** associated with a context or situation.

Example 6.3

Exploring register through genre sets

You have just travelled to Manchester to visit your cousin. The coach broke down and you arrived two hours late. Working in pairs or small groups, write an email:

- to a friend, describing the experience;
- to the transport company.

Questions to consider before writing:

- How will you address the friend or the company?
- What kind of language will you use in each case?

Whole-group discussion after writing:

- Compare the register of the two texts; project them on to a screen and ask the group to pick out specific uses of language and other features such as punctuation, which create the register. This is important as it shows how register works – it is not a mystery, but is founded in choices made by the writer:

  Hi Tom, here I am but what a journey!! ☹

  Dear Sir/Madam, I wish to complain about the appalling service provided by your company ...

Exploring genre variation and change

Genres not only shift over time but vary between languages and cultures. Writing 'appropriately' is not just a matter of following conventions; it also means using language that is up to date and culturally sensitive.

One way of exploring genre variation is to read and compare sample texts before writing.

Example 6.4

Discussing changing genres

Embedded literacy: business administration
Learners compare samples, ranging from contemporary emails to memoranda from earlier decades. They look at salutations and endings such as *Hi guys, Dear*

all, Esteemed colleagues, Respectfully, Kind regards, etc. This enables them to place themselves, as contemporary writers, in a historical context and make choices when writing their own emails at work or for course assignments.

Task 6.4

Exploring differences in genre conventions across generations and cultures

A literacy group is preparing to write to friends and family, telling them of their success in gaining a literacy qualification and inviting them to the award ceremony. One learner has decided to invite the Learning Support Assistant who worked with him during the course:

- As oral preparation for writing, what questions might you ask the group in order to explore:
   - cultural and intergenerational differences in forms of address;
   - ways of reflecting the degree of intimacy between writer and reader.

- What additional resources might be useful?

Comment 6.4

Some possible questions you might ask the group are:

- How would you begin or end an email or letter to an older person in your family, a friend or a child?
- Would your children begin and end the letter/email to each other in a different way?
- What would you use in your first language? Would it sound right in English? (For example, in Mexico, people say 'many kisses' rather than 'love').
- What would the Learning Support Assistant think if she got an email which ended 'Lots of love'? What would be more appropriate? Why?

Resources could include a bank of salutations and endings for people to comment on, add to and select from, for their own texts.

Working on coherence

A text must be coherent if it is to be effective. A writer can build a coherent text, in which the structure and ideas are clear to the reader, by using a number of devices, including: **signposts** such as headings and illustrations; **discourse markers** such as connectives; and **lexical sets**: words and phrases that express the main themes of the text (See Chapter 3).

One way to explore coherence is to compare sample texts, one coherent and the other not, asking learners to find the features that make them coherent or incoherent. Another way is to use a single model text. In both cases it is helpful to project the texts on to a screen and discuss key features as a group.

Sometimes it is best to focus on one feature at a time. Subheadings are the main organizing device in certain kinds of text, such as recipes:

> Ingredients
>
> Directions
>
> Cooking time
>
> Serves

In other kinds of writing, connectives are more important. For example, in **Sean's** personal narrative (**Text 4**), clear cohesive links are needed because the narrative does not develop in a linear way but is interspersed with comments on the general theme of education. In the final paragraph **Sean** signals to the reader that he is returning from these broader issues to his own personal story:

> *So getting back to my first day at collage ...*

Having analysed sample texts, learners then compose their own, using similar devices, with scaffolding provided for those who need it.

An alternative to a model of coherence is one of incoherence. Here, the use of humour can be effective, for example a text that is a ridiculous muddle, veering between one topic and the next or endlessly repeating itself. The challenge for learners is to turn it into a coherent text.

Students can also use non-text based approaches, as in the example below.

Example 6.5

Using images to create coherent texts

Images can be used to organize a text on screen or on the page. The basic structure is provided by the sequence of pictures and the text is then developed further. Working in pairs or small groups, learners:

- Select images and sequence them according to the purpose of the writing (e.g. narrative or persuasive);
- Write a caption for each picture;
- Use each caption as the topic sentence of a paragraph;
- Revise and edit the text and present it to the whole group.

Part 3: Developing writing at sentence level

In this section we move on to writing at sentence level, looking at ways of approaching **grammar** and **punctuation**. We can't cover these comprehensively here, so we focus on some issues that arise frequently in literacy learners' writing.

Grammar and writing development

In previous chapters (3 and 4) we have discussed how writing can differ significantly from speech, particularly informal speech The following issues have particular implications for learner writers.

- Most published writing is in Standard English. In some varieties of English the grammar is very different to the Standard.
- The syntax of writing is different from that of speech. It is based on complete sentences (rather than phrases or fragments) and in more formal texts the use of complex sentences, with embedded clauses and other features, is common.
- In writing, punctuation is used to mark the boundaries of sentences and clauses; these boundaries do not always correspond with pauses in speech.
- In speech we often omit parts of words, such as verb endings, or pronounce them indistinctly, but we need to use them if we are writing in Standard English.

In this section of the chapter we discuss practical ways of approaching all these issues.

From speech into writing

Sharon's home language is a London variety of English, in which the past and present tenses of verbs are similar to Standard English. Yet in '*Scary Story*' (**Text 2a**), her inconsistent use of tenses affects the coherence of the text:

> I <u>walk</u> into the woods at nighttime and <u>try</u> to get my dogs and then I <u>saw</u> werewolves running towards us. We <u>run</u> to get to my car. I <u>got</u> one of my dogs into the car ...

There are a number of possible explanations for **Sharon's** inconsistent use of tenses here.

- She is moving between past and present as she might do in informal speech when recounting an anecdote. She is using the present tense for dramatic effect but reverts to the past tense at intervals.
- She may not be aware that each component of a word must be written down even if it is not pronounced (*walk + ed*).

- She finds it difficult to hear the separate sounds within a word.
- She thinks of the root word (*walk*) as being the most important part, and the ending as relatively unimportant.

Whichever of these is true, the issue is not that **Sharon** is unable to use language grammatically, but that she is still developing her understanding of written language and how it differs from speech. In the final section of this chapter, we give an example of **formative dialogue** (see Chapter 8) that could be used when working with **Sharon** on this piece of writing.

Teaching grammar for writing: inductive and deductive approaches

As discussed in Chapter 4, learners whose home language is a spoken variety of English may need to learn Standard English grammar explicitly, so that they can compare it with the grammar of their own varieties and make informed choices when they write, weighing up which variety best serves their purpose and fits the context in which they are writing.

There are two key approaches to working explicitly on grammar. In a **deductive** approach, the teacher teaches the 'rules' or general principles and learners practise applying them. In an **inductive** approach, learners 'discover' these themselves by analysing examples; the role of the teacher is to provide authentic examples, using questions and prompts as needed.

The activities described below, in which learners analyse the grammar of a model text, are part of an inductive method.

Example 6.6

Identify past tense verbs in narrative texts
Examples of narrative texts

- Personal narrative
- Biography
- Story
- Health or social care report
- Accident report
- Witness statement
- Record of a work procedure

Choosing models

Choose a model text according to the interests and needs of the group, for example a children's story with a family learning group, a formal report for a vocational course, or, in a discrete literacy class, any kind of narrative text that members of the group are interested in.

Setting a context

Begin by discussing the context and purpose of the text, using questions, prompts and aids such as photos or recordings, to elicit learners' prior knowledge and experience.

Past simple tense practice activities

These could include the following:

- Follow a narrative and pick out key events
  - watch/listen to/read an audio/video clip or written text.

- Highlight the verbs
  - *–ed* endings of regular verbs;
  - common irregular verbs.

- Carry on the story
  - finish an incomplete narrative;
  - put in the missing verbs (choose from a word bank if needed).

- Create a narrative
  - use their own verbs or choose from words generated by the group.

It is helpful to do worked examples first before asking learners to work independently, and to cater for different learning styles, for example providing colour highlighters or using cards or other tactile approaches rather than relying exclusively on worksheets.

With many groups it is best to start with regular verbs ending in *-ed*. Initially you might need to write a model text in which most of the verbs are regular; this is unlikely to happen in a real text, as most common verbs in English are irregular. In the long term, aim to use authentic texts as far as possible, including examples brought in by learners themselves, as these reflect language as it is used in real life.

Learning written grammar through 'immersion'

As mentioned in the introduction to this chapter, a recent research study (Andrews *et al.* 2004) suggests that young learners *acquire* knowledge of written grammar through reading, rather than through explicit teaching, whether deductive or inductive.

In an approach based on this idea of *acquisition*, learners read model texts, but there is no explicit teaching of grammar before writing; instead, the emphasis is on *experiencing* language through reading and reproducing it when writing. Proponents of this approach argue that, by frequently reading certain types of text, we internalize their grammatical features and reproduce these naturally in our own writing.

Example 6.7

Learning grammar through immersion

Learners have been reading different kinds of texts over a period of time. In this activity they are given the beginning of a text in which the language of a familiar genre is exemplified, for example:

> Dear Mama, you ask me what I'm doing. Well, I'm thinking about you and hoping that you are well...

STRETCHING AND RELAXING

Lie down flat on the floor, arms at sides, feet slightly apart. Inhale deeply and stretch your arms above your head along the floor, your fingers apart. Stretch your feet with toes apart ...

RUOK

Learners then develop the text further, writing in the same style as the original. They can do this individually or in pairs. The point at this stage is for them to enjoy using the language and let the grammar emerge naturally. Once the group has produced drafts, specific points of grammar are identified and analysed, for example:

I'm doing ... I'm thinking ... and [I'm] hoping:

- present continuous tense;
- ellipsis (if appropriate for the level of the group) – see Chapter 3.

Lie down ... inhale ... stretch:

- imperative form of the verb

RUOK:

- the abbreviated nature of 'text speak', in which words that would normally be separate are compacted together (*areyouok*)

Most formal evidence of people's ability to acquire knowledge of written syntax without explicit teaching is to be found in research studies focusing on children. Purcell-Gates *et al.* (2004) in the United States found that pre-school children growing up in literate, English-speaking households, whose parents read them a story at bedtime, could easily reproduce the language of children's fiction, including the kind of syntax not normally found in speech.

Not all adult literacy students have grown up in these circumstances. Nonetheless, in some learners' writing there is evidence of the influence of reading on their syntax. For example, the sentences in **Geraldine's** Mills and Boon synopsis (**Text 1a**) are fluent and complex, featuring constructions often found in popular fiction:

> Having just moved to London after the death of her mother, she has no friends, no family and no job. She moved to London hoping to make a new life for herself and find her father. Little does she know she will also meet her future husband.

A favourite device used here is inverted word order for dramatic effect:

> Little does she know ...

Sean's personal narrative (**Text 4**) shows attempts to reproduce formal written syntax. His sentence structure is ambitious and works well up to a point, though he is not fully in control:

> On my first day back in education as an adult at Shoreditch college in Hackney, was very daunting. In the first place it was hard to relate to the boy who from the age of four to sixteen didn't enjoy his time at school also in Hackney and Tower Hamlets.

Sean's text, though it shows the positive impact of reading on his ability to use varied and complex sentences, also suggests the limitations of relying solely on acquisition. He has many skills, but would benefit from working explicitly on sentence structure and punctuation, while continuing to read as widely as possible.

Combining acquisition and explicit teaching approaches

Most tutors combine explicit teaching, both inductive and deductive, with approaches based on the concept of acquisition. In addition to reading and analysing model texts and providing support for people to try things out informally, they work on sentence structure, using learners' own writing and supporting them with developing their syntax as part of the revision process.

It can be helpful to writers to break down complex constructions and rebuild them in stages, eventually adding the punctuation needed to make the structure clear. This can be done interactively, with the tutor asking questions and giving prompts to draw out implicit knowledge. Colour coding makes the syntax easier to 'see', both literally and metaphorically.

In the first sentence of **Sean's** text, removing the embedded phrase, *as an adult at Shoreditch College in Hackney*, would reveal the basic structure of the sentence and **Sean** could later put the phrase back in, with commas to mark its boundaries:

> My first day back in education was very daunting.

> My first day back in education, *as an adult at Shoreditch College in Hackney*, was very daunting.

Similarly, when working on his second sentence **Sean** could remove the phrase, *from the age of four to sixteen*, and put it back in with punctuation:

> the boy who didn't enjoy his time at school …

> the boy who, *from the age of four to sixteen*, didn't enjoy his time at school …

Ultimately **Sean** could rebuild the whole sentence, adding the main clause and using the past perfect tense in the subordinate clause (*hadn't enjoyed*) to refer to a time further back in the past:

> It was hard to relate to the boy who, *from the age of four to sixteen*, hadn't enjoyed his time at school, also in Hackney and Tower Hamlets.

It is likely that **Sean**, who reads widely, knows the past perfect tense implicitly, though he may not use it when he speaks. The tutor could use questions and prompts to elicit this form of the verb, or offer an amended version of the sentence, drawing attention to the two contrasting tenses and asking **Sean** to explain the difference:

> It was hard to relate to the boy who … hadn't enjoyed his time at school

This kind of activity can work on paper, with cards or on screen. In group activities an interactive whiteboard is helpful: learners remove and replace key elements (such as subjects and objects or main clauses and relative clauses) in order to explore their role in the sentence.

In **Sean's** case an auditory approach to syntax might also work, as there is evidence that his approach to spelling is often based on the sounds of words rather than visual memory.[24] In the case of syntax an auditory strategy would consist of reading the sentence aloud, exaggerating the phrasing and elongating the pauses, in order to draw attention to the different syntactic units within the sentence.

Sean is keen to work closely on this aspect of his writing. He is aware that he needs to develop greater accuracy and control if he is to fulfil his goal of studying at university.

Working on syntax with beginning writers: building sentences and texts

With beginning writers, Language Experience, an approach which is outlined in Chapter 5, provides opportunities to work on syntax. One benefit of this method is that it draws on the communicative skills learners already have. Another benefit is that, in using their own language, it helps them move from speech into writing.

This is particularly important for those whose spoken grammar differs significantly from Standard English. Rather than asking a beginner writer to move from one grammar into another at the same time as producing a written text, the tutor uses the learner's own grammar, negotiating changes only if the meaning is unclear. This avoids making unrealistic demands on the learner during the writing process. For example, if a learner said "In 1976 I come to England", the tutor would write the word come, as it is clear from the context that the action took place in the past.

Another way for inexperienced writers to work on syntax is by generating words around a topic and using these to build sentences. The tutor uses discussion, questions, prompts, model texts and audiovisual aids to elicit and create a word bank, usually on cards. Each person chooses words she wants for her text, makes them into sentences and uses the sentences to build a text.

Sometimes the tutor writes all the words needed for a sentence, in a circle or on cards, and the learner uses these to construct the sentence:

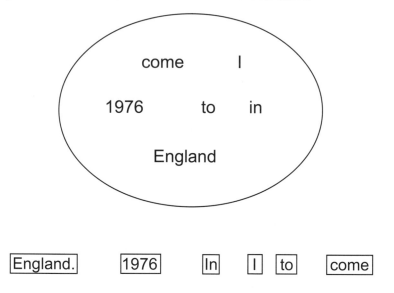

At other times the tutor provides more difficult words and the learner combines these with words she already knows. In **Yvonne's** case (**Text 16**), the tutor provided:

Yvonne was able to write some of the words independently, including:

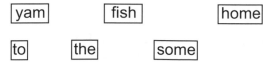

At this stage the focus is on building sentences, rather than on practising new spellings, which is best done afterwards to avoid distraction and overload.

Sometimes the focus can be on a particular **word class**. In the activity below, using one of the model texts discussed earlier in the chapter (Williams 2003), learners fill in the missing adjectives. Later they build their own texts using the same adjectives or others of their choice.

My house is big.

My kitchen is nice.

My bedroom is warm.

My house is ...

My kitchen is ...

My bedroom is ...

Grammar needed for writing: bilingual learners

Generally speaking, when working on grammatical aspects of writing with groups that include bilingual learners, some different or additional issues need to be addressed, as there are likely to be features of English grammar that differ from the grammar of their home languages and they may need to learn them explicitly.

For example, when working on past tense verbs, bilingual learners may need to clarify the distinction in meaning between the **past simple** and **past continuous**.

For those who speak English as a first language these tenses can also be challenging, though for different reasons: sometimes the form of the verb is different in their spoken variety or, as we saw with **Sharon**, phonological features of informal speech carry over into their writing, including indistinct verb endings.

When working on the past simple and past continuous tenses, begin by exploring the context of a narrative and demonstrating the different meanings of the two tenses. Provide opportunities for bilingual learners to practise these orally (if necessary focusing on one tense initially and the other one at a later date, to avoid confusion). Choose a model text that exemplifies the use of past simple and past continuous verbs and ask learners to consider the role that each plays in the narrative.

Example 6.8

Identifying past simple (ps) and past continuous (pc) verbs in a text
Different kinds of narrative text can be used, depending on their relevance to the group and the context for learning, for example:

Care worker's report:
Mr Patel was sitting up (pc) in bed when I arrived (ps).

Accident report:
I was standing (pc) on the corner of Blackstock Road and Seven Sisters Road when a blue VW Golf approached (ps) the junction very fast and crashed (ps) into a stationary red van.

Story:
Daylight was fading (pc) and the wind was howling (pc) in the trees. She felt (ps) a light tap on her left shoulder and screamed (ps)...

This is just one example of a grammar point that is likely to be particularly important for bilingual learners. Other examples are discussed in Chapter 4. For approaches to working on spoken and written grammar with bilingual learners, see the partner volume to this one: Paton and Wilkins (2009).

Approaches to developing punctuation

Punctuation marks are symbols that carry meaning; writers use them to send 'signals' to readers to guide them through a text. At sentence level they clarify the grammatical structure and at text level they work alongside other symbols to create an overall design. As with grammar, it is helpful to approach punctuation through looking at its use in context.

Changing conventions in punctuation and capitalization

All literacy conventions vary according to genre and change over time. As technology develops and new genres come into being, different 'rules' apply and new symbols emerge (recent examples are bullet points and emoticons such as smileys ☺).

Since Shakespeare's time there have been a number of small shifts in the use of punctuation marks and capital letters. This is shown clearly in the famous title page below.

Task 6.5

Changing conventions of punctuation and capitalization

Look at the title page of the first complete works of Shakespeare, published in 1623. Can you identify uses of punctuation and capitalization that are different from what they would be today?

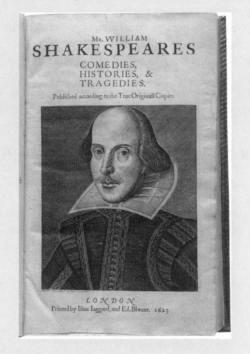

Comment 6.5

This text is a little over-punctuated and over-capitalized by today's standards. The writer has used:

- a full stop at the end of each heading/subheading;
- a full stop after the abbreviated version of a name (*Ed*);
- commas before *and;*
- initial capitals in *True Original Copies*.

One missing punctuation mark which would normally be used today is the apostrophe for possession:

MR WILLIAM SHAKESPEARES COMEDIES
MR WILLIAM <u>SHAKESPEARE'S</u> COMEDIES

Activities for exploring changing conventions in punctuation

It can be empowering for people to explore changes in punctuation, as it challenges the view that punctuation is always 'right' or 'wrong', by showing that it is based on social convention.

- Investigate the punctuation used in a range of texts (e.g. advertisements, menus, recipes, TV listings, food labels, emails, text messages). Ask learners to bring in their own texts; add samples to illustrate particular changes or innovations. Invite learners to:
  - discuss how punctuation marks are used and find any differences between genres;
  - identify new symbols that have come into use in their lifetime.

- Research the history of punctuation, using sample texts from different historical periods and drawing on published books and web-based sources.

Activities focusing on the role of punctuation and other symbols

- Examine a particular feature in a text, such as the use of bullet points, and discuss its purpose.
- In small groups people share what they already know about punctuation marks and other symbols, and feed back to the whole group. The tutor provides questions, ensuring that the range of punctuation covered and the wording of the questions are appropriate to the level of the group:

  Which punctuation mark would you use?
  - *To show that a question is being asked?*
  - *To express surprise or strong feeling?*
  - *To indicate that another person is being quoted?*
  - *To separate items in a list?*
  - *To convey friendliness and informality (in a text message or email)?*
  - *To make a list of items stand out from the body of the text?*

Scaffolding can be provided for this activity, such as a bank of symbols on cards and/or a bank of terms:

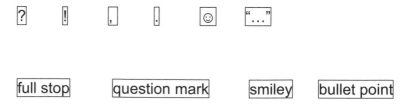

- Working in pairs, learners try out a particular symbol in a short text and share their drafts with other pairs.
- In small groups, learners read a story aloud, with one person playing the part of the narrator and the others reading the words of characters in the dialogue, using the line breaks and speech marks as a guide.

Punctuation and syntax

The greatest challenge punctuation presents comes from its relationship with syntax. Punctuation is part of the written code and is based on written sentences rather than units of speech. The most 'basic' punctuation marks, the full stop and comma, are used to mark the boundaries of sentences and clauses. This is not as easy as it sounds, because syntactic units in written language do not wholly correspond with units of meaning and sound in speech.

As Mina Shaughnessy (1977) and Roz Ivanic (1996) found in their research with adult learners, learner writers tend to apply the logic of meaning and prosody when using punctuation.

In this extract (**Text 14**) **Joyce** has used a capital letter and full stop to mark a **topic unit** or unit of meaning beyond the level of a sentence, and a comma to divide it into smaller units:

> The plane journey was something I can never forget, I was sick all the way the experience was unforgettable.

This 'sentence' is about her journey as a whole; the smaller units consist of an introduction (*The plane journey was something I can never forget*) and an elaboration (*I was sick all the way the experience was unforgettable*).

In conventional punctuation, the introductory clause would end with a full stop, as it is a complete sentence with a subject (*The plane journey*) and a finite verb (*was*), but **Joyce**, looking at it from the point of view of meaning, sees it as an introduction and only uses a comma.

She also sees the second and third clauses, *I was sick all the way* and *the experience was unforgettable*, as part of a single thought or utterance and does not break them up with punctuation, whereas conventionally they would be marked as separate sentences.

Joyce's use of full stops and commas is logical, but incorrect in terms of current conventions in English.

Joyce also uses punctuation as a rhetorical tool. Twice in the same text she uses a capital letter and full stop to mark a short, technically incomplete sentence, in order to heighten the impact of her words:

> The land that pave with that proverbial gold.

> Still living the dreams of one day.

Sometimes it is acceptable in standard written English to use incomplete sentences rhetorically; indeed it is a favourite device of many fiction writers, as in the famous opening sentence of *Bleak House*:

Fog everywhere.[25]

But fundamentally writers need to understand what a 'complete sentence' is if they are to use punctuation conventionally. As Roz Ivanic (1996) points out, teachers often give advice based on 'common-sense' definitions, such as 'a sentence is a group of words that makes complete sense' or 'a full stop marks a long pause and a comma marks a shorter one'. Unfortunately, these are not always a reliable basis for making punctuation decisions, though they can be useful as starting points.

For learners at higher levels of literacy, accuracy in punctuation may be an important aim, particularly if they want to gain a vocational or academic qualification. For learners whose literacy skills are less developed, it is unrealistic to expect total accuracy in the use of full stops, however 'basic' this skill may seem to those who have managed to acquire it.

Developing a sense of what a 'sentence' is

Tutors can help learners at all levels develop their understanding of what a 'sentence' is, beginning with simple sentences before moving on to compound or complex sentences. With some groups technical terms such as **subject**, **verb** and **predicate** are useful, as they identify the key components explicitly. With others it is essential to find more concrete ways of making the concepts clear. In most of the examples below, the technical terms can be used or not, as appropriate to the group.

One of the simplest ways of introducing the idea of a 'sentence' is to identify two main components, **subject** and **predicate**.

Example 6.9

Activities focusing on *subject* and *predicate*

1   Learners make sentences from colour-coded components: subjects and predicates. The full stops are on separate cards, to highlight their role as symbols and so that learners will use them actively to mark the ends of sentences.

   With basic literacy learners, and initially at all levels, it's best to begin with short or single-word subjects. In the examples below, predicates are shown in italics.

She | *went shopping* | .

. | *is a hundred and fifty years old* | Her house

climbed through the window | . | A burglar

Eventually use longer, multi-word subjects to show that a subject can be long or short, a single word or a *noun phrase*. Use different colour fonts to illustrate the concept visually.

My cousin Yvonne | . | *went shopping*

. | *climbed through the window* | A burglar wearing a balaclava

The house where my grandmother used to live | .

is a hundred and fifty years old

As with earlier activities, some learners like using cards they can handle, while others prefer to move things around on a screen.

2   A fun activity is to have a 'lucky dip' of subjects and predicates, which can lead to incongruous results:

My cousin Yvonne is a hundred and fifty years old.

A burglar wearing a balaclava went shopping.

3   Subjects and predicates, separately and combined, can be used to contrast 'complete' and 'incomplete' sentences. A subject or predicate on its own is a fragment, but combined they make a complete sentence. With the help of prompts if needed, learners identify incomplete sentences, discuss what makes them incomplete, and add subjects or predicates to make them complete:

climbed through the window (Who climbed through the window?)

The house where my grandmother used to live (What about the house?)

4   At higher levels of literacy it is important to be able to identify the subject and verb in a sentence and to be aware that in Standard English the verb is sometimes **inflected** to indicate **person** or **tense**, as in this activity.

Ask learners to underline the subjects and circle the verbs. Do worked examples and discuss them first:

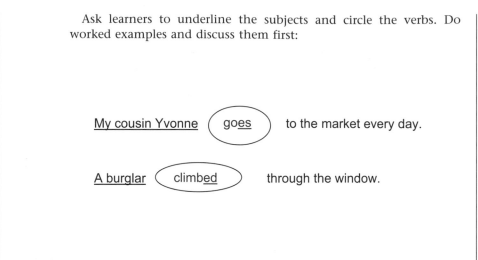

My cousin Yvonne (goes) to the market every day.

A burglar (climbed) through the window.

All these activities can be made more effective by using sentences from texts that learners have been reading or, even more importantly, from their own writing.

Punctuation and the writing process

Learners develop punctuation skills as they compose whole texts. Having a reader in mind encourages a writer to use punctuation to convey meaning. Activities to develop a sense of authorship in relation to punctuation include the following.

- **Formative dialogue**: ask learners to explain their punctuation choices, one-to-one or in pairs.
- **Peer review**: display a draft on screen and discuss the use of punctuation.
- **Revision**: encourage learners to revise for punctuation, focusing on how effectively they have used it to communicate with the reader.
- **Proofreading**: ask learners to focus on a single punctuation mark that they've been working on individually or in the group.

Punctuation and capitalization

Capitalization is partly a word-level process in writing: it involves forming upper case letters when handwriting or selecting them when keyboarding. It is also a sentence-level skill, involving the use of capital letters, along with full stops, to mark the boundaries of sentences.

Task 6.6

Analyse the use of capital letters, full stops and paragraphs in this piece of writing by **Yvonne** (**Text 16**). For the purposes of the task we have amended **Yvonne's** spelling.

> *I went to the market to do some shopping When I got to the market I bought some potato and spinach some fruit with onions and rice at same market And yam and fish and chicken and some milk Some cod and chips I bought some orange juice and banana.*
> *And come back home.*

Comment 6.6

Yvonne's text is an example of written language that is close to speech, but showing some knowledge of writing conventions. On the basis of her limited experience, **Yvonne** appears to have formed a hypothesis about the role of capital letters, using them to break down her text into manageable chunks. Each chunk is about the length of a sentence and sometimes corresponds to a sentence syntactically:

> I went to the market to do some shopping When I got to the market ...

At other times **Yvonne's** use of capitals seems to reflect her thought processes during the production of the text, with each new thought marked by a capital letter:

> And yam and fish and chicken and some milk Some cod and chips ...

Yvonne's writing shows partial knowledge of the function of paragraphs and full stops. She understands that a new paragraph indicates a new idea or event, and has divided her text into paragraphs, one about going to the market and buying food, the other about coming home again. She knows that a full stop is used at the end of a unit or chunk of text, and has marked the end of each paragraph with a full stop.

To help **Yvonne** see the difference that punctuation makes, the tutor could begin by pointing out one or two places where a full stop or comma would make it easier to follow, and then ask **Yvonne** to carry on the process. To allow her to experiment, the full stops and commas should be movable symbols, either on cards or on screen.

Yvonne could also benefit from working with a partner on matching subjects and predicates, as described earlier, using simple sentences from their own speech or writing.

Part 4: Developing writing at word level

Vocabulary[26]

English vocabulary is very large and capable of expressing many nuances and shades of meaning. This is a wonderful resource for writers which, if explored, can enhance their pleasure and confidence in the writing process.

Range and precision: taking risks

In **Sean's** personal narrative (**Text 4**), the word *daunting* vividly conveys how he feels at the prospect of returning to education as an adult. It captures the exact quality of the feeling in a way that a more everyday word such as *worrying* would not have done. **Sean** took risks when he drafted this text, using many words he was unsure of, like *apprehension, techniques* and *disrespectful* (*aprehenchon, texneces, disrespectable*). This resulted in a much more powerful piece of writing than he could have produced had he limited himself to words he could spell.

One way that learners can begin to take risks is by engaging in 'low-stakes' writing practice[27] – trying out new ways of expressing thoughts, ideas and feelings. This kind of writing can help people develop the self-assurance and flexibility they need for writing in general, including more 'functional' writing. In some contexts, such as family learning or creative writing with literacy, the arts of storytelling and poetry are part of the curriculum. In discrete literacy classes many people also enjoy this kind of writing and value the increased confidence it gives them.

Unfortunately, what is often promoted in textbooks and educational websites, in exercises devoted to 'descriptive' writing, is an overwhelming focus on adjectives, despite the fact that overusing them leads to writing that is flowery or unnatural. In exercises using kernel sentences, simple statements like

> The man went down the street.

can end up as:

> The tall, thin, blond man went happily down the wet street.

Notice that the verb in this sentence (*went*) is lifeless and uninformative: it reveals nothing of the man's state of mind, or the state of the pavement. It would have been more effective, and more economical, to let the verb show that the man was happy (he *danced*) or that the street was wet (he *skidded*). It's also worth asking whether the adjectives describing the man's appearance, *tall*, *thin* and *blond* contribute anything to the story.

'Low-stakes' activities for developing vocabulary

Example 6.10

Verbs for storytelling

- **Miming**: Verbs are written on cards (e.g. *dance, skid, creep, tiptoe, dash*). Learners take it in turns to pick up a card and act out the verb written on the card. Others guess what the verb is. The word on the card is eventually revealed. (This can be a small group activity if people feel too shy to mime in front of the whole group.)
- **Pictures**: Each card has a picture illustrating an action in the story. Learners think of a verb for each picture or match two sets of cards, one with pictures and the other with verbs.
- **Going round the group**: Each person suggests a more interesting verb to replace went. The tutor gives prompts such as 'How was he feeling as he went down the street'? 'How would he move if he were drunk/injured/excited/scared?'

It's a good idea for the teacher to join in these activities, sharing the risk taking with learners and providing models, miming a particular verb to get the story going or suggesting a word that reveals a character's physical or mental state and setting off a chain of related words (*stumbled, staggered, swayed*, etc.).

Vocabulary for specific contexts

Different kinds of vocabulary are needed for different types of text, and word choice depends on the audience and purpose of the writing. In an embedded literacy course, vocabulary development can be linked to a writing assignment; in a discrete literacy course it can relate to learners' roles as parents, workers or members of the community.

A useful pre-writing activity is to elicit and build a **lexical** or **semantic set** of words and phrases needed for the type of text and its purpose. As well as extending vocabulary, this enables people to build more coherent texts by means of **lexical cohesion**.[28]

EXAMPLE 6.11

Building lexical sets for writing

> **Motor vehicle assignment**: *mechanic, hub, chassis, align, alternator*
> **Meetings and minute taking**: agenda, matters arising, point of order, chair's action.
> **Job application**: substantial experience, hardworking, conscientious, motivated.

Learning words in a meaningful context makes them easier to remember. It's also helpful to limit the number of new words and phrases being learned at any one time.

Passive and active vocabulary

A person's *active vocabulary* consists of the words they know and use. Their *passive vocabulary* consists of words they know but are less likely to use, as discussed in Chapter 3. Pre-writing activities, to enable people to access passive vocabulary and use it actively, could include asking them to:

- suggest key words for a topic;
- pick words from a bank and match them to definitions;
- discuss the meanings of words in a text and choose some to practise in sentences;
- compose a text, using words they have generated and practised.

Bilingual learners, who have grown up speaking another language or languages, may not have a large passive vocabulary in English, as they have not been immersed in English since childhood (see Chapter 4). They may need additional input from the tutor, including pre-teaching of words and phrases needed for a writing task. For discussion of this aspect of second language learning see the partner volume of this book, *Teaching ESOL* (Paton and Wilkins 2009).

Spelling

Spelling is a complex and much debated issue in adult literacy. This complexity arises from the interplay of a number of factors, including:

- **linguistic**: the nature of the alphabetic system and the difficulties posed by the 'opaque' spelling system of English;
- **cognitive**: the role of memory in spelling, and the need for individuals to develop their own strategies according to their learning style;
- **social**: the value attached to conventional spelling and the fact that it is often equated with competence or even 'intelligence';[29]
- **affective**: the distress caused by the stigma attached to 'poor' spelling, and the fact that many learners are understandably anxious to improve their spelling skills above all others.

In this section we will look at each of these factors and consider implications for practice.

Linguistic factors

The alphabetic code and the writing process

In an alphabetic writing system, individual speech sounds are represented by abstract symbols. The shapes of words and letters do not reflect either their sound or their meaning. The shape of the symbol *t*, which represents the sound of the first letter in *tree*, is entirely random; the word *elephant* does not look like a real elephant any more than *house* looks like an actual house.

So spelling involves drawing on a body of abstract knowledge during the already complex process of composing a text. Some people develop automaticity in spelling, but many people writing in English, including experienced writers, find it hard to produce conventional spellings as they write.[30] A writer in this situation must use other strategies, such as skipping over words at the drafting stage (as **Geraldine** did in **Text 1b**), using a personalized checklist for proofreading, or asking a tutor or friend for support. It is important to discuss these strategies with learners, so they can decide what works best for them.

Sound–symbol correspondence

As explained in Chapter 3, every alphabetic language has a set of regular sound–symbol correspondences, but in English this set is very large because of the number of variations. Irregular words are an added complication.

Many people argue that English spelling is unnecessarily difficult and call for it to be reformed. They point out that many of the variations and exceptions exist for purely historical reasons, often arbitrary ones, and that a more consistent system would remove at least some of the barriers people face when learning to write in English.

The *schwa* presents a particular challenge for the learning and teaching of spelling. This vowel sound, the most common one in the English language, can be spelled in many different ways (see Chapter 3).

Proponents of **synthetic phonics** argue that the entire set of regular sound–symbol correspondences, including all the variations, can be learned, stored in the memory and retrieved when writing. They suggest an order in which to study them and recommend that people master each new pattern before moving on to the next one. However, for many adult literacy learners this would be extremely difficult. An added problem is that, if divorced from writing whole texts for real purposes, learning spelling in this way can feel pointless and alienating.

On the other hand, knowledge of sound–symbol relationships is an important tool for writing, without which writers would only be able to use words whose spelling they could recall visually. Learners need access to this body of knowledge and tutors need to find ways of incorporating it into the writing curriculum.

One approach is to focus on groups of words with the same spelling patterns, generating these from words in texts that learners are reading or writing. The rationale for this is twofold:

- people are motivated to learn words they want or need for a purpose;
- learning a type of word or a pattern is more useful than learning an individual word, as it gives the learner underpinning knowledge that can be applied to other words.

Eddie's text (**Text 3**) contains many spelling errors, from which he and a tutor would need to select.

One word that could be grouped with others of the same pattern is *would*. Using an *onset-rime* approach (see Chapter 5), learners could:

- divide *would* into its onset and rime:

  w + ould = would
- add the onsets *c* and *sh* to the same rime:

  c + ould = could
  sh + ould = should
- learn and practise the whole group: *would, could, should.*

These words are difficult, but they are among the most common words in the language.

Another way of working on sound–symbol correspondence is to incorporate regular work on phonics into a literacy course. In adult contexts this means devoting a small proportion of each lesson to learning or revising a new pattern, following a logical order such as the one recommended in the English adult literacy core curriculum (DfES 2001). To take an example from **Eddie's** text, it would be logical to work on consonant–vowel–consonant (CVC) words such as *fed* and *bed*, before tackling more difficult words like *write* and *like*, in which the long vowel sound is represented by the middle *i* combined with the final *e*.

For all learners, knowledge of sound–symbol relationships is a step towards more accurate spelling, but for many it remains extremely difficult and they need to combine it with other strategies (see the section on cognitive factors below).

Accent and pronunciation

Adult learners come from varied language backgrounds and speak English with many different accents. Vowel sounds vary from one region to another, and learning how to represent them in writing can be difficult in a group. For example, the vowel sound in *bed* is different in different accents, and for some people the pronunciation of *bed* and *bad* is almost identical. This is an enormous complication when using phonics for spelling.

For tutors the challenge is to support individuals in moving from the sounds of their own natural speech into the letter patterns of conventional English spelling.

Morphology and spelling

As discussed in Chapter 3, morphology is the study of the structure of words.

From the point of view of spelling, what writers need to know about morphology is that:

- spelling longer words can be easier if you divide them into components such as 'roots', prefixes and suffixes;
- a suffix (and occasionally a prefix) can change the spelling of the root word;
- this happens in predictable ways which can be learned;
- there are exceptions.

Morphology is usually a core part of a spelling curriculum. As the concepts being learned are very abstract, teachers often help learners gain 'ownership' of them by using an inductive approach. This involves providing models and asking learners to look for patterns, for example how and when a plural or past tense ending affects the spelling of a root word:

family/families

hurry/hurried

'Imported' words

All languages absorb words from other languages. In terms of spelling, the problem with this process in English is that imported words tend to retain their original form, or at least a version of it that does not fit within the normal range of English spelling patterns. This makes the words difficult to spell, for example *technique*, *rhythm* and *psychiatrist*. (Strategies for learning difficult words are discussed below in the section on cognitive factors.)

There are particular issues for speakers of other languages when dealing with English spelling (see Chapter 4). Tutors need to be aware of these when supporting bilingual learners.

Cognitive factors

People's ability to remember spellings depends on many factors, including age and cognitive style. People who are dyslexic can have difficulties arising from visual or auditory processing problems or inefficiency in the working memory. Finding strategies which draw on their distinctive strengths, as well as addressing weaknesses, is particularly important for these learners.

Some people use knowledge of word structure or sound-symbol correspondence to apply spelling rules when writing. Others draw on their visual memory of words and their implicit knowledge of patterns: they go by the 'look' of the word:

easily 'looks' right, whereas *easyly* doesn't

Another visual strategy is finding words-within-words. Do carnivores eat *meat* or *meet*? In this case it's easy to choose the right spelling, as the word *eat* is contained within the word *meat*.

Some people like to have an overview of all the possible letters or combinations that can be used to represent a sound, but for many literacy learners this kind of global approach only leads to confusion. For them, trying to learn more than one spelling pattern at a time is not a good idea, particularly if the patterns are similar.

Example 6.12

Homophones *there, their* and *they're*
Many people understand the distinction in meaning between these words, but still get them confused when they write them. This is because the main factor in choosing the correct spelling is memory. For these learners it is better to concentrate on one word at a time, exploring its uses and building up associations to which the memory of the word can be 'pegged':

- using a drawing, photograph or other visual image.
- grouping words of the same pattern and learning them together

    h<u>ere</u>, th<u>ere</u> and everyw<u>here</u>.

The strategy adopted depends partly on the word itself and partly on the learning style of the individual. When working in a group, it is best to assume that there will be as many preferred ways of learning spelling as there are people in the group, and use a variety of approaches.[31]

Task 6.7

Developing strategies for spelling difficult words
How would you remember the spelling of the words *rhythm* and *necessary*?

Comment 6.7

Ways of tackling these words could be:

- Highlight single and double letters in contrasting colours:
- Learn the necessary letters by heart:
    r-h-y-t-h-m
- Use a mnemonic:
    Rhythm **h**as **y**our **t**wo **h**ips **m**oving.
    It is ne<u>c</u>essary to have one <u>c</u>ollar and two <u>s</u>ocks.

Social and affective factors

As discussed earlier, social pressure to spell conventionally is very strong and conventional spelling is often regarded as a sign of 'intelligence', despite the fact that it depends more on memory than on higher order intellectual processes. The stigma attached to 'poor' spelling causes problems for many people, including lack of confidence, a distorted view of their own abilities and a tendency to focus on spelling as if it were the most important aspect of literacy.

On the positive side, there are affective factors that can help with spelling, such as motivation to learn words that are personally significant to the learner. In **Text 12**, there is evidence that **Aftab** can learn personal key words, including long ones like *Bangladesh.*

In **Eddie's** text (**Text 3**): most key words are misspelt, including *bricklayer, fed up, learn, read, write* and *help.* However, he wrote this text before he started a literacy course and it is likely that he could learn some personal key words with the support of a tutor, choosing words that he needs for his goal of becoming a bricklayer:

mix + er = mixer

brick + lay + er = bricklayer

Literacy tutors can respond to positive and negative affective factors in spelling in several ways, including:

- taking into account learners' interests and priorities;
- giving constructive feedback;
- discussing the reasons for the difficulty of English spelling, including historical reasons;
- working on spelling regularly and systematically, in the context of meaningful writing tasks.

Approaches to learning and teaching spelling

Having explored some of the factors that impact on the learning and teaching of spelling, we now consider a number of established approaches.

Making a link with reading: text-based activities

As with other aspects of writing, whole texts can be used as a starting point for work on spelling. Using a text that the group has been reading,

- explore spelling issues arising from words in the text;
- ask learners to suggest strategies for difficult words;
- devise practice activities;
- set up a writing task drawing on the themes of the text, using a selection of the words.

To take just one example, the word 'favorite' in the text 'Baked Bananas' (page 205) could be used in a number of ways:

- To compare British and American spelling: ask the group to compile a list of words with the same patterns, such as

favor	favour
flavor	flavour
color	colour
neighbor	neighbour

- To explore the broader social issues arising from this example: the global spread of American English, the current trend towards US spelling, and the reasons behind it. This kind of discussion enables learners to take a longer view of spelling and helps demystify current conventions by putting them in a historical context.
- To identify and discuss the *schwa*. The middle syllable in the word *favourite* is normally swallowed and the word is pronounced something like *fave / rit*.
  Sometimes the spelling of the schwa can be revealed by going back to the root word, where the syllable is a little more distinct and the pattern can be seen more easily:
  fav<u>ou</u>r
  fav<u>ou</u>rite

Diagnostic assessment: identifying strengths and areas for development

One way to meet individual needs in a spelling programme is through diagnostic assessment and dialogue. In this part of the chapter, we will refer to writing by **Aftab** and **Eddie**.

Aftab: Text 12

Aftab is a bilingual learner who had limited access to literacy as a child, and for whom English is not a first language. In view of this, his spelling in English is remarkably strong.

- Personal key words are spelt correctly:

  Aftab, Bangladesh, England, family, problem, college, English.
- Phonic strategy is often successful. Even when a word is not completely correct it is based on existing words or patterns (in this example *add*, *mesh*, *on*):

  addmeshon (for admission);

  or he uses a logical phonic alternative (*oz*), combined with visual memory of the word as a whole:

  bec<u>oz</u>e (for because).

- Vowel sound confusion reflects the pronunciation patterns of Sylheti:

  smool (for small).
  live (for leave);
  batter (for better).

Eddie: Text 3

It is evident from this piece of writing that **Eddie**, unlike **Aftab**, has fundamental problems with spelling, though he does have some knowledge that can be used as a starting point.

- He uses initial consonants correctly.
- He remembers the spelling of two personal key words: *work* and *hope*.
- He knows the consonant digraph *-ck* and uses it in *backlald* (*bricklayer*) in which the vowel sound is short, but incorrectly in *lick* (*like*), in which the vowel is long and the final *-e* is needed.
- He uses the consonant blend *-lp* correctly in *help* (*holp*), but misses the blend *br-* in *bricklayer* (*backlald*).
- He can't always identify the component sounds of words; sometimes he adds an extra phoneme: *lont* for *lot*, or an extra syllable: *reder* for *read*.

Spelling in the context of learners' own writing

It is clear that **Aftab** would benefit from continuing to learn personal key words, as this is something he already does successfully. **Eddie** could also try this strategy; his motivation for writing is linked to a vocational goal and he could pick words he needs for this context.

Aftab could extend his knowledge of sound–symbol correspondence in regular words, learning new patterns and clarifying confusions. For **Eddie** this is also very important but he is likely to find it difficult.

Both learners could set up a regular spelling routine in which they choose words they want to learn; decide on strategies for learning them; practise them and test themselves at frequent intervals. A well-known framework for doing this is *Look, Say, Cover, Write, Check*.[32] Two basic principles underpinning this approach are:

- the words must be useful to the learner, who chooses them from his own writing;
- the tutor's role is to help the learner explore strategies that will work for him as an individual.

Aftab could work towards developing proofreading skills, though at present this would be difficult for him, as his knowledge of English spelling is still fairly limited. In **Eddie's** case it would only be realistic to proofread for a very small number of words that he has been working on.

Dyslexia and spelling

Eddie's problems with spelling affect his ability to produce a legible text or use writing to express his ideas. There is a discrepancy between this extreme difficulty with spelling and the qualities in his writing, including clarity and coherence at text and sentence level, and logical, if not completely accurate, use of punctuation and capitalization. This combination of notable strengths and difficulties can be a sign of dyslexia.

Eddie has some knowledge of spelling to build on. A tutor would have to be encouraging, realistic and selective in her feedback and her suggestions for learning, and support him in trying out different strategies. He would probably find it helpful to work with a specialist tutor one-to-one, as this would give him scope to investigate his strengths and difficulties and find strategies for moving forward with spelling.

Learning and teaching spelling: putting it all together

When working on spelling with groups and individuals it is worth remembering some basic principles:

- Practise regularly and for short periods.
- Concentrate on one pattern or aspect at a time.
- If working regularly on phonics, follow a recommended sequence.
- Provide opportunities for review and consolidation.
- Vary the activities and use a multi-sensory approach.
- Use technical terms to shed light on useful concepts, as appropriate to the group (e.g. *vowel, consonant, prefix, suffix*).

- Use contexts that are meaningful and relevant to adult learners.
- Use words from texts that people are already reading.
- Make links with learners' own writing.
- Provide opportunities for active and collaborative learning.
- Explore the history of English spelling and discuss the difficulties it presents.
- If possible, make spelling fun!

Part 5: Supporting the writing process as a whole

As suggested in the introduction to this chapter, people learn to write by writing. Learners need opportunities to compose whole texts, with support from tutors on both the technical skills of writing, like punctuation and spelling, and the strategic skill of producing an effective text within a given social context. They need opportunities to develop confidence, a sense of themselves as writers and a repertoire of 'voices' for the different kinds of writing they want or need to do.

A recent NRDC research study (Grief *et al.* 2007) suggests that it is important for teachers to:

- set up writing tasks carefully, using pre-writing activities to prepare for writing;
- make the composition process explicit;
- engage in formative dialogue with learners;
- give useful feedback.

In this section we discuss each stage of the process, drawing on theory and practice covered earlier in the chapter. These are only examples; when planning, tutors have to take into account a wide range of factors, including the writing people do and aspire to do outside the classroom, how they feel about writing, how they work together as a group, the ways they prefer to learn and the sub-skills they need to develop.

Effective teaching depends on being responsive and flexible, going with the 'teachable moment', picking up on issues as they arise and responding effectively.[33] This is often quite subtle, requiring skill on the part of the tutor. In the case of writing, it means noticing and analysing how learners use spoken and written language and being aware of the social, affective and cognitive factors that can impact on writing, as discussed throughout this chapter.

Before writing

Generating ideas

Pre-writing activities are important because they enable learners to:

- draw on their knowledge of the topic, genre and wider social context;
- express ideas orally first, as a bridge into writing;
- practise language or literacy skills needed for the task;
- build confidence and motivation for writing.

Examples of pre-writing activities from earlier in this chapter are the 'credit crunch' debate on page *219* and the community workers' discussion on page 226, in which learners share ideas, explore themes and work on the grammar or vocabulary they need for the topic.

Exploring the writing cycle

Writing is a process which, though individual in many ways, has elements that can be identified and practised. Learners may have implicit knowledge of this which the tutor can draw on.

Example 6.13

Visually representing the writing cycle

One way of showing the cyclical nature of writing is to use cards with different 'stages' written on them and ask learners to sequence them. This can lead to discussion of what writing involves, including the fact that it is not a linear process.[34]

Planning

When working on the planning stage of writing, it can be helpful to:

- offer a framework – a spider–gram or other visual tool - or invite learners to create their own planning tools;
- help people draw up plans, using questions and prompts;
- discuss options, including the option *not* to plan, for example when spontaneity is more important than structure, as in a personal email or text message.

During writing

Providing scaffolding for a first draft

The point of scaffolding is to give support that frees up the learner to express ideas and develop a text.

Scaffolding can include:

- a writing frame;
- grammar and vocabulary needed for the topic and type of text;
- spellings of difficult words.

The type and amount of scaffolding will depend on the learners and the tutor must make a judgement about what kind of support to offer, how much structure to provide and how best to use learners' own language and ideas as a starting point.

Responding to drafts

This is one of the most significant aspects of teaching writing and demands sensitivity and skill on the part of the tutor.

Research with adult learners in the UK and USA (Grief *et al.* 2007 and Condelli *et al.* 2003) suggests that it is important to respond to drafts as a *reader*, not just as an assessor, using formative feedback and dialogue to:

- support the development of a sense of authorship;
- build confidence;
- develop awareness of audience, discussing the needs of the reader and the impact of the writer's choices;
- offer support with technical aspects of writing.

When responding to a draft:

- respond with interest to the content;
- use open questions to help the writer develop her ideas;
- highlight aspects of the writing that are effective and explain why;
- point out errors that might cause problems for a reader;
- explore the choices open to the writer.

When a learner is 'stuck' during drafting, remind him or her of ideas he or she expressed earlier and give prompts to help the learner clarify what he or she wants to say.

If the learner is worried about technical problems:

- remind him or her to stay focused on the overall purpose of the text;
- suggest short-term strategies, such as asking for spellings of words he or she needs, using a word bank or writing the first letter of an unknown word and moving on.

Most literacy learners need assurances that there will be opportunities to work on spelling and other technical aspects of writing later, if not at the drafting stage.

All these ways of responding to drafts can be used in small groups as well as one-to-one.

Formative feedback and dialogue

Example 6.14

Formative feedback to Sharon (Text 2a)

Formative feedback to **Sharon** on her draft of *Scary Story* could cover many issues. To avoid overload or demoralization, it would be important to be selective and highlight qualities as much as areas for development. Here are some examples of comments the tutor might make, each of which could be the beginning of a dialogue:

This really is a 'scary story': there's a lot of running and tripping and an atmosphere of panic! You've created this effect very well, using the words 'run' and 'running' several times. Did you enjoy writing the story? Did you make it up or is it based on one you've read?

Sometimes I got a bit lost in the story. For example, when you say 'they' in the fifth line, who do you mean? Who are 'they'? Who do you mean by 'the other person'? If you make these things clear, your story will be easier to follow.

Your use of punctuation is very strong. You have used full stops to mark the ends of sentences. Did you use the grammar check on the computer (the squiggly green line)?

*Let's talk about the verbs you've used in the story. Verbs can make a big difference to how easy it is to follow. Do you know what a verb is? Let me show you some examples … (See pages 212–13 for discussion of **Sharon's** use of tenses.)*

Are you thinking of putting this story in the class magazine? If so, how will you illustrate it? How will you make the title stand out? Can you make it look scary?

After writing

Revision

To revise effectively we must be readers of our own texts. When a teacher responds to a draft as a *reader* she is modelling the revision process, focusing on the effectiveness of the text, discussing issues such as clarity, expressiveness, coherence and fitness for purpose. These are the kinds of issues that a writer needs to consider when revising a text.

Recent research in the area of *assessment for learning* (Black *et al.* 2005) suggests that it is important for learners to draw up their own criteria and apply these when revising. This can work especially well as a group activity when working on a particular type of text.

Example 6.15

Eliciting criteria for effectiveness in writing

- Project a sample text on to a screen or interactive whiteboard.
- Evaluate it as a group: analyse what makes it more effective or less effective.
- The group draws up a set of criteria related to the genre and the purpose.
- Learners now apply these criteria collaboratively in assessing other texts (e.g. each other's drafts).
- Finally, each person uses the criteria independently to revise her own writing.

Many learners are unused to the idea of revision and have the unrealistic expectation that a first draft, if written by an experienced writer, is already perfect. Many people confuse revision with proofreading and it's important for tutors to make a clear distinction between the two processes: **revision** is for **effectiveness**, **proofreading** is for **correctness**.

It can be helpful for people to draw up their own revision checklists. For example, while some people find it hard to maintain a consistent register in a piece of writing, others have problems with sequencing or using suitable headings.

Revision as a creative process

Revision need not be just a hard slog but can be a creative process. For a writer, the purpose of revision is to find better ways to express what she wants to say and achieve the effects that she wants to create. This can be enjoyable and satisfying. For example, **Sharon** could make her *Scary Story* more effective visually, using 'scary' pictures or a font like Chiller for the title; she could also get satisfaction from making the story more coherent and enabling her readers to follow the plot.

Even in more formal or impersonal writing the creative aspect of revision is important. For example, when revising a persuasive text like a letter of request, a writer might choose new words or phrases that make the points more clearly or heighten the impact of the text.

Teachers can help by supporting the redrafting process, focusing on both linguistic and visual features, as in **Sharon's** case. Skilful questioning can help people develop their drafts, improve their use of language and other modes of expression and make their writing more effective.

Proofreading

Even proofreading, which means checking for errors and correcting them, can be enjoyable, especially if done in a group. Some tutors use games, such as *the first team to find the twenty deliberate mistakes wins*, which many learners enjoy (though this can be undermining for some people).

It's often a good idea to focus on just one issue, for example verb endings, plurals, full stops or capital letters, depending on what people have been working on recently.

As with revision, each person can draw up her own checklist, in response to formative feedback from the tutor. Many learners will need extra support, especially those at an early stage of literacy.

Conclusion

Writing is a difficult but potentially rewarding activity for adult literacy learners, and one that is important to them for many reasons, as discussed at the beginning of this chapter. They aspire to use writing to fulfil a variety of personal and social goals, and they bring funds of knowledge and experience as a resource for learning.

Further reading and resources

Grief, S. and Chatterton, J. (2007) *Writing*. London: NRDC.
Moss, W. (1999) Talk into text: reflections on the relationship between author and scribe in writing through language experience, *RaPAL Bulletin*, 40.
NRDC, *Voices on the Page*, www.nrdc.org.uk/voices accessed 17 June 2009.

Notes

1. For discussion of the debate around 'genre' and 'process' theories, see Wray D. (2004) *Literacy: Major Themes in Education, Vol. 3. Writing: Processes and Teaching*. Routledge/Falmer.
2. See National Literacy Trust website for a summary of this debate, including brief historical overview and references: www.literacytrust.org.uk/database/Writing/grammar.html. Accessed 15 June 2009.
3. See Crystal, D. (2008) *Txtng: The Gr8T Db8*. Oxford: Oxford University Press. See also '2b or not 2b?', article by David Crystal, with contributions by Will Self and Lynne Truss, in the *Saturday Guardian Review*, 5 July 2008.
4. For discussion of this issue with reference to literacy, see Purcell-Gates, Jacobson and Degener (2004) especially chapter 7, 'Print literacy development through a widened lens', pp. 81–125.
5. Named after a child who participated in research on this issue.
6. See Clark, R. and Ivanic, I. (1997) *The Politics of Writing*. London: Routledge.
7. For example, Bereiter, C. and Scardamalia, M. (1987) *The Psychology of Written Composition*. Mahwah, NJ: Lawrence Erlbaum Associates.
8. Goode, P. (1985) A beginner reader is not a beginner thinker, in G. Frost and C. Hoy (eds) *Opening Time*. Manchester: Gatehouse, cited in Woodin, T. (2008) ' "A beginner reader is not a beginner thinker": student publishing in Britain since the 1970s', Paedagogica Historica, 44 (1&2).
9. In some communities the practice of collaborative writing, in which everyone contributes ideas and more literate members of the community take the role of scribe, is still strong. See Mace, J. (2002) *The Give and Take of Writing: Scribes, Literacy and Everyday Life*. Leicester: NIACE; and Saxena, M. (1994) Literacies among the Panjabis in Southall in Mary Hamilton *et al.* (eds), *Worlds of Literacy*. Clevedon: Multilingual Matters.
10. *Guardian* (2007) Guide, 14 March: 34. 'Home-clubber' cartoon by Modern Toss, website: www.moderntoss.com accessed 15 June 2009.
11. See also Kress, G. (2003) *Literacy in the New Media Age*. London: Routledge.
12. From Clark and Ivanic (1997), *op. cit.*
13. The NRDC practitioner guide, *Writing* (Chatterton and Grief 2007, *op. cit.*), suggests activities for 'bringing the outside in'. See also: Appleby, A. and

Barton, D. (2008) *Responding to People's Lives*. London: NRDC; and Fowler, E. and Mace, J. (2005) *Outside the Classroom: Researching Literacy with Adult Learners*. Leicester: NIACE.

14. See *Voices on the Page* www.nrdc.org.uk/voices accessed 15 June 2009.
15. See Woodin (2008), *op. cit.*
16. From Williams (2003).
17. This piece of writing was produced using Language Experience. It illustrates how beginner writers can be eloquent speakers, using rhetorical devices intuitively to create powerful texts. See *Voices on the Page, op. cit.*
18. *Guardian*, 26 May 2008.
19. From the poem by Robert Frost, 'Stopping by woods on a snowy evening', in E.C. Latham (ed.) (2001) *The Poetry of Robert Frost*. London: Vintage, p. 224.
20. See for example: Hyland K. (2004) *Genre and Second Language Writing*. Ann Arbor, MI: Michigan University Press; Wray, D. (2004) *op. cit.*; Spiegel, M. and Sunderland, H. (1999) *Writing Works: Using a Genre Approach for Teaching Writing to Adult and Young People in ESOL and Basic Education Classes*. London: LLU+, London South Bank University.
21. See Fawns, M. and Ivanic, R. (2001) Form-filling as a social practice: taking power into our own hands, in J Crowther, M. Hamilton and L. Tett (eds) *Powerful Literacies. Leicester: NIACE*.
22. See Moon, P. and Sunderland, H. (2008) *Reflect for ESOL Evaluation: Final Report*. London Language and Literacy Unit at London South Bank University.
23. Thanks to Becky Winstanley, Tower Hamlets College, for this example.
24. For example, he writes *indivigle* for *individual*, *perants* for *parents* and *apprehencon* for *apprehension*.
25. Dickens, C. (2003) *Bleak House*. Harmondsworth: Penguin Classics.
26. In the English Adult Literacy Core Curriculum, vocabulary is listed as a word-level element in reading but a text-level element in writing. In this book, for reasons of consistency, we discuss vocabulary under word level.
27. For discussion of this approach, see Vacca, R.T. and Vacca, J.L. (2000) Writing across the curriculum, in R. Indrisano and Squire. (eds) (2000) *Perspectives on Writing: Research, Theory and Practice*. Newark, DE: International Reading Association.
28. See Chapter 3.
29. See Clark and Ivanic (1997), *op. cit.*
30. See Peters, M. (1985) *Spelling: Caught or Taught? A New Look*. London: Routledge.
31. For examples see Basic Skills Agency (2008).
32. *Ibid.*
33. See Grief *et al.* (2007).
34. See Grief and Chatterton (2007).

7 Speaking and listening

Irene Schwab and Nora Hughes

Introduction

The first thing to be said about speaking and listening, as with reading and writing but to a greater extent, is that literacy learners already do it; indeed they began in early childhood.

Chomsky has argued that we are all born with an innate faculty for learning any language.[1] Of course, the actual language we learn depends on which language or languages we are exposed to. If we have been exposed to English from birth, we will acquire English and by the age of 5 we will be competent oral users of that language. We will have learned our speaking and listening skills by interacting with family, friends and others in our community, hearing and using the language. Acquiring the skills of listening and speaking is very different from learning to read and write, about which there is nothing instinctive, innate or natural.

For bilingual learners in literacy groups the issue of speaking and listening is a little different. They are fluent speakers of English but may still not be as comfortable or proficient in the language as someone who grew up using it.

In literacy classes the focus, in terms of speaking and listening, is on the 'strategic' or 'higher order' aspects of oral communication. These include understanding, selecting and interpreting when listening, and coherence, register and rhetorical strategies when speaking – in other words, the overall effectiveness of the communication in relation to the context and purpose.

Many learners bring transferable skills from their own cultures and subcultures. In some cases, the oral traditions of the community are still strong and people rely on the spoken word because access to literacy is not universal. In other cases there is simply a wealth of creativity in spoken language, including dexterity in areas as diverse as street talk, rapping, storytelling, poetry, jokes and offering advice.[2]

Historically, we are living in a time of rapid change in communication techniques, with a marked shift in the balance of visual and linguistic elements in written texts and a blurring of boundaries between speech and writing, for example in emails and text messages in which the interaction is often more akin to a conversation with both people present than a traditional written interaction.

However, the considerable oral skills and abilities of some learners may not entirely match those required for formal spoken genres, whose characteristics mirror those of formal written language. On the other hand, as with reading and writing, learners can build on their skills, confidence and fluency in listening and speaking, extending their repertoire to encompass a wider range of contexts and types of communication.

Contexts for speaking and listening

Learners bring to literacy classes funds of knowledge about listening and speaking. As members of communities and the wider society, they participate in events and practices in which they frequently use oral language, drawing on skills that are both personal to them and cultural or social in origin. Many are good storytellers, eloquent speech makers or good listeners.

Effective speaking and listening depend not only on linguistic skill but also on knowledge of context. For example, a care worker, when assessing a client's support needs, listens in particular ways, noticing factual details that may be important and also picking up on more implicit facts or feelings. A parent uses a range of skills to communicate effectively with a child. A friend or family member recounts an anecdote or makes a speech at a social gathering, using language and gesture that are appropriate to the situation and the participants.

Many of these skills are transferable, for example listening for implicit meanings or speaking consistently in a chosen register. Other aspects may be specific to one context and less transferable to others, for example in-jokes or exophoric references (references to things outside the text that are known only to people within that context).

As with written language, oral communication can be categorized in terms of **genre**. Spoken genres range from everyday conversations to more formal interactions like interviews and presentations. All of these have recognizable features that have been identified and described by linguists.[3] In the case of more 'vernacular' or everyday genres, most people know the unwritten 'rules' already if they are operating within a culture that is familiar to them.[4] In the case of more 'dominant' or formal genres, most literacy learners are less experienced and less confident, and could benefit from studying the features of these explicitly.

It is in these formal contexts that many learners aspire to be more powerful; for example they want to use oral communication skills to get a job or qualification, or to negotiate effectively with someone in power, like a head teacher, local councillor or MP.

Task 7.1

What do you think were the main barriers to effective speaking and listening for this learner in this situation?

Sean came into his literacy class greatly troubled. Earlier that day, he had made representations to the school disciplinary committee to try and prevent his son from being excluded from school and he felt the meeting had been a disaster. He had tried to explain why his son had been fighting, but the committee had just brushed his justification aside. He felt intimidated by the committee and did not put his case as coherently as he felt he should have done. 'I just got angry and got sidetracked into complaining about all the other things Tom hates about the school' he sighed. 'What were the school's reasons for imposing such a long exclusion?' asked one of the other learners in the group. **Sean** stared at her, 'I'm not sure', he replied. 'They talked and talked and I wasn't sure which were the important bits.'

Comment 7.1

1   In attending the committee, **Sean** had been placed in an unfamiliar situation and was not able to draw on his usual linguistic resources. He didn't entirely understand the role of the formal committee meeting in which he had to defend his son and felt overawed by the situation. He wasn't confident about his ability to convince the committee of his argument or to understand what they said to him.

2   Although **Sean** knew that he had to attend the meeting to make representations on behalf of his son, he wasn't completely sure what this involved. His presentation was not clearly structured to this purpose and, at times, strayed off the point. He was not able to respond to particular points, because he was not sure which were the key points being made.

3   During the meeting, **Sean** recognized that things had gone wrong but he wasn't sure what he needed to do to retrieve the situation. Because of his unfamiliarity with this context and his associated lack of confidence, **Sean** could not engender the flexibility needed here. He was unable to adapt his normal facility with language to meet the challenge of a new and different context.

Three key issues in successful speaking and listening are raised by this case study:

1   Confidence.
2   Clarity of purpose.
3   Awareness of context and the ability to adapt to its needs.

Whilst these are also important issues in reading and writing, the immediacy of situations involving oral communication make them even more crucial in these contexts.

Oral and written communication

Making a comparison of the skills involved in oral and written language can be a useful one for teachers. Whilst it is sometimes difficult to think about how to develop speaking and listening skills when learners are clearly already proficient (even if only in certain situations), if we consider the range of skills and sub-skills involved, we can design a programme of work for their development.

In many ways communicating orally is similar to written communication: in both cases the conventions of the genre have to be taken into account and the context and purposes of the communication drive its style and content.

As with writing, a speaker needs to be clear about her message and organize it for optimum coherence and clarity to suit the audience, which means using rhetorical devices, selecting an appropriate register, vocabulary and language variety and choosing an appropriate length.

The listener, like the reader, will need to draw on her background knowledge and use her schemata to make sense of the message. She will make predictions and guesses as she takes in information and interprets it.

Both speakers and listeners will apply their critical faculties to the utterances and consider how they are positioning and being positioned. In these cases, teachers can draw on the skills they use in teaching reading and writing to assist learners to develop these sub-skills.

However, as we saw in Chapter 3, there are also significant differences between spoken and written language and these create new challenges for the teacher of oral language.

For example, the speaker uses some different rhetorical devices from the writer. When her audience is able to watch her, she can use paralinguistic features to create the effect she wants, such as body language including posture, gesture, facial expression and positioning (near or distant from her audience); she can also make use of her voice, over and above the words she speaks – control of the pitch, volume, speed of delivery and rhythm of her speech all assist the message.

The listener will make use of these effects to assist her interpretation. She is also able to ask for clarification, repetition, rephrasing of any part of the utterance she doesn't understand. A speaker's likely use of more informal language will generally be helpful to the learner, although for some bilingual learners the use of idiomatic and colloquial language might be difficult.

A synchronous interchange between speaker and listener will draw on turn-taking conventions and the conversation can be supported by back channelling (utterances signalling understanding to the speaker like 'uh huh', 'mmmm', 'yes I see').

The increased flexibility and immediacy of an oral interaction can be stimulating but also nerve-wracking, as we saw with **Sean**.

Task 7.2

If **Sean** had asked his literacy tutor for support before the meeting

- How could she have helped him prepare for it?
- What group activities could she have organized to help all learners in the group develop their speaking and listening skills?

Comment 7.2

Three key issues came up for **Sean** in putting his case effectively:

- confidence;
- clarity of purpose;
- awareness of context and the ability to adapt to its needs.

To build **Sean's** confidence, she could offer opportunities to practise speaking and listening in formal situations. These types of activities put **Sean** in a 'sandpit' situation where he can try out different ways of arguing a case without fear of losing face and with the support of his class, for example:

- making a presentation;
- actively listening to someone else giving a presentation (making notes, preparing questions to ask the presenter);
- taking part in more formal discussions where he has to present a case and support it;
- reading (or listening to) an argument and either summarizing the writer's point of view or producing a counter-argument. He could work with a partner who would present the opposite point of view. Their classmates could be asked to vote on the most convincing argument;
- balloon debates (where each member of the group has to pick a famous person and justify why he or she should not be thrown from the balloon)
- problem-solving exercises, where learners have to defend their solution to the problem and persuade others to agree.

One reason for **Sean** being so nervous at the committee meeting was that he felt powerless in the face of authority figures – the head teacher and governors of the school. This is partly to do with inequality and social class and in **Sean's** case it may also have brought back memories from his own school days. His literacy teacher will not, of course, be able to wave a magic wand here but she might feel that discussing issues like this with the group could help learners share their experiences and resources for dealing with such concerns.

As well as being able to speak assertively, **Sean** also needs to become more confident in his listening skills, so that he can pick up the main points of other people's arguments and respond to them quickly and appropriately.

If **Sean** is clear about the purpose of his talk, it will help him to organize it appropriately. If he is to present a case against exclusion, he needs to consider the overall structure and content. This will include the length and range of what he says; how many points he wants to make and how he will support each of them with evidence, examples or illustrations. He might explore ways of carrying out research prior to the event, looking at relevant books, leaflets, newspaper articles or interviewing another parent who has been through the same disciplinary procedure. The preparation for his input to this meeting could be compared to that required for planning a piece of persuasive writing; he might use the same approach and methods and his teacher might draw on some of the same resources.

Similarly, clarity about purpose is important in developing his listening skills. If he is clear what he is listening for, he will be able to apply the most appropriate listening techniques to his task. He could draw on his perception of the main issues (perhaps derived from the research he has done beforehand) to make predictions about what he will hear, which will help him to sift rapidly through what is being said by the panel, deciding which points are most important and discarding those he feels to be irrelevant. He will simultaneously apply his critical listening and thinking skills so that he is constantly analysing what is being said to him and assessing its strength as an argument. If he is able to focus on the main points, he can begin to consider his response and formulate his counter-argument. Again, an understanding of the genre of persuasive texts and an analysis of their features could be helpful to him.

The third issue in putting an effective case, as we noted above, was an awareness of the context and the ability to adapt to its needs. **Sean** is very aware that this meeting is an important one. This is partly the source of his worries. He has some knowledge of the way powerful institutions operate through his reading of newspapers and books, and through his membership of a trade union. He could build on this and his teacher could help him to see the connections between speaking to a union motion and presenting a case to the disciplinary committee. As well as research to support his case, he could prepare himself by checking relevant websites to find out what his rights are in this context. This might also boost his confidence and enable him to act strategically. He can make tactical decisions about his input, using knowledge of the context and the participants, maybe prioritizing certain aspects of his case, 'pressing the right buttons' to make himself heard.

Sean's awareness of the context will help him to understand the structure of the meeting and assess which parts of it are merely formal procedures and which parts require a real contribution. He will be able to decide on content and register appropriate to his audience and adjust this as necessary during the proceedings, in response to their input. A realistic appreciation of the context will allow him to operate more flexibly within it.

Sean spent his childhood in London. This gives him insights into the English education system which he might not have if he had been educated elsewhere. Through his active membership of a trade union, he is also aware of the norms and conventions of formal meetings of this sort. However, if he had not had this broader contextual knowledge, for example of the norms and expected behaviours of the people involved in the interaction, this would be something that could be investigated further in his literacy class.

Other contexts

Sean's experience is a familiar one, an example of a formal interaction in everyday life in which the personal and public domains (in this case family and education) overlap. Many literacy learners communicate formally in other contexts too, for example as learners on vocational courses, or as employees or volunteers working as part of a team. The kinds of speaking and listening they do include giving a presentation and responding to questions, listening to a talk and taking notes or planning a project or event in collaboration with colleagues or peers.

Some of the same skills and strategies are needed for these, including selecting, organizing, synthesizing, interpreting and making strategic or tactical decisions with reference to the context, the other participants and the purpose of the interaction.

Task 7.3

What specific listening and/or speaking skills are needed for the activities below? In what ways are they similar or different to the ones **Sean** needed?

1 Giving a presentation and responding to questions.
2 Listening to a talk and taking notes.
3 Planning a project or event as part of a team.

Comment 7.3

Similarities

There are some skills and strategies that speakers and listeners need for any situation using oral language. **Sean** might have made use of these generic skills and they would also be of use in the contexts listed in the task:

- understanding and making use of the context;
- having a clear purpose which will determine the strategies that are used;
- drawing on knowledge of the genre;
- following or building a sequence of ideas;
- being selective and analytical in terms of content;
- having a critical viewpoint;
- being confident and assertive;
- being aware of the balance of power in the situation;
- using paralinguistic features (body language and voice).

Differences/additional elements

1 Giving a presentation

In a formal presentation a speaker will often use other modes of expression in addition to spoken language and gesture. For example, in a PowerPoint presentation she might use written text, graphics and possibly sound effects.

This has implications for planning, as she will need to think ahead about how to combine spoken words with other elements. There are implications for pace, timing and co-ordination, such as leaving time for listeners to read the words on the screen, or limiting the amount of written text so as not to distract from what she is saying.

A multimodal presentation involves using a wider range of rhetorical strategies, combining the resources of spoken and written words, image and gesture and making them complement and enhance each other.

In vocational and academic settings there are different kinds of presentations. The purpose may be to demonstrate knowledge and understanding of a subject or procedure, rather than to make a case or persuade a group of listeners to adopt a course of action. In this case the presentation is explanatory rather than persuasive and the speaker doesn't have to be tactical in quite the same way as **Sean** did. The criteria for effectiveness would include scope and accuracy of content as well as clarity of expression.

Giving a presentation in an academic context is 'high-stakes' when it is part of a formal assessment for a qualification, or it can be 'low-stakes' when it is an informal practice with classmates. This makes a difference to how the speaker feels, her choice of topic and the kind of preparation she does.

In the case of a formally assessed presentation, the range of possible topics may be prescribed, especially if part of the point is to demonstrate subject knowledge. In this case the presenter will need to prepare the content carefully. She may also decide to do a practice run to ensure that the timing is right and to help overcome 'nerves'.

Preparing for an informal practice with classmates need not be so thorough and the presenter, though she may still feel nervous at the prospect of addressing a group of people, may be able to enjoy it more and can use it as an opportunity to develop new skills and confidence.

2 Listening to a talk

A talk may last for an hour or more. The listener needs to concentrate carefully and maintain that concentration over an extended period. This can be physically and mentally tiring and listeners need to think how they can keep listening actively for this period of time.

The environment may support or hinder listening: there may be noise or distractions from outside; the room might be uncomfortable; it may be difficult to hear the speaker. These can get in the way of concentrating on what the speaker says.

The talk might deal with new and difficult concepts. If the listener does not already have a schema for the subject matter, she would have to build one up. She could prepare for the talk by finding out about the subject beforehand. She could come to the talk with some questions she would like answered; this will help her to listen actively.

If the speaker is skilful, she will signpost the structure of her talk to the audience (this is what I am going to talk about today ... ; there are three main points I want to make – first ...; in summary the point I am making is ...). The teacher could help the learner make effective use of these types of discourse markers.

However, the speaker might be nervous or her talk might lack structure or coherence. It may be that she used specialist or technical vocabulary, long and complex idea units[5]; or that her structure was unclear. Learners need to devise strategies to deal with 'inconsiderate' spoken texts as well as written ones.

Particularly important is whether the speaker has provided any visual aids to assist her audience. If she provides something to look at, such as PowerPoint slides, the learner can use these to orientate herself and see where the talk is leading.

A talk does not usually require a verbal response until after it has finished, but an active listener might be considering throughout the talk what questions are being raised. Note-taking can help concentration and encourage active listening. Because the process of writing notes is slower than the speech of the speaker, it also forces the listener to be selective and pick out the main points. Learners may well find it difficult to listen and write at the same time and learning techniques for effective note-taking is helpful.

3 Planning a project or event as part of a team

When planning a project or event in a group, achieving an agreed final product is complex and challenging because it is a synthesis of different people's ideas.

Far from convincing others of a single point of view, this task is about working together to a common end. The aim of the task is to reach consensus and the group will need to establish a way of working that allows them to do this. The teacher could model tactful and sensitive language to use ('That's a good idea but have you also considered ... ?' 'Can we agree on that before we move on ... ?') and paralinguistic features such as nodding to signal agreement, maintaining eye contact with all members of the group, avoiding confrontational language and gestures.

The team is likely to be made up of learners from diverse backgrounds and varying amounts of experience of this type of task. The group need to be aware of different cultural norms in existence and respond sensitively and inclusively.

Working as part of a team, learners will need to set up a structure for the group, deciding who, if anyone, is to chair the group and how they are going to record their decisions. The group has a responsibility for setting up a workable structure that will help it achieve its ends.

Having looked at different kinds of speaking and listening and the skills and strategies involved, we will end this chapter by suggesting some approaches that can be used by the teacher to develop these skills, followed by a worked example of activities around giving a presentation.

Developing speaking and listening skills

Before listening	Before speaking
• Draw on learners' existing skills; many people who struggle with reading are thoughtful and perceptive listeners; think about how you can use these skills as a resource.	• Draw on learners' existing skills; many people who struggle with writing are fluent and expressive speakers; think about how you can use these skills as a resource.
• Choose a listening text that is relevant, authentic and appropriate. Adults are used to dealing with complex spoken texts, so it doesn't usually have to be simplified – it is the task that needs to be made appropriate for the learners' skill level rather than the text.	• Agree on a speaking task that is relevant, authentic and appropriate. In real life adults use speaking skills in situations that are complex and challenging.
• Activate the learners' schemata by discussion or use of pre-listening activities including predictive and genre recognition tasks.	• Prepare by using pre-speaking activities, including exploring the social context, the relationship between the participants and the topic.
• Agree on the purpose for listening so learners can choose how to approach the spoken text. They need to know the task *before* they start listening so that they can apply the appropriate strategies e.g. listening for gist or listening for specific information.	• Agree on the purpose for speaking; discuss the language and organizational features of this type of speaking (persuasive, explanatory, descriptive, etc.).
• Authentic listening often (but not always) involves watching the speaker as well as listening to her. Valuable support can be derived from non-verbal messages, so don't always use tape recorders – make use of video, DVD, websites such as YouTube (www.youtube.com) and, of course, the resources to hand: yourself and the learners in the room.	• Elicit what makes this kind of speaking effective or not effective: discuss use of language, use of voice and body language. It can be helpful to watch or listen to a model of a speech or interaction, using a video or audio recording.
• Elicit and pre-teach vocabulary that could cause problems or words/phrases that might be used in an unfamiliar way.	• Elicit and pre-teach vocabulary needed for the speaking. Discuss word choice (not just 'big words' but words and phrases that will convey what the speaker wants to say). Give an example of how a new word or phrase is used.
	• Support learners with planning the speaking part of the interaction (using planning tools such as graphic organizers to generate and sequence ideas); this works well in pairs or small groups.

During listening	During speaking
• Keep tasks during listening to a minimum. If you set a task to do while listening, make sure it promotes active listening rather than impedes it.	• Respond to the speaker as a listener, not just an assessor: show interest in the content
• While listening to a recording, make strategic prompts which remind learners of their purpose for listening and encourage them to use strategies related to that purpose.	• During a presentation, if a speaker gets 'stuck', ask exploratory questions, refer back to ideas she expressed earlier in the group; give prompts to help her clarify her ideas; give reassurance.
• Model approaches to listening just as you might model reading strategies. For example, when listening to a broadcast/audiotape, stop it after a section to monitor understanding and point out clues to draw on. ('How many points is the speaker going to make?' 'How do we know this?' 'How does he signal that he is moving on to another subject?')	• When the speaking is part of an interaction, give prompts and suggestions to make it more effective, e.g. ask the learner to rephrase a question in order to get a different kind of answer.
• When using a recording, allow the learners to hear the text several times as this helps to allay anxiety and allows the learners more control over accessing content.	• Allow the learners to have a practice run where appropriate.
• Encourage learners to make notes or record key words or points on a pro forma where appropriate	
• Encourage learners to stop the speaker where appropriate and request clarification or repetition.	• Encourage speakers to notice the reactions of their listeners and check from time to time that they are following.
• Encourage learners to respond to a speaker at appropriate times. This might be while they are listening, rather than waiting till the end.	
• Listening can be tiring – where possible, break long passages into small chunks; give breaks; allow responses; change speakers.	• Address individual difficulties (e.g. a speaker gets lost, forgets the point she was making, can't articulate a word because it's long or difficult to pronounce). Suggest strategies for managing these (e.g. use cue cards, choose a shorter or easier word that means the same thing, take a few minutes to get yourself back on track).

After listening	After speaking
• Literacy learners may well find it hard to listen and write at the same time so they may be more confident completing written tasks after they have finished listening.	• Model constructive feedback: congratulate the people who have spoken; give examples of things you found interesting, informative, well expressed.
• As beginner readers and writers are likely to find reading and writing difficult, try to avoid setting tasks that require extended reading or writing. If you are working on listening, this should be the focus. Use tasks that involve images, diagrams, box ticking, true/false, cloze completion or one-word answers.	• Review the criteria for effectiveness that the group have already agreed; invite those who spoke to evaluate how they did, invite other group members to give constructive feedback; make one suggestion for development and invite other group members to do likewise.
• If you do set questions that need longer answers, perhaps for more confident writers, it is a good idea to give the questions out in advance.	
• Encourage note-taking for stronger writers; notes can be used authentically to write a summary or a review of what has been heard.	
• Not every listening activity needs a written response. Oral activities such as giving opinions and holding discussions are often more relevant, immediate and appropriate.	

Example 7.1

An informal presentation[6]

Learners on a discrete literacy course want to practise presentation skills. They agree that each person will give a one-minute presentation to the group on a subject of her choice. The work on this is spread over three sessions.

Activities

Session 1: Initial discussion and planning

- **Topics**: the kinds of topics people might choose (something they would enjoy telling others about).

- **Skills**: the speaking skills they have already, where they've used them and how they feel about speaking.
- **What makes a good presentation?** Using examples from television such as politicians, TV presenters and sports celebrities, the group produces a list of criteria and the tutor adds her own suggestions.
- **Planning**, using a graphic organizer and/or cue cards.

Session 2: Preparation for presenting and evaluating

- **Review of what makes a good presentation**: the tutor has written ideas, based on the previous session, on sets of cards. Working in pairs, learners categorize them into **do's and don'ts** and the group discusses them, adding any more that they think should be there. Examples could be:
  - ○ look at the ground;
  - ○ mumble;
  - ○ use hand gestures;
  - ○ make eye contact;
  - ○ Look at the audience;
  - ○ take your time;
  - ○ keep talking until you run out of breath.

- **How to link ideas when speaking**: an activity focusing on **sequence markers** (e.g. *first of all, secondly, finally*)
  - ○ review these in the group;
  - ○ listen to a short talk and tick the phrases and linking words that the speaker uses.

- **Evaluation and feedback: preparation**
  - ○ go through the feedback form together, so that learners will be able to record their feedback during the presentations;
  - ○ talk about constructive feedback, what this would involve.

Session 3: During and after the presentations

- **Listening and recording feedback**: each learner has a partner, with whom she gives and receives feedback; she ticks the boxes on the form (*Yes/No/Sometimes*). These are based on criteria agreed earlier e.g.:
  - ○ took your time and didn't rush;
  - ○ made eye contact;
  - ○ appeared nervous;
  - ○ used some sequence words.

- **Self-assessment:** learners generate useful words for self-assessment and each learner completes a self-evaluation form.

- **Feedback** from partner and tutor.
- **Review**: group discussion focusing on:
  - the experience of giving and listening to presentations, including how people might use the knowledge and understanding they gained for another occasion or context;
  - the experience of self-assessment and of giving and receiving feedback.

Further reading and resources

Carter, R. (2004) *Language and Creativity: The Art of Common Talk*. London: Routledge.

Carter, R. and McCarthy, M. (1997) *Exploring Spoken Language*. Cambridge: Cambridge University Press.

See also NIACE website for recent publications by the Basic Skills Agency which focus on speaking and listening: www.niace.org.uk

Notes

1. See for example Smith, N. (2004) *Chomsky: Ideas and Ideals*, 2nd edn. Cambridge: Cambridge University Press.
2. See Carter, R. (2004). *Language and Creativity: The Art of Common Talk*. London: Routledge.
3. See for example Carter, R. and McCarthy, M. (1997) *Exploring Spoken Language*. Cambridge: Cambridge University Press.
4. See Section 2.2 for discussion of cultural variations in discourse conventions. See also Liddicoat, A. and Crozet, C. (eds) (2000) *Teaching Languages, Teaching Cultures*. Melbourne: Language Australia.
5. See Chapter 3.
6. Thanks to Christina Barrett for this activity.

8 Planning and assessment
Jay Derrick and Judith Gawn

In this chapter we look at planning and assessment within adult literacy teaching and learning. The two are very closely connected and we will explore this connection throughout the chapter.

Assessment and planning – principles

Three purposes for assessment

In this section we look at assessment and its implications for planning. Much of what we say here applies to teaching and learning in any subject and in any situation. However, getting the approach to assessment right is even more important for learners with negative previous experiences of education, and with less confidence in themselves as learners. Many adult literacy learners are likely to fall into this group. We start by distinguishing between three types of assessment, based on different purposes, all more or less important in adult literacy learning:

- **summative assessment**: for certification and/or progression;
- **formative assessment**: for planning teaching and learning;
- **formative assessment**: for the development of judgement, self-evaluation and sustainable learning.

Summative assessment: for certification and/or progression

Most people have a 'common-sense' idea that assessment is about exams: indeed, many adult literacy learners may worry about assessment because they associate it with previous experience of failure. They think of tests, or perhaps of written assignments, and of getting grades or marks. They may have experienced their grades or marks being compared publicly with other learners, and may have felt humiliated if they didn't do well. Assessment does have an important role in providing public recognition of achievement; it provides evidence that learners can take to future employers, for example. Many adult literacy learners, while perhaps nervous of failure, are still very keen to gain certificates and qualifications: to help directly with

Humiliating + scary experience. if failure.

*Confidence boost.
Sense of achievement
+ motivation to work
harder still.*

employment, or just to prove to themselves that they can be successful in education. Achieving a certificate for the first time, at any level, can be a powerful factor in improving learners' confidence and motivating them to persist and continue improving their literacy.

This kind of assessment, or 'summative' assessment, often comes at the end of a programme of learning, for example in a test, but it can also take place during courses. Some courses consist of the steady collection by the learner and the tutor of evidence demonstrating the learner's performance against a set of assessment criteria, which the learner builds into a final portfolio. In this case assessment for certification is taking place throughout the course. The evaluation of this evidence, or marking of tests, is usually carried out either independently or by the tutor whose marking is then moderated internally and externally. The learner's own view about how she has done and what she has learned is rarely taken into account. Summative assessment is sometimes referred to as **assessment *of* learning**. In England and Wales, though not in many other countries, the results of this kind of assessment are numerically aggregated and used to determine funding, and to compare the performance of teachers, provider organizations, regions, and even countries.

*Tutor marking
moderated internally
+ Externally*

Formative assessment: for planning teaching and learning

Alongside its important role in certificating learning, assessment has other critical roles. In its second key role, assessment is the main means by which teachers find out, and keep revising, what needs to be taught. Assessment for planning, teaching and learning starts at the very beginning of the course, or even before it, in processes known as screening, initial assessment and diagnostic assessment. These will be discussed later in the chapter, but for now we will just note that their purpose is to find out about the learners' abilities and dispositions at the outset. Any information about new adult literacy learners can be crucial in helping them to learn successfully. Assessment here includes not just finding out about how fluent they are with spelling or punctuation but also, for example, about what their schooling was like and how they feel about it.

Assessment for planning, teaching and learning, starting right at the beginning of a course, needs to continue all the way through, so that the teacher can constantly update his information about the development of learners. He needs to adjust the teaching plan accordingly, both on a moment-by-moment basis and from lesson to lesson. This type of assessment aims to improve teaching and learning by continually increasing the accuracy of its focus. It concerns not just what happens within the course but events and episodes in the learners' lives outside the course and the influence they may have on learning. The key activity is *dialogue* between the learner and teacher. The teacher's role is to enable, stimulate and develop this dialogue through constructive and open-ended questioning, and through generating thinking and reflection about learning. Again, we will look at this in more detail later in this chapter.

flexibility

Teacher's role.

Formative assessment: for the development of judgement, self-evaluation and sustainable learning

[handwritten margin note: Judgement]

The third type of assessment activity adds a critical dimension to learning, as something which, *when practised by learners themselves,* is concerned with the development and exercise of judgement: judgement of performance, appropriateness, accuracy and authenticity. It is through these activities that learners develop their capacity to make critical, aesthetic and practical judgements of the quality and effectiveness of their literacy activities. If they are not encouraged to practise these skills as part of their literacy learning, the skills they learn will be decontextualized and more difficult to transfer between different situations. Learners will be less aware of the importance of using differentiated literacy practices in different social settings, and less able in relatively unfamiliar situations to gauge how to interact successfully in their use of language.

The focus of this type of assessment is on successful performance, which is usually largely a matter of personal judgement or opinion. We can compare this to the kind of judgements people make when they are talking about the quality of performance of a play or a music concert. These mostly reflect the personal preferences of those involved. People may justify their opinions by referring to various norms or rules, but these too may be rejected by others in favour of another set of norms and different rules. Similarly, any use of language in real-life situations tends to be evaluated immediately and intuitively by the people involved in the exchange.

It follows that it is vital that literacy learners are given support in developing their fluency and confidence in using language in a wide range of situations, and in developing the ability to monitor and evaluate their own language use. This fluency can only be developed through practice. Literacy classes need to provide learners with relevant conceptual tools, and practical collaborative experience of making, exchanging and discussing judgements of the quality of literacy work. There are examples of activities that promote critical reading in Chapter 5.

Language use is not simply a matter of speaking, reading or writing correctly. It is, in practice, a matter of interaction, negotiation, intuition and empathy, and includes such forms as irony, dishonesty and dramatic impersonation as well as openness and authenticity. Literacy learners need support in developing fluency, confidence and discrimination in their use of language in all its forms. Otherwise, although they may gain useful qualifications, they may not have improved their literacy *in practice*. This type of assessment focuses on 'sustainable learning' oriented towards the future (Boud 2000). It implies that the teacher's role is more like a facilitator or mentor. We will look at how teachers can play this role in practice later on.

The second and third types of formative assessment distinguished above are often called **assessment *for* learning** (ARG 2002). Each calls for a high level of rich, interactive, two-way communication between learners themselves and between learners and teachers. While there are important differences between assessment *of* learning and assessment *for* learning, both are important for adult literacy learners.

There is an important link between both formative and summative assessment, and the motivation and persistence of learners (Ward and Edwards 2002). Teachers need to have a clear understanding of the differences between them and use this to inform their lesson plans and schemes of work.

The role of formative assessment

Assessment is often looked at as a process starting with initial and diagnostic assessment, moving through **on-course** assessment and finishing with summative assessment. Although this sounds like common sense, it can lead to confusion about the different purposes of assessment mentioned above. For example **formative assessment** is sometimes confused with **continuous assessment**, in which assessment for certification and/or progression is spread throughout the learning programme rather than just at the end.

There is powerful evidence from school-based research that in **high-stakes** systems (where the formal outcomes of learning are used for funding, performance management purposes and league tables), teachers do not pay sufficient attention to formative assessment as they are over-focused on grades and 'getting the learners through the test' (see for example Black and Wiliam 1998). The research found that shifting the focus to formative assessment developed broader and deeper learning and markedly improved achievement and the longer term capacity and motivation of learners. This research is now being replicated in the post-compulsory sector (Derrick *et al.* 2007, 2008). Importantly for adult literacy teachers, these results apply more strongly to learners with less confidence and success in previous education and training.

This chapter aims to support teachers in providing the most effective and sustainable learning for their learners: this requires them to keep in mind at all times the different roles of assessment in learning and the three different types of assessment. *The essential ingredient of effective learning is continuous interaction and dialogue with learners about the processes of learning.* There are three practical benefits of this approach: first it recognizes the status of the learners as adults and enables them to use and express their accumulated experience and knowledge for the benefit of everyone in the group. Secondly, it is through extended dialogue with the learners themselves that the teacher can best discover how to differentiate the learning programme so that the diversity of needs and purposes amongst learners can be addressed. Thirdly, dialogue enables teachers to orient the learning programme towards the particular everyday tasks each group of learners is most concerned with. This can lead to increasing the learners' understanding of their own learning processes, help them connect their learning with what they do outside the classroom and build their capacity for self-assessment and independence.

In the rest of this chapter we consider:

- the teaching and learning cycle;
- planning and record keeping;
- screening and initial assessment;

- integrating formative assessment with teaching and learning;
- feedback and marking; and
- summative assessment (including the formative uses of tests).

We include case studies and tasks to illustrate the discussion.

The teaching and learning cycle

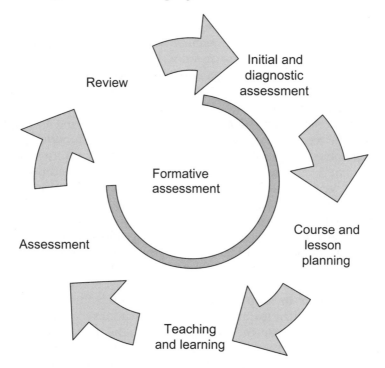

The teaching and learning cycle above shows the stages of teaching and learning, and how assessment informs planning. In practice, the cycle involves a complex inter-weaving of the two. Planning is inevitably influenced by external factors such as funding, government guidance on policy and the needs of local circumstances. It will also naturally take into account the demands of any accreditation being offered. However, the key starting point of the planning process is initial assessment, and it continues to be informed by ongoing assessment of learners' progress, or formative assessment. The final outcomes and achievements (summative assessment) of learners in a particular group will inform planning for the next group or stage of learning.

First contact, screening and initial assessment

Screening usually refers to the identification of a literacy need. It may result in signposting to provision or advice about an appropriate course. This may occur during initial contact with a prospective learner, either in conversation or by information given on an application form. The first person a new learner speaks to when they make an enquiry about learning has a crucial role to play here as their attitudes and welcome can make a significant difference to the confidence of learners, who may easily be discouraged.

The purpose of **initial assessment** is to begin to build up a picture of the learner, his literacy needs, abilities and short- and long-term goals. Many paper and online assessments give a very limited insight into learners' strengths and areas for development. Whether or not teachers use tests, initial assessment can also be an opportunity to establish some essential information through a one-to-one conversation. Learners need to understand the reasons they are being asked particular questions and how that relates to their future learning. (The focus of discussion at this stage should always be on what people *can* do rather than what they can't.) For the teacher, it is an opportunity to clarify the learner's beliefs and feelings about learning and about his expectations of a good teacher. It is critical that the teacher has an understanding of the learner's likely responses to particular pedagogical approaches or learning activities (Belzer 2004). For example, learners who feel strongly that learning is a matter of individual practice, involving silent concentration and hard work, may feel that classroom discussion is a waste of their limited time with the teacher. The initial assessment process needs to establish:

- what the potential learner wants to do and why;
- information about her previous educational experiences;
- some information about her previous achievement and skills;
- how the learner likes to learn;
- mother tongue and/or variety of English language used;
- an indication of what her current strengths are;
- an indication of some areas for development;
- issues which may affect her learning, e.g. health problems, dyslexia, work/personal commitments;
- any longer term goals;
- availability and time constraints;
- an indication of additional support needs.

It is important also to explain to learners why they are being asked to complete initial assessment tasks and how the information gained will be used to help plan future learning with them.

Task 8.1

Initial assessment in your organization

- What is the initial assessment process in your organization?
- Using the criteria above, consider how effective it is?
- What suggestions, if any, would you make for improvement?

Diagnostic assessment

The aim of diagnostic assessment is to draw up an in-depth profile of the learner's strengths and areas for development. As in initial assessment, there are plenty of online and paper-based assessment materials and toolkits to draw on, but teachers need to ensure that they are appropriate for the learners and provide all the information required for effective planning. Sitting a learner down with a form or in front of a screen will not be sufficient as it won't uncover *why* the learner finds it difficult to structure sentences or understand what they have read. Diagnostic assessment requires skill in identifying why people are making 'mistakes', rather than just identifying what those mistakes are. It means assessing the learner's level of competence in, for example, constructing and deconstructing words, or their familiarity with a range of texts and how language works in formal and informal registers. It also requires an awareness of the social and cultural dimensions of the uses of literacy – how people use reading and writing in their everyday lives – in order to contextualize the learner's own use of language. (There is an example of detailed diagnostic assessment in Chapter 3.)

The diagnostic assessment process is also an opportunity to discuss with learners the strategies they use round literacy, their preferences in relation to their own learning and their purposes and their motivation for coming. Jane Mace argues for the importance of this kind of dialogue with learners, including discussing their previous experiences of schooling and assessment. Only from such a dialogue can the teacher fully understand the motivation, the ability to engage in formal learning and the formation of their attitudes and ideas about assessment and perceptions of 'success' (Mace 1979). Considerable skills, knowledge and empathy are needed in order to analyse the information gathered and then to set relevant and realistic learning goals with the learner. As a result of diagnostic assessment, teachers should be able to build up a profile of individual learners in a group.

Planning

Planning is an essential part of any teacher's work. One of the primary purposes of assessment and evaluation is to support ongoing planning by suggesting directions for change (Rogers 2002). Effective teachers change and develop their plans based on evidence derived from learners from the initial assessment process and formative assessment of their ongoing learning and progress. This also allows the teacher to differentiate plans to suit individual learners. The skill of the teacher is in planning for the whole group whilst addressing the needs of individuals.

Course planning

A scheme of work provides an overview of learning activities over a specified period of time, but this does not mean that it should be set in stone and never veered away from. Teachers working within an externally accredited system have a difficult balancing act – to support learners to make progress towards the intended outcomes as well as any other learning objectives individual learners may have.

The adult literacy scheme of work is likely to include:

- the formal outcomes the course is defined as covering;
- any other learning objectives the learners may have;
- the content to be covered (topics);
- how skills, knowledge and understanding will be addressed (teaching methods, resources and activities);
- how individual learning needs will be met (differentiated strategies and preferred modes of learning);
- the context for learning (may affect the content, e.g. workplace, family learning);
- the assessment processes.

Schemes of work clearly have an administrative role, but it is important that teachers use them as working documents, which change as a result of the development of the skills and motivation of the learners during the course.

Developing a scheme of work

A tutor drew up a draft ten-week scheme of work for an Entry Level 2[1] literacy group at the beginning of Term 1. The scheme focused on skills development in reading and writing. The tutor did not plan to work explicitly on speaking and listening skills at this point in the course, though of course she fully intended to encourage discussion and sharing of ideas in the group.

The draft scheme of work was informed by the limited information she had gleaned from initial assessment, which gave only a partial overview of individuals' strengths and areas for development and provided no information about their interests and priorities. From Week 3 onwards the tutor amended her scheme in order to respond to the group's interest in reading children's books (they were all parents or grandparents and wanted to be able to read to young children). She also built into the new scheme a stronger focus on particular skills in order to address gaps in understanding which she had gathered from observation, discussion and feedback from learners. Ongoing assessment allowed her to make further adaptations.

From discovering more about the learners' lives and interests, she continued to note topics and themes to provide new contexts for skills development, some of which would inform the scheme of work for Term 2. She had the opportunity to use ICT facilities and as the learners expressed a keen interest, she began to build this into her scheme to support learning. The teacher used ongoing assessment and negotiation with learners to inform teaching and planning in an integrated way.

Her revised scheme of work is shown below. It is not intended as a model in terms of its format, headings or the amount of space devoted to each aspect. There are many different ways of drawing up a scheme of work and every institution has its own procedures that teachers are asked to follow. What is important is that course planning is an organic and responsive process, in which the tutor amends her plans in the light of her growing understanding of learners' interests, abilities and priorities for learning.

Note on terminology

Course aims

These are broad, long-term, developmental aims, encompassing knowledge, understanding and skills that the learners are working towards during the course. They can also include 'soft' outcomes such as confidence, for example the confidence to read a story aloud to a child or to write a letter to the school.

Lesson aims

These are what the tutor wants learners to achieve in one lesson.

Lesson objectives

These are statements of specific things that the learners should be able to do by the end of the session, and which will provide evidence of new knowledge, understanding and skills.

Example 8.1

Scheme of work

Group: Entry Level 2 – Adult Literacy (10 weeks)

Course aims

For learners to develop:

- clarity about their own learning goals;
- increased confidence, especially for reading and speaking in a group;
- skills and strategies for reading children's stories, including reading aloud;
- awareness of differences between writing and speaking;
- strategies for spelling.

Week	Content	Curriculum ref.	Lesson objectives	Tutor comments
1	Welcome/New enrolments/Induction activities/Introduction to the course			
2	Agreement on topics and themes for learning. Introduction to reading – what do we read, why do we read it, what do we want to be able to read?	Rt/E2.2	Identify some purposes for reading.	Topics of interest: helping children to read finding out more about the local area. Group goals agreed.
3	Review of purposes for reading. Reading – becoming familiar with different text types. Choose one text type to focus on; paired reading of chosen text. Oral questioning on comprehension of text.	Rt/E2.2 Rt/E2.1	Recognize different purposes of texts. Gain meaning from chosen text.	Implement personal reading programme, learners to choose and review texts for children. Identify individual goals on ILPs. Organize visit to children's library.

4	Learners to bring in a children's book from home. Strategies for comprehending text (prediction; text features, vocabulary). Read books (or excerpts) to each other in small groups. Discuss strategies for reading aloud to children. Prepare for visit to library.	Rt/E2.1 Rt/E2.4 Rs/E2.3	Read and understand a text written for children. Use pictures in text to contribute to interpretation. Identify strategies for reading aloud to a child.	Need regular focus on spelling strategies – weekly review. Learners to build own word banks.
5	Visit to library. Set tasks to help learners choose appropriate books for their child(ren). Each learner to choose one book to focus on. Small presentation where each learner explains why she chose a certain book.	Rt/E2.3 SLc/E2.3	Use strategies to select appropriate books for reader. Give short presentation to their peers on reasons for choosing a book.	Learners building up collection of stories they like – explore telling own story onto tape? S, L, M and G found it hard to find books – need to work on alphabetical order. Build in more structured work on presentations. Another visit next term? Museum?
6	Share chosen book (use big book so all can see it or scan and project book). Apply reading strategies. Discuss what makes a good story. Work on spellings from text – apply strategies.	Rt/E2.1 Rt/E2.4 Rs/E2.3 Ww/E2.2	Gain meaning from narrative text. Identify a range of strategies for dealing with comprehension breakdown. Apply strategies for learning spelling to key words.	More work on decoding strategies next term, particularly for learners D, J and S.
7	Revise what makes a good story (for children). Think of a story and practise telling it to a partner. Paired feedback. Tape each learner telling a story for their children.	SLc/E2.1 SLc/E2.3 SLlr/E2.6	Relate a story suitable for a child to listen to. Listen and respond to story and offer constructive feedback .	Build in ICT time, for writing activities. Copy onto separate tapes for each learner (and use for *as evidence for* S+L assessment).

8	Play back tapes from last week. Decide what might need changing for a written version of the story. Discussion about the writing process. Draft story. Spelling strategies for chosen words from story drafts.	SLlr/E2.1 Wt/E.2.1 Ww/E2.2	Listen to oral stories and identify differences between oral and written stories. Make a first draft of a written version of story. Apply strategies for learning spelling to key words.	Bring copies of tapes so that they can take home and play to their children. D and S word processing their writing – make more of a feature of ICT next term?
9	Elicit criteria for a good written story. Learners use these criteria for revision of drafts. Final proofreading. Choose images to go with stories.	Wt/E2.1 Ws/E2.3 Ws/E2.4 Wt/E2.1	Revise draft of short text. Proofread writing to identify and correct errors. Link an appropriate image to text.	Transcripts of tapes contributed to writing – focus on language use, particularly on adjectives and verbs. Produce photocopies of each story for each learner in group and copies of tapes so that they can take home and play to their children.
10	Revise techniques for reading aloud. Practise reading aloud with fluency. Each learner reads aloud their story; other learners in group read along. Review of work covered and evaluation of term. Planning for Term 2.	Rt/E2.1	Read aloud a short text with enough fluency to enable others to follow.	Pictures make big difference to comprehension of stories – develop further next term?

Lesson planning

An effective lesson plan should also be a working document and a guide, rather than a straitjacket. There needs to be a cyclical element to planning so that sessions are structured coherently to build in review, recap and forward planning in a way that is clear to learners.

There is plenty of material elsewhere on lesson planning, so below is a brief guide to an effective plan for an adult literacy class.

A lesson plan will normally include:

- aims and objectives for the session;
- teaching and learning activities and resources;
- assessment approaches;
- post-session notes reviewing the session and follow-up for individuals.

Lesson objectives

In setting out the objectives for the session, it's useful to consider whether all learners will be able to achieve the objective to the same degree and develop differentiated objectives to meet the needs of individual learners.

Teaching and learning activities and resources

A session plan includes a detailed breakdown of activities and resources. An effective plan includes a good variety of methods, for individual and group work, and opportunities for peer and individual reflection and dialogue with the teacher. The plan should indicate where activities are differentiated for different learners.

Assessment

The plan will show how assessment is built into activities at each stage – and not simply focus on an end product.

Review

Effective sessions will include recap and review, both of the previous session and the current session. These need to be more than just routine exercises, checking, for example, whether learners remember the last session's topic. They should provide meaningful opportunities to check learner's understanding of and feelings about sessions, as well as being an opportunity to reinforce important learning points. Reviews are a source of evidence to support planning for future sessions. The session plan itself needs sufficient space for the tutor to write her own review, and notes on individual progress. Pre-set formats adopted by the whole organization may not have sufficient space to record the results of detailed observations or one-to-one conversations with learners, so literacy teachers should be willing to adapt these appropriately.

Example 8.2

Lesson plan

Note: This session is taken from a different scheme of work to the example above.

Adult Literacy Group: Entry Level 2
Date: 24 March   Time: 10.30–12.30   Room 23

Aims of session
For learners to write a simple set of directions using a London tube map.

Learning objectives at completion of lesson:
Less confident learners will

- find a simple route on the tube map;
- use a grid to find a station on the map;
- scan the index for underground stations using alphabetical order;
- use the imperative form to write a simple instruction.

More confident learners will also be able to

- find routes on the tube map using several tube lines;
- use the terms 'key' 'grids' and 'coordinates';
- use the imperative form to write more complex directions.

Time	Content	Learner groupings	Tutor activities (incl. assessment)	Curriculum Ref:
				Rt/E2.2
				Rw/E3.5
				Rw/E2.5
				Ws/E3.1
				Resources
2.00	Introduction + discussion to recap alphabetical order. Why is alphabetical order used? Where do we find things in alphabetical order?	Whole group discussion.	Elicit and provide prompt questions.	Record answers on board.

2.10	Recap: What do we know about alphabetical order? Whole class: quiz.	Whole group. Individual – 2 versions/pair checking.	Elicit understanding, prompt questions. Monitor, encourage sts to check answers.	Whiteboard. Worksheets.
2.30	Introduction to Tube maps. How many people travel by tube? What are difficulties in reading tube maps?	Whole group learners work in pairs to discuss.	Elicit, listen. Monitor pair discussions, support use of internet.	Enlarged tube maps. Internet: online maps.
3.00	Grids and co-ordinates.	Whole group – agree correct co-ordinates on board. Small group – agree and mark correct co-ordinates on task sheet.	Elicit, explain, observe, directed questions, check answers and encourage small group checking.	Enlarged map on board. Task sheets.
3.20	Use underground maps, introduce index, remind learners of alphabetical order.	Learners work in pairs to identify simple routes by tube.	Monitor, observe, check answers, encourage pair checking.	Worksheet: how do you get from—to—? (Extension exercises with more complex routes for quicker learners).

4.00	Writing directions. Look at language of directions: Point out sentences that start with imperative form – *Change at ..., Take the ... Get on at ...*	In small groups, learners write directions to get from (a) to (b).	Write starting phrases on board. Monitor, observe, listen, support.	Differentiated worksheets with simple and more complex scenarios needing directions.
4.20	Recap and review of session.	Whole group.	What helped? New learning points? What needs to be followed up?	
4.25	Homework: use same worksheet to plan another tube journey.	Whole group.	Explain task, check everyone clear.	Worksheet: How do you get from — to —?

Review of session:

Large maps were good for learners with poor eyesight. Pairs worked well and were evenly balanced – learners worked together and supported those with less experience of using maps. Need recap on terms such as northbound, southbound and on reading of unfamiliar place names. Provide simplified map with fewer tube lines for less confident readers. Use of internet worked well but too brief. Follow-up on using online maps and getting information from Transport for London website. However, learners found looking at different maps of London interesting.

Individual follow-up:

Need extension activities for learners P, J and D.
Prepositional practice to support sentence structure for A and S.

Task 8.2

Staging a lesson

Staging is an important aspect of lesson planning. Having designed activities that will enable learners to achieve the aims of the lesson, the tutor must sequence the activities in a way that allows learners to develop their skills incrementally. In other words, each activity should be a step towards achieving the overall aim.

- How has the tutor staged the learning in the sample lesson above?
- How do you think this would help learners build their knowledge, understanding and skills incrementally?

Comment 8.2

In this session, in order to achieve the aim of writing directions for a tube journey, learners needed to be able to: find the names of stations in an alphabetical index; locate these stations on a tube map using a grid; and write directions using the imperative form of the verb.

The tutor began by reviewing alphabetical order, discussing where and why it is used, and enabling learners to consolidate skills they had learned in a previous lesson. She then introduced the tube map, once again beginning with the wider context and inviting learners to discuss their own experiences before identifying specific difficulties with map reading. This led naturally to a focus on grids, as this was the aspect of map reading that was likely to be unfamiliar and pose a challenge to learners. The next activity provided practice in using grids, more specifically the skill of using coordinates to find a particular location. Learners then applied this skill to finding tube stations and working out routes between them. Finally, before asking students to write directions, the tutor illustrated the particular form of the verb they would need, to ensure that they were equipped for the task. So the lesson was carefully staged to equip learners for tasks at each stage of the process.

However, as she noted in her evaluation, the tutor did underestimate some of the knowledge and skills needed for these activities, including the meaning of 'northbound' and 'southbound', the skill of decoding unknown words and, for a small group of bilingual learners, the use of prepositions in sentences. Her evaluation was thorough, based on close monitoring of how people learned and the difficulties they encountered, and she planned to address these issues in the next lesson.

Recording teaching and learning

The recording of learning is all too often little more than a paper exercise designed to meet the requirements of funding and inspection regimes. The bodies that provide funding for provision and those that monitor quality obviously need to know that money is being spent well and therefore require evidence of effective practice. However, a system that is driven solely by such requirements can all too often lead to these processes being implemented in a bureaucratic way rather than based on the needs of learners. The processes of recording learning must be underpinned by sound pedagogical considerations and informed by the ongoing dialogue with learners that we have already referred to.

Individual Learning Plans (ILPs), Individual Training Plans (ITPs), Work Records – call them what you will – have caused an enormous amount of debate and anguish since their introduction in England in the late 1990s. Seen as time-consuming and pointless by some teachers, they are valued by others as a vital tool for planning and recording progress. At the bottom line, this record of learning needs to be a real working document with a clear benefit to both learner and teacher. If possible, the learner should have a copy. But in any case, the learner needs to have a real sense of 'ownership' of this document. It is useful if the ILP has space to record discussions with learners about their progress, rather than being a simple checklist of skills or tasks to be achieved. However, the format of the document is much less important than the process.

Later in this chapter we will discus how self-assessment is a crucial dimension to learning. Discussions around the ILP are a prime opportunity to enable learners to practise making judgements about the quality and effectiveness of their literacy activities.

Learners in adult literacy classes are often encouraged to keep a record of what they have done or what they have learnt in each session. Whilst it is useful for learners to reflect on the session, this activity can involve learners simply copying from the board what the teacher has written or ticking a box to indicate whether they have completed a particular piece of work or need to do more. A more useful exercise might be to encourage learners to talk or write about specific aspects of the session. For example:

- What do you know now that you didn't know at the beginning of the session (or part of the session)?
- What can you do now that you couldn't do at the beginning of the session?
- What was the most interesting thing about what you have read today? Why?
- Tell the person next to you about ... / how to ....

Providing a variety of questions or ways of encouraging learners to think about learning can reduce the likelihood of this becoming routine and help learners to build up a repertoire of modes of reflection.

Example 8.3:

Learner record sheet

> **At the start of the class**
>
> Today's topic/skill:
> _____
>
> What does this mean to you? What do you already know?
> Even if you're not sure, try to think what it might mean.
> _____
> _____
> _____
> _____

> **At the end of the class**
>
> What have you learned, understood or worked out since we started the lesson?
> _____
> _____
> _____
> _____
> _____
>
> What more work would you like on this topic/skill?
> _____
> _____

Integrating formative assessment into teaching and learning

Dialogue and discussion

Alexander (2004), writing about the education of children, argues that learning is a process in which teachers and learners are interactive participants. He characterizes **dialogic teaching** as collective, reciprocal, supportive, cumulative and purposeful. In dialogic teaching, knowledge is open to discussion rather than given and closed. This is a view also held by Freire (1972), who wrote of liberating education as consisting of shared acts of cognition. Through problem-posing and dialogue be-tween learners and teachers, the world is recreated and unequal power relations addressed.

Teaching and learning through dialogue sees the development of knowledge and understanding, as a process. This dialogue is important not just between teacher and learners but between learners themselves. It assumes that responsibility for the development of learners' knowledge, skills and understanding does not rest only with the teacher.

In a class based on dialogue, learning is structured as far as possible around discussion between teachers and learners and between learners. Talk is open-ended and exploratory, rather than a series of routine exchanges and simple encouragement. It is organized so as to encourage reflection, supporting learners to develop their confidence and autonomy and to see themselves as planners and architects of their own learning. Learning itself and how that is evaluated are explicit topics for regular discussion focusing on how people learn, remember and approach difficult areas.

Task 8.3

Dialogue through a reflective diary

Tutor M is working with a group of Level 1 literacy learners in an inner-city adult education college. Because it is an evening class there is minimal time for lengthy conversations on a one-to-one basis. M wanted to set up a conversation with her learners that would involve them in the process of learning and make planning and teaching more learner-centred.

Her intervention has been to implement a 'reflective diary' – this works as both a mode of communication about how the learners feel about their learning as well as a tool for working on writing skills. The questions in the diary change regularly so that M can focus on particular activities or skills. She then replies in writing to their comments and uses what she has learnt about their interests and level of skills to plan her future sessions. Learners have all written something about how they like to work in the classroom. The learners themselves asked M to use diaries to correct their mistakes.

What teacher M said

> It has helped us to grow as a group. It was not received particularly positively at first, but it started a conversation that has grown. The main reticence is that at first they didn't know what to write. But it has encouraged the learners to reflect on their learning, to think about what they want to do, to think about who they are and where they want to go. I thought it would help with planning and focusing on what they wanted to learn, but in fact it has meant a lot more than that. It has helped me to create activities that I know they will be interested in and will suit their personalities, ways of working.
>
> In future I would like the learners to be more active participants in deciding what should go into the diary. I would like to involve them more in the creation of it.

Suggested activities

Discuss this idea with at least one other teacher.

- In what ways could a diary like this help the teacher to understand more about her learners' learning?
- What might be the difficulties in implementing this activity and what could be done to overcome them?
- How could learners become more active participants in the creation of a diary?

Questioning

Research on effective formative assessment in schools (e.g. Black *et al.* 2003) has demonstrated that effective questioning is a key formative strategy. Asking the right questions can help learners to explore ideas and solve problems rather than just coming up with 'right' answers, and it also models for learners how to formulate questions for themselves.

It is always useful to develop a repertoire of questioning techniques. Hodgen and Wiliam (2006) recommend that teachers share, talk about and reflect upon questioning with other teachers. In research with teachers they found this 'to be a very valuable way of increasing their repertoire of questions and their ability to use these questions in the classroom'.

It is important for teachers to avoid leading questions, rhetorical questions and closed questions as these all discourage learners from reflection or from revealing a lack of understanding. Questions that require learners to find their own words are much more useful:

Why did you decide to put a full stop/comma there?

What do you think happens next in this story?

What do you like about your piece of writing?

What parts did you find hard?

Adult literacy teachers who use these sorts of questions will discover more about their learners' knowledge of how language works and gain a greater understanding of how they are approaching the literacy tasks. In addition, expressing their ideas and listening to others will provide learners with opportunities to develop those skills at the same time. This is another example of learning and assessment being effectively the same thing.

Questioning is a complex process and there are no easy answers about how best to respond 'in the moment' to learners' ideas and questions.

Example 8.4

Using formative questioning with a group of Entry 2/Entry 3 literacy learners

The teacher is helping the learners prepare for the tests they will be taking at the end of the term. Most of them have already completed a practice paper, which involved planning, drafting, editing and rewriting a short informal text.

Tutor: Ok, last week we did a practice paper for the test you're going to do in a few weeks' time. How did you feel that went?

Student 1: I didn't think I did very well.

Student 2: It was hard, but I think I did OK.

Student 3: It wasn't as bad as I thought it was going to be.

Student 4: No, I felt nervous, I didn't really like it.

Tutor: Well, what I'm going to do is give you back the papers I have marked and I'd like you to go through them and decide what you've done well on and where you need to do some more work. I suggest you work in pairs. D, can you move and sit with P? How about if you two (S and K) work together and J, you join them – I know you haven't done the practice test, but have a look and see if you'd like to try doing it.

(Tutor hands back the practice tests and goes to sit with two of the pairs.)

Tutor: Well, how do you think you did now you've had a look at the paper?

Student 1: Well, I still think I didn't do very well, but I can see I did alright on this (the planning).

Tutor: You did do well – and did it help you to think about what you wanted to write?

Student 3: It's difficult to know what to write – the spidergram helped me.

Tutor: How did the spidergram help you?

Student 3: Well, it made me think about the different points I wanted to make and then I used a new paragraph for each point.

Student 4: I didn't really write much on the spidergram.

Tutor: K (S3) – can you explain to P (S4) how you used the spidergram, what you did?

Student 3 (showing her spidergram to S4): See this is what I did: I put something at the end of each leg – the place, the journey, the weather, the food, then it made me think about starting a new paragraph for each idea.

Tutor: Do you think that would help, P?

Student 4: Yes, I think that's a good idea because I didn't have any new paragraphs, it's just one.

Student 5: It's important to read what it says you have to do – it's worth taking the time to read it carefully. Because it tells you at the top of each page what you have to do.

Tutor: What do you think, P?

Student 5: Yes, I didn't really read it; I just started writing. I didn't really plan what I was going to write.

Student 1: I did the planning, that was OK, but then it was changing what I'd written; I didn't know what to change.

Tutor: Well, what did you want to change? What are you looking for?

Student 13: Spelling – the right spelling.

Student 3: And if it's in the past, what is it – the right tense?

Student 5: It's hard not having any lines on the paper, my writing went down like this, look ...

Tutor (turning to the groups): Has anybody else had that difficulty, of not being able to write on a straight line? (Nods and assent) Anybody got any suggestions what we can do about that in future?

Student 6: How about if we use one of those sheets like you get with letter paper, with thick lines on, and put it underneath, that might help.

Tutor: Great – that's a brilliant idea. I'll make sure I get some for next time.

Building in self- and peer-assessment activities

In assessment for learning, developing self- and peer-assessment activities ise central. This requires the adult literacy teacher to construct a safe learning environment where learners feel comfortable with each other and confident about taking some risks. This can be difficult with learners who may have received their earlier education in traditional settings where learners are expected to be passive and to see the teacher's judgement as paramount. It can take time for some learners to feel comfortable with the processes of self- and peer-assessment, but with careful preparation learners at any level can benefit from being involved in these activities. One of the case studies below suggests how this can be organized.

Activities that encourage self- and peer-assessment include:

- paired reading;
- paired or small group discussions on ideas for writing;
- exchanging drafts for comments;
- setting each other spelling tests.

Learners need to be supported to understand the processes of assessment and the criteria on which it is based. For many learners the language of assessment can seem highly technical and inaccessible. If teachers encourage pairs and groups of learners to discuss and agree upon their own criteria for assessment, and then apply them to their own work and that of others, this can help them understand and put into perspective the status of the official criteria. This promotes an essential part of learning – to be able to evaluate their own performance in real-life situations without the support of the teacher.

Example 8.5

Self- and peer-assessment

This case study is based on Example 7.1 in Chapter 7, which looks at a short series of lessons on giving an informal presentation.

Ruth is a teacher working with a group of eight literacy learners in an inner-city further education college. There are varying degrees of confidence in the group. Some learners are relaxed about participating in group activities, while others find it difficult to speak to the group as a whole and tend to speak only to the teacher in one-to-one situations, or when asked a direct question.

Ruth wants to incorporate simple self- and peer-assessment activities into learning activities and she decides to build these around learners making short spoken presentations to the group, as this is something they have said they would like to do. In particular, she wants learners to evaluate their own and each other's presentations.

A principle that underpins Ruth's approach is that adult learners, through their experience of everyday life, have already developed the speaking skills needed for many different contexts. They may not be aware of these skills and some of them will be more effective speakers than others. However, she hopes that, by reviewing the situations where they already speak effectively, and by practising a new kind of speaking in a supportive group environment, they will become more confident about speaking in a wider range of contexts.

The activities are planned to take place over three sessions, so that people get used to the ideas and to working in a group. Ruth is careful to ensure that each member of the group is involved in the activities, though this is difficult at times. If someone feels unable to speak to the whole group, she asks them to work with a partner at first.

Ruth discusses the aims of the three sessions with learners and the new skills they will be working on, including the skills of self- and peer-assessment. She emphasizes that the activity is meant to be constructive and supportive.

She focuses first on the speaking skills learners already have and moves on to a discussion of what makes a good presentation. The group produces a list of criteria for a successful presentation. In the second and third sessions, learners review the criteria and use them to evaluate their own and others' performance.

The tutor spends significant amounts of time on this process of learners devising their own assessment criteria. At times it is a struggle, as one or two of the learners are not used to being in this role. But even if the process doesn't go perfectly at all times, overall it does result in learners taking responsibility for, and having ownership of, their learning in a way that they have never done before. It also helps less confident learners to participate more confidently, which Ruth sees as a crucial learning objective:

> Presenting, discussing or even implementing imperfect strategies can be of great value as it forces the learners to identify the criteria by which to plan and judge future assessments. How often does a teaching strategy work absolutely perfectly?

The planning and preparation of the learners' presentations is another stage of this extended process. Ruth offers them various forms of 'scaffolding' and allows time for revisions and reworking. Some work on individual presentations, and others do them in pairs.

The learners' actual presentations are followed by the self- and peer-assessment stage. This starts with group discussion, followed by individual learners making their personal assessments. The teacher organizes simple record sheets on which learners assess their own performance and that of their peers against the criteria already agreed by the group. They use a very simple classification system: the point is not the actual results as much as the practical learning fostered by the process. She then adds her own assessments. The differences between these three distinct assessments are then discussed. Most learners find that they have assessed themselves at a lower level than their peers' assessments of them.

Ruth's conclusions are that:

> The learner input appears to lead to increased motivation. It's easy, when working with learners at this level of literacy, to forget that they are sophisticated, thinking people. The focus on trust and respect worked: at the beginning of the year some of them wouldn't listen to each other, but now they are all happily doing self- and peer-assessment. It doesn't all work perfectly every time, but I now make this kind of activity a central element of my teaching strategy. The fact that they are 'low-level' learners only means that my preparation has to be more careful, not that they can't do it.

Feedback and marking

> Action without feedback is completely unproductive for the learner.
>
> (Laurillard 1997: 61)

Oral and written feedback is a key part of the interactive dialogue that goes on all the time between teacher and learners, and a central element of teaching and learning. Teachers need to know as much as possible about their learners' previous experiences of education and assessment, their perceptions of their own strengths and weaknesses, which specific literacy tasks and situations are important to them and, most importantly of all, how they think they learn best.

Teachers will always give informal feedback, and more formal feedback (widely described as 'marking') of learners' work is now a more common feature of adult literacy teaching. Formal feedback clearly overlaps with formal record-keeping requirements and thus potentially can embody both formative and summative assessment purposes at the same time. It is important not to let record keeping become the dominant reason for carrying it out, for, if so, the formative potential of feedback and marking may be diminished. As with all such interactions, the purpose is two-way:

the teacher aims to give the learner information about the progress she has made and practical advice about what to do next, and to listen to the learner's responses, check her understanding and motivation and monitor any changes in her purposes and aspirations.

Research shows that effective feedback:

- is given regularly and as soon as possible;
- gives clear reasons for the learner's success or failure;
- gives factual descriptions of the performance of the learner, such as 'you have used linking words to make your story read better' rather than non-specific comments such as 'good';
- offers constructive and practical guidance about how to improve;
- is given privately (at least at first);
- avoids the teacher correcting the work of the learner;
- agrees what should be done next with the learner.

Guidelines about feedback apply equally to marking learners' written work. Learners tend to value comments which are practical, descriptive and constructive rather than opinionated: 'You have used apostrophes correctly except in this one case – isn't this a plural?', rather than 'Excellent use of apostrophes for the most part'.

Two ideas for developing constructive approaches to formal feedback are:

- to treat the feedback as if it is a brief research report on a study of learning carried out jointly with the learner;
- particularly for a piece of writing, to see feedback as a comment on an artistic performance, in which issues of 'correctness' need to be balanced with the expression of an authentic voice.

Taking a research perspective should ensure that feedback is based firmly on the evidence of the learner's work and offers constructive ways forward. It should also take account of the views of the learner, who should be seen as a fellow researcher in this context.

Gardener (1985) offers detailed advice on the marking of written work:

Marking clearly needs to be related to past and future teaching. Even with marking for correctness, we respond differently to persistent errors on points we think the writer is aware of, ambitious new errors, or confusions that grow from part-learning or misapplying hard won learning. Most of us surely mark selectively, with an eye to how much the writer can act on. We also need to use a code the *learner* can read. If we underline a spelling mistake, what do we expect to happen? If we don't mark something, is it necessarily right? If we write 'tenses' in the margin, is it related to past discussions and proposals for work? Do we want to code differently our marking of 'exercise' work and of free writing, where communication is the main aim? Does the *learner* feel 'Good' has a known value, or no value? Are our responsive comments readable (and I mean handwriting as well as language) and stimulating? Do we want to suggest a grade of any kind, even related to the writer's own previous work? If we don't comment, is this read as rejection? We won't know any of this unless we make marking a running topic of discussion with *learners*

(Gardener 1985; section B2, 7)

Task 8.4

Feedback on learner writing

Below are brief profiles of two literacy learners followed by an example of their writing and the feedback given by each of the writer's tutors.

For each one, consider:
- In what ways is the feedback formative?
- Which features, if any, are not formative?
- In what ways could the feedback be made more formative?

Learner A

Profile

Learner A is a young man who was born in the UK and attended primary school. At the age of 11 he went back to Bangladesh for three years and then came back to the UK for the final two years of secondary school. He wants go back to college to get some qualifications. He is good at maths. He is quite shy and nervous about writing – he's very keen to 'get it right'.

Text

My name is ... I was born on the 8th October 1984 I attend at M ... **** School for just two year's. and left, **** **** then to go and work for my Dad on car's. I am a polite young man and willing ** to ** learn.

Note: **** This symbol replaces words vigorously crossed out in the original hand-written text.

Feedback

Good.
   I have marked the corrections I want you to make. Also, just remember you don't use an apostrophe for plurals, such as years, cars.
   Now write some more about what you want to do at work in the future.

Learner B

Profile

Learner B is attending a literacy course. He speaks Turkish as his first language and was educated up to the age of 14 in Turkey. He came to the UK 12 years ago. Although he speaks English well, he finds writing difficult. He wants to improve his reading and writing in English in order to improve his career prospects and to help his young son with his school work. He would be interested in setting up and running his own restaurant.

Text

My hobbies at the weeks are. to go see my son and thank him to the pictures, also thank him to the pank prork prank palyind football together, and finding the ducks with beard beard.
  I like to do joking very moring to keep myself feet.
  My hobbies to cooked.

Written feedback

This is an interesting piece of writing: you have said clearly what your hobbies are. I enjoyed reading about your trips to the park with your son.
  You have used paragraphs well, with one paragraph for each hobby.
  You have used full stops well, to mark the ends of sentences.
  Your spelling is getting better – well done! You have got some difficult words right. Can you pick out three or four words you're not sure of? We can talk about these.

Oral feedback/dialogue

When you wrote about going to the park with your son, you gave some nice examples of things you did, like feeding the birds together. I could easily picture you doing it. What's your son's name? How old is he?
  What about the other two hobbies? Do you enjoy jogging or is it just hard work? Can you say more about this?
  What do you like to cook? Are you a good cook? If you had your own restaurant would you do the cooking yourself?
  Your paragraphing is good, but you could improve it more by leaving a space after each paragraph, before going on to the next one. What difference would this make to how your story looks on the page? How would it help the person reading it?
  You've used full stops very well, but in the first line there is a full stop in the middle of the sentence. Can you find it? I think I know why you used a full stop here but can you explain it to me?

> You've spelt some difficult words correctly, for example 'pictures', 'hobbies' and 'together'. Well done! Did you remember these or did you find them in a dictionary?
>
> Have you picked out some words to talk about?

Comment 8.4

Effective feedback involves

- deciding on the particular points in a piece of work to give feedback on (it may well not include everything);
- deciding on the focus of the feedback (text-level, sentence-level, and/or word-level skills);
- giving suggestions or prompts about how the piece of work can be improved;
- discussing with learners what makes good pieces of work.

Learner A

It is unlikely that this feedback will help the learner develop his skills or confidence. The tutor gives no clear explanations that the learner can use to improve his writing. For example, the word 'Good' would not help him understand the strengths in his writing. The feedback on apostrophes is unclear and it's unlikely that he will understand it.

The tutor has taken ownership of the writing away from the learner by simply telling him what she wants him to correct. She could make her feedback more formative by engaging in dialogue with him, using questions and prompts and offering practical suggestions on how to develop his writing further.

The tutor has not taken into account the learner's feelings about writing. Her feedback would be likely to undermine him further. She could make it more formative by showing an interest in what he wants to say. Instead of focusing exclusively on a punctuation error that does not seriously affect the overall clarity of the piece, she could focus on meaning, suggesting ways of improving the writing that would make the meaning clearer. She could also ask him what words he crossed out and why, and explain that even experienced writers do not get everything right in a first draft.

Learner B

In this case the tutor has given the learner feedback on what works well in his piece of writing and why it works well, with examples that he can understand. She identifies specific strengths and areas for development at text, sentence and word level.

> Rather than just correcting him, she asks questions and engages in dialogue with him, to find out what he already knows and to stimulate him to develop his writing further, drawing on what he has told her about his interests and aspirations. She makes practical suggestions about how to improve and what to work on.
>
> Her feedback is selective and realistic, but to avoid overloading the learner she may need to spread her comments over more than one conversation, as part of the process of supporting him in developing his text. She can make a judgement about this by observing his response to feedback and assessing how much he is able to make use of at any one time.

For more examples of formative feedback and dialogue with learners on their reading and writing, see Chapters 5 and 6.

Summative assessment (including formative use of summative tests)

As discussed at the start of this chapter, summative assessment can take many forms, including tests, written examinations and teacher/student assessment; it can take place in one go at the end of the course of learning or in stages throughout the course, or it could be a combination of any of these. The particular form and mode of summative assessment required is usually stipulated by the funding or awarding body for a particular course. There is, however, strong evidence that adult literacy learners prefer assessment 'based on discussion and portfolio building supported by tutor feedback and individual reflection' to 'tests and exams' (for example, Ward and Edwards 2002).

It is a vital part of the teacher's role to encourage 'sustainable' learning, even if this means that some learning activities may seem only indirectly related to the summative assessment process. It is not enough, for example, to produce a single piece of writing that has no grammatical errors, even if that is all that is required by the awarding body for the course. Learners need to have the confidence, knowledge and experience to weigh up the grammatical quality of a range of different possible ways of expressing the same points. Without this kind of understanding of the issues involved, learners may not be able to transfer their learning between different tasks and contexts and are not necessarily becoming more autonomous. In fact they may be becoming less autonomous, even if they can satisfy the requirements of the course: 'There is all the difference in the world between having to say something and having something to say' (Dewey 1907).

How can teachers encourage and support this kind of sustainable learning, particularly when the demands of summative assessment may discourage it? It is essential to remember that all assessment activities have the potential to be used both formatively and summatively: it all depends on how they are used. Brookfield (1990) suggests organizing group activities which highlight elements of summative assessment regimes, in order to problematize them and encourage learners to consider alternatives to them, such as:

- critically examining the published assessment criteria for their prospective summative assessment tasks;
- producing alternative summative assessment activities;
- producing alternative assessment criteria;
- looking at particular real life literacy tasks and discussing ways of talking about how well or badly they are carried out;
- revisiting previously assessed work, comparing the marks or comments with the original assessment criteria and suggesting alternatives or improvements;
- critically examining judgements of quality by their own teacher.

Brookfield and others argue that teachers need to focus attention on 'success criteria' rather than 'assessment criteria'. This reminds learners of the subjective and provisional nature of most judgements of quality in everyday life. Learners can work together and with the teacher to reflect on and develop criteria to assess the quality of their own writing, taking account of its appropriateness for purpose, its accuracy, its technical correctness and its authenticity in terms of that learner's voice (see Chapter 6). Again, it is important that there is an emphasis on developing critical judgement, not just on technical 'correctness'. This stage of the work, which begins towards the end of the technical production of writing, is what connects literacy learning with the learning of 'English'.

From a learning perspective, assessment activities which do not contribute to learning are wasted opportunities. So, for example when a learner takes an online multiple choice literacy test, the more teachers can find ways to use aspects of these activities for learning, the better. Reflecting on the experience of doing such tests, collectively devising and evaluating alternative test questions, or group discussions of the effectiveness of such tests as tools for accurately measuring literacy capabilities in real-life situations are all legitimate and valuable classroom activities for learning. Moderation meetings among teachers can also be rich sources of professional development in assessment for learning – if they are structured and organized at least partly for this purpose.

In conclusion, then, most teaching and learning situations are circumscribed by policy and organizational systems and summative assessment processes such as examinations, portfolios or tests. In principle, these processes are necessary and valuable in their own terms: whatever their main purposes are, imaginative adult literacy teachers will find ways to use them to support learning rather than simply measuring it.

Further reading and resources

Black, P. and Wiliam, D. (1998) Assessment and classroom learning, *Assessment in Education*, 5(1): 7–74.

Derrick, J., Gawn, J. and Ecclestone, K. (2008) Evaluating the 'spirit' and 'letter' of formative assessment in the learning cultures of part-time adult literacy and numeracy classes, *Research in Post-Compulsory Education*, 13(2): 173–84.

Derrick, J. Gawn, J. and Ecclestone, K. (in press) *Using Classroom Assessment in Adult Literacy, Language and Numeracy Teaching and Learning*. Leicester: NIACE.

Note

1. Entry 2 is a level of skill identified in the English Core Curriculum for Adult Literacy. To see the curriculum go to www.dcsf.gov.uk/curriculum literacy/ accessed 18 June 2009.

Acknowledgements

We wish to thank the teachers who have contributed or helped with material for this chapter: Kay Rodbourn, Katrina Blannin and Sue East.

Section 4

Inclusive learning

9 Dyslexia

Margaret Herrington

Introduction

This chapter is written for adult literacy teachers working in a wide range of educational and vocational contexts. It is an invitation to participate in a discussion about dyslexia and as such may also interest specialist dyslexia support tutors.

The rationale for a chapter on dyslexia in this book is threefold. First, educational providers have a legislative responsibility under the Disability Discrimination Act (DDA) 2005 to *promote equality* for disabled students and to involve students in such processes. Dyslexia is designated as a disability. Second, adult literacy teachers have a professional responsibility to be able to respond to learning difficulties/differences within teaching groups, however these may be labelled. Third, in assuming such a professional responsibility, it is important for tutors to **construct for themselves** a narrative about dyslexia drawn from their own experience and that of dyslexic students, researchers, writers and tutors. *They should do so reflexively –* that is, always be aware of the impact of their own experience and standpoint when they interpret what students present. Tutors and students are active makers of knowledge about dyslexic differences and not just recipients of the knowledge made by professional researchers or experts.

The purpose of the chapter is thus to encourage teachers to develop sufficient confidence and competence to explore dyslexia for themselves, to investigate individual dyslexic profiles in partnership with their students and to develop effective, and potentially new, practice. This chapter will first examine competing and coexisting ways of thinking about dyslexia, then explore how dyslexia is identified and finally look at methods of supporting dyslexic students.

Ways of thinking about dyslexia

> **Task 9.1**
>
> **Check your assumptions and preconceptions about dyslexia**
>
> 1   You are told that one of your adult learners is dyslexic. Do you think any of the following?
>   • the learner will be unable to read;

- the main problem will be with spelling;
- dyslexia is all about not knowing the sounds of letters;
- dyslexia is not related to your general level of intellectual ability;
- dyslexia involves rapid multi-dimensional thinking;
- dyslexic people write without any sense of structure;
- dyslexic learners are different to 'ordinary' adult literacy students;
- I am dyslexic and I got through without extra support.

2   What kind of employment do you expect a dyslexic person to have?
3   What is the basis of your assumptions? Size and type of your sample? In which contexts have you gathered your evidence?

Return to this exercise when you have finished reading this section.

Three competing narratives about dyslexia

At the heart of the debate about dyslexia in the adult literacy field lies a claim of **otherness**, that is, within the diversity of general adult literacy students, there is something essentially different about certain learners and that this difference can and should be identified so that specialist teaching methods can be employed. Some of the contrasting ideas about this 'difference' are illustrated below.

1   Dyslexia does not exist – it is a cultural myth

This 'story' uses the confusing definitions of dyslexia, the weaknesses in the methods of identification and the lack of research evidence from large-scale, random samples of dyslexic people regarding the effectiveness of special teaching methods as reasons for denying the existence of dyslexia. Generations of adult literacy tutors have thus seen no reason to separate out any such sub-groups among their students, nor to grant any extra teaching or technological resources to them.

A variant of this stance suggests that dyslexia is a myth which has been created by those who have most to gain from such a label ('middle-class parents'). The claim is that they use the label as a means of accessing resources for their children, at the expense of poorer children with literacy difficulties. This therefore involves issues of equality, class perceptions of illiteracy and professional knowledge versus parental protection.

The advantages of this narrative lie in its continuing focus on the whole group of literacy learners and in some cases on inclusiveness without 'labelling'. The disadvantages, however, are considerable. In practice this view may leave many learners with a sense that their experiences are not named and recognized. The 'something to explain' is still there for these learners. This view may also have contributed to the lack of qualitative research based on talking and listening to dyslexic learners themselves.

2 Dyslexia is an identifiably distinct set of weaknesses, deficits or difficulties in processing text with an in-person, biological basis

This narrative recognizes an 'otherness' in some learners. This account of dyslexia began when researchers identified unusual perceptual deficits in perceiving symbols among those with literacy problems; and 'unexpected deficit' stories of different kinds have continued to this day. Dyslexia is thus often discussed as **a set of specific learning difficulties** in contradistinction to a **global** learning difficulty. The claim is that dyslexic people have unexpected difficulties with learning language/ literacies, despite average or above-average levels of intelligence.

The majority of books and websites devoted to dyslexia focus on what has emerged as a classic set of difficulties:

1. Marked effects on reading. For example:
   - **visual disturbance***:* blurred letters; moving, shimmering text; words running off the page;
   - **tracking difficulties**: finding oneself on different lines as one is reading or having missed lines altogether;
   - **blanks in text**: not seeing particular letters or words; filling in gaps with other words;
   - **decoding problems**: difficulties with segmenting sounds, general phonic analysis and synthesis, word recognition;
   - **Syntax awareness difficulties**: not handling complex sentence formation – problems with memory for processing complex sentences can affect fluency;
   - **reading aloud**: often particularly problematic because of reading, memorising and speaking at the same time;
   - **comprehension**: this can be delayed because of needing to know what something is about first or needing several reads to construct the framework within which comprehension can occur.
   - **delays in reading speed**;
   - **concept and word reversal**;
   - **fatigue and physical symptoms; avoidance**.

2. Handwriting difficulties (discomfort and/or lack of control in letter formation, size and joins and delay in writing speed).
3. Spelling weakness (identifiable kinds of spelling error; weak ability to self-correct).
4. Marked effects on writing (delays in word finding; weakness in organization, sequencing, proof reading; absence of words and links.

5 Effects on speech (pronunciation; delay in word finding; controlling speech flow; 'round the houses' explanations, unpredictable loss of access to usual level of speech).

6 Particular weaknesses in numeracy (language of maths; sequences; particular computations; classification).

7 Visual and auditory short-term memory difficulties.

8 Inability to multi-task in relation to literacy, e.g. listening and writing at the same time.

9 Marked variations in performance within and between days, weeks, etc.

10 Experiencing time as a dimension into and out of which one moves and thence experiencing organization and time management difficulties.

Whilst many adult literacy tutors would not think these unusual, dyslexia is often identified when:

- **the distinctiveness of an individual element**; or
- **the nature of the clusters of difficulties**; and/or
- **the degrees of intractability** experienced stand out **within a diverse group.** More formally, students are identified as dyslexic when their difficulties are not expected in relation to measured IQ levels.

Researchers look for explanations in either a single perceptual and cognitive processing weakness which accounts for a range of dyslexic characteristics, or in multiple cognitive and motor inefficiencies. The neurobiological bases of these are still being explored, including genetic factors, structures and functions of the brain (mapping); hemisphericity and magnocellular impairment (Stein 2001).

This narrative has some advantages. In articulating the deficits associated with dyslexia, it does explicitly acknowledge some of the particular and sometimes extreme difficulties experienced by many learners. It also challenges the conventional wisdom among many educators that literacy skills are always a proxy for intellectual quality. Finally, though offering policy makers and researchers an over-simple view about literacy failings and disability, it has contributed to a high policy profile. This has resulted in a raft of support measures which actually help dyslexic learners in educational settings.

The weaknesses, however, are marked. There is a growing consensus that there is no valid case for separating out those with an average or above-average IQ score from the rest and calling the former 'dyslexic'. And, whilst finding a 'discrete' definition of dyslexia may be convenient for policy makers, students can demonstrate very different clusters and degrees of difficulties. Tutors have to find out *how* someone is dyslexic in order to work effectively, and so the label of 'dyslexic' is not sufficient in itself. The 'discrete' view also implies that it is possible to distinguish between dyslexic and non-dyslexic across the adult population, but such distinctions are not so clear-cut as this suggests. Further, this **specific deficits** view of dyslexia sends the unremitting message that dyslexic people have something wrong with them, diverting attention from their learning strengths and transmitting an incomplete description of their learning profiles. (The exception is Stein's (2001) findings of biological difference at cell level, which he believes may account both for the weaknesses associated with dyslexia and for some of the cognitive 'holistic thinking' strengths.) Finally, this position tends to be based on a view of literacy as a set of discrete skills, rather than as a set of social practices (see Chapter 1). It takes little account of the texts and contexts – in life, work and study – within which dyslexic learners acquit themselves successfully. The overall impact of the specific deficits view, therefore, is to fuel the ongoing suspicion about the educability and employability of dyslexic adults, especially in professions such as medicine and teaching.

3   Dyslexia can be seen as unfolding *differences* in the ways people think and learn, which include both difficulties and cognitive strengths – dyslexia has to be understood in a broader social context, not as an individual 'problem'

Though literacy weaknesses may be the most obvious signal, and present the greatest difficulties in education, this narrative questions the idea of dyslexia as an 'impairment'. Instead, it heeds the suggestion from dyslexic writers and some researchers that there is a broader underpinning thinking and learning profile which includes both cognitive strengths and weaknesses. Dyslexia is about *difference* rather than simply about 'deficit'.

A number of variations in this 'differences' story are available: some consider Gardner's (1983) multiple intelligences framework to be an important tool for understanding differences (Kallenbach and Viens 2001) and models of neurodiversity are also being explored (Pollak 2007).

Hence, this is essentially an unfolding narrative with key questions concerning:

- the ways in which dyslexic adult learners get around their weaknesses and the neurological processes involved in this compensating activity;
- dyslexic literacies – the forms of reading and writing which come easily to many dyslexic adults;
- the intensity of the relationships between thinking and emotion as described by dyslexic adults;
- the particular claims for enhanced cognitive and affective strengths such as fast, global and multidimensional, visual spatial thinking skills; intuitive and empathetic strengths, and creativity (West 1991; Hetherington 1996; Everatt 1997; Brigden and McFall 2000).

The narrative also places these differences and the questions about them within a social context. It focuses on the ways in which certain social contexts (families, schools, colleges, workplaces) have particular values and practices regarding literacy and how these result in dyslexia being constructed as a disability. For example, publishing practices govern textual layout, colours and forms, some of which are extremely difficult for dyslexic adults to negotiate. The rapidly changing literacy and cultural practices that have resulted from changes in technology can also change the experience of dyslexia (West 1991).

This holistic and critically aware view offers a number of key advantages: it helps us to make sense of accounts by dyslexic learners of their experiences which extend far beyond literacy difficulties; it suggests that we simply do not yet know enough to discuss dyslexia as an *entirely* discrete phenomenon; and finally, by focusing on social context, it removes the enduring emphasis on dyslexia as simply a set of individual weaknesses.

However, as a more open-ended, sophisticated narrative, it represents something of a challenge for those policy makers who find simple ideas about literacy problems easier to manage. Tutors, too, are left with the task of looking for unfolding patterns of learning strengths and weaknesses, rather than simply identifying and addressing literacy 'deficits'.

But isn't dyslexia a disability?

Do these different views matter if dyslexia has been already defined as a disability by policy makers? We must be clear about how we use the term 'disability'. A common distinction is made between individual (or medical) and social models of disability. The former sees individual impairment – i.e. there is something wrong with the individual – as constituting **disability**. Disability activists have long challenged this (Barnes and Mercer 2005) by distinguishing between *impairment* and *disability*, and have argued that the latter is constructed by social attitudes, conventions and policies. In other words, it is society that disables people. The long fight by activists to have this 'social model' accepted has resulted in legislation which requires colleges and other organizations to make 'reasonable adjustments' to enable all learners to have equal access to learning and to challenge discriminatory structures.

In relation to dyslexia, this distinction between the medical and social models can be clearly seen. Those who focus on dyslexia as a set of impairments in processing symbolic text, stemming from neurological disorders, use an individual/medical model of disability: there is something wrong with the individual. In contrast, a social model focuses on how the disability is constructed by the literacy practices and conventions around learners. It is only when dyslexic learners are required to do *particular kinds of literacy* that they are 'disabled'. More recently the social model has itself been challenged (Tremain 2005), primarily because it fails to acknowledge that impairment itself is also socially constructed by cultural perceptions and measures of 'normality'. Whose cognitive styles are 'normal' – dyslexic learners or non-dyslexic learners?

In this chapter, I am using what I have termed a *critical social interactive model* of disability (Herrington and Hunter Carsch 2001). This means that I recognize that social practices result in people being seen as 'impaired' or 'disabled', that social action is required and that the learner is entitled to actively investigate and challenge such practices.

Individual narratives about dyslexia

The three broad brush 'stories' about dyslexia outlined above give a sense of the landscape within which the battle over the nature of dyslexia occurs. However, there is no compelling reason why many lines of enquiry, providing multiple insights, should not continue. Indeed, it is of critical importance for the field as a whole for dyslexic learners, tutors and researchers to explore those insights. The truth of dyslexia is not to be found *in telling it like it is* in some absolute sense but *telling it like each* narrative maker *sees it* (Badley 2003).

Tutors usually find themselves in the middle of these competing perspectives within their workplaces. They may be asked to implement institutional policies that are at odds with their own developing views as professionals. Students, too, may have particular views, which could be at odds with those of the tutor or each other. Notwithstanding such complexities, tutors must continue to work closely with learners to devise an understanding of what the issues are for that learner.

Ways of identifying dyslexia

The first view above – the 'cultural myth' view – suggests that it is unnecessary and even impossible to identify dyslexia. The latter two views claim dyslexia is important to identify both for educational reasons and to trigger additional support arrangements. However, these two views have quite different emphases: one is concerned with measuring expected deficits, the other with exploring the complexity of students' thinking and learning preferences and allowing the unknown to emerge. At the time of writing in the UK, identification is formally undertaken by educational psychologists or by specialist support tutors, but it is vitally important for all adult literacy tutors to understand the methods used in order to make sense of the reports and to some extent explain them to the learners. It is also important for dyslexic learners to have an opportunity to discuss all the methods described below.

Three principles currently underpin the identification of dyslexia:

- **exclusion of other factors**: that is, the 'otherness' cannot stem from poor teaching or socio-economic disadvantage and so, in the final analysis, all other potential causes can be excluded;
- **discrepancy**: in terms of unexpected difficulties for those with average or above-average IQ;
- **positive indicators**: both specific, selected characteristics which define the 'condition' *or* a checklist of all characteristics which are associated with dyslexia.

In practice, all forms of identification involve some aspect of **profiling**. Whilst educational psychologists may still focus on discrepancy, they compile histories and often also invite learner accounts of their experience of dyslexia, and tutors who focus on positive indicators and exclusion usually also gather background data from the student.

Identification tools

- **Screening checklists**: These are designed as a first indicator of dyslexia. They consist of twenty or so questions such as the following (taken from a list compiled by the Dyslexia Institute):

       ○   Do you find difficulty in telling left from right?

       ○   Do you find it difficult to remember the sense of what you have read?

       ○   Do you dislike reading long books?

       ○   Is your spelling poor?

       ○   Do you find it difficult to take messages on the phone and pass them on correctly?

(www.dyslexiaaction.org.uk)

All are deficit-oriented, leading questions with only yes/no as possible answers. Yet many dyslexia specialists consider them to have some predictive value in identifying dyslexia.

- **Distinctive groups of short tests** including the Aston Index, the Bangor Test, and the Dyslexia Adult Screening Test (DAST.) This approach is based on the idea that there are key identifiers of dyslexia, not all of which are confined to literacy. The Bangor Test (Miles 1993), for example, includes exercises to explore left-right delays and confusions.
- **IT-based tests**, for example, LADS, Instines, Quickscan, etc. These were designed to identify the likely presence of dyslexia without the tutor being present, thus saving both tutor time and student embarrassment during the assessment process. However, the theoretical bases of the methods are not always identified, the results are not self-explanatory and the actual tasks presented can cause distress when students feel they are getting behind. The process of explaining the reports can be just as long as the more formal reports described below.
- **Psychometric tests**: These are used by educational psychologists and other specialists and usually include verbal and non-verbal IQ tests (WAIS – Wechsler Adult Intelligence Scale) with a battery of literacy and other processing tests designed to identify particular weaknesses. The resulting measurements allow **discrepancy** to emerge. These 'timed' tests are still cited as the only 'objective' method of identifying dyslexia despite cogent critiques.
- **Structured and structuring interviews**: A tutor gathers a learning history from the student and builds up a comprehensive individual learning profile. She also asks the learner to complete selective tasks (Klein 1993; Herrington 2000). This approach is rooted in the importance of the student's version of himself. Various 'tests' are often used within this format to establish the nature of a particular difficulty while also drawing out student strengths. In practice, the quality of the student–tutor dialogue and the knowledge and attitudes of the tutor determine the usefulness of the findings (in the case of some ESOL students, interpreters are necessary for this).

Knowledge of the above methods is particularly important given the problems associated with assessment: learner fearfulness, reinforced sense of failure, and limited criteria. Learners rarely have one assessment – both screening and formal testing is not unusual – and this can be confusing and in some cases distressing. The measurements can be difficult to interpret for both learners and tutors. The emotional impact for some learners of having a positive identification of dyslexia can be profound, and tutors need to be ready for that. Some learners may be unwilling to be labelled with a condition which may carry a stigma of disability (especially when they may face family or community stigma regarding disability). Others are deeply relieved to have the analysis and what they see as a more accurate label than the ones given throughout their schooling.

What is possible/reasonable in the classroom?

Large classes and heavy teaching loads can make it seem almost impossible to notice the complexity of a learner's strengths and weaknesses. In such circumstances tutors may only notice those for whom the 'otherness' is marked in terms of degree and intractability of difficulty, but this can underestimate the overall incidence of dyslexic patterns.

Here I describe a proactive approach.

Listen out

Whether you are working on a one-to-one basis or within a group, listen out for descriptions of reading and writing (Herrington, 2001d) which indicate what learners are actually experiencing. For example:

> When I read the word (red) I am immediately in a room with a fire and dog and cat sitting on mat … orange emerges … I don't know where it will go next … (impact of colour leading away from the rest of the text).
> (Mature student at University of Wolverhampton, 2006)

This is not foolproof because many students have never had the opportunity to name or discuss their experience. This usually needs dialogue for further clarification:

> *Student*: It's as if my language suddenly goes.
> *Tutor*: What do you mean?
> *Student*: It all suddenly seems like a foreign language.
> *Tutor*: How long does this happen for?
> *Student*: Varies.
> *Tutor*: What do you do?
> *Student*: Feel very panicky.
> *Tutor*: And you don't know when it will come back?
> *Student*: No.
> *Tutor*: But it always does eventually?
> *Student*: Yes.

> *Tutor*: So what do you want me to do in class if this happens to you? Suggest you leave the work until it comes back?
> *Student*: Sometimes I would rather keep going and not give in to it. Other times, I just can't do anything and have to leave it.
> (Based on student–tutor dialogues in Leicestershire, 1990)

This kind of naming work can be built into the general curriculum conversations and will lead to descriptions of thinking and learning which tend to be far more useful than test findings.

Look out

Sometimes there are very early clues: a refusal to do any reading or writing even in individual teaching sessions, inability to write one's own name despite years of compulsory schooling, extreme difficulty with the movements involved in handwriting, high degrees of stress and discomfort when tackling any aspect of literacy, complete memory blanks despite intensive learning, etc. Often the clues only emerge later when the classic difficulties (see view 2 above) become apparent.

Dyslexic characteristics are more obvious when a discrepancy emerges, for example highly developed verbal fluency and presentation skills alongside acute spelling difficulties, or well-developed reading skills alongside acute handwriting problems. As students progress in education the discrepancies become more subtle. However, when students reveal difficulties across the board – in speech (especially), reading, writing, spelling, maths, sequencing, organization, time management, etc. they can often be seen as having general learning difficulties when they actually are experiencing *all the dyslexic characteristics together*. Adult literacy students have explained to me how, as children, they were sent to special schools because no one could understand their collection of difficulties. The dangers of ignorance in this field are stark.

Referral and beyond

If you think someone may be dyslexic, refer to specialist support tutors if they are available, but also recognize that the learning investigation will continue between you and the learner after any formal assessment. Explain as best you can the basis of the tests, and the emerging pattern of strengths and weaknesses. Use analogies, encourage students to express their own, draw diagrams and pictures, quote other student descriptions and explain in relation to the different views of dyslexia mentioned above. Be prepared to discuss the findings in an unpressured and exploratory way.

Ways of teaching and supporting dyslexic learners

> *Question:* Do I need to do anything different with dyslexic learners?
> *Answer:* It depends on what you do now!

The different views of dyslexia carry different implications for teaching. Those who deny its existence would say that no special teaching is required. Those arguing for the second, 'classic' view traditionally believe that dyslexic learners require specialist teaching based on 'structured, sequential, multi-sensory methods'. This has become something of a mantra in relation to dyslexia, despite different interpretations in use. For some it refers to the breaking down of language into its smallest components and the sequential learning and synthesizing of these in chunks by using as many of the senses as possible (Hornsby and Shear 1980). For others it means analysing any adult literacy activity with the learner in terms of which senses or combination of senses are necessary for them to learn. Both of these suggest learners need something quite different and separate from standard teaching methods.

More recently the idea of separate teaching methods for dyslexic learners has evolved into a reverse argument that the methods necessary for dyslexic learners are desirable for all. This suggests that there is no need for any differentiation so long as the methods used for dyslexic learners are used with all students. There is some merit in this argument. It encourages all teachers to learn about and draw upon the specialist methods. It ensures that any student who has not been officially assessed as dyslexic will have a more accessible curriculum. It is a positive tool in the battle to change attitudes among non-specialist tutors in adult, further and higher education.

However, it is rare to find any detailed analysis of what this actually means. Very obvious examples are used to carry the weight of the argument: showing all students how to change the colour of their computer screens, or encouraging all students to learn using a range of senses. Yet, not all methods which help dyslexic learners are necessary for all learners and some may even prove problematic. For example, a PowerPoint presentation with its accompanying *hum,* which suits a particular dyslexic learner, may be anathema to learners with hearing difficulties.

The argument here is not for a superficial integration of methods but for a more sophisticated ongoing exploration of the relationships between traditional and specialist ones. This suggests a curriculum for all, which includes core central approaches and an ongoing active exploration of the 'edges', including the bringing in of specific methods for particular learners. Both elements feed each other and are underpinned by a central investigative drive with the learner about how learning can be achieved.

Core elements for all?

In this section I shall identify five core elements and their particular significance for dyslexic learners.

Commitment and values of the tutor

This sounds like a statement of the obvious but the tutors must care about the learner and about whether or not learning occurs and must convey this to the learner. Whilst this is important for all students, dyslexic students have regularly identified this emotional and professional connection as *essential* to their development (Palfreyman Kay 2001; Davies 2007).

The knowledge base of the tutor

This must include: models of literacy and learning (including literacies as social practice); current narratives about dyslexia and the implicit power relationships within them; and some awareness of how disability is constructed and deconstructed. Without this knowledge base it is difficult for tutors to help students to reframe past experience of failure, construct a different learning identity and contribute to our general knowledge about learning differences. Any such reframing must include reference to how literacy and power works in social and economic contexts – the workplace, communities, prisons, educational institutions and the internet – and how values and practices construct disability (see Chapter 1).

Tutor self-awareness

Tutors must be clear about their own 'literate' identities, their histories and their limitations. Tutors are labelled by society as literate compared with adult literacy students and are employed as gatekeepers to standard forms of English. Yet adult literacy professionals know that:

- Standard English is not linguistically superior to other varieties/dialects;
- literateness is a multi-dimensional, moving cultural feast rather than a single scale with the 'literate' at one end and the 'illiterate' at the other;
- we do not know how someone else experiences literacy and so are often operating in unknown territory.

Tutors (both dyslexic and not) must be aware of their own limited perspectives, listen very carefully to the clues provided by learners and always be prepared to find out something new. Above all they must be sensitive to how their perceptions may contribute to creating environments which 'disable'.

Exploratory, analytical, investigative, collaborative teaching

Teachers should work with learners to investigate which teaching approaches work best. To this end, they must ensure that students learn to name their experiences and develop their **voices**. This is particularly important for dyslexic students, who have long complained that their descriptions of learning are ignored, as if irrelevant to the teaching process. If teachers will only listen, students will explain the nature of their dyslexia and then methods can be generated accordingly.

At the heart of this way of working is student–tutor dialogue in which the student and tutor are exploring together. Students must be acknowledged as knowledge-holders about their own experience, as well as knowledge-makers about how they can learn.

Here is a flavour of the kind of exchanges possible. The two examples are based on actual dialogues within my own teaching.

Example 9.1

Tutor: What is reading like for you?

Student: It is like building a framework and filling it in as I read and reread.

Tutor: How many times do you need to read something to fill it in?

Student: Depends on what it is.

Tutor: (*Discuss different kinds of text*) Take this passage … will you read it as often as you need and then let me know when you feel you can tell me what it is about.

Student: (*Reads four or five times*) Well, it is about Iraq and about soldiers getting killed in Basra …a mess.

(*Student and tutor discuss the war issues*)

Tutor: Can you now look again at the passage and mark with a pencil the words you hesitated over or couldn't get? This has worked quite well for other people …see how you go … I will leave you to it.

Student: (*Reads silently and marks the text frequently*)

(*The tutor returns and discusses the delaying factors with the student: synthesizing segments of sounds, length and complexity of sentence, lack of visual clues etc. The tutor reads out the problem parts, indicating meaning in the tone. The student mimics this.*)

Tutor: Have another go and see how you do

(*Student returns to text and reads silently*)

Tutor: What do you think?

Student: I can make more sense of it now …but I still struggle here (*pointing to a compound sentence*).

Tutor: If I made it into two sentences would that be more readable (*shows student*).

Student: Yes (*reads the two*)… yes.

And this word, I just do not like (*one with a double consonant in the middle*).

Tutor: What do you mean you don't like it?

Student: It is uncomfortable to look at …ugh …I can't look at it (*laughter*).

Tutor: (*laughter*) Just the look of it?

Student: Yes. Couldn't they use another word?

Example 9.2

Student: I just don't get it … I learned these spellings weeks ago but I just forget them so easily.
Tutor: Are these words you really want to be able to spell?
Student: Yes, I chose them.
Tutor: Why do you think you cannot remember them?
Student: No idea really … just blanks.
Tutor: How did you learn them in the first place?
Student: I had this list … and we went through them one at a time … looking, saying, covering and writing … and then I practised and the teacher checked me on them the following week.
Tutor: And could you remember any the following week?
Student: Yes, about half … say four out of the eight.
Tutor: Why do you think some stayed and some disappeared?
Student: Some just clicked straightaway … some were easy to just work out but the rest … ? It is so frustrating … I'm coming to classes but am not sure I have made that much progress with spelling at all.
Tutor: You just have to develop a system which will work for you. There is no point in keep learning and forgetting. From what you have said, your memory is like a resistant surface which words bounce off. You have to somehow cut a groove in the surface for it to stick. You are the one in charge of this.
Student: I see it more as if there are very few … only one or two … channels for the words to get through … so many words … so few channels.

These represent dialogues with individual learners, but the same issues are easily and valuably discussed in groups. It is particularly helpful to organize discussions about memory and to discuss claims about the particular memory weaknesses and strengths of dyslexic adults (Saunders and White, 2002).

Building on knowledge from dyslexic learners

Here are some key lessons taught to us by dyslexic learners:

- It is vital to build on dyslexic strengths within curriculum content and process. For example, the claim is often made that creativity is a dyslexic strength and though much more research is needed, my own experience with dyslexic learners has lent some support to this. A recent piece of work (Herrington *et al.* 2005), which focused on encouraging students to make learning materials using digital cameras, created an environment in which learners could release their imaginations and energy for learning. It involved them actively in discussion, physical movement and decision making in a way they needed. Encouraging dyslexic learners to monitor and manage their own creative energy levels is essential.

- Understanding students' experience of 'visual disturbance' or 'visual stress' in relation to text is vital for any tutor. By this I mean the range of effects on text, such as shimmering, moving, letters running off the page, sentences eliding, etc. (Szumko and Beacham 2006). There is no consensus that the visual disturbance which many dyslexic adults experience is an essential part of dyslexia, given that not all dyslexic people experience it, but it does happen sufficiently often to alert all teachers to check for it. Whenever it exists, it demands a response from tutors.

- It is particularly important to explore and discuss the effects of colour. For some students the effect of changing the combination of black text on white paper for black/dark blue on yellow or blue is dramatic and surprising to a non-dyslexic tutor. It is not simply a matter of being slightly more comfortable. It can sometimes mean really seeing letters stand out for the first time. Once preferences are found, then the student can use specific colours of fonts, backgrounds or screens. Optimal colours and shades change over time and so the challenge for the learner is to find a way of managing arrangements for lenses, overlays, paper colour, etc. The challenge for the tutor is to assist with this within the general classroom and to consider the implications for assessment of an individual's reading skills. Clearly if someone is experiencing extreme disturbance and the tutor is unaware of it, then it will be difficult to assess reading competence.

- Tutors must be aware that students vary in their use of different sensory pathways. This does not mean simply labelling someone as a 'visual' or 'auditory' or 'kinaesthetic' learner. It is a matter of being willing to explore the sensory palate with students in order to see the kind and mix of inputs which *make sense* and *their relative impact on memory*. Some students, for example, cannot learn from hearing material alone. They must see a visual representation or must learn kinaesthetically. It is important to encourage self-awareness in dyslexic students about how they learn most effectively and therefore how they can tackle new learning.

- One of the single most important methods of teaching reading when someone has an intractable difficulty is to provide the student with a recording of their chosen text to use in class or at home. This gives the student an overview about what the piece is about and an opportunity to listen and read along with any text for as many times as necessary, without monitoring by a tutor. It involves a sequential or simultaneous looking, listening and speaking. The control over the size of text rests with the student.

Some methods of teaching spelling are particularly effective with dyslexic learners. Many now use spellcheckers but when spellings need to be learned, the student needs to discover a way of doing this. For example, a hybrid method involving:

  o   student selecting words to be learned;
  o   analysing the known and unknown parts of the word;
  o   chunking the bit to be learned in a way which makes sense to the learner;

○ using Simultaneous Oral Spelling (SOS) – sounding out the *names* of the letters which gives the learner a precise auditory clue;

○ use of colour to highlight parts of the word, if helpful;

○ student taking responsibility for writing the word once each day for a number of days, stopping for several days and then testing self to see if the word is still there. If not, student and tutor revisit the word and check the original chunking, etc. (Herrington 2001c).

We know that simply offering a range of methods to all students is not sufficient. The method must be adapted to fit the particular memory profile of the learner. Without this, some students will continue to learn and forget spellings over many years.

● The value of **assistive technology** has also been clarified by dyslexic learners. This 'necessary, good thing' helps dyslexic learners to access language, literacy and learning in general. Students have found word processing software particularly helpful for their writing, providing:

○ a keyboard for those who struggle with handwriting;

○ a clean, legible final product which gives the writer a sense of pride;

○ spelling and grammar checking facilities;

○ cut and paste facilities which allow writers to reorder their ideas;

○ the possibility of changing the screen colour, font colour, size and type;

○ allowing line spacing which makes reading easier for the writer.

Other software has been reported as useful by dyslexic learners:

○ **predictive** software which enables students to write without typing every individual word;

○ **mindmapping** software such as *Inspirations* or *Mind Manager* which allow them to create an easy visual representation of ideas for writing;

○ software which allows the writer **to speak into the computer** and see it created on-screen (viz. *Dragon, Kurzweil*). This can enable students to start writing without worrying about spelling (Morgan 1995).

○ software which provides an electronic voice **to read back the writer's text** has proved very popular (e.g. *Text Help Read and Write*). A major difficulty for many dyslexic students is the gap between what they think they have written and what they have actually written. This software is often very helpful for such students. When used with scanners (and *OCR – Optical Character Recognition* software) any text can be placed onto the computer, allowing learners to listen to the text in front of them.

Dyslexic learners have noted that other equipment is invaluable too, such as **digital recorders** for recording teaching points and for capturing ideas (for writing), and **reading pens**, which offer the chance for learners to hear individual words as they read.

Finally, the use of the **internet and intranets** within institutions offers an escape from book-based learning and literacies, which is so essential for some dyslexic learners.

Overall this is an emerging story in which student accounts about their interactions with technology are vital. However, it is particularly important to remember that this technology has not been devised specifically for dyslexic learners: some learners experience great frustration with what they feel is the slow speed of IT processors, or with the embodied voices in the voice input and voice output software, and the initial training and set-up can prove difficult. In short, assistive technology is not a panacea for independent learning for all, but for some it is a necessary prerequisite for reading and writing progress. As such, this provision cannot be an optional or occasional extra in the adult literacy classroom.

- It is important for tutors to investigate emerging claims about supporting dyslexic learners which come from outside mainstream research. Recent examples have included: the Davis Reorientation Programme (2001); Brain Gym Exercises (Dennison and Dennison); DDAT (Dyslexia, Dyspraxia, Attention Deficit Disorder Treatment Centre) established by Wynford Dore; Brightstar (Blackfriar's House, London); and complementary therapies such as cranial osteopathy. They are all asking questions which mainstream thinking has yet to answer and emerging findings and insights should be offered to students for critical analysis. It is fundamental to the tutor's role to scrutinize such developments closely and not dismiss them out of hand.

Conclusion

The argument within this chapter has been that it is essential for adult literacy tutors to be prepared to investigate and respond to claims of 'otherness' within their practice and that this does not automatically threaten equality for all. Indeed, it is centrally involved in constructing equality for all and is the business of all tutors.

This does not mean that tutors must unquestionningly accept existing notions of dyslexic impairment but that they must work carefully with all their students, acknowledging the importance of individual testimony, and be prepared to learn about and be surprised by emerging differences. It also means being prepared to see clusters and patterns in these respects and to explain these to students.

Tutors are also asked to be more alert to broader thinking and learning strengths among dyslexic learners. It is not helpful to see dyslexia as entirely about literacy problems or difficulties. We may yet be unsure of the extent to which cognitive and other strengths are intrinsic to dyslexic profiles, or simply often accompany them, because we are still finding our way in understanding the experience of dyslexia. We are also still exploring the disabling/enabling roles of some literacies that are specific to education, and questioning their value in supporting learning.

It may be helpful to note finally that these explorations are continuing in all phases of post-compulsory education. Many teaching and support staff are working to counter the view of dyslexic learners as a 'problem' , encourage a sense of what dyslexic learners should reasonably expect by way of individual support, assist in devising the reasonable adjustments to curricula and highlight the dyslexia-friendly thinking and learning spaces within their organizations. Dyslexic learners, teachers and researchers are also increasingly speaking and writing about their experience. It is an important time for adult literacy tutors to highlight their own knowledge-making role.

Further reading and resources

Chappell, D. (2008) Discrete dyslexia groups for adults – what is their value in raising self-esteem and developing confidence? in C. Atkin and A. Convery (eds) *Adult Learning in Lincolnshire and Rutland: Voices from Practice.* Practitioner-led research projects, Volume 2. Nottingham: Unesco Centre for Comparative Education Research, School of Education, University of Nottingham.

Hetherington, J. (1996). Approaches to the development of self-esteem in dyslexic students in higher education, *Dyslexic Students in Higher Education: Practical Responses to Student and Institutional Needs.* Conference Proceedings, Joint Skill/University of Huddersfield Conference, January.

Saunders, K. and White, A. (2002) *How Dyslexics Learn: Grasping the Nettle.* Evesham: PATOSS.

10 Literacy learning for adults with global learning difficulties

Sam Duncan

Introduction

If adult literacy teaching is an under-researched field, teaching literacy to adults with global learning difficulties is a *very* under-researched field. More research, writing and thinking needs to be done. Many more links need to be made between those teaching in this area and those researching relevant aspects of psychology, linguistics and sociology. A chapter like this, in a book like this, will be much longer in five years. For now, I will look at the meaning and development of the term 'global learning difficulties' (hereafter GLD), how it relates to models of disability, and key issues surrounding its provision, before identifying potential teaching and learning issues with suggested strategies.

Definitions and labelling

GLD is the current umbrella term for a range of cognitive processing differences that were once labelled 'mental disabilities', 'mental handicaps', 'mental deficiencies' or 'mental retardation', terms now considered offensive. Many people with GLD prefer the term global learning difficulties to global learning disabilities, though both are used. The 'global' in GLD differentiates it from specific learning difficulties (hereafter SLD), such as dyslexia, dyspraxia and dyscalculia (see previous chapter), indicating that, unlike SLD, which affect a particular aspect of a person's learning (for example, difficulty with numbers), GLD affect a wider range of cognitive functions. The definitions of SLD and GLD both hinge, problematically, on a notional norm.

GLD are a lifelong condition (they cannot be 'cured') and are often categorized as mild, moderate, severe or profound. In the past, and in some present contexts, these categories were bound by IQ (intelligence quotient), with 'mild' signifying an IQ of 50–69, moderate 35–49, severe 20–34 and profound below 20 (with 'normal' IQ ranging between 90 and 110) (Reber 1995; Walker Tileson 2004; British Institute of Learning Disabilities 2007). IQ is rarely used by those teaching adult literacy, so these categories are more often understood in terms of a person's ability to lead an independent life. The definitions from Alice Bradley's *Starting Work with People With Learning Disabilities* are useful:

> Mild learning disability usually means that someone has obvious difficulties in learning most things, especially formal educational skills, but can acquire the skills of everyday living.
>
> (Bradley 2001: 44)

while

> Profound learning disability usually means that someone will have extreme difficulty in all learning. He or she will have limited communication ... and will be highly dependent on others for personal care.
>
> (Bradley 2001: 44)

People with 'profound and multiple learning disabilities' (PMLD) have profound GLD as well as physical disabilities, sensory or mental health issues and often other health needs.

Around 1.5 million people in the UK have GLD (Mencap 2007); the cause is frequently unknown. GLD can be caused by hereditary factors, or factors (such as illnesses or injury) affecting brain development during pregnancy, birth or childhood. The two most common genetic causes are Fragile X syndrome and Down's syndrome. Not everyone with Fragile X syndrome has GLD, while everyone with Down's syndrome does, but whether mild, moderate, severe or profound varies. A person with GLD and physical disabilities is more likely to be *seen* as having severe or profound GLD, rather than mild or moderate, though this is not always the case.

It is therefore important to distinguish between GLD and other conditions. Cerebral palsy is a physical condition, distinct from GLD, but many people who have GLD also have cerebral palsy. Likewise, epilepsy is not a GLD, but almost a third of those with GLD also have epilepsy (MENCAP 2007). People with autism may have GLD, but not always.

GLD are also distinct from mental health issues. Mental health issues are psychological or behavioural concerns, while GLD relate to cognitive processing. However, a person with GLD is more likely than most people to have a mental health issue, such as acute anxiety or depression (British Institute of Learning Disabilities, 2007). As with any learners, adults with GLD and physical disabilities, illnesses or mental health issues may be taking medication, which could affect learning.

This chapter concerns GLD rather than mental health issues or physical disabilities. However, the general principles of inclusive learning apply to each, which brings us back to the social model of disability mentioned in the previous chapter. A medical model of disability is based on a post-enlightenment scientific tradition, where knowledge is used to identify a condition and work to cure it, or make it as close to 'normal' as possible. In this model, the condition, or the person with the condition, is 'the problem' needing to be solved. A social model, on the other hand, sees the inflexible, norm-bound society as 'the problem' and so works with the social structures to accommodate those different, for example, legislating for more disabled access in tube stations or assistive technology for those with SLD at university.

While it is clear that a functioning society needs both models, the social model is favoured in adult literacy teaching, for both ideological and pragmatic reasons. Many new teachers of adults with GLD are surprised at not receiving a report of each learner's condition, which they could then research and find out how best to work with this learner. Many learning providers won't have this information, as often no one knows the cause of a GLD, and the very nature of an umbrella term like GLD means that for every definition, there is a huge amount of variation. Yet, even if a teacher did know the cause of a learner's GLD and did research its typical manifestations, there is nothing to say how it will manifest in this particular learner. Some learners with autism and GLD have problems differentiating between the pronouns I, you and he/she – but does this particular person? The teacher will check, but wouldn't they have tried to figure out this learner's strengths and areas for development anyway? Could knowledge of medical conditions associated with a learner's GLD limit a teacher's expectations of that learner? The social model involves working from each person's unique needs and desires, which means working from the individual to diagnose learning needs.

However, most teachers agree that some more information about conditions would be useful, not to replace the 'seeing for ourselves' but rather as a tool in that seeing process: a reminder of what to look out for and ask about in order to expand our awareness of what GLD could mean for different people.

Provision

An adult with GLD wanting to develop her literacy may face a diversity of provision: from groups specifically for adults with GLD (discrete provision) to groups for adults with or without GLD (integrated or 'mainstream' provision), and from groups focused specifically on literacy to groups where literacy is embedded in other subjects, such as gardening or retail skills. One-to-one provision is common in some countries and less common in others. Each of these models offers a different set of advantages and disadvantages to each learner. Some choices are relatively simple: if a woman with GLD wants to become a gardener, and recognizes that she needs to develop her literacy skills to do this, she will probably opt for a gardening class with embedded literacy. If the same woman wants to develop her literacy so she can read and write her own letters, beyond her gardening ambitions, then she may prefer to join a literacy class, perhaps as well as the gardening class. One-to-one provision, where available, allows some learners to make greater progress, while others find the exclusive attention too intense and miss the social aspect of group learning.

The choice between discrete provision (which tends to be offered mainly at beginning levels) and integrated provision (generally a wider range of levels) is more complex and emotive. What kind of class does a learner want to be in? What kind of class will she learn best in? Learners with GLD often process information more slowly than most adults in integrated classes, so may find the pace of an integrated class unhelpfully fast. Yet, the paces of integrated classes obviously vary a huge amount, as do the learning needs of adults with GLD. Some adults with learning difficulties prefer to be in integrated groups as they feel they move faster and let them 'get on with their work' better. Others prefer to be in classes especially for those with GLD where they may feel more relaxed and accepted.

Other students in integrated classes may (or may not) have reactions to someone with GLD joining their group. To an adult who has overcome considerable personal and external stigma to join a literacy class, the presence of someone with GLD may make them feel out of place (as they may have felt at school) or indicate that they too have GLD, potentially confusing their sense of self. Unconventional behaviours such as constant murmuring or frequent crying – though absolutely not exclusive to, or always an aspect of, GLD – may be problematic in integrated classes, whether disruptive to other learners or alienating to the learner in question. However, many learners with GLD are highly skilful at making others feel welcome and at ease in a group situation, so would be valued members of any class. A teacher of an integrated group needs to balance the needs of everyone in the group, and the learner or learners with GLD as much as everybody else.

Whether discrete or integrated, literacy-focused or embedded, most teachers agree that learning is most effective when what is learnt within the class is strongly linked to life outside the class. Wilson and Hunter (2007) have concluded that, for literacy learning to be effective, literacy tutors need to work together with carers and others supporting adults with GLD, on particular learning goals. This view is reinforced by the argument of Clarke *et al.* (2005) for 'social coherence', a joining up of those who make up the community of adults with GLD, and is a valuable reminder of the vital importance of communication between teachers and care/support workers and that, however provision is organized, the link between what happens in the learning group and what happens outside the group is integral to the significance and validity of literacy learning.

Provision, progression and politics

There are many competing tensions in adult literacy teaching, causing American teacher/researcher Tom Valentine to make the comment many would recognize: 'I do not find adult literacy work comfortable' (Ireland *et al.* 1997: 6). Helping learners decide what kind of provision is best for them, working out what changes to existing provision are needed, and planning, teaching and assessing learning, involve negotiating a philosophical, political and social minefield. Is it true that adults with GLD have a 'ceiling' to their literacy development, beyond which they cannot progress? Or is this a dangerous myth leading to low expectations? Do most adults with GLD make little progress? Or are we measuring progress in the wrong ways? Are literacy classes for adults with GLD sometimes used as 'dumping grounds' (Sutcliffe 1994: 8) for people who have nowhere else to go? And if so, is this a problem of inappropriate literacy provision or of a lack of other services? Who decides if provision is appropriate or not for a particular learner? And is this decision based on what a learner can do or what a learner wants to do?

Does state-funded education have to show certain types of measurable progress in order to justify its cost? Does this progress have to relate to employability or other forms of societal 'usefulness'? And speaking of employability, are there jobs or voluntary opportunities for those adults with GLD who want them? And who judges what is useful to, or about, another person? If someone wants to spend three hours a week in a state-funded adult literacy class, perhaps for ten or twenty years, because she wants to learn to write and is still, after many years, struggling to do so, should we be fighting for her right to continue? Or investigating whether there are other ways to learn which may suit her better? Or trying to unpack that desire to learn to write? Or all three? Is literacy learning only about learning a set of skills that can be taken out of the group and used in a variety of contexts, or could it also be about a social practice that takes place only within the group, a way for learners to participate in a literate culture in a supported way?

Each of these questions raises many more, all important for us to think about when contributing to decisions about funding and provision and when developing our teaching. As teachers we have to balance our attention. We have to keep one eye on how to influence the bigger picture – on how courses are funded, how provision is organized and accredited, curricula for teaching and teacher training – and the other eye on how best to work within our present teaching situations. To forget either one could damn the other.

Learning and teaching

The ideals and ideas of good adult literacy teaching and learning, discussed in this book, stand here too. What is good practice teaching literacy to any group of adults is good practice teaching literacy to adults with GLD and vice versa. Yet – and as important as it is to avoid deficit thinking – when I asked learners with GLD what they think teachers should know in order to teach them better, they explained (in one woman's words) that they may 'have extra difficulty' in certain areas that teachers should 'be ready for'.

TASK 10.1

The following issues are common to all learning situations (and so could equally apply to a numeracy or drama class). What strategies could you use to help learners in each of these cases?

1 **Memory**: Learners may have trouble remembering things said or done earlier in the same learning session or in previous sessions.
2 **Concentration/attention span**: Learners may not be able to concentrate or pay attention to one topic or activity for very long.
3 **Emotions**: Learners may be more likely to have overt emotional reactions, like tears of anger or sadness while learning.

4   **Work arrangements**: Some learners with GLD may find working alone, in pairs or small groups (considered good practice in most areas of education to maximize individual thinking, learner collaboration and provide variety), daunting, preferring the security of the teacher's attention in one-to-one or whole-group work.

5   **Talking and appropriacy**: Learners may be more likely to talk while others are talking, or have difficulty with conventions of turn-taking and relevance in group discussions.

Comment 10.1

Memory

- Repetition, variety and repetition: cover learning points again and again in the same and different ways. Keep reviewing past learning and connecting past learning to present.

- Contextualize and practise as much as possible. Many people remember best when we learn things in a particularly memorable context. (For example, learn about capital letters in place names from reading a postcard from a group member. The memory of that person and that trip may help learners remember the rule.) Encourage active production immediately (ask learners to think of a favourite town, city or borough and ask them to write it up, using a capital letter in the same way).

- Encourage learners to discover learning points for themselves. For example, use a text you are reading or writing to elicit words with the '**sh**' phoneme (David/Wendy – are you using phonemic symbols? If so, put in the '**sh**' phoneme symbol please). Write them up on the board and ask learners to notice how this sound is written, noting the most common spelling and any alternatives, if appropriate.

- Ask learners to recap past work, remembering for each other. Some learners may find remembering difficult; others will remember in great detail. Asking learners to recap for each other challenges those with good memories and creates an environment where learners learn from each other.

- Discuss memory explicitly: talk as a group about what it means to remember, whether or not memory is important, when and what we have to remember, and any ideas for how we can remember better.

- Play games that use and potentially develop the short-term memory, like pelmonism card games (learners could make these themselves in order to practise certain words or letters/sounds) or games where objects are remembered and then one removed. Make these games fun. Sometimes memory can be developed; sometimes it can't.

Concentration/attention span

- Provide a variety of pace, activity (using sight, sound, touch and movement, including experimenting with ICT, while making sure that any learners with physical difficulties can take part) and work arrangements. Experiment and ask learners for feedback.

- Think about provision – would shorter, more frequent classes work better? Have breaks, where learners can move about, eat or drink and get fresh air.
- Be explicit about what you are learning, how and why; most of us concentrate better when we have a good reason. Motivation, interest and ownership: are learners interested? Did you give them a say in what you are doing? Try assigning roles in organizing or deciding what the group is working on. Discuss concentration/attention span with the group. Does anyone have any ideas when and why it becomes difficult to concentrate or how we can concentrate better?

Emotions

- Overt emotion may be distressing to other learners (such as sadness or anger).

  If the class is double-staffed, then try asking the emotional student if he wants to leave the teaching room with you for a while. This way, hopefully, you can calm down the emotional student (remembering always that you are a literacy teacher and not a counsellor) while the other teacher gets the other students focused back on learning. If appropriate, communicate with carers and refer learners to counselling services.
- Talk through text/discussion topics you or other students have chosen before you start, to get an idea of how learners feel about these topics. For example, some learners cared for by elderly parents may have huge anxieties about the idea of a parent dying and may find texts on this topic unbearable. Others may choose this topic for exactly this reason. Ask for, and listen carefully to, all opinions in the group.
- You can also have a discussion, or ask a counsellor to run a session, on how these strong emotions feel, why someone might need to, for example, cry in class and how it might feel to have other learners staring at you when you are feeling particularly vulnerable.

Work arrangements

- Explain that many people like learning in pairs (or small groups or individually) and that you are interested in their opinions on this. Ask them to give a certain arrangement a try, stressing that you'll be asking for feedback afterwards and then as a group you'll decide whether to do it again and get volunteers for particular roles (for example deciding who sits where, keeping time, or how big or small the groups should be).

Talking and appropriacy

- Set aside time each session for learners to talk about whatever they want to talk about, so that you can all be more focused when you move on to the planned learning. Ask how everyone feels about different people talking at once; most learners argue for clear turn taking and no interrupting. Some groups write these down as 'class rules', allowing the teacher and other members of the group to point to these rules when appropriate. This way it is clear that these are rules created by the group for the sake of the happy workings of the group – not the teacher imposing authority for the sake of it.

- Stress that the idea of taking turns when speaking is so that you can all hear each other's contributions, to listen to and learn from each other. If a learner starts talking while someone else is talking, responses of, for example, 'Sorry Sophie, could you please wait, we're trying to listen to Semira', or 'Just a second, Robert is explaining something important to us' avoid getting anywhere close to the inappropriate situation of 'telling off' an adult in front of other adults.

- Some learners who talk to themselves throughout a class may not realize they are doing it. Talk to them alone about it, involving carers if appropriate.

- Relevance is a relative thing. If, for example, during a conversation about recycling, a learner interjects with details of her next holiday, you could feel torn between not wanting to dismiss any learner contribution but also not wanting to distract from the present discussion. Try acknowledging the response while putting it on hold: 'OK, thanks, we'd like to hear about that but right now we're all talking about recycling. Let's come back to your holiday later; I'll note it down.' And do note it down, and do come back to it. (However, the learner may have been about to talk about flights and global warming, related to the topic of recycling, so, to state the obvious, be careful about dismissing or assuming that you're a better judge of appropriacy than others.)

A note on communication: For groups to work, learners need to be able to communicate with each other. This may include learners using British Sign Language with a signer, or lip reading. Additionally, some adults with severe and profound learning difficulties, their carers and teachers, use communication systems developed from sign language, such as Makaton, which involve varied combinations of speech, gestures, facial expressions, eye contact and body language. Some teachers of adults with GLD use such systems to enhance whole-group communciation.

TASK 10.2

These three literacy learning challenges seem more common with learners with GLD. Again, what strategies could you use to help learners in each of these cases, bearing in mind the above *potential* concerns of memory and concentration?

1 Writing sentences with words in an unconventional/incomprehensible order (perhaps with words left out) even when the learner speaks with conventional word order. (For example, a learner says 'I went shopping with my friend' and writes 'Shopping my friend went with') and when it is clearly not an issue of the influence of other languages (check to make sure!).
2 Mixing up capital and lower case letters.
3 Some learners feel there are some words they can read and others they can't, and they will never be able to read those they can't.

Comment 10.2

Writing sentences with words in a non-conventional order

- Sit beside the learner and read his sentence, or ask him to read the sentence, word for word, pointing to each word. He may comment that it doesn't make sense (if not, involve another learner and see what that learner thinks). If the learner decides, alone or with others, that the sentence doesn't work as effective communication (rather than you marking it wrong for reasons he may not understand), then it is an area to address.
- You can also audio-tape the learner saying the sentence she wants to write and play it back several times, using the pause function, so she can notice the order of each word and write it down (scribing for learner as appropriate). You can ask the learner to write her sentence on a whiteboard (large or individual) and sit beside her. Together read, rearrange and add words until it matches the sentence the learner says she wants to write. Electronic whiteboards can work well here, where learners can drag words around (using just fingers with some programmes) until happy.
- Use language experience to write up one or more sentences. Write – or ask learners to write – sentences on a large piece of card cut up into words and invite learners to order into sentences that make sense to them. Ask learners to look at each other's work, comment and discuss.
- Try having discussions about the usual order of words in sentences, eliciting sentences from the group and writing them up on the board (or getting learners to write them up). Read and notice how sentences usually start. Work towards a general observation that *most* sentences

are about someone or something doing or being something, in this order. You may, or may not, want to try introducing terms like subject or verb/predicate.

Mixing up capital and lowercase letters

- Clarify whether the learner doesn't understand the rules of capital letter use, or doesn't realize that there are two distinct forms of each letter or, in handwriting, isn't sure how to form one or the other form, or, in keyboarding, doesn't know how, or doesn't have the motor skills, to switch between capital and lower case – or a combination.
- If the learner has trouble understanding the rules of use, elicit and discuss when and why capital letters are used, and so why it could be confusing for a reader to see a capital *R* in the middle of a word or in the word *Rat* in the middle of a sentence. (Is this a person called Rat or an actual rat, the animal?) If rules are taught without emphasis on the *why*, it's hard for anyone to grasp them.
- If the learner isn't sure of the two different forms of each letter, try some letter tiles, sandpaper letters or 3D letters, so that learners can match capitals with lower case into clear, physical pairs – or get learners to make their own letter tiles of capital and lower case letters and then match them.
- Ask one learner to write a letter on the board and another to write the corresponding capital/lower case – vary and make into games. Or get learners to circle particular letters in texts you've been reading and note if they are capital or lower case (and why).
- Both handwriting and keyboard skills can be practised but this is also an issue of learner priority. One learner may have great difficulty writing/forming letters but really want to develop readable handwriting, while another learner with the same difficulty forming letters may prefer to concentrate on keyboard skills instead.
- What if a learner knows when to use capital and lower case letters and knows how to form each letter but simply prefers to write a capital R whenever an *r* is needed? Here issues of audience and purpose (and the larger issue of what literacy provision is for) come into play. If a learner wants to improve her writing so she can write for herself only, for example in a diary and isn't interested in writing for others, then does it matter if she always writes a capital *R*?

Some learners feel that there are some words they can read and others they can't, and that they will never be able to read those they can't

- Learners may feel that their GLD will prevent them from learning to read new words. This is very rarely the case. Talk explicitly about ways that we can learn to read new words. Ask the learners how they think this happens; they may well come up with the two main (though of course overlapping) categories of phonic decoding and whole-word recognition. Point out that this is how they learnt the words they can already read.

- Try a combination of phonics and whole-word recognition work (contextualized as much as possible, using words from the texts learners want to read and write) and see how it goes with each student. The use of phonics and whole-word recognition has been dealt with in Chapter 5, and what applies to any developing reader applies here. There is a myth floating around that adults with GLD cannot work with a phonic approach, or that those with GLD cannot develop phonemic awareness. In my experience this isn't true of all, or even most, learners. A phonic approach will be very useful for some learners but not for others. Some learners may have bad memories associated with phonic or other approaches to learning to read at school; others will not. Try as many approaches as possible, but avoid materials created for children.

Note

on selecting texts to read, write and discuss: Adults with GLD are likely to be interested in the same range of reading, writing and discussion topics as any adults – from war and dreams to politics and housing. Don't assume any topic is taboo or beyond the philosophical understanding of adults with GLD. As this chapter demonstrates, relatively little is known about GLD, and there is no reason to believe that adults with GLD can't, or don't, think about the same human issues as anyone else.

Ask learners what they need and want to read and write, and why. Invite learners to bring in texts. Bring in texts yourself. Try texts specifically created for literacy learners, adapt texts yourself and use unadapted texts, sometimes grading the task rather than the text. Think widely. Use literature and song, magazines and newspapers. Read texts written by other learners.

Encourage critical thinking by asking why a text has been written, what for, who for, who would read it, who would like it, who might not like it, what makes it 'good' or 'bad'. Think about what we need to do to make our writing effective. How and why can it be a pleasure to read or write? Make books of learner writing, display writing, share writing with other groups. Use language experience. See if learners are interested in setting up pen pal systems with other groups. Set up learner readings as a focus for creating and developing pieces of writing. Don't limit your expectations and in doing so limit the learning and enjoyment that could take place.

Conclusion

Adult literacy learners are the best resource we have for understanding more about teaching and learning reading and writing. Unlike many of us who can't really remember how we learnt to read or write, adult literacy learners are self-consciously developing their reading and writing as part of their adult lives. They have insights into reading, writing and teaching, and to be better teachers we need these insights. Ask your learners what they want to do, why and how. Ask them what helps them learn, and why. Ask them what they find useful and not so useful. Constantly ask for their ideas and suggestions. This is not to say that your professional knowledge, of language and pedagogy, isn't vitally important, or that you shouldn't have clear ideas yourself about things to learn, why and how, but your knowledge and ideas have to react to theirs (not to an externally set curriculum or form of accreditation).

I asked my Entry Level 1 literacy workshop, for adults with GLD, what advice they would give to someone teaching a class like ours. They talked a lot, I scribed their ideas and they made changes to wording and order until they were happy with this:

- help us get better at reading by getting us to do as much reading in class as possible;
- we get better at reading by breaking words down – sounds and letters and parts of words;
- go on lots of trips; we can read signs on trips and write about trips;
- be patient with students – some people do things slower and you have to wait for us;
- help us with spelling; give us spelling quizzes;
- do some work as a big group so we can learn more from each other and some work in small groups so it's quieter and easier to concentrate;
- students and teachers should all be polite and nice to each other: no swearing, shouting or fighting;
- we want a mix of some time to laugh and chat and some time to work hard,
- ask us what we want to do and don't want to do;
- help us with confidence – tell us when we are doing well so we can be more confident.

They also asked me to pass on an invitation to 'come and visit our class'. That, like the rest of their ideas, is an important point. It's difficult to read (and write) about teaching; instead, visit other classes, watch other teachers, ask questions, email and exchange ideas, attend conferences or set up smaller meetings to share perspectives. Like all teaching, working with adults with GLD takes patience (the learners' as much as the teachers'). There will be days when it may feel like you're doing everything wrong, but if you're thinking about it, then you're doing a lot right. So keep trying. It's hard, but it should be.

Further reading and resources

Atkinson, D. (2004) Research and empowerment: involving people with learning difficulties in oral and life history research, *Disability & Society*, 19(7): 691–702.

Bradley, A. (2001) *Induction: Starting Work with People with Learning Disabilities*. Kidderminster: BILD.

British Institute of Learning Disabilities website: www.bild.org.uk accessed 22 June 2009.

Brooks, G. and Green, D. (2003) *Literacy and Numeracy for Adults with Disabilities and Learning Difficulties: A Review and Exploration*. London: National Research and Development Centre for Adult Literacy and Numeracy.

Clarke, C.L., Lhussier, M., Minto, C., Gibb, C.E. and Perini, T. (2005) Pararefdoxes, locations and the need for social coherence: a qualitative study of living with a learning difficulty, *Disability & Society*, 20(4): 405–19.

DfEE (Department for Education and Employment) (2000) *Freedom to Learn: Basic Skills for Learners with Learning Difficulties and/or Disabilities*. London: The Stationery Office.

DfES (Department for Education and Skills) (2001a) *Adult Literacy Core Curriculum*. London: The Stationery Office.

DfES (2001b) *Adult Pre-Entry Curriculum*. London: The Stationery Office.

DfES (2001c) *Access for All: Guidance on Making the Adult Literacy and Numeracy Core Curricula Accessible*. London: The Stationery Office.

DfES/NIACE (2001a). *Basic Skills for Adults with Learning Difficulties or Disabilities: A Resource Pack to Support Staff Development*. London: The Stationery Office.

DfES/NIACE (2001b) *Yesterday I Never Stopped Writing: Community-based Basic Skills for Adults with Learning Difficulties or Disabilities*. London: The Stationery Office.

DfES/NIACE (2001c) *Living Our Lives (10 Readers Written by Learners for Learners)*. London: The Stationery Office.

DfES/NIACE (2006) *Learning for Living*. London: The Stationery Office.

DoH (Department of Health) (2001a) *Valuing People: A New Strategy for Learning Disability for the 21st century*. London: The Stationery Office.

Ivanic, R., Appleby, Y., Hodge, R., Tusting, K. and Barton, D. (2006) *Linking Learning and Everyday Life: A Social Perspective on Adult Language, Literacy and Numeracy Classes*. London: National Research and Development Centre for Adult Literacy and Numeracy.

Leavey, J. and Wilson, A. (2007), Effective learning for adults with learning difficulties: engaging carers and supporters in the literacies learning process. Paper presented at NRDC International Conference: Nottingham, April.

Makaton website: www.makaton.org accessed 22 June 2009.

MENCAP website: www.mencap.org.uk accessed 22 June 2009.

National Autistic Society website: *www.nas.org.uk*. Accessed 22 June 2009.

Nightingale, C. and Maudslay, L. (2004) *Achievement in Non-accredited Learning for Adults with Learning Difficulties*. Leicester: NIACE.

Scottish Consortium for Learning Disability website: www.scld.org.uk accessed 22 June 2009.

Sutcliffe, J. (1994) *Teaching Basic Skills to Adults with Learning Difficulties*. London: The Adult Literacy and Basic Skills Unit and NIACE.

Acknowledgements

Thank you Pelin Ova, **George** Cochrane, **Eddie** McDoughnah, Amie Njie, Claire Bonncy, Iris Browne, **Wayne** Godding, Janet Phillips and Paulette Tivy.

11 Embedding literacy
Theresa Latham

Introduction

There is nothing particularly new about the idea of developing a learner's literacy alongside her study in another subject, and the link between progress in the former and success in the latter has long been established. Programmes designed to develop literacy through other subjects have been around since the 1970s. In a 1994–95 study of further education colleges in England, Nankivell (1996) found that learners needing literacy, language and numeracy support were more likely to stay on the programme, complete their courses and achieve their main qualification aim if they received support for literacy and numeracy. In the intervening years, embedding literacy, language and numeracy in learning programmes has become a key component of the national adult literacy and numeracy strategies of many western countries and substantial investment has been made in a number of research and pathfinder programmes.

Principles and definitions

Not all learners who have literacy needs want to attend a discrete literacy class, and learners can be more motivated to work on their literacy skills when they have the opportunity to improve it as part of a vocational or other programme. One definition of embedded literacy, language and numeracy is teaching and learning that:

> combines the development of literacy, language and numeracy with vocational and other skills. The skills acquired provide learners with the confidence, competence and motivation necessary for them to succeed in qualifications, in life and at work.[1]

Between 2004 and 2006 the National Research and Development Centre for Adult Literacy and Numeracy (NRDC) in England carried out two research studies on embedding literacy, language and numeracy. The first was a series of in-depth case studies of embedded practice across a range of providers, including training providers, colleges and adult and community learning (Roberts *et al.* 2005). The second (Casey *et al.* 2006) focused on embedding literacy and numeracy in vocational programmes in further education colleges. The findings of this study supported the conclusions from Nankivell's earlier research. It found that where literacy and language development were fully embedded in the subject programme, more learners were retained on the programme and completed their vocational qualification. It also found that learners on embedded programmes were significantly more likely to achieve qualifications in literacy, language or numeracy than learners on programmes where these subjects were not embedded.

In order to undertake the analysis the research team identified four different degrees of 'embeddedness'. These ranged from completely separate or discrete classes in language and literacy to fully embedded or integrated support. In developing these categories they placed emphasis on the way in which the learners experience the provision of literacy, language and numeracy teaching.

- **Separate elements**: Learners experience their literacy and language development and vocational studies as entirely, or almost entirely, separate. Literacy and language teaching is provided through an additional programme, rather than being based on the vocational or subject context. Any connections between the different areas are made by the learners themselves.
- **Partly embedded**: Learners experience their literacy and language development and vocational studies as integrated to some degree, or only in some aspects.
- **Mostly embedded**: Learners mostly experience literacy and language development as an integral part of their vocational studies, but some aspects of their literacy and language development and vocational studies remain unco-ordinated.
- **Fully embedded or integrated**: Learners experience their literacy and language development as an integral part of their vocational or other studies. Literacy and language teaching is organized in such a way that it is an integral part of the vocational and other programme itself, but may include explicit work on literacy and language.

The team found that embedded teaching of literacy, language and numeracy is successful when the following are in place.

- Teaching and learning practices:
  - link literacy teaching to subject content and practical activities;
  - use materials contextualized to the subject area;
  - use initial and diagnostic assessment of literacy to inform differentiation in the subject teaching;
  - take as a starting point that literacy development is relevant to *all* learners – not just those with identified literacy needs and essential to their success in their vocational or subject area.

- Teamwork between subject and literacy staff which requires:
  - time for formal planning meetings;
  - opportunities for informal shared planning.

- Staff understandings and beliefs which include:
  - literacy teachers being seen to contribute to learners' vocational aspirations;
  - literacy teachers and subject teachers being willing to engage with each other's subjects and to develop their skills in relation to these.

- A whole-organization approach to embedding which requires:
    - support from senior and middle managers in terms of policy and practice;
    - organizational arrangements, resources and working conditions that support embedding.

The second NRDC research project found evidence that learners achieve best in literacy, language and numeracy when they are taught by a team of specialists rather than by one teacher who teaches both the main subject and LLN. This did not mean team teaching in all lessons, but did require a team approach that ensured literacy, language and numeracy was experienced by learners as a fully integrated part of the overall programme. Literacy and numeracy teaching are complex areas which require input from specialists.

What follows in this chapter is an expansion of the key principles and features based on the research findings and how you might adapt these into your working practice as a literacy teacher.

Structure of provision

Each educational organization is very individual; the way each is structured, and where its sites are, often reflect its historical development and the way that provision has grown to respond to local need. Consequently, there is no one perfect model for embedding or integrating literacy and language. For instance, you may be employed in a prison where movement around the environment is highly structured and it is not possible for education staff to teach jointly in the training workshops, or you may be team teaching with subject teachers in a variety of 'off-site' locations working far from the main centre. However, past research has shown us that there are a number of generic features of good practice we can draw on; research also provides us with case studies of provision that can be transferred to other organizations.

Task 11.1

Case study: further education college
A literacy teacher working on embedded literacy support describes her college below. Consider the challenges you might encounter as a specialist literacy teacher working in this organization.

> I am a literacy teacher in a general further education college which operates over several different campuses. We take a 'multi-layered' approach to embedding literacy in vocational programmes and I think it works quite well. We screen *all* our learners using a nationally published assessment. In previous years, learners had the choice about accepting literacy support and not all of them accepted the offer, but this year we made it compulsory with a positive result.

We were particularly concerned about providing the right amount of literacy teaching and support for learners on Entry and Level 1 programmes, because these learners were less successful on their programmes. This year a new model was introduced, and now the staffing and group sizes reflect the level of the programme of study.

At Entry Level, the group size is kept small, usually 10 learners, and each session is double staffed with literacy and vocational teachers working together. This means that there is substantial integration of literacy teaching within the course. However, all the group also attend Key Skills sessions for one and a half hours each week.

On Level 1 programmes, the teacher–learner ratio is 1:16 on average. These courses have two to three hours of literacy and numeracy a week, jointly taught by a literacy and a vocational teacher.

At Level 2, the college offers additional workshops, with additional pastoral support if it is needed. There is no embedded literacy at this level but students still attend Key Skills sessions.

I plan the course with the vocational teachers. I help them to identify the literacy and language aspects of each course and to develop this aspect of the schemes of work. We have dedicated time to work jointly on this and on writing joint lesson plans for when we team teach. When literacy is taught in a separate session, the lesson plan is my responsibility.

I both team teach with vocational teachers and deliver separate key skills communication sessions. Some vocational teachers I work with are very experienced and have taken specialist literacy qualifications themselves. Others are new to teaching and need more support and advice from me. The make-up of teaching teams can vary from year to year because of staff turnover.

Students record their literacy goals on their Individual Learning Plans, which are shared with all their teachers. Their progress is monitored by the vocational teacher.

The college has three review days a year when the team meets to review the progress of each learner, and I contribute to these reviews.

Comment 11.1

In terms of the challenges facing literacy teachers, you might have identified the following:

Working in partnership
- The need for close collaboration between literacy and vocational teachers to do an audit: to go through the scheme of work together and draw out the key aspects of literacy and language needed on the course.
- The importance of timetabled time for joint planning and preparation and other meetings between vocational and literacy teachers.

- The need for the specialist literacy teachers to attend course team meetings as part of the whole teaching team – in this case to discuss individual students' progress.
- The need to cope with changes to the subject teaching team. You may have built up a good relationship working in a team of experienced vocational teachers and find, as staff change, that you are working with teachers who are less experienced or new and need more support and guidance from you.
- This teacher is working on several sites, and so she will have to work out the logistics of moving around to carry out initial assessments, and meet and plan with her colleagues.

Knowing the subject and the learners

- The need to develop expertise in the subject your students are learning. In some organizations, you might be attached to one or two vocational teams and this will allow you to build up a lot of knowledge about the area. In others, your work may vary from year to year across a range of different subjects.
- In this case study, the vocational teacher monitors learners' progress, but you would still be expected to keep your own records of progress so you can feed back at team meetings.
- Where literacy is taught in separate classes, you will need to check this is linked to the vocational scheme of work, so that learners develop the reading, writing and speaking and listening skills they need at the appropriate time for their vocational study.
- An important role for the specialist is to support vocational teachers in giving feedback to learners, particularly with regard to separating feedback on literacy and language development from progress in vocational skills.

Teaching teams

The seven case studies undertaken by the NRDC (Roberts *et al.* 2005) found that the key aspect of successful embedded support was the quality of the teachers, and good working relationships between them. It is vital that there is a culture of empathy and mutual respect between literacy and other subject teachers. When jointly developing embedded provision with others, you should remember that you are a partner in the teaching and not be tempted to take the role of a 'missionary'. You may also need to be aware that some subject teachers are not fully confident about all aspects of their own literacy skills, for instance spelling or punctuation.

There are a number of existing models across a variety of organizations for embedded teaching arrangements to draw on, for instance, teaching:

- by a vocational teacher who is also qualified to teach literacy;[2]
- by a literacy teacher who is also qualified to deliver the vocational or subject context;

- by team teaching with subject and literacy teachers working together;
- by a subject teacher with input from a literacy teacher in timetabled classes.

One of the key findings of the case studies was the way that learners were motivated by acquiring a new 'professional' identity and the skills and language this involves. One of the most important roles of a vocational or subject teacher is to model the literacy and language of the chosen profession or subject and to demonstrate the behaviour, values and ways of communicating in that occupation – for instance, as a child care worker. The literacy teacher's role here might be to help the subject teacher identify the literacy and language skills needed to become a member of her 'community of practice' (Chaiklin and Lave 1996). Subject teachers have already demonstrated the literacy and language required to be a member of that profession. What they need from literacy teachers is the specialist support to assess the literacy skills of their learners, and guidance on developing those skills through their subject teaching.

Task 11.2

Supporting literacy and language in community education

Read this case study of one learner's experience in community education. If you were a literacy teacher working with the craft teacher, what suggestions would you make to support the learner's literacy and language development in preparation for teaching this course?

A learner's experience in community education

I joined the *Jewellery Craft and Design* course in our community centre last year with a friend of mine because I had never had the chance to design anything before. When we started the course, the teacher handed out a list of assignments we had to do and told the class that we would be making a portfolio, although no one had told us this before we started.

As the course went on some of the other people in the class got quite worried about keeping the portfolio so the teacher brought an example to the class so people could look at it. There was quite a lot of writing – for example about using equipment safely, and I knew from conversations at break that some people in the group were quite anxious about having to do written work.

The portfolio building took a large amount of time. I had to describe how I soldered the metals and which tools I used and why. We had been given some bad photocopies from books with some of the information we needed, but it took time to write it out. Some people in the group needed a bit of support, and the teacher tried when she could. My friend and I also helped people out at break times.

We had not thought when we enrolled that we would be doing so much written work. Because it was a craft class we expected it to be very 'hands on'. Instead we had to write about each design we did and item we made. The teacher did not seem to realize some of us would need so much help. Later on in the course we found out that getting a certificate and preparing the portfolio was an option and not compulsory.

How could you have supported the craft teacher in preparing for the literacy demands of this course?

Comment 11.2

- The course teacher did not have any background information about the learners' previous educational experiences. Where this is available within an organization, you could help the teacher interpret what the available information means in terms of expected levels of literacy. As we have stated previously, learners do not always expect to undertake an assessment of their literacy. However, as we know, most educational programmes make some kind of literacy demand on learners, if only about the introduction of new vocabulary, so for any teacher it is useful to have a broad indication of learners' levels. You also need to consider the nature of the course, its length, the level of qualification (if there is one) and the learners' motivation for studying You could work with the teacher on developing an informal 'light touch' initial assessment to be introduced during the first session, for instance a traffic light self-assessment asking learners to indicate their writing skills on a 'not confident' 'can do with support' 'can do independently' basis.

- Work through the course with the craft teacher to identify the text types that learners will be expected to produce for their portfolios. Help the teacher to draft a writing frame identifying the structural features of the relevant text type with some suggested sentence stems (see below).

- Each new area of study introduces new specialist vocabulary to learners. The craft teacher could identify these from the course specification and produce a glossary of terminology for the programme. You could also show the craft teacher some spelling strategies to help him support learners to write the new vocabulary during lessons. Having identified key words and terminology, the craft teacher could prepare a 'word grid' and make a poster for the new vocabulary to be introduced in a particular lesson.

- If information technology is available, you could show learners' progress through recording sound files. You could suggest some sentence stems to help learners explain what they have done and place the recording alongside an image of their work. These can be placed in an 'e-portfolio'.

Finding a starting point

As mentioned before, not all learners join programmes with the intention of developing their literacy and language skills. There are a variety of reasons why people decide to enrol on learning programmes and these need to be taken into consideration when you work with the subject teacher to consider how you assess learners' literacy skills. In the table below, consider the range of educational programmes that are generally available and what the learner's motivation for joining such a programme might be.

Task 11.3

Learners' motivations

Type of programme	Learner motivation
Vocational e.g. catering, construction Academic e.g. English literature, social studies Personal development e.g. assertiveness Work-based training Informal adult education e.g. art or craft, fitness Return to study Family learning Independent living	

Comment 11.3

You might have identified a list which included:

- getting a job;
- preparing for higher level study;
- seeking promotion at work;
- building self-development and increasing personal confidence;
- learning a new skill;
- training for a particular job;
- meeting a group of people with similar interests;
- returning to study;
- supporting child development; or
- taking increased responsibility for personal affairs.

On some programmes, learners will have enrolled expecting to develop their literacy and language skills as part of their study. On some other courses, as identified in the community programme case study, learners might not expect this at all although, as we know, the delivery of the subject content will make demands on their literacy skills. In either case, however, it is an important part of any teaching preparation to identify what those demands are so that, having made an assessment of learners' literacy strengths and areas for development, teachers can identify which aspects of literacy and language elements they may need to support.

In England, you may find some guides suggest mapping the course syllabus or criteria to adult national standards or the curriculum for literacy and language as a starting point. However, many published case studies demonstrate that embedding literacy in the delivery of other subjects is *not just about matching different curricula together*. The process of mapping literacy curriculum elements to another set of vocational or other criteria can also undermine the subject teacher's confidence to teach the literacy content, as the result often describes what is to be taught or learnt in an impenetrable meta-language when the reality is much simpler.

A more suitable starting point used by many experienced organizations is for the literacy and subject teacher jointly to undertake an audit of the syllabus, to identify the literacy and language elements:

- to be developed for learners to take part in the learning sessions themselves (and for coursework or portfolio evidence if appropriate);
- required for the occupation or subject expertise (as part of the learner's new identity as a member of a 'community of practice');
- to be developed in accord with learners' wishes to enhance their personal skills and confidence.

If we take this approach, an audit of the National Occupational Standards for Animal Care at Level 1 could produce a profile of literacy and language skills as shown in Example 11.1. Then, when you develop the scheme of work, cross-referencing can be made (in England) to the relevant Adult Literacy or Pre-Entry Curriculum Framework at the appropriate level for the learners. You will have a guide to learners' individual literacy strengths and needs from the initial assessment of the group. Following this method, you support the subject teacher in clearly identifying the literacy skills that learners need to develop and explore how learners need to use them as part of their programme of study and for the subject itself.

Example 11.1

A literacy and language audit for animal care at Level 1

Literacy and language for course work/class work/portfolio			Literacy and language for occupation or subject		
Speaking and listening	**Reading**	**Writing**	**Speaking and listening**	**Reading**	**Writing**
Follow instructions. Use subject vocabulary. Give oral presentations. Participate in role play. Participate in paired/group work. Participate in class/group discussion. Participate in group enquiry. Ask questions to obtain information and check own understanding.	Get information from a range of texts: • reports • instructions • explanations using: • skimming • scanning • close reading.	Take notes from oral presentations, demonstrations and written texts. Produce written text for: • course assignments • recounts[3] • reports • explanations • instructions • portfolio statements. Use clear handwriting. Spell regularly used and specialist words correctly.	Participate in workplace interactions: • report health and safety issues • make Health and Safety suggestions • deal with enquiries • ask questions to obtain information • refer enquiries • take part in formal and informal conversations with other staff.	Read a range of workplace texts: • policy documents • stock records • care records • instructions • health and Safety signs. Use close reading for detailed information. Read technical terms and specialist vocabulary.	Produce a range of written texts: • stock records • client appointments • accident reports • messages • care records. Spell common, regularly used and specialist words correctly. Use clear handwriting.

This particular audit has identified:

- the range of text types that the learner will need to read and write both for the learning programme and for the chosen occupation;
- the range of speaking and listening interactions which will take place both on the programme and in the workplace.

Task 11.4

Auditing a course

Take a look at two of the performance criteria taken from the unit specification for 'Prepare and Mix Concrete and Mortars'. If you were working with the vocational teacher, what aspects of literacy and language could you draw out as part of your audit for the scheme of work, breaking down the skills between speaking and listening, reading and writing?

Performance criteria	Knowledge and understanding relating to performance criteria
You must be able to:	*You must know and understand:*
1 Comply with given, relevant legislation and official guidance to carry out your work and maintain safe work practices.	Different types of instructions. About relevant, current legislation and official guidance and how it is applied. How emergencies should be responded to and who should respond. Security procedures for tools, equipment and personal belongings. What the accident reporting procedures are and who is responsible for making the reports. What personal protective equipment should be used and when.
2 Select the required quantity and quality of resources for the methods of work.	The characteristics, quality, uses, limitations and defects associated with different materials. How the materials should be used. The hazards associated with the materials and methods of work.

Comment 11.4

You might have identified:

Speaking and listening	Reading	Writing
Listen to and follow detailed guidance, explanations and instructions. Report any issues to do with health and safety, working method, hazards and accidents. Take part in workplace discussions on: • health and safety • use of personal protective equipment • selection of resources, tools and equipment • methods of work • hazards associated with the resources and working methods. Ask questions to get information and check own understanding. Speak clearly and use language that is appropriate to the situation.	Read and find information from a range of workplace texts: • health and safety documents • detailed instructions • Health and Safety and COSHH signs • diagrams, for instance, management structure tree. Read regular and commonly used words and specialist, technical vocabulary.	Write: • notes • reports • recounts • instructions. Spell regularly and commonly used words and specialist, technical vocabulary. Produce clear, legible text.
Provide explanations about health and safety issues and safe use of tools and equipment.		

You might also add a numeracy and ICT column if you are responsible for these skills too.

When you develop the scheme of work with the subject teacher, you will want to identify when particular literacy and language skills will be taught so that delivery coheres with the delivery of specific aspects of the subject syllabus. Throughout the scheme of work and lesson planning, you will also be supporting the differentiation of literacy learning objectives, activities, resources and outcomes based on learners' individual starting points and the results of initial and diagnostic assessment. For instance, if we take the writing aspects from the last example, at lesson planning level, the literacy objective might look like this:

> We are learning to write an account of how we made the cement mix.

If you differentiate the learning outcomes, based on the target level learners are aiming for, they might look like this:

At text level

What I'm looking for is that you can:
- present your writing in short paragraphs (Entry level);
- organize your writing in paragraphs that show the sequence of events (Level 1);
- organize your writing showing the structural features of a recount text (Level 2).

At sentence level

What I'm looking for is that you can write:
- in simple sentences (Entry level);
- in simple and compound sentences (Level 1);
- in simple, compound and complex sentences (Level 2).

At word level

What I'm looking for is that you can spell:
- words you use regularly and some key words for work (Entry level);
- a range of regularly used words including plurals and some specialist vocabulary (Level 1);
- a range of specialist and technical words you use regularly at work (Level 2).

Always remember that, tempting though it is to start with spelling, objectives for writing should always start at text level, particularly focusing on the structure of the target text type. Then devise appropriate outcomes at sentence and word level, according to the target level learners are aiming for. When you define spelling objectives, you may find that it is helpful to support learners with a word grid of a range of work-related words at the appropriate level. This defines the range of words they are aiming to spell when you negotiate their individual learning targets.

It can be an easy trap to agree an individual target with learners to *'improve my spelling'* because most of us worry about spelling when we write, particularly when we are learning a new subject which is introducing us to new vocabulary. It will be more supportive to identify the new vocabulary with learners according to their target level and then prepare spelling strategies to support them, as they can identify their progress in reviews against a specific goal. 'Improving my spelling ...' is a vague, immeasurable target and, rather like painting the Forth Rail Bridge, learners will never know when they have finally achieved it.

Lesson planning

After you have undertaken the literacy and language audit, the information flow chart through to developing the scheme of work and lesson planning stage can be summed up as follows:

> Subject specifications, qualification unit specification or personal development programme outcomes.

> Describe the literacy and language elements for the scheme of work in terms of:
> - those skills to be developed for the learning sessions (and course-work);
> - those skills to be developed for the occupation or subject;
> - those skills to be developed for personal/social aims.

> On a lesson planning level, identify the subject and literacy/language objectives and learning outcomes expressed in a way that learners can understand.

> Make links or reference to key skills or Pre-Entry Curriculum Framework/Adult Literacy Core Curriculum to describe skills to be developed.

With the subject teacher, throughout the entire scheme of work, you will have identified the range of literacy and language skills to be developed both for the subject and for the learner to take part in the programme. The next step at individual lesson planning level is to work with the subject teacher to draw out the literacy lesson objectives alongside those for the subject. For instance, the table below shows the national occupational standards for making an appointment in animal care at Level 1.

Example 11.2

Standards for making an appointment in animal care at Level 1

Element AC7.2 Make appointments	
Performance criteria	**Knowledge and understanding**
You must: 1 Deal with all requests for appointments politely and promptly. 2 Accurately identify client requirements 3 Schedule appointments to satisfy the client and to ensure the most productive use of time. 4 Confirm the availability of services, where necessary with relevant colleagues. 5 Confirm appointment details are acceptable to the client. 6 Ensure all appointment details are accurate, recorded in the right place and are easy to read.	You must know and understand: • the importance of making appointments correctly; • the importance of communicating effectively; • how to make appointments; • how to ask the right questions and give suitable answers to questions; • the services available; their duration and cost; • how the appointment system works; • the limits of your own authority when making appointments.

If you work in England and did a direct mapping exercise to an Adult Literacy Core Curriculum at Level 1, the learning objectives could read:

SLc/L1.1   Speak clearly in a way which suits the situation.
SLC/L1.2   Make requests and ask questions to obtain information in a familiar context.
Ww/L1.1   Spell correctly words most often used at work.
Ww/L1.1   Produce legible text.

As we have discussed before, this approach uses a meta-language that the subject teacher might find daunting as it does not clearly identify the skills to be developed in the context in which the learners will be using them. However, if you draw out the relevant literacy and language aspects of the task with the subject teacher, the learning objective for the lesson might be expressed in a clearer way that learners will understand, like this:

We are learning to make appointments for clients and deal with them appropriately.

The level of performance (that is the learning outcomes or success criteria) that you expect from learners could be expressed as:

What I am looking for is that you can:
- talk to the client politely;
- ask the right questions to get the information you need;
- speak to work colleagues to check any details;
- agree a date and time with the client;
- confirm the appointment to the client;
- write the appointment clearly and correctly in the appointment book so that other people can read it.

If you take an audit rather than a mapping approach, you will work through a hierarchy with the subject teacher that starts with clear identification of the literacy and language skills to be developed throughout the scheme of work and at individual lesson planning level. This method produces clear literacy learning aims and outcomes that you can cross-reference to the relevant curricula, rather than using curriculum references and elements as the starting point for planning teaching and learning.

The next stage is to identify how you, the literacy teacher, can support the subject teacher in preparing to teach and support literacy and language skills development throughout:

- the teaching and learning activities;
- the checks that are made on learners' understanding;
- giving constructive feedback to learners on their work;
- conducting a plenary or lesson review; and
- supporting the learners' self-evaluation of progress.

Consider the learning objective we discussed previously.

We are learning to make appointments for clients and deal with them appropriately.

If you were planning the lesson with the vocational teacher, what teaching and learning activities would you suggest that support the development of language and literacy against the learning outcomes?

You might have considered any of the following:

- Listening activities, for instance watching a video extract of an assistant booking an appointment and asking learners to identify key words, questions and phrases used.
- Small or whole-group discussions about use of formal and informal language and cultural/generational attitudes about politeness.
- Role plays about dealing with a range of customers including handling difficult or problem situations.

- A thinking frame to support the development of critical thinking about problem solving, solutions, outcomes and consequences for discussions about handling difficult or problem situations.
- Sentence stems (see below) to support learners in asking questions for information and clarification (modelled by teachers). This can be developed with an oral questioning game such as 'Crime and detection' where one group is given individual character and information cards about a fictional crime, and the detective group is given a limited number of questions they can ask to solve it. Other games include 'Guess the mystery object' or 'Missing maps', where each small group has the same street map as other groups but each map has different items of information. Each group can only ask one question in turn of any other group to complete the blanks on their map. The winning team is the first with a complete map. This exercise is also useful for developing positional language in addition to framing questions.
- A handwriting game for pairs such as 'Consequences' supports the importance of writing so that others can read it. The game can be put in the context of the lesson, for instance: 'In a veterinary practice in ... the client said ... the assistant said ... the consequence was ...' Obviously, set ground rules for the game.
- Support learners in identifying when performance reaches the success criteria or learning outcomes. For instance, give the learners the success criteria and show a range of video extracts between a client and assistant booking an appointment. Ask learners to use the success criteria to assess whether the interaction reaches the expected performance. Where it does, ask them to explain why, where it does not, ask them to suggest what the assistant could have done to achieve it.

Effective stems for questioning

How can we be sure that ... ?
What is the same and what is different about ... ?
Why do —, — and — all give the same answer?
How do you ... ?
How would you explain ... ?
What does that tell us about ... ?
Why is — true?
What do you think ... ?
How do you know ... ?
Why do you think that ... ?
How can you be sure ... ?
Is there another way/idea ... ?
What if ... ?
Where is there an example of this?
What do you think happens next?

Task 11.5

Planning a hairdressing lesson

If you were working with the hairdressing teacher, consider the strategies for teaching and supporting literacy and language that you could suggest, using the following frame as a prompt.

Learning objective We are learning to carry out a scalp condition check with a client and write a report.		
Lesson stage	**Teaching and learning activity**	**Strategies for supporting the teaching of speaking and listening, reading and writing**
Introduction and learning objectives.	Recap of last lesson. Explanation of learning objective.	
Main part of session.	Teacher demonstrates undertaking a scalp condition report with a 'client'.	
	Learners each work with a 'client' to undertake a scalp condition report.	
Formative feedback and dialogue about learning.	Teacher discusses progress with learners and checks that they know what they need to do to reach the learning outcomes.	
Plenary and learner self-review.	Teacher and learners measure their progress against the intended learning outcomes. Learners review their progress. Learners prepare portfolio statements and reports if required.	

Comment 11.5

You could suggest a number of scaffolded approaches to support the development of literacy and language in the lesson delivery, including some of the following:

Introduction and learning objectives
- Learning objective(s) and outcomes displayed on whiteboard or interactive whiteboard.
- Question bank for teacher to check understanding of learning objective.

Main part of session
- Teacher models key language and terminology during the demonstration.
- Note-taking frame for steps in a sequence for use on paper or laptop/writing tablet.
- Personal glossary of new vocabulary as handout either on paper or ICT format.
- Key word grid of new specialist vocabulary on display in learning environment either paper or on interactive whiteboard.

Learner activity
- Sentence stems to prompt discussion with client, e.g. 'Do you have any problems with ...'?
- Writing frame for a scalp condition report either on paper or for use on laptop or writing tablet.
- Exemplars of scalp condition reports written at a range of literacy levels.
- Teacher has prepared strategies to support learners in spelling new specialist vocabulary.

Formative feedback and dialogue
- Question bank for teacher to check learner progress and understanding against learning objective(s) and outcomes.
- Reminder prompt sheet for teacher to frame constructive feedback e.g. 'Remember when we/that we ...' (followed by an improvement prompt and an example of target skill).

Plenary: Stems for plenary review
    I can ...
    My strengths are ...
    My targets are ...
    I need to work on ...
    I understand ...
    I learned something new when ...
    I found ... difficult.

I need more help with ...
I want to improve ...
I learned best when ...

- Oral or written plenary such as learner presentation or graffiti board exercise.
- Effective question stems for teacher to model language to learners.
- Key review word grid and sentence stems on display for learners to use in self-review.
- **KWL** thinking frame to support learners in reflecting on what they **k**now, what they **w**ant to find out and what they **l**earned.
- Writing frame either on paper or electronically for e-portfolio to support writing evidence report.
- Use of oral recordings and sound files for e-portfolio reflection on learning.

Summary

Embedding literacy in teaching and learning

- Embedded approaches require teachers with different expertise to work together in a complementary way to meet learners' needs.
- The approach to embedded literacy has to be across the whole organization so that it is part of every programme and learners have equal opportunities to develop their literacy skills.
- Embedding literacy is not just about just about mapping a subject curriculum to the literacy and language curricula. The specialist teacher needs to learn how literacy is used for the particular vocational or subject area and in each different learning environment.
- The integration and timing of literacy is crucial. It needs to be integrated not just with the vocational or subject context in general but with the specific vocational or subject task the learner has in hand at the time.
- Good relationships between teachers are vital. Vocational/subject and literacy teachers should plan and work closely together as a teaching team. They should share the same vocational objectives for their learners, be strongly learner-centred and prepared to learn from each other.
- The way in which teachers, both vocational and literacy specialists, introduce literacy is crucial to motivating learners and developing positive learner attitudes.

Further reading and resources

Casey et al (2006) *'You wouldn't expect a maths teacher to teach plastering'. Embedding literacy and language in post 16 vocational programmes - the impact on learning and achievement.* London: NRDC

Eldred, J. (2005) *Developing Embedded Literacy, Language and Numeracy: Supporting Achievement.* Leicester: NIACE.

Learning for Work (2007) *Improving Initial Assessment: Guide to Good Practice. Initial Assessment Toolkit* (Key Skills Support Project). London: Learning and Skills Network. www.lsneducation.org.uk accessed 4 April 2009.

Roberts, C. et al (2006) *'Embedded teaching and learning of adult literacy, numeracy and ESOL' Seven Case Studies.* London: NRDC

Notes

1. www.dfes.gov.uk/readwriteplus/embeddedlearning accessed 30 March 2009).
2. The NRDC Study (Casey 2006) found, however, that where one teacher is required to teach both the vocational subject and LLN, the learners are twice as likely to fail their language, literacy and numeracy qualifications. This suggests that asking vocational teachers to take on literacy teaching without collaborating with literacy colleagues is a less successful option for embedding. Hence the title of the report: 'You wouldn't ask a maths teacher to teach plastering'.
3. A 'recount' is a text type commonly used in reports or in education. It is an account of something that has occurred in time sequence. It starts with an introduction setting the context, followed by a temporal sequence. It concludes with conclusions, feelings or thoughts about the event described.

Glossary

ABE	Adult Basic Education (early name for adult literacy and numeracy classes in England)
ALBSU	Adult Literacy and Basic Skills Unit (national agency for supporting literacy and numeracy in the 1980s)
BSA	Basic Skills Agency (national agency for supporting literacy and numeracy in the 1990s)
BBC	British Broadcasting Corporation
ESOL	English for Speakers of Other Languages (usually used to describe English language teaching for those making their home in the UK)
EU	European Union
FLCs	Family Learning Classes, usually based in schools, where children and adults learn together
FE	Further education (distinguished from Adult and Community Learning and higher education), Further education colleges provide largely vocational qualifications for 14- to 19-year-olds and adults
GCSE	General Certificate of Secondary Education (national qualifications sat at 16 in schools in the UK)
IALS	International Adult Literacy Survey
ICT	Information and communication technology
LSC	Learning and Skills Council (government agency responsible for national funding of all lifelong learning in England, except for universities)
LEA	Local education authority
UNESCO	United Nations Educational, Scientific and Cultural Organization
OECD	Organization for Economic Cooperation and Development
DfES	Department for Education and Skills
Learn Direct	Government provision, based locally, offering online and distance learning opportunities for adults.
Ofsted	Office for Standards in Education (responsible for inspecting all provision in the lifelong learning sector, apart from universities)
Skills for Life	Adult literacy, numeracy and English for speakers of other languages (ESOL). More recently, information and communications technology has been added as a 'basic skill'

References

ALBSU (Adult Literacy and Basic Skills Unit) (1985) *Adult Literacy: The First Decade*. London: ALBSU.

Alexander, R. (2004) *Towards Dialogic Teaching: Rethinking Classroom Talk*. York: Dialogos.

Anderson, L.W. and Krathwohl, D.R. (eds) (2001) *A Taxonomy for Learning, Teaching and Assessing: A Revision of Bloom's Taxonomy of Educational Objectives*, Complete edn. New York: Longman.

Andrews, R., Torgerson, C., Beverton, S. *et al.* (2004) The effect of grammar teaching (syntax) in English on 5 to 16 year old accuracy and quality in written composition, *Research Evidence in Education Library*. London: EPPI-Centre, Social Science Research Unit, Institute of Education. http://eppi.ioe.ac.uk/cms/Default.aspx?tabid=229 accessed 28 March 2009.

Appleby, Y. (2008) *Bridges into Learning for Adults Who Find Provision Hard to Reach*. Leicester: NIACE.

Appleby, Y. and Barton, D. (2008) *Responding to People's Lives*. Leicester: NIACE.

Appleby, Y. and Barton, D. (2009) Adults' lives and learning in different contexts: a view over time, in S. Reder and J. Bynner (eds) *Tracking Adult Literacy and Numeracy Skills: Findings from Longitudinal Research*. London: Routledge.

Appleby, Y. and Hamilton, M. (2006) Literacy as social practice: travelling between the everyday and other forms of learning, in P. Sutherland and J. Crowther (eds) *Lifelong Learning: Contexts and Concepts*. London: Routledge/Falmer.

ARG (Assessment Reform Group) (2002) *Assessment for Learning: 10 Research-based Principles to Guide Classroom Practice*. http://arg.educ.cam.ac.uk/CIE3.pdf accessed 22 September 2006.

Badley, G. (2003) The truth of stories: Graham Badley reviews, narratives and fictions in educational research by Peter Clough, *Post-Compulsory Education*, 8(3): 441–6.

Barnes, C. and Mercer, G. (eds) (2005) *Implementing the Social Model of Disability: Theory and Research*. Leeds: The Disability Press.

Barton, D. (2007) *Literacy: An Introduction to the Ecology of Written Language*, 2nd edn. Oxford: Blackwell.

Barton, D. and Hamilton, M. (2000) *Local Literacies: Reading and Writing in One Community*. London: Routledge.

Barton, D., Hamilton, M. and Ivanic, R. (2000) *Situated Literacies: Reading and Writing in Context*. London: Routledge.

Barton, D., Appleby, Y., Hodge, R., Tusting, K. and Ivanic, R. (2006) *Relating Lives and Learning: Adults' Participation in a Variety of Settings*. London: National Research and Development Centre for adult literacy and numeracy (NRDC).

Barton, D., Ivanic, R., Appleby, Y., Hodge, R. and Tusting, K. (2007) *Literacy, Lives and Learning*. London: Routledge.

Belzer, A. (2004) 'It's not like normal school': the role of prior learning contexts in adult learning, *Adult Education Quarterly*, 55(1): 41–59.

Besser, S. *et al.* (2004) *Adult Learners' Difficulties in Reading: An Exploratory Study*. London: NRDC.

Black, P. and Wiliam, D. (1998) Assessment and classroom learning, *Assessment in Education*, 5(1): 7–74.

Black, P., Harrison, C., Lee, C., Marshall, B. and Wiliam, D. (2003) *Assessment for Learning: Putting It Into Practice*. Buckingham: Open University Press.

Black, P., Harrison, C., Lee, C., Marshall, B. and Wiliam, D. (2005) *Assessment for Learning*, 3rd edn. Oxford: OUP.

Boud, D. (2000) Sustainable assessment: rethinking assessment for the learning society, *Studies in Continuing Education*, 22(2): 151–67.

Bradley, A. (2001) *Induction: Starting Work with People with Learning Disabilities*. Kidderminster: BILD.

Brandt, D. (2005) Writing for a living: literacy and the knowledge economy, *Written Communication*, 22(2) (April): 166–97.

Bransford, J.D. and Johnson, M.K. (1972) Contextual prerequisites for understanding: some investigators of comprehension and recall, *Journal of Verbal Learning and Verbal Behavior*, 11: 717–26.

Brigden, A. and McFall, C. (2000) Dyslexia in Higher Education Art and Design: A Creative Opportunity, Surrey Institute of Art and Design University College, Farnham, Surrey, GU9 7DS (Available from the Academic Registrar).

Briggs, A. and Burke, P. (2005) *A Social History of the Media: From Gutenberg to the Internet*. Cambridge: Polity Press.

British Institute of Learning Disabilities (2007) www.bild.org.uk accessed 24 June 2009.

Brookfield, S. (1990) *The Skilful Teacher: On Technique, Trust and Responsiveness in the Classroom*. San Francisco, CA: Jossey Bass.

Brooks, G. *et al.* (2007) *Effective Teaching and Learning: Reading*. London: NRDC.

BSA (Basic Skills Agency) (1997) *Annual Report 1996/7*. London: Basic Skills Agency.

BSA (2008) *The Spelling Pack: 21st Century*. Leicester: NIACE.

Burton, M. (2007) *Oral Reading Fluency for Adults*. London: NRDC.

Bynner, J. and Parsons, S. (2006) *New Light on Literacy and Numeracy*. London: NRDC.

Campbell, B. and Bradshaw, D. (eds) (2007) *Fancy Footwork: Adult Educators Thinking on their Feet*. Melbourne: Victoria Adult Literacy and Basic Education Council.

Casey, H. *et al* (2006) *'You Wouldn't Expect a Maths Teacher to Teach Plastering ...' Embedding Literacy, Language and Numeracy in Post-16 Vocational Programmes – The Impact on Learning and Achievement*. London: NRDC.

Carter, R. (1995) *Keywords in Language and Literacy* London: Routledge.

Chaiklin, S. and Lave, J. (1996) *Understanding Practice: Perspectives on Activity and Context*. Cambridge: Cambridge University Press.

Clarke, C.L., Lhussier, M., Minto, C., Gibb, C.E. and Perini, T. (2005) Paradoxes, locations and the need for social coherence: a qualitative study of living with a learning difficulty, *Disability & Society*, 20(4): 405–19.

Condelli, L., Wrigley, H., Yoon, K., Seburn, M. and Cronen, S. (2003) *What Works. Study for Adult ESOL Literacy Students*. Washington, DC: US Department of Education.

Cookson, H., Hale, G., Menist, C. and Rice, B. (2006) *'I Can': Demonstrating Soft Outcomes for Homeless and Vulnerable Learners*. London: NRDC.

Crystal, D. (2003) *English as a Global Language*, 2nd edn. Cambridge: Cambridge University Press.

Davies, R. (2007) The experience of dyslexia: some personal accounts, *REFLECT* (NRDC), Issue 8 (June).

Davis, R.D. with Eldon, M. Braun (1994) *The Gift of Dyslexia. Why Some of the Brightest People Can't Read and How They Can Learn*. London: Souvenir Press.

Denny Taylor (1996) *Toxic Literacies: Exposing the Injustice of Bureaucratic Texts*. Portsmouth, NH: Heinemann.

Derrick, J., Gawn, J. and Ecclestone, K. (2007) Improving formative assessment: looking at pedagogy in post-compulsory education, including adult literacy, numeracy and ESOL, *Research and Practice in Adult Literacy Journal*, 62 (Spring).

Derrick, J., Gawn, J. and Ecclestone, K. (2008) Evaluating the 'spirit' and 'letter' of formative assessment in the learning cultures of part-time adult literacy and numeracy classes, *Research in Post-Compulsory Education*, 13(2).

Dewey, J. (1907) *The School and Society*. Chicago, IL: University of Chicago Press.

DfEE (Department for Education and Employment) (1999) *Improving Literacy and Numeracy: A Fresh Start. The Report of the Working Group Chaired by Sir Claus Moser*. London: HMSO.

DfEE (2001) *Skills for Life – The National Strategy for Improving Adult Literacy and Numeracy Skills*, White Paper. London: HMSO.

DfES (Department for Education and Skills) (2001) *Adult Literacy Core Curriculum*. London: DfES.

DfES (2004a) *The Skills for Life Annual Review 2003–04*. London: DfES.

DfES (2004b) *Delivering Skills for Life. A Framework for Understanding Dyslexia*. Leicester: NIACE.

DfES (2005) *Disability Discrimination Act (DDA)*. London: The Stationery Office.

D. Nuccio *et al.* (eds) (1994) *The Macintosh Bible*, 5th edn. Berkeley, CA: Peachpit Press, quoted in De Silva, J. H. and Burns, A. (1999) *Focus on Grammar*. Sydney: National Centre for English Language Teaching and Research.

Dore, W. (2000) *The Wynford Dore Programme. Dyslexia, Dyspraxia, Autism Treatment Centres*, www.Dore.co.uk accessed 24 June 2009.

Edward, S., Coffield, F., Steer, R. and Gregson, M. (2007) Endless change in the learning and skills sector: the impact on teaching staff, *Journal of Vocational Education and Training*, 59(2): 155–73.

Eldred, J. (2002) *Moving On with Confidence*. Leicester: NIACE.

Everatt, J. (1997) The abilities and disabilities associated with adult developmental dyslexia, *Journal of Research in Reading*. 20(1), 13–21.

Fawcett, A. (2001) *Dyslexia: Theory and Good Practice*. London: Whurr.

Freebody, P. and Luke, A. (1999) *Further Notes on the Four Resources Model*. www.readingonline.org/research/lukefreebody.html accessed 31 March 2009.

Freire, P. (1972) *Pedagogy of the Oppressed*. Harmondsworth: Penguin Books.

Gardener, S. (1985) *Conversations with Strangers*. London: ALBSU/Write First Time.

Gardiner, A. (2008) *Revision Express A5 and A2 English Language*. Harlow: Pearson Education.

Gardner, H. (1983) *Frames of Mind: The Theory of Multiple Intelligences*. New York: Basic Books.

Gilbert, K. and Appleby, Y. (2005) 'Sometimes I tell them from my old family.' Bi-lingual family language, literacy and numeracy learning. Working Paper No. 10. Lancaster: Lancaster Literacy Research Centre.

Glover, J., Bruning, R. and Ronning, R. (1990) *Cognitive Psychology For Teachers*. New York: Macmillan.

Goodman, K. [1973] Miscues: windows on the reading process, in A. Flurkey and X. Jingguo (eds) (2003) *On the Revolution of Reading: The Selected Writings of Kenneth S. Goodman*. Portsmouth, NH: Heinemann.

Goswami, U. (2002) Rhymes, phonemes and learning to read, in M. Cook (ed.) *Perspectives on the Teaching and Learning of Phonics*. Royston: United Kingdom Reading Association.

Goswami, U. and Bryant, P. (1990) *Phonological Skills and Learning to Read*. Hove: Lawrence Erlbaum.

Grief, S. and Chatterton, J. (2007) *Writing*. London: NRDC.

Grief, S., Meyer, B. and Burgess, A. (2007) *Effective Teaching and Learning: Writing*. London: NRDC.

Halliday, M.A.K. (1985) *Spoken and Written Language*. Victoria: Deakin University. Quoted in De Silva, J. H. and Burns, A. (1999) *Focus on Grammar*. Syndey: National Centre for English Language Teaching and Research.

Hamilton, M. and Hillier, Y. (2006a) *A History of Adult Literacy, Numeracy and ESOL 1970–2000*. Stoke on Trent: Trentham Books.

Hamilton, M. and Hillier, Y. (2006b) *Changing Faces of Adult Literacy, Language and Numeracy: A Critical History*. Stoke on Trent: Trentham Books.

Harris, R. Disappearing language: fragments and fractures between speech and writing, in J. Mace (1995) *Literacy, Language and Community Publishing*. Clevedon: Multilingual Matters.

Harrison, C. (2003) *Understanding Reading Development*. London: Sage Publications.

Haviland, R. (1973) *Survey for Provision of Adult Illiteracy in England*. Reading: Centre for the Teaching of Reading, Reading University.

Heath, S.B. (1983) *Ways with Words: Language Life and Work in Communities and Classrooms*. Cambridge: Cambridge University Press.

Herrington, M. (2000) Dyslexia interview schedule. Internal document in the Nottingham University Study Support Centre.

Herrington, M. (2001a) Adult dyslexia – partners in learning, in M. Hunter Carsch and M. Herrington (eds) *Dyslexia and Effective Learning in Secondary, and Tertiary Education*. London: Whurr.

Herrington, M. (2001b) An approach to learning support in HE, in M. Hunter Carsch, and M. Herrington (eds) *Dyslexia and Effective Learning in Secondary and Tertiary Education*. London: Whurr.

Herrington, M. (2001c) Conversations about spelling, in M. Hunter Carsch and N. Herrington (eds) *Dyslexia and Effective Learning in Secondary and Tertiary Education*. London: Whurr.

Herrington, M. (2001d) The continuing exploration. Insights for literacy educators, *RaPAL Bulletin*, 46.

Herrington, M. and Hunter Carsch, M. (2001) A social interactive model of specific learning difficulties, in M. Hunter Carsch and M. Herrington (eds) *Dyslexia: A Psycho Social Perspective*. London: Whurr.

Herrington, M. and Kendall, A. (2005) Introduction, *Insights from Research and Practice. A Handbook for Adult Literacy Practitioners in Post-Compulsory Education*. Leicester: NIACE.

Herrington, M., Whitehouse, G., Davis, G. and Warren, P. (2005) Creativity and the core curriculum? *RaPAL Bulletin*, 57: 2–6.

Hetherginton, J. (1996) Approaches to the development of self-esteem in dyslexic students in higher education, in Higher Education: Practical Responses to Student and Institutional Needs, Conference Proceedings, Jointskill/University of Huddersfield Conference, January.

Hodgen, J. and Wiliam, D. (2006) *Mathematics inside the Black Box: Assessment for Learning in the Mathematics Classroom*. London: Kings College London/NFER Nelson.

Hoover, W. and Gough, P. (1990) The simple view of reading, *Reading and Writing*, 2: 127–60.

Hornsby, B. and Shear, F. (1980) *Alpha to Amega: The A–Z of Teaching Reading, Writing and Spelling*, 3rd edn. London: Heinemann.

House of Commons Public Accounts Committee (2009) *Skills for Life: Progress in Improving Adult Literacy and Numeracy*. London: The Stationery Office.

Howard, U. (2004) Hearing 'the learner's voice, *Adults Learning*, February: 23–4. Leicester: NIACE.

Hurry, J., Brazier, L., Snapes, K. and Wilson, A. (2005) *Improving the Literacy and Numeracy of Disaffected Young People in Custody and in the Community. A Summary Interim Report*. London: NRDC.

Illeris, K. (2002) *The Three Dimensions of Learning: Contemporary Learning Theory in the Tension Field between the Cognitive, the Emotional and the Social*. Trekroner: Roskilde University Press, distributed by NIACE.

Ireland, T., Mace, J., Ntseane, G. and Valentine, T. (1997) Articulating the structural and personal boundaries of adult literacy education: a comparative analysis of four nations. Paper presented at the 27th annual Standing Conference on University Teaching and Research in the Education of Adults, University of London, 1–3 July.

Ivanic, R. (1996) Linguistics and the logic of non-standard punctuation, in N. Hall and A. Robinson (eds) *Learning about Punctuation*. Clevedon: Multilingual Matters.

Ivanic, R. (1997) *Writing and Identity: The Discoursal Construction of Identity in Academic Writing*. Amsterdam/Philadelphia, PA: John Betjamins Publishing Company.

Ivanic, R. (ed.) with Beck, D., Burgess, G., Gilbert, K., Hodson, R. and Hudson, A. (2004) *Listening to Learners: Practitioner Research on the Adult Learners' Project*. London: NRDC.

Ivanic, R., Appleby, Y., Hodge, R., Tusting, K. and Barton, D (2006) *Linking Learning and Everyday Life: A Social Perspective on Adult Language, Literacy and Numeracy Classes*. London: NRDC.

Kallenbach, S. and Viens, J. (2001) *Multiple Intelligences in Practice: Teacher Research Reports from the Adult Multiple Intelligences Study*. Cambridge, MA: NCSALL, University of Harvard.

Klein, C. (1993) *Diagnosing Dyslexia: A Guide to the Assessment of Adults with Specific Learning Difficulties*. London: Basic Skills Agency.

Kress, G. (1985) *Linguistic Processes in Sociocultural Practice*. Oxford: OUP.

Kress, G. (2000) The futures of literacy, *RaPAL Bulletin*, 42: 1–19.

Kress, G. (2007) *Multimodality: Exploring Contemporary Methods of Communication*. London: Routledge.

Kruidenier, J. (2002) *Research-based Principles for Adult Basic Education Reading Instruction*. Portsmouth, NH: National Institute for Literacy.

Laurillard, D. (1997) *Rethinking University Teaching*. London: Routledge.

LSC (Learning and Skills Council) (2005) *National Learner Satisfaction Survey: Adult and Community Learning Providers Report 2003/04*. Coventry: Learning and Skills Council.

Leavey, J. and Wilson, A. (2007). Effective learning for adults with learning difficulties: engaging carers and supporters in the literacies learning process. Paper presented at the NRDC International Conference, Nottingham, April.

Leitch, S. (2006) *Prosperity for All in the Global Economy: World Class Skills. Final Report*. Norwich: The Stationery Office.

Lisbon European Council (2000) *An Agenda of Economic and Social Renewal for Europe*. http://ec.europa.eu/growthandjobs/pdf/lisbon_en.pdf accessed 29 March 2009.

Lunzer, E.A. and Gardner, K. (1984) *Learning from the Written Word*. Edinburgh: Oliver & Boyd.

Mace, J. (1979) *Working with Words*. London: Chameleon.

Mace, J. (1995) *Literacy, Language and Community Publishing*: Clevedon: Multilingual Matters,.

Mace, J. (2002) *The Give and Take of Writing: Scribes, Literacy and Everyday Life*. Leicester: NIACE.

Marshall, B. and Wiliam, D. (2003) *Assessment for Learning: Putting It Into Practice*. Maidenhead: Open University Press.

Marshall, B. and Wiliam, D. (2006) *English Inside the Black Box: Assessment for Learning in the English Classroom*. London: Kings College London/NFER Nelson.

McNeil, B. and Dixon, L. (2005) *Success Factors in Informal Learning: Young Adults' Experiences of Literacy, Language and Numeracy*. London: NRDC.

McShane, S. (2005) *Applying Research in Reading Instruction for Adults: First Steps for Teachers*. Portsmouth, NH: National Institute for Literacy. www.nifl.gov/partnershipforreading/publications/applyingresearch.pdf accessed 30 March 2009.

Medwell, J., Wray, D., Poulson, L. and Fox, R. (1998) *Effective Teachers of Literacy*. Exeter: University of Exeter School of Education.

Mencap (2007) *Mencap: Understanding Learning Disability*. www.mencap.org.uk

Miles, T.R. (1993) *Dyslexia: The Pattern of Difficulties*, 2nd edn. London: Whurr.

Morgan, E. (1995) Releasing potential in the dyslexic writer (using voice recognition software), *RaPAL Bulletin*, 27. Republished in Herrington, M. and Kendall, A. (eds) (2005) Introduction, in *Insights from Research and Practice: A Handbook for Adult Literacy Practitioners in Post Compulsory Education*. Leicester: NIACE.

Morgan, E. and Klein, C. (2000) *The Dyslexic Adult in a Non-Dyslexic World*. London: Whurr.

Moseley, D. and Poole, S. (2001) The advantages of rime-prompting: a comparative study of prompting methods when hearing children read, *Journal of Research in Reading*. 24(2) (June): 163–72.

Nankivell, C. (1996) *Building the Framework*. London: Basic Skills Agency.

Nation, P. (2002) *Managing Vocabulary Learning*. RELC Portfolio Series 2. Singapore: SEAMED Regional Language Centre.

National Reading Panel (2000) *Report of the National Reading Panel: Teaching Children to Read*. Washington, DC: National Institute of Child Health and Human Development. www.nationalreadingpanel.org/Publications/summary.htm accessed 24 June 2009.

(OECD) Organization for Economic Co-operation and Development (OECD) (1997) *Literacy Skills for the Knowledge Society*. Paris: OECD.

Palfreyman Kay, J. (2001) Students' views of learning support, in M. Hunter Carsch and M. Herrington (2001) *Dyslexia and Effective Learning in Secondary and Tertiary Education*. London: Whurr.

Palincsar, A.S. and Brown, A.L. (1986) Interactive teaching to promote independent learning from text, *The Reading Teacher*, 39(8): 771–7.

Papen, U. (2005) *Adult Literacy as Social Practice: More than Skills*. London: Routledge.

Paton, A. and Wilkins, W. (2009) *Teaching ESOL: Principles and Practice*. Maidenhead: NRDC/Open University Press.

Pollak, D. (2005) *Dyslexia, the Self and Higher Education. Learning Life Histories of Students Identified as Dyslexic*. Stoke-on-Trent: Trentham Books.

Pollak, D. (2007) *Neurodiversity*. www.brainhe.com.

Preston, J. (2006) (Mis)recognising lifelong learning in non-formal settings, in P. Sutherland and J. Crowther (eds) *Lifelong Learning: Concepts and Contexts*. London: Routledge.

Purcell-Gates, V., Jacobson, E. and Degener, S (2004) *Print Literacy Development: Uniting Cognitive and Social Practice Theories*. Cambridge, MA: Harvard University Press.

Raphael, T., Highfield, K. and Au, K. (2001) *QAR Now*. New York: Scholastic.

Reber, A.S. (1995) *The Penguin Dictionary of Psychology*. Harmondsworth: Penguin.

Rice, M. with Brooks, G. (2004) *Developmental Dyslexia in Adults: A Research Review*. London: NRDC.

Roberts, C., Baynham, M., Shrubshall, *et al.* (2005) *Embedded Teaching and Learning of Adult Literacy, Numeracy and ESOL: Seven Case Studies*. London: NRDC.

Robinson, F. (1970) *Effective Study*. New York. Harper and Row.

Rogers, A. (2002) *Teaching Adults*, 3rd edn. Buckingham: Open University Press.

Rose, J. (2006) *Final Report of the Independent Review of the Teaching of Early Reading*. www.standards.dfes.gov.uk/phonics/report.pdf accessed 31 March 2009.

Saunders, K. and White, A. (2002) *How Dyslexics Learn: Grasping the Nettle*. Evesham: PATOSS.

Schuller, T., Preston, J., Hammond, C., Brasset-Grundy, A. and Bynner, J. (2004) *The Benefits of Learning: The Impact of Education on Health, Family Life and Social Capital*. London: Routledge Falmer.

Schwab, I. and Stone, J. (1986) *Language, Writing and Publishing: Work with Afro-Caribbean Students*, ILEA Afro-Caribbean Language and Literacy Project in Further and Adult Education. London: ILEA.

Scribner, S. and Cole, M. (1981) *The Psychology of Literacy*. Cambridge, MA: Harvard University Press.

Shaughnessey, M. (1977) *Errors and Expectations: A Guide for the Teacher of Basic Writing*. New York: Oxford University Press.

Stanovich, K. (1980) Toward an interactive–compensatory model of individual differences in the development of reading fluency, *Reading Research Quarterly*, 16(1): 32–71.

Stanovich, K. (1986) Matthew effects in reading: some consequences of individual differences in the acquisition of literacy, *Reading Research Quarterly*, 21(4): 360–407.

Stein, J. (2001) The magnocellular theory of developmental dyslexia, *Dyslexia*, 7(1): 12–36.

Street, B. (1984) *Literacy in Theory and in Practice*. Cambridge: Cambridge University Press.

Sutcliffe, J. (1994) *Teaching Basic Skills to Adults with Learning Difficulties*. London: Adult Literacy and Basic Skills Unit and NIACE.

Szumko, J. and Beecham, N. (2006) *Dyslex Siim Materials Pack*. Loughborough: English Language Study Unit, Loughborough University.

Taylor, D. (1996) *Toxic Literacies. Exposing the Injustice of Bureaucratic Texts*. Portsmouth: N. H Heinemann.

Taylor, S. (1995) Improving on the blank page, in J. Mace (ed.) *Literacy, Language and Community Publishing*. Clevedon: Multilingual Matters.

TES (Times Educational Supplement) (2004) Survey suggests shortage of suitably qualified teachers holds back adult literacy, 14 May.

Tett, L., Hall, S., Maclachlan, K., *et al.* (2006) *Evaluation of the Scottish Adult Literacy and Numeracy (ALN) Strategy*. Glasgow: Scottish Executive.

Thornbury, S. (1998) The lexical approach: a journey without maps? *Modern English Teacher*, 9(4): 7–13.

Topping, K. (1995) *Paired Reading, Spelling and Writing: The Handbook for Teachers and Parents*. London: Cassell Education.

Tremain, S. (2005) Foucault, governmentality and critical disability theory, in Tremain, S. (ed.) *Foucault and the Government of Disability*. Ann Arbor, MI: University of Michigan Press.

Trollope, J. (2006) *The Book Boy* (Quick Reads). London: Bloomsbury.

Walker Tileson, D. (2004) *What Every Teacher Should Know About Special Learners.* Thousand Oaks, CA: Corwin Press.

Ward, J. and Edwards, J. (2002) *Learning Journeys: Learners' Voices. Learners' Views on Progress and Achievement in Literacy and Numeracy.* London: Learning and Skills Development Agency.

Warner, J. and Vorhaus, J. (2008) *Summary Report: The Learner Study. The Impact of the Skills for Life Strategy on Adult Literacy, Language and Numeracy Learners.* London: NRDC.

Weinreich, M. (1973) *History of the Yiddish Language.* Chicago, IL: University of Chicago Press.

West, T. (1991) I*n the Mind's Eye: Visual Thinkers, Gifted People with Learning Difficulties, Computer Images and the Ironies of Creativity.* New York: Prometheus.

Whitehouse, G. (1995) Dyslexia: an FE student's experience of assessment, or 'It's a big shock finding out you are disabled', *RaPAL Bulletin,* Summer.

Williams, J. (2003) *Teaching Literacy in ESOL Classes,* available from www.avantibooks. com.

Wilson, A. and Hunter, K. (2007) *Effective Learning for Adults with Learning Difficulties: Engaging Carers and Supporters in the Literacies Learning Process.* Edniburgh: Scottish Government.

Wolfe A., Evans, K. and Emslie-Henry, R. (2004) *Identifying Effective Workplace Basic Skills Strategies Enhancing Employee Productivity and Development.* London: NRDC.

Index

Locators shown in *italics* refer to diagrams, boxed examples, tasks and comments.